a year of
desserts

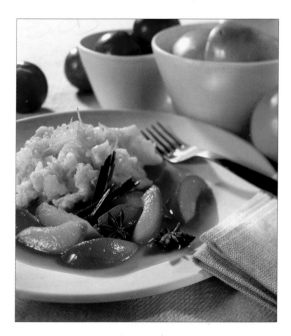

365 Delicious Step-By-Step Recipes

Martha Day

southwater

This edition is published by Southwater, an imprint of Anness Publishing Ltd,
108 Great Russell Street, London WC1B 3NA; info@anness.com

www.southwaterbooks.com; www.annesspublishing.com; twitter: @Anness_Books

If you like the images in this book and would like to investigate using them for publishing, promotions or advertising,
please visit our website www.practicalpictures.com for more information.

Publisher: Joanna Lorenz
Project Editor: Finny Fox Davies
Designer: Ian Sandom
Recipes: Catherine Atkinson, Alex Barker, Michelle Berriedale-Johnson, Angela Boggiano, Janet Brinkworth,
Carla Capalbo, Jacqueline Clark, Francis Cleary, Carol Clements, Roz Denny, Patrizia Diemling, Nicola Diggins,
Joanna Farrow, Christine France, Sarah Gates, Shirley Gill, Rosamund Grant, Carole Handslip, Deh-Ta Hsiung,
Shehzad Husain, Sheila Kimberley, Gilly Love, Norma MacMillan, Sue Maggs, Maggie Mayhew, Maggie Parnell,
Anne Sheasby, Liz Trigg, Laura Washburn, Stephen Wheeler, Kate Whiteman, Elizabeth Wolf-Cohen, Jeni Wright
Photographers: William Adams-Lingwood, Karl Adamson, Edward Allwright, David Armstrong, Steve Baxter,
James Duncan, Michelle Garrett, Amanda Heywood, David Jordan, Don Last, Patrick McLeavy,
Michael Michaels, Thomas Odulate

© Anness Publishing Ltd 2015

A CIP catalogue record for this book is available from the British Library.

NOTES
For all recipes, quantities are given in both metric and imperial measures and, where appropriate, in standard cups and spoons.
Follow one set of measures, but not a mixture, because they are not interchangeable.
Standard spoon and cup measures are level. 1 tsp = 5ml, 1 tbsp = 15ml, 1 cup = 250ml/8fl oz.
Australian standard tablespoons are 20ml. Australian readers should use 3 tsp in place of 1 tbsp for measuring small quantities.
American pints are 16fl oz/2 cups. American readers should use 20fl oz/2.5 cups in place of 1 pint when measuring liquids.
Electric oven temperatures in this book are for conventional ovens. When using a fan oven, the temperature will probably need to be reduced
by about 10–20°C/20–40°F. Since ovens vary, you should check with your manufacturer's instruction book for guidance.
The nutritional analysis given for each recipe is calculated per portion (i.e. serving or item), unless otherwise stated. If the recipe gives a range,
such as Serves 4–6, then the nutritional analysis will be for the smaller portion size, i.e. 6 servings.
The analysis does not include optional ingredients, such as salt added to taste.
Medium eggs are used unless otherwise stated.

Main front cover image shows Greek Chocolate Mousse Tartlets – for recipe, see page 162

PUBLISHER'S NOTE
Although the advice and information in this book are believed to be accurate and true at the time of going to press, neither the authors
nor the publisher can accept any legal responsibility or liability for any errors or omissions that may have been made nor for any inaccuracies
nor for any loss, harm or injury that comes about from following instructions or advice in this book.

Contents

INTRODUCTION 6

BEST-EVER DESSERTS 8
HOT PUDDINGS AND DESSERTS 22
COLD PUDDINGS AND DESSERTS 62
CAKES AND GÂTEAUX 96
PASTRIES AND PIES 128
CUSTARDS, SOUFFLÉS AND WHIPS 166
FRUIT SALADS, ICES AND SORBETS 204

LOW-FAT DESSERTS 258
HOT LOW-FAT PUDDINGS AND DESSERTS 272
COLD LOW-FAT PUDDINGS AND DESSERTS 340
LOW-FAT PASTRIES, CAKES AND PIES 380
LOW-FAT CUSTARDS, SOUFFLÉS AND WHIPS 416
LOW-FAT FRUIT SALADS 444
LOW-FAT ICES AND SORBETS 482

INDEX 506

Introduction

DESSERT RECIPES CAN RANGE from the lightest sorbet to the most substantial steamed chocolate pudding, so there are several decisions to be made when planning a menu. Your choice of what to serve will be influenced by the season, the occasion and the dietary requirements of your guests. If you are serving a filling main course you will invariably choose a light or fruity dessert to follow it, or if you plan to make a rich, creamy dessert you will deliberately pick a light main course. To help you maintain a healthy balance this book includes a wide range of delicious low-fat desserts that can make the decision reassuringly easy.

Many of the desserts in this selection can be made a day or two in advance, others can be started early in the day and finished off just before you eat, while frozen desserts and ice creams can be made weeks in advance, ready to serve whenever you need them. If you are planning a festive meal or entertaining a large number of people make sure you leave plenty of time for preparation, choose one of the desserts that can be made in advance and do at least some of the work for the other courses earlier in the day. That way your guests *and you* can enjoy the meal.

All the recipes have clear instructions, so that even the potentially difficult desserts, such as soufflés and roulades, will be easy to make, and look and taste delicious. For certain results, read the recipe through before you start and follow the step-by-step instructions.

The book is divided into two sections. *Best-ever Desserts* contains all the old favourites, such as Sticky Toffee Pudding, Crème Caramel and Trifle, along with some more unusual recipes that are destined to become your new favourites. There are chapters on hot puddings and desserts, cold puddings and desserts, and many more, to make sure you serve a best-ever dessert for every occasion. *Low-fat Desserts* contains recipes that are just as delicious, but are carefully designed to fit into a healthy, lighter diet. Nearly all recipes have no more than 5g of fat per portion, and many have fewer than 200 calories.

BEST-EVER DESSERTS

Desserts are irresistible at any time of day: with morning coffee or afternoon tea, as the perfect end to a lazy lunch, as a special indulgence or treat, or as the grand finale to a romantic evening. This section of the book presents recipes for the most luxurious, sumptuous desserts imaginable, including classics such as Peach Melba and Black Forest Gâteau, as well as innovative ideas such as Chocolate and Cherry Polenta Cake and Kiwi Ricotta Cheese Tart. There are six easy-to-use chapters that cover every kind of dessert for all occasions – hot and cold puddings, cakes and gâteaux, pastries and pies, custards and soufflés, fruit salads, ices and sorbets.

◆ ◆ ◆

Making Shortcrust Pastry

A meltingly short, crumbly pastry sets off any filling to perfection, whether sweet or savoury. The fat content of the pastry dough can be made up of half butter or margarine and half white vegetable fat or with all one kind of fat.

For a 23cm/9in pastry case (pie shell)
225g/8oz/2 cups plain (all-purpose) flour
1.5ml/¼ tsp salt
115g/4oz/8 tbsp fat, chilled and diced

1 Sift the flour and salt into a bowl. Add the fat. Rub it into the flour with your fingertips until the mixture is crumb-like.

2 Sprinkle 45ml/3 tbsp of iced water over the mixture. With a fork, toss gently to mix and moisten it.

3 Press the dough into a ball. If it is too dry to hold together, gradually add another 15ml/1 tbsp of iced water.

4 Wrap the ball of dough with clear film (plastic wrap) or baking parchment and chill it for at least 30 minutes.

5 To make pastry in a food processor: combine the flour, salt and cubed fat in the work bowl. Process, turning the machine on and off, just until the mixture is crumbly. Add 45–60ml/3–4 tbsp iced water and process again briefly – just until the dough starts to pull away from the sides of the bowl. It should still look crumbly. Remove the dough from the processor and gather it into a ball. Wrap and chill.

SHORTCRUST PASTRY VARIATIONS

For Nut Shortcrust
Add 30g/1oz/¼ cup finely chopped walnuts or pecan nuts to the flour mixture.

For Rich Shortcrust
Use 225g/8oz/2 cups flour and 175g/6oz/¾ cup fat (preferably all butter), plus 15ml/1 tbsp caster (superfine) sugar if making a sweet pie. Bind with 1 egg yolk and 30–45ml/2–3 tbsp water.

For a Two-crust Pie
Increase the proportions for these pastries by 50%, thus the amounts needed for basic shortcrust pastry are: 340g/12oz/3 cups flour, 2.5ml/½ tsp salt, 175g/6oz/¾ cup fat, 75–90ml/5–6 tbsp water.

PASTRY MAKING TIPS

It helps if the fat is cold and firm, particularly if making the dough in a food processor. Cold fat has less chance of warming and softening too much when it is being rubbed into the flour, resulting in an oily pastry. Use block margarine rather than the soft tub-type for the same reason.

When rubbing the fat into the flour, if it begins to soften and feel oily, put the bowl in the refrigerator to chill for 20–30 minutes. Then continue to make the dough.

Liquids used should be ice-cold so that they will not soften or melt the fat.

Take care when adding the water: start with the smaller amount (added all immediately, not in a dribble), and add more only if the mixture will not come together into a dough. Too much water will make the dough difficult to handle and will result in tough pastry.

When gathering the mixture together into a ball of dough, handle it as little as possible: overworked dough will again produce a tough pastry.

To avoid shrinkage, chill the pastry dough before rolling out and baking. This 'resting time' will allow any elasticity developed during mixing to relax.

Making French Flan Pastry

The pastry for tarts and flans is made with butter or margarine, giving a rich and crumbly result. The more fat used, the richer the pastry will be – almost like a biscuit (cookie) dough – and the harder to roll out. If you have difficulty rolling it, you can press it into the tin instead, or roll it out between sheets of clear film (plastic wrap). Flan pastry, like shortcrust, can be made by hand or in a food processor. Tips for making, handling and using shortcrust pastry apply equally to this type of pastry.

INGREDIENTS

For a 23cm/9in flan case (pie shell)

200g/7oz/1¾ cups plain (all-purpose) flour

2.5ml/½ tsp salt

115g/4oz/½ cup butter or margarine, chilled

1 egg yolk

1.5ml/¼ tsp lemon juice

1 Sift the flour and salt into a bowl. Add the butter or margarine. Rub into the flour until the mixture resembles fine breadcrumbs.

2 In a small bowl, mix the egg yolk, lemon juice and 30ml/ 2 tbsp of iced water. Add to the flour mixture. With a fork, toss gently to mix and moisten.

3 Press the dough into a rough ball. If it is too dry to come together, add 15ml/1 tbsp more water. Turn on to the work surface or a pastry board.

4 With the heel of your hand, push small portions of dough away from you, smearing them on the surface.

5 Continue mixing the dough in this way until it feels pliable and can be peeled easily off the work surface or pastry board.

6 Press the dough into a smooth ball. Wrap in clear film (plastic wrap) and chill for at least 30 minutes.

FLAN PASTRY VARIATIONS

For Sweet Flan Pastry
Reduce the amount of salt to 1.5ml/¼ tsp, add 15ml/1 tbsp caster (supefine) sugar with the flour.

For Rich Flan Pastry
Use 200g/7oz/1¾ cups flour, 2.5ml/½ tsp salt, 150g/5oz/10 tbsp butter, 2 egg yolks, and 15–30ml/ 1–2 tbsp water.

For Rich Sweet Flan Pastry
Make rich flan pastry, adding 45ml/3 tbsp caster sugar with the flour and, if liked, 2.5ml/½ tsp vanilla extract with the egg yolks.

Making Choux Pastry

Unlike other pastries, where the fat is rubbed into the flour, with choux pastry the butter is melted with water and then the flour is added, followed by eggs. The result is more of a paste than a pastry. It is easy to make, but care must be taken in measuring the ingredients.

INGREDIENTS

For 18 profiteroles or 12 eclairs

115g/4oz/½ cup butter, cut into small pieces

10ml/2 tsp caster (superfine) sugar (optional)

1.5ml/¼ tsp salt

150g/5oz/1¼ cups plain (all-purpose) flour

4 eggs, beaten to mix

1 egg, beaten with 5ml/1 tsp cold water, for glaze

1 Preheat the oven to 220°C/425°F/Gas 7. Combine the butter, sugar, if using, salt and 250ml/8fl oz/1 cup of water in a large heavy pan. Bring to the boil over moderately high heat, stirring occasionally.

2 As soon as the mixture is boiling, remove the pan from the heat. Add the flour all immediately and beat vigorously with a wooden spoon to mix the flour smoothly into the liquid.

3 Return the pan to moderate heat and cook, stirring, until the mixture will form a ball, pulling away from the side of the pan. This will take about 1 minute. Remove from the heat again and allow to cool for 3–5 minutes.

4 Add a little of the beaten eggs and beat well to incorporate. Add a little more egg and beat in well. Continue beating in the eggs until the mixture becomes a smooth and shiny paste.

5 While still warm, shape choux puffs, éclairs, profiteroles or rings on a baking sheet lined with baking parchment.

6 Glaze with 1 egg beaten with 5ml/1 tsp of cold water. Put into the preheated oven, then reduce the heat to 200°C/400°F/Gas 6. Bake until puffed and golden brown.

SHAPING CHOUX PASTRY

For Large Puffs

Use two large spoons dipped in water. Drop the paste in 5–6cm/2–2½in wide blobs on the paper-lined baking sheet, leaving 4cm/1½in between each. Neaten the blobs as much as possible. Alternatively, for well-shaped puffs, pipe the paste using a piping (pastry) bag fitted with a 2cm/¾in plain nozzle.

For Profiteroles

Use two small spoons or a piping bag fitted with a 1cm/½in nozzle and shape 2.5cm/1in blobs.

For Eclairs

Use a piping bag fitted with a 2cm/¾in nozzle. Pipe strips 10–13cm/4–5in long.

For a Ring

Draw a 30cm/12in circle on the paper. Spoon the paste in large blobs on the circle to make a ring. Or pipe two rings around the circle and a third on top.

BAKING TIMES FOR CHOUX PASTRY

Large puffs and éclairs	30–35 minutes
Profiteroles	20–25 minutes
Rings	40–45 minutes

Rolling Out and Lining a Tin

A neat pastry case that doesn't distort or shrink in baking is the desired result. The key to success is handling the dough gently. Use the method here to line a round pie or tart tin (pie pan) that is about 5cm/2in deep.

Remove the chilled dough from the refrigerator and allow it to soften slightly at room temperature. Unwrap and put it on a lightly floured surface. Flatten the dough into a neat, round disc. Lightly flour the rolling pin.

1 Using even pressure, start rolling out the dough, working from the centre to the edge each time and easing the pressure slightly as you reach the edge.

2 Lift up the dough and give it a quarter turn from time to time during the rolling. This will prevent the dough sticking to the surface, and will help keep the thickness even.

3 Continue rolling out until the dough circle is about 5cm/2in larger all round than the tin. It should be about 3mm/⅛in thick.

4 Set the rolling pin on the dough, near one side of the circle. Fold the outside edge of the dough over the pin, then roll the pin over the dough to wrap the dough round it. Do this gently and loosely.

5 Hold the pin over the tin and gently unroll the dough so it drapes into the tin, centring it as much as possible.

6 With your fingertips, lift and ease the dough into the tin, gently pressing it over the bottom and up the side. Turn excess dough over the rim and trim it with a knife or scissors, depending on how you want to finish the edge.

Finishing the Edge

1 *For a forked edge*
Using a knife, trim the dough even with the rim and press it flat. Firmly and evenly press the prongs of a fork all round the edge. If the fork sticks, dip it in flour every so often.

2 *For a crimped edge*
Using scissors, trim the dough to leave an overhang of about 1.5cm/½in all round. Fold the extra dough under. Put the knuckle or tip of the index finger of one of your hands inside the edge, pointing directly out. With the thumb and index finger of your other hand, pinch the dough edge around your index finger into a "V" shape. Continue all the way round the edge.

3 *For a ruffled edge*
Using scissors, trim the dough to leave an overhang of about 1.5cm/½in all round. Fold the extra dough under. With the thumb and index finger of one hand about 2.5cm/1in apart, gently pinch the dough around the index finger of your other hand. Continue this all the way round the edge.

4 *For a cutout edge*
Using a knife, trim the dough even with the rim and press it flat. With a small pastry cutter, cut out decorative shapes from the dough trimmings. Moisten the edge of the pastry case and press the cutouts in place, overlapping them slightly if you like.

5 *For a ribbon edge*
Using a knife, trim the dough even with the rim and press it flat. Cut long strips about 2cm/¾in wide from the dough trimmings. Moisten the edge and press one end of a strip on to it. Twist the strip gently and press it on to the edge again. Continue this all the way round the edge.

Preparing Fresh Fruit

PEELING AND TRIMMING FRUIT

Citrus fruit
To peel completely: cut a slice from the top and from the base. Set the fruit base down on a work surface. Using a small sharp knife, cut off the peel lengthways in thick strips. Take the coloured rind and all the white pith (which has a bitter taste). Cut, following the curve of the fruit.

To remove rind: use a vegetable peeler to save off the rind in wide strips, taking none of the white pith. Use these strips whole or cut them into fine shreds with a sharp knife, according to recipe directions. Or rub the fruit against the fine holes of a metal grater, turning the fruit so you take just the coloured rind and not the white pith. Or use a special tool, called a citrus zester, to take fine threads of rind. (Finely chop the threads as an alternative method to grating.)

Kiwi fruit
Follow the citrus fruit technique, taking off the peel in thin length-ways strips.

Apples, pears, quinces, mangoes, papayas
Use a small sharp knife or a vegetable peeler. Take off the peel in long strips, as thinly as possible.

Peaches, apricots
Cut a cross in the base. Immerse the fruit in boiling water. Leave for 10–30 seconds (according to ripeness), then drain and immerse in iced water. The skin should slip off easily.

Pineapple
Cut off the leafy crown. Cut a slice from the base and set the pineapple upright. With a sharp knife, cut off the peel lengthways, cutting thickly to remove the brown "eyes" with it.

Bananas, lychees, avocados
Make a small cut and remove the peel with your fingers.

Passion fruit, pomegranates
Cut in half, or cut a slice off the top. With a spoon, scoop the flesh and seeds into a bowl.

Star fruit (carambola)
Trim off the tough, darkened edges of the five segments.

Rhubarb
Cut off the leaves and discard them (they are poisonous). Peel off any tough skin.

Fresh currants (red, black, white)
Pull each cluster through the prongs of a fork to remove the currants from the stalks.

Fresh dates
Squeeze gently at the stalk end to remove the rather tough skin.

CORING AND STONING OR SEEDING FRUIT

Apples, pears, quinces
For whole fruit: use an apple corer to stamp out the whole core from stalk end to base. Alternatively, working up from the base, use a melon baller to cut out the core. Leave the stalk end intact.

For halves: use a melon baller to scoop out the core. Cut out the stalk and base using a small sharp knife.
For quarters: cut out the stalk and core with a serrated knife.

Citrus fruit
With the tip of a pointed knife, nick out pips from slices or segments.

Cherries
Use a cherry stoner (pitter) to achieve the neatest results.

Peaches, apricots, nectarines, plums
Cut the fruit in half, cutting round the indentation. Twist the halves apart. Lift out the stone (pit), or lever it out with the tip of a knife.

Fresh dates
Cut the fruit lengthways in half and lift out the stone. Or, if the fruit is to be used whole, cut in from the stalk end with a thin-bladed knife to loosen the stone, then remove it.

Mangoes

Cut lengthways on either side of the large flat stone (pit) in the centre. Curve the cut slightly to follow the shape of the stone. Cut the flesh from the two thin ends of the stone.

Papayas, melons

Cut the fruit in half. Scoop out the seeds from the central hollow, then scrape away any fibres.

Pineapple

For spears and wedges: cut out the core neatly with a sharp knife.
For rings: cut out the core with a small pastry cutter.

Gooseberries

Use scissors to trim off the stalk and flower ends.

Grapes

Cut the fruit lengthways in half. Use a small knife to nick out the pips. Alternatively, use the curved end of a sterilized hair grip.

Star fruit (carambola), watermelon

With the tip of a pointed knife, nick out pips from slices.

Strawberries

Use a special huller to remove the leafy green top and central core. Or cut these out with a small sharp knife.

Avocado

Cut the fruit in half lengthways. Stick the tip of a sharp knife into the stone and lever it out without damaging the surrounding flesh.

CUTTING FRUIT

Apples, quinces

For rings: remove the core and seeds with an apple corer. Set the fruit on its side and cut across into thick or thin rings, as required.

For slices: cut the fruit in half and remove core and seeds with a melon baller. Set one half cut side down and cut it across into neat slices, thick or thin according to recipe directions. Or cut the fruit into quarters and remove core and seeds with a knife. Cut lengthways into neat slices.

Pears

For fans: cut the fruit in half and remove the core and seeds with a melon baller. Set the halves cut side down and cut lengthways into thin slices, not cutting all the way through at the stalk ends. Gently fan out the slices so they are overlapping each other evenly. Transfer the pear fans to the plate or pastry case (pie pan) using a palette knife.
For slices: follow apple technique.

Citrus fruit
For slices: using a serrated knife,
cut the fruit across into neat slices.

For segments: hold the peeled fruit
in your cupped palm, over a bowl
to catch the juice. Working from the
side of the fruit to the centre, slide
the knife down one side of a
separating membrane to free the
flesh from it. Then slide the knife
down the other side of that segment

to free it from the membrane there.
Drop the segment into the bowl.
Continue cutting out the segments,
folding back the membrane like
the pages of a book as you work.
When all the segments have been
cut out, squeeze all the juice from
the membrane.

**Peaches, nectarines, apricots,
plums**
For slices: follow apple technique.

Papayas, avocados
For slices: follow apple technique.
Or cut the unpeeled fruit into
wedges, removing the central seeds
or stone. Set each wedge peel side
down and slide the knife down the
length to cut the flesh away from
the peel.
For fans: follow pear technique.

Melon
For slices: follow papaya technique.
For balls: Use a melon baller.

Mangoes
Cut the peeled flesh into slices
or cubes, according to recipe
directions.

Pineapple
For spears: cut the peeled fruit
lengthways in half and then into
quarters. Cut each quarter into
spears and cut out the core.
For chunks: cut the peeled fruit
into spears. Remove the core. Cut
across each spear into chunks.
For rings: cut the peeled fruit
across into slices. Stamp out the
central core from each slice using a
pastry cutter.

Kiwi fruit, star fruit (carambola)
Cut the fruit across into neat slices;
discard the ends.

Banana
Cut the fruit across into neat slices.
Or cut in half and then lengthways
into quarters.

Gelatine

DISSOLVING GELATINE

It's important to dissolve gelatine correctly, or it can spoil the texture and set of your finished dessert.

1 Place 45ml/3 tbsp of very hot water per sachet of gelatine in a small bowl.

2 Sprinkle the gelatine over the liquid. Always add the gelatine to the liquid.

3 Stir briskly until the gelatine is completely dissolved. There should be no visible crystals and the liquid should be clear. If necessary, stand the container in a pan of hot water over a low heat until dissolved. Do not allow the gelatine to boil.

VEGETARIAN ALTERNATIVE

There is a vegetarian alternative to gelatine, which can be used in the appropriate recipes, if you wish. Follow the instructions on the packet, but in general you should sprinkle the alternative on to cold liquids and stir until completely dissolved. Next, heat the mixture to near boiling. (If setting proves difficult add more of the gelatine alternative to the mixture and reheat.) It is now ready to be used as specified in the recipe, but should be allowed to set for about 1 hour, or until firm and should always be allowed to cool.

Redcurrant and Raspberry Coulis

A dessert sauce for the height of summer to serve with light meringues and fruit sorbets. Make it particularly pretty with a decoration of fresh flowers and leaves.

INGREDIENTS

Serves 6

225g/8oz/2 cups redcurrants
450g/1lb/2⅔ cups raspberries
50g/2oz/½ cup icing (confectioners')
  sugar
15ml/1 tbsp cornflour (cornstarch)
juice of 1 orange
30ml/2 tbsp double (heavy) cream,
  to decorate

1 Strip the redcurrants from their stalks using a fork. Place in a food processor or blender with the raspberries and sugar, and purée until it it smooth.

2 Press the mixture through a fine sieve (strainer) into a bowl and discard the seeds and pulp.

3 Blend the cornflour with the orange juice then stir into the fruit purée. Transfer to a pan and bring to the boil, stirring continuously, and cook for 1–2 minutes until smooth and thick. Leave until cold.

4 Spoon the sauce over each plate. Drip the cream from a teaspoon to make small dots evenly around the edge. Draw a cocktail stick (toothpick) through the dots to form heart shapes. Place the meringue or scoop sorbet into the middle and decorate with flowers.

Crème Anglaise

Here is the classic English custard, light, creamy and delicious – far superior to packet versions. Serve hot or cold.

INGREDIENTS

Serves 4

1 vanilla pod (bean)
450ml/¾ pint/1⅞ cups milk
40g/1½oz/3 tbsp caster (superfine) sugar
4 egg yolks

1 Split the vanilla pod and place in a pan with the milk. Bring slowly to the boil. Remove from the heat, then cover and infuse for 10 minutes before removing the pod.

2 Beat together the sugar and egg yolks until thick, light and creamy.

3 Slowly pour the warm, infused milk on to the egg mixture, stirring constantly.

4 Transfer to the top of a double boiler or place the bowl over a pan of hot water. Stir constantly over a low heat for 10 minutes or until the mixture coats the back of the spoon. Remove from the heat immediately as curdling will occur if the custard is allowed to simmer.

5 Strain the custard into a jug if serving hot or, if serving cold, strain into a bowl and cover the surface with buttered paper or clear film (plastic wrap).

VARIATION

Infuse a few strips of thinly pared lemon or orange rind with the milk, instead of the vanilla pod.

Sabayon

Serve this frothy sauce hot over steamed puddings or chill and serve just as it is with light dessert biscuits or whatever you prefer. Never let it stand for any length of time, as it will collapse.

INGREDIENTS

Serves 4-6

1 egg
2 egg yolks
75g/3oz/⅔ cup caster (superfine) sugar
150ml/¼ pint/⅔ cups sweet white wine
finely grated rind and juice of 1 lemon

1 Whisk the egg, yolks and sugar until they are pale and thick.

2 Stand the bowl over a pan of hot – not boiling – water. Add the wine and lemon juice, a little at a time, whisking vigorously and constantly.

3 Continue whisking until the mixture is thick enough to leave a trail. Whisk in the lemon rind. If serving hot serve immediately over pudding or fruit salad.

4 To serve cold, place over a bowl of iced water and whisk until chilled. Pour into small glasses and serve immediately.

Butterscotch Sauce

A deliciously sweet sauce which will
be loved by adults and children
alike! Serve with ice cream or with
pancakes or waffles.

INGREDIENTS

Serves 4–6

75g/3oz/6 tbsp butter
175g/6oz/¾ cup soft dark brown sugar
175ml/6fl oz/¾ cup evaporated milk
50g/2oz/½ cup hazelnuts

1 Melt the butter and sugar in a heavy pan, bring to the boil and boil for 2 minutes. Cool for 5 minutes.

2 Heat the evaporated milk to just below boiling point, then gradually stir into the sugar mixture. Cook over a low heat for 2 minutes, stirring frequently.

4 Tip the nuts on to a clean dish towel and rub them briskly to remove the skins.

3 Spread the hazelnuts on a baking sheet and toast under a hot grill (broiler).

5 Chop the nuts roughly and stir into the sauce. Serve hot, poured over scoops of vanilla ice cream, or warm waffles or pancakes.

Brandy Butter

This is traditionally served with
Christmas pudding, but is equally
delicious on a hot baked apple.

INGREDIENTS

Serves 6

100g/4oz/½ cup butter
100g/4oz/½ cup icing (confectioners'),
   caster (superfine) or soft light
   brown sugar
45ml/3 tbsp brandy

1 Cream the butter until very pale and soft, then beat in the sugar gradually until mixed.

2 Add the brandy, a few drops at a time, beating continuously. Add enough for a good flavour but take care it does not curdle.

3 Pile into a small serving dish and allow to harden. Alternatively, spread on to foil and chill until firm. Cut into shapes with small fancy cutters.

VARIATION

Cumberland Rum Butter
Use soft light brown sugar and rum instead of brandy. Grate the rind of 1 orange and beat in with the sugar, adding a good pinch of mixed spice.

Chocolate Fudge Sauce

*A real treat if you're not counting
calories. Fabulous with scoops of
vanilla ice cream.*

INGREDIENTS

Serves 6

150ml/¼ pint/⅔ cup double
  (heavy) cream
50g/2oz/4 tbsp butter
50g/2oz/¼ cup granulated (white) sugar
175g/6oz plain (semisweet) chocolate
30ml/2 tbsp brandy

VARIATIONS

White Chocolate and Orange Sauce:
40g/1½oz/3 tbsp caster (superfine) sugar,
  to replace granulated (white) sugar
175g/6oz white chocolate, to replace plain
  (semisweet) chocolate
30ml/2 tbsp orange liqueur,
  to replace brandy
finely grated rind of 1 orange

Coffee Chocolate Fudge:
50g/2oz/¼ cup light brown sugar, to
  replace granulated (white) sugar
30ml/2 tbsp coffee liqueur or dark rum,
  to replace brandy
15ml/1 tbsp coffee extract

1 Heat the cream with the butter
and sugar in the top of a
double boiler or in a heatproof
bowl over a pan of hot water. Stir
until smooth, then cool.

2 Break the chocolate into the
cream. Stir until it is melted
and thoroughly combined.

3 Stir in the brandy a little at a
time, then cool to room
temperature.

4 For the White Chocolate and
Orange Sauce, heat the cream
and butter with the sugar and
orange rind in the top of a double
boiler, until dissolved. Then, follow
the recipe to the end, but using
white chocolate and orange
liqueur instead.

5 For the Coffee Chocolate
Fudge, follow the recipe, using
light brown sugar and coffee
liqueur or rum. Stir in the coffee
extract at the end.

6 Serve the sauce over cream-
filled profiteroles, and serve
any that is left over separately.

Glossy Chocolate Sauce

*Delicious poured over ice cream or
on hot or cold desserts, this sauce
also freezes well. Pour into a freezerproof container, seal, and keep
for up to three months. Thaw at
room temperature.*

INGREDIENTS

Serves 6

115g/4oz/½ cup caster (superfine) sugar
175g/6oz plain (semisweeet) chocolate,
  broken into squares
30ml/2 tbsp unsalted butter
30ml/2 tbsp brandy or orange juice

1 Place the sugar and 60ml/
4 tbsp of water in a pan and
heat gently, stirring occasionally,
until the sugar has dissolved.

2 Stir in the chocolate, a few
squares at a time, until melted,
then add the butter in the same
way. Do not allow the sauce to boil.
Stir in the brandy or orange juice
and serve warm.

HOT PUDDINGS & DESSERTS

❖ ❖ ❖

Warm Lemon and Syrup Cake

The combination of pears, sticky syrup and lemon makes this a real winner. Drizzle with single cream for extra luxury.

Serves 8

3 eggs

175g/6oz/¾ cup butter, softened

175g/6oz/¾ cup caster (superfine) sugar

175g/6oz/1½ cups self-raising
   (self-rising) flour

50g/2oz/½ cup ground almonds

1.5ml/¼ tsp freshly grated nutmeg

50g/2oz/5 tbsp candied lemon peel,
   finely chopped

grated rind of 1 lemon

30ml/2 tbsp lemon juice

poached pears, to serve

For the syrup

175g/6oz/¾ cup caster (superfine) sugar

juice of 3 lemons

1 Preheat the oven to 180°C/
350°F/Gas 4. Grease and base-line a deep, round 20cm/8in cake tin (pan).

2 Place all the cake ingredients in a large bowl and beat well for 2–3 minutes, until the mixture is light and fluffy.

3 Tip the mixture into the prepared tin, spread level and bake for 1 hour, or until golden and firm to the touch.

4 Meanwhile, make the syrup. Put the sugar, lemon juice and 75ml/5 tbsp water in a pan. Heat gently, stirring until the sugar has dissolved, then boil, without stirring, for 1–2 minutes.

5 Turn out the cake on to a plate with a rim. Prick the surface of the cake all over with a fork, then pour over the hot syrup. Leave to soak for about 30 minutes. Serve the cake warm with thin wedges of poached pears.

Chocolate and Orange Scotch Pancakes

Fabulous baby pancakes in a rich creamy orange liqueur sauce.

INGREDIENTS

Serves 4

115g/4oz/1 cup self-raising
   (self-rising) flour
30ml/2 tbsp cocoa powder
2 eggs
50g/2oz plain (semisweet) chocolate,
   broken into squares
200ml/7fl oz/⅞ cup milk
finely grated rind of 1 orange
30ml/2 tbsp orange juice
butter or oil for frying
60ml/4 tbsp chocolate curls, for sprinkling

For the sauce

2 large oranges
30ml/2 tbsp unsalted butter
45ml/3 tbsp light muscovado
   (brown) sugar
250ml/8fl oz/1 cup crème fraîche
30ml/2 tbsp Grand Marnier or Cointreau
chocolate curls, to decorate

1 Sift the flour and cocoa into a bowl and make a well in the centre. Add the eggs and beat well, gradually incorporating the surrounding dry ingredients to make a smooth batter.

2 Mix the chocolate and milk in a pan. Heat gently until the chocolate has melted, then beat into the batter until smooth and bubbly. Stir in the grated orange rind and juice.

3 Heat a large heavy frying pan or griddle. Grease with a little butter or oil. Drop large spoonfuls of batter on to the hot surface. Cook over a moderate heat. When the pancakes are lightly browned underneath and bubbly on top, flip them over to cook the other side. Slide on to a plate and keep hot, then make more in the same way.

4 Make the sauce. Grate the rind of 1 of the oranges into a bowl and set aside. Peel both oranges, taking care to remove all the pith, then slice the flesh fairly thinly.

5 Heat the butter and sugar in a wide, shallow pan over a low heat, stirring until the sugar dissolves. Stir in the crème fraîche and heat gently.

6 Add the pancakes and orange slices to the sauce, heat gently for 1–2 minutes, then spoon over the liqueur. Sprinkle with the reserved orange rind. Scatter over the chocolate curls and serve the pancakes immediately.

Gingerbread Upside-down Pudding

A proper pudding goes down well on a cold winter's day. This one is quite quick and easy to make and looks very impressive.

Serves 4–6

sunflower oil, for brushing

15ml/1 tbsp soft brown sugar

4 medium peaches, halved and stoned
    (pitted), or canned peach halves

8 walnut halves

For the base

130g/4½oz/generous 1 cup wholemeal
    (whole-wheat) flour

2.5ml/½ tsp bicarbonate of soda
    (baking soda)

7.5ml/1½ tsp ground ginger

5ml/1 tsp ground cinnamon

115g/4oz/½ cup dark muscovado
    (molasses) sugar

1 egg

120ml/4fl oz/½ cup skimmed milk

50ml/2fl oz/¼ cup sunflower oil

1 Preheat the oven to 180°C/ 350°F/Gas 4. For the topping, brush the base and sides of a 23cm/9in round springform cake tin (pan) with oil. Sprinkle the sugar over the base.

2 Arrange the peaches cut-side down in the tin with a walnut half in each.

3 Sift together the flour, bicarbonate of soda, ginger and cinnamon, then stir in the sugar. Beat together the egg, milk and oil, then mix into the dry ingredients.

4 Pour the mixture evenly over the peaches and bake for 35–40 minutes, until firm to the touch. Turn out and serve hot.

Rhubarb-Strawberry Crisp

Strawberries, cinnamon and ground almonds make this a luxurious and delicious version of rhubarb crumble.

INGREDIENTS

Serves 4

225g/8oz strawberries, hulled

450g/1lb rhubarb, diced

90g/3½oz/½ cup granulated (white) sugar

15ml/1 tbsp cornflour (cornstarch)

85ml/3fl oz/⅓ cup fresh orange juice

115g/4oz/1 cup plain (all-purpose) flour

90g/3½oz/1 cup rolled oats

115g/4oz/½ cup light brown sugar, firmly packed

2.5ml/½ tsp ground cinnamon

50g/2oz/½ cup ground almonds

150g/5oz/generous ½ cup cold butter

1 egg, lightly beaten

1 If the strawberries are large, cut them in half. Combine the strawberries, rhubarb and granulated sugar in a 2.4 litre/ 4 pint/10 cup baking dish. Preheat the oven to 180°C/350°F/Gas 4.

2 In a small bowl, blend the cornflour with the orange juice. Pour this mixture over the fruit and stir gently to coat. Set the baking dish aside while making the crumble topping.

3 In a bowl, toss together the flour, oats, brown sugar, cinnamon and ground almonds. With a pastry blender or two knives, cut in the butter until the mixture resembles coarse bread-crumbs. Stir in the beaten egg.

4 Spoon the oat mixture evenly over the fruit and press down gently. Bake until browned, 50–60 minutes, then serve warm.

Baked Apples with Caramel Sauce

The creamy caramel sauce turns this simple country dessert into a more sophisticated delicacy.

INGREDIENTS

Serves 6

3 Granny Smith apples, cored but
   not peeled
3 Red Delicious apples, cored
   but not peeled
150g/5oz/¾ cup light brown sugar
2.5ml/½ tsp grated nutmeg
1.5ml/¼ tsp ground black pepper
40g/1½ oz/¼ cup walnut pieces
40g/1½ oz/scant ¼ cup sultanas
   (golden raisins)
50g/2oz/4 tbsp butter or margarine, diced
For the caramel sauce
15g/½ oz/1 tbsp butter or margarine
120ml/4fl oz/½ cup whipping cream

1 Preheat the oven to 190°C/
375°F/Gas 5. Grease a baking
tin (pan) just large enough to hold
the apples.

2 With a small knife, cut at an
angle to enlarge the core
opening at the stem-end of each
apple to about 2.5cm/1in in
diameter. (The opening should
resemble a funnel in shape.)

3 Arrange the apples in the
prepared tin, stem-end up.

4 In a small pan, combine
175ml/6fl oz/¾ cup of water
with the brown sugar, nutmeg and
pepper. Bring the mixture to the
boil, stirring. Boil for 6 minutes.

5 Mix together the walnuts and
sultanas. Spoon some of the
walnut-sultana mixture into the
opening in each apple.

6 Top each apple with some of
the diced butter or margarine.

7 Spoon the brown sugar sauce
over and around the apples.
Bake, basting occasionally with the
sauce, until the apples are just
tender, 45–50 minutes. Transfer the
apples to a serving dish, reserving
the brown sugar sauce in the
baking tin. Keep the apples warm.

8 For the caramel sauce, mix the
butter or margarine, cream
and reserved brown sugar sauce in
a pan. Bring to the boil, stirring
occasionally, and simmer until
thickened, about 2 minutes.
Leave the sauce to cool slightly
before serving.

VARIATION

Use a mixture of firm red and gold
pears instead of the apples,
preparing them in the same way.
Cook for 10 minutes longer.

Cabinet Pudding

A rich, baked custard, flavoured with glacé and dried fruit.

INGREDIENTS

Serves 4

25g/1oz/2½ tbsp raisins, chopped
30ml/2 tbsp brandy (optional)
25g/1oz/2½ tbsp glacé (candied)
  cherries, halved
25g/1oz/2½ tbsp angelica, chopped
2 trifle sponge cakes, diced
50g/2oz ratafia biscuits (almond
  macaroons), crushed
2 eggs, plus 2 egg yolks
30ml/2 tbsp sugar
450ml/¾ pint/1⅞ cups single (light)
  cream or milk
few drops of vanilla extract

1 Soak the raisins in the brandy, if using, for several hours.

2 Butter a 750ml/1¼ pint/3 cup charlotte mould and arrange some of the cherries and angelica in the base.

3 Mix the remaining cherries and angelica with the sponge cakes, ratafia biscuits and raisins and brandy, if using, and spoon into the mould.

4 Lightly whisk together the eggs, egg yolks and sugar. Bring the cream or milk just to the boil, then stir into the egg mixture with the vanilla extract.

5 Strain the egg mixture into the mould, then leave for 15–30 minutes.

6 Preheat the oven to 160°C/325°F/Gas 3. Place the mould in a roasting pan, cover with baking parchment and pour in boiling water to come halfway up the side of the mould. Bake for 1 hour, or until set. Leave for 2–3 minutes, then turn out on to a warm plate, to serve.

Eve's Pudding

The tempting apples beneath the sponge topping are the reason for the pudding's name.

INGREDIENTS

Serves 4–6

115g/4oz/½ cup butter
115g/4oz/generous ½ cup caster
  (superfine) sugar
2 eggs, beaten
grated rind and juice of 1 lemon
90g/3½oz/scant 1 cup self-raising
  (self-rising) flour
40g/1½oz/⅓ cup ground almonds
115g/4oz/scant ½ cup soft brown sugar
675g/1½lb cooking apples, cored and
  thinly sliced
25g/1oz/¼ cup flaked (sliced) almonds

1 Beat together the butter and caster sugar in a large mixing bowl until the mixture is very light and fluffy.

2 Gradually beat the eggs into the butter mixture, beating well after each addition, then fold in the lemon rind, flour and ground almonds.

3 Mix the brown sugar, apples and lemon juice, tip into the dish, add the sponge mixture, then the almonds. Bake for 40–45 minutes, until golden.

Chocolate Crêpes with Plums and Port

A good dinner party dessert, this dish can be made in advance and always looks impressive.

INGREDIENTS

Serves 6

50g/2oz plain (semisweet) chocolate,
  broken into squares
200ml/7fl oz/⅞ cup milk
120ml/4fl oz/½ cup single (light) cream
30ml/2 tbsp cocoa powder
115g/4oz/1 cup plain (all-purpose) flour
2 eggs
For the filling
500g/1¼lb red or golden plums
50g/2oz/¼ cup caster (superfine) sugar
30ml/2 tbsp port
oil, for frying
175g/6oz/¾ cup crème fraîche
For the sauce
150g/5oz plain (semisweet) chocolate,
  broken into squares
175ml/6fl oz/¾ cup double (heavy) cream
30ml/2 tbsp port

1 Place the chocolate in a pan with the milk. Heat gently until the chocolate has dissolved. Pour into a blender or food processor and add the cream, cocoa powder, flour and eggs. Process until smooth, then tip into a jug (pitcher) and chill for 30 minutes.

2 Meanwhile, make the filling. Halve and stone (pit) the plums. Place them in a pan and add the sugar and 30ml/2 tbsp of water. Bring to the boil, then lower the heat, cover, and simmer for about 10 minutes or until the plums are tender. Stir in the port and simmer for a further 30 seconds. Remove the pan from the heat and keep warm.

3 Have ready a sheet of baking parchment. Heat a crêpe pan, grease it lightly with a little oil, then pour in just enough batter to cover the base of the pan, swirling to coat it evenly.

4 Cook until the crêpe has set, then flip it over to cook the other side. Slide the crêpe out on to the sheet of parchment, then cook 9–11 more crêpes in the same way.

5 Make the sauce. Combine the chocolate and cream in a pan. Heat gently, stirring until smooth. Add the port and heat gently, stirring, for 1 minute.

6 Divide the plum filling between the crêpes, add a dollop of crème fraîche to each and roll them up carefully. Serve in shallow plates, with the chocolate sauce spooned over the top.

Pears in Chocolate Fudge Blankets

Warm poached pears coated in a rich chocolate fudge sauce – who could resist?

INGREDIENTS

Serves 6

6 ripe eating pears
30ml/2 tbsp lemon juice
75g/3oz/scant ½ cup caster
   (superfine) sugar
1 cinnamon stick
For the sauce
200ml/7fl oz/⅞ cup double (heavy) cream
150g/5oz/scant 1 cup light muscovado
   (brown) sugar
25g/1oz/2 tbsp unsalted butter
60ml/4 tbsp golden (light corn) syrup
120ml/4fl oz/½ cup milk
200g/7oz plain (semisweet) chocolate,
   broken into squares

1 Peel the pears thinly, leaving the stalks on. Scoop out the cores from the base. Brush the cut surfaces with lemon juice to prevent browning.

2 Place the sugar and 300ml/ ½ pint/1¼ cups of water in a large pan. Heat gently until the sugar dissolves. Add the pears and cinnamon stick with any remaining lemon juice, and, if necessary, a little more water, so that the pears are almost covered.

3 Bring to the boil, then lower the heat, cover the pan and simmer the pears gently for 15-20 minutes.

4 Meanwhile, make the sauce. Place the cream, sugar, butter, golden syrup and milk in a heavy pan. Heat gently until the sugar has dissolved and the butter and syrup have melted, then bring to the boil. Boil, stirring constantly, for about 5 minutes or until thick and smooth.

5 Remove the pan from the heat and stir in the chocolate until it has melted.

6 Using a slotted spoon, transfer the poached pears to a dish. Keep hot. Boil the syrup rapidly to reduce to about 45–60ml/3–4 tbsp. Remove the cinnamon stick and gently stir the syrup into the chocolate sauce.

7 Serve the pears in individual bowls or on dessert plates, with the hot chocolate fudge sauce spooned over.

Sticky Toffee Pudding

Filling, warming and packed with calories, but still everyone's favourite pudding.

INGREDIENTS

Serves 6

115g/4oz/1 cup toasted walnuts, chopped
175g/6oz/³⁄₄ cup butter
175g/6oz/scant 1 cup soft brown sugar
60ml/4 tbsp single (light) cream
30ml/2 tbsp lemon juice
2 eggs, beaten
115g/4oz/1 cup self-raising
   (self-rising) flour

1 Grease a 900ml/1½ pint/ 3¾ cup heatproof bowl and add half the walnuts.

2 Heat 50g/2oz/4 tbsp of the butter with 50g/2oz/4 tbsp of the sugar, the cream and 15ml/ 1 tbsp lemon juice in a small pan, stirring until smooth. Pour half into the heatproof bowl, then swirl to coat it a little way up the sides.

3 Beat the remaining butter and sugar until light and fluffy, then gradually beat in the eggs. Fold in the flour and the remaining nuts and lemon juice and spoon into the bowl.

4 Cover the bowl with baking parchment with a pleat folded in the centre, then tie securely with string.

5 Steam the pudding for about 1¼ hours, until it is set in the centre.

6 Just before serving, gently warm the remaining sauce. Unmould the pudding on to a warm plate and pour over the warm sauce.

Chocolate and Orange Soufflé

The base in this soufflé is an easy-to-make semolina mixture, rather than the thick white sauce that most soufflés call for.

INGREDIENTS

Serves 4

600ml/1 pint/2½ cups milk
50g/2oz/generous ⅓ cup semolina
50g/2oz/scant ¼ cup brown sugar
grated rind of 1 orange
90ml/6 tbsp fresh orange juice
3 eggs, separated
65g/2½oz plain (semisweet)
   chocolate, grated
icing (confectioners') sugar, for sprinkling

1 Preheat the oven to 200°C/400°F/Gas 6. Butter a shallow 1.75 litre/3 pint/7½ cup ovenproof dish.

2 Pour the milk into a heavy pan and sprinkle over the semolina and brown sugar. Bring to the boil, stirring the mixture all the time, until thickened.

3 Remove the pan from the heat, beat in the orange rind and juice, egg yolks and all but 15ml/ 1 tbsp of the grated chocolate.

4 Whisk the egg whites until stiff, then lightly fold into the semolina mixture in three batches. Spoon into the buttered dish and bake for about 30 minutes, until just set in the centre. Sprinkle with the reserved chocolate and the icing sugar.

Queen of Puddings

*This hot pudding was developed
from a 17th-century recipe by
Queen Victoria's chefs.*

Serves 4

75g/3oz/1½ cups fresh breadcrumbs

60ml/4 tbsp caster (superfine) sugar,
   plus 5ml/1 tsp

grated rind of 1 lemon

600ml/1 pint/2½ cups milk

4 eggs

45ml/3 tbsp raspberry jam, warmed

1 Preheat the oven to 160°C/
325°F/Gas 3. Stir the breadcrumbs, 30ml/2 tbsp of the sugar
and the lemon rind together in a
bowl. Bring the milk to the boil in
a pan, then stir into the breadcrumb mixture.

2 Separate three of the eggs and
beat the yolks with the whole
egg. Stir into the breadcrumb
mixture, pour into a buttered
baking dish and leave to stand for
30 minutes, then bake the pudding
for 50–60 minutes, until set.

3 Whisk the three egg whites in a
large, clean bowl until stiff but
not dry, then gradually whisk in
the remaining 30ml/2 tbsp caster
sugar until the mixture is thick and
glossy, taking care not to overwhip.

4 Spread the jam over the
pudding, then spoon over
the meringue to cover the top
completely. Sprinkle the remaining
sugar over the meringue, then bake
for a further 15 minutes, until the
meringue is beginning to turn a
light golden colour.

COOK'S TIP

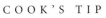

Ring the changes by using
another flavoured jam, lemon
curd, marmalade or fruit purée.

Magic Chocolate Mud Pudding

*A popular favourite, which
magically separates into a light and
luscious sponge and a velvety
chocolate sauce.*

INGREDIENTS

Serves 4

50g/2oz/4 tbsp butter

200g/7oz/generous 1 cup light
    muscovado (brown) sugar

475ml/16fl oz/2 cups milk

90g/3½oz/scant 1 cup self-raising
    (self-rising) flour

5ml/1 tsp ground cinnamon

75ml/5 tbsp cocoa powder

Greek (US strained plain) yogurt or
    vanilla ice cream, to serve

1 Preheat the oven to 180°C/
350°F/Gas 4. Lightly grease a
1.5 litre/2½ pint/6 cup ovenproof
dish and place on a baking sheet.

2 Place the butter in a pan. Add
115g/4oz/¾ cup of the sugar
and 150ml/¼ pint/⅔ cup of the
milk. Heat gently, stirring from
time to time, until the butter has
melted and all the sugar has
dissolved. Remove the pan from
the heat.

COOK'S TIP
~

A soufflé dish will support the
sponge as it rises above the sauce.

---

3 Sift the flour, cinnamon and
15ml/1 tbsp of the cocoa
powder into the pan and stir into
the mixture, mixing evenly. Pour
the mixture into the prepared dish
and level the surface.

4 Sift the remaining sugar and
cocoa powder into a bowl, mix
well, then sprinkle over the
pudding mixture.

5 Pour the remaining milk over
the pudding.

6 Bake for 45–50 minutes or
until the sponge has risen to
the top and is firm to the touch.
Serve hot, with the yogurt or
vanilla ice cream.

Christmas Pudding

This recipe makes enough to fill one 1.2 litre/2 pint/5 cup bowl or two 600ml/1 pint/2½ cup bowls. It can be made up to a month before Christmas and stored in a cool, dry place. Steam the pudding for 2 hours before serving. Serve with brandy or rum butter, whisky sauce, custard or whipped cream.

INGREDIENTS

Serves 8

115g/4oz/½ cup butter
225g/8oz/1 heaped cup soft dark brown sugar
50g/2oz/½ cup self-raising (self-rising) flour
5ml/1tsp ground mixed spice
1.5ml/¼ tsp grated nutmeg
2.5ml/½ tsp ground cinnamon
2 eggs
115g/4oz/2 cups fresh white breadcrumbs
175g/6oz/generous 1 cup sultanas (golden raisins)
175g/6oz/generous 1 cup raisins
115g/4oz/½ cup currants
25g/1oz/3 tbsp mixed candied peel, chopped finely
25g/1oz/¼ cup chopped almonds
1 small cooking apple, peeled, cored and coarsely grated
finely grated rind or 1 orange or lemon
juice of 1 orange or lemon, made up to 150ml/¼ pint/⅔ cup with brandy, rum or sherry

1 Cut a disc of baking parchment to fit the base of the bowl(s) and butter the disc and bowl(s).

2 Whisk the butter and sugar together until soft. Beat in the flour, spices and eggs. Stir in the remaining ingredients thoroughly. The mixture should have a soft dropping consistency.

3 Turn the mixture into the greased bowl(s) and level the top with a spoon.

4 Cover with another disc of buttered baking parchment.

5 Make a pleat across the centre of a large piece of baking parchment and cover the bowl(s) with it, tying it in place with string under the rim. Cut off the excess paper. Pleat a piece of foil in the same way and cover the bowl(s) with it, tucking it around the bowl neatly, under the frill. Tie another piece of string around and across the top, as a handle.

6 Place the bowl(s) in a steamer over a pan of simmering water and steam for 6 hours. Alternatively, put the bowl(s) into a large pan and pour round enough boiling water to come halfway up the bowl(s) and cover the pan with a tight-fitting lid. Check the water is simmering and top it up with boiling water as it evaporates. When the pudding(s) have cooked, leave to cool completely. Then remove the foil and baking parchment. Wipe the bowl(s) clean and replace the baking parchment and foil with clean pieces, ready for reheating.

TO SERVE

Steam for 2 hours. Turn on to a plate and leave to stand for 5 minutes, before removing the heatproof bowl (the steam will rise to the top of the bowl and help to loosen the pudding). Decorate with a sprig of holly.

Steamed Chocolate and Fruit Puddings

Some things always turn out well, including these wonderful little puddings. Dark, fluffy chocolate sponge with tangy cranberries and apple is served with a honeyed chocolate syrup.

INGREDIENTS

Serves 4

115g/4oz/⅔ cup dark muscovado (molasses) sugar

1 eating apple

75g/3oz/¾ cup cranberries, thawed if frozen

115g/4oz/½ cup soft margarine

2 eggs

75g/3oz/⅔ cup plain (all-purpose) flour

2.5ml/½ tsp baking powder

45ml/3 tbsp cocoa powder

For the chocolate syrup

115g/4oz plain (semisweet) chocolate, broken into squares

30ml/2 tbsp clear honey

15ml/1 tbsp unsalted butter

2.5ml/½ tsp vanilla extract

1 Prepare a steamer or half fill a pan with water and bring it to the boil. Grease four individual heatproof bowls and sprinkle each one with a little of the muscovado sugar to coat well all over.

2 Peel and core the apple. Dice it into a bowl, add the cranberries and mix well. Divide equally among the prepared heatproof bowls.

3 Place the remaining muscovado sugar in a mixing bowl. Add the margarine, eggs, flour, baking powder and cocoa; beat until combined and smooth.

4 Spoon the mixture into the bowls and cover each with a double thickness of foil. Steam for about 45 minutes, topping up the boiling water as required, until the puddings are well risen and firm.

5 Make the syrup. Mix the chocolate, honey, butter and vanilla extract in a small pan. Heat gently, stirring, until melted and smooth.

6 Run a knife around the edge of each pudding to loosen it, then turn out on to individual plates. Serve immediately, with the chocolate syrup.

COOK'S TIP

The puddings can be cooked very quickly in the microwave. Use non-metallic bowls and cover with baking parchment instead of foil. Cook on High (100% power) for 5–6 minutes, then stand for 2–3 minutes before turning out.

Hot Chocolate Cake

This is wonderfully wicked served as a pudding with a white chocolate sauce. The basic cake freezes well – thaw, then warm in the microwave before serving.

INGREDIENTS

Makes 10–12 slices

200g/7oz/1¾ cups self-raising (self-rising) wholemeal (whole-wheat) flour
25g/1oz/¼ cup cocoa powder
pinch of salt
175g/6oz/¾ cup soft margarine
175g/6oz/¾ cup soft light brown sugar
few drops vanilla extract
4 eggs
75g/3oz white chocolate, roughly chopped
chocolate leaves and curls, to decorate

For the white chocolate sauce

75g/3oz white chocolate
150ml/¼ pint/⅔ cup single (light) cream
30–45ml/2–3 tbsp milk

1 Preheat the oven to 160°C/ 325°F/Gas 3. Sift the flour, cocoa powder and salt into a bowl, adding in the whole wheat flakes from the sieve (strainer).

2 Cream the margarine, sugar and vanilla extract together until light and fluffy, then gently beat in one egg.

3 Gradually stir in the remaining eggs, one at a time, alternately folding in some of the flour, until the mixture is blended in.

4 Stir in the white chocolate and spoon into a 675–900g/ 1½–2lb loaf tin (pan) or a 18cm/ 7in greased cake tin. Bake for 30–40 minutes, or until just firm to the touch and shrinking away from the sides of the tin.

5 Meanwhile, prepare the sauce. Heat the white chocolate and cream very gently in a pan until the chocolate is melted. Add the milk and stir until cool.

6 Serve the cake sliced, in a pool of sauce and decorated with chocolate leaves and curls.

Bread Pudding with Pecan Nuts

A version of the British classic deliciously flavoured with pecan nuts and orange rind.

INGREDIENTS

Serves 6

400ml/14fl oz/1⅔ cups milk

400ml/14fl oz/1⅔ cups single (light) or
 whipping cream

150g/5oz/¾ cup caster (superfine) sugar

3 eggs, beaten to mix

10ml/2 tsp grated orange rind

5ml/1 tsp vanilla extract

24 slices of day-old French bread,
 1.5cm/½in thick

75g/3oz/½ cup toasted pecan nuts,
 chopped

icing (confectioners') sugar, for sprinkling

whipped cream or sour cream and maple
 syrup, to serve

1 Put 350ml/12fl oz/1½ cups each of the milk and cream in a pan. Add the sugar. Warm over low heat, stirring to dissolve the sugar. Remove from the heat and cool. Add the eggs, orange rind and vanilla and mix well.

2 Arrange half of the bread slices in a buttered 23–25cm/9–10in baking dish. Scatter two-thirds of the pecans over the bread. Arrange the remaining bread slices on top and scatter on the rest of the pecans.

3 Pour the egg mixture evenly over the bread slices. Soak for 30 minutes. Press the top layer of bread down into the liquid once or twice.

4 Preheat the oven to 180°C/ 350°F/Gas 4. If the top layer of bread slices looks dry and all the liquid has been absorbed, moisten with the remaining milk and cream.

5 Set the baking dish in a roasting pan. Add enough water to the tin to come halfway up the sides of the dish. Bring the water to the boil.

6 Transfer to the oven. Bake for 40 minutes or until the pudding is set and golden brown on top. Sprinkle the top of the pudding with sifted icing sugar and serve warm, with whipped cream or sour cream and maple syrup, if you like.

Chocolate Chip and Banana Pudding

Hot and steamy, this is a superb light pudding.

INGREDIENTS

Serves 4

200g/7oz/1¾ cups self-raising
    (self-rising) flour
75g/3oz/6 tbsp unsalted butter
    or margarine
2 ripe bananas
75g/3oz/⅓ cup caster (superfine) sugar
60ml/4 tbsp milk
1 egg, beaten
60ml/4 tbsp plain (semisweet) chocolate
    chips or chopped chocolate
Glossy Chocolate Sauce (see Basic
    Techniques) and whipped cream, to serve

1 Prepare a steamer or half fill a
pan with water and bring it to
the boil. Grease a 1 litre/1¾ pint/
4 cup heatproof bowl. Sift the flour
into a bowl and rub in the butter
or margarine until the mixture
resembles breadcrumbs.

2 Mash the bananas in a bowl.
Stir them into the creamed
mixture, with the caster sugar.

3 Whisk the milk with the egg in
a jug (pitcher) or bowl, then
beat into the pudding mixture. Stir
in the plain chocolate chips or
chopped chocolate.

4 Spoon the mixture into the
prepared bowl, cover closely
with a double thickness of foil, and
steam for 2 hours, topping up the
water as required during cooking.

5 Run a knife around the top
of the pudding to loosen it,
then turn it out on to a warm
serving dish. Serve hot, with the
chocolate sauce and a spoonful of
whipped cream.

COOK'S TIP

If you have a food processor,
make a quick-mix version by
processing all the ingredients,
except the chocolate, until
smooth. Stir in the chocolate and
proceed as in the recipe.

Hot Plum Batter Pudding

Other fruits can be used in place of plums, depending on the season. Canned black cherries are a convenient substitute to keep in the store cupboard.

INGREDIENTS

Serves 4

450g/1lb ripe red plums, quartered and
    stoned (pitted)
200ml/7fl oz/⁷⁄₈ cup skimmed milk
60ml/4 tbsp skimmed milk powder
15ml/1 tbsp light muscovado
    (brown) sugar
5ml/1 tsp vanilla extract
75g/3oz/²⁄₃ cup self-raising
    (self-rising) flour
2 egg whites
icing (confectioners') sugar, to sprinkle

1 Preheat the oven to 220°C/ 425°F/Gas 7. Lightly oil a wide, shallow ovenproof dish and add the plums.

2 Pour the milk, milk powder, sugar, vanilla, flour and egg whites into a blender or food processor. Process until smooth.

3 Pour the batter over the plums. Bake for 25–30 minutes, or until puffed and golden. Sprinkle with icing sugar and serve immediately.

> ### COOK'S TIP
> ～
> If you don't have a food processor, then place the dry ingredients for the batter in a large bowl and gradually whisk in the milk and egg whites.

Glazed Apricot Sponge

Proper puddings can be very high in saturated fat, but this healthy version uses the minimum of oil and no eggs.

INGREDIENTS

Serves 4

10ml/2 tsp golden (light corn) syrup
411g/14½oz can apricot halves in
    fruit juice
150g/5oz/1¼ cups self-raising
    (self-rising) flour
75g/3oz/1½ cups fresh breadcrumbs
90g/3½oz/½ cup light muscovado
    (brown) sugar
5ml/1 tsp ground cinnamon
30ml/2 tbsp sunflower oil
175ml/6fl oz/¾ cup skimmed milk

1 Preheat the oven to 180°C/ 350°F/Gas 4. Lightly oil a 900ml/1½ pint/3¾ cup heatproof bowl. Spoon in the syrup.

2 Drain the apricots and reserve the juice. Arrange about 8 halves in the bowl. Purée the rest of the apricots with the juice and set aside.

3 Mix the flour, breadcrumbs, sugar and cinnamon then beat in the oil and milk. Spoon into the bowl and bake for 50–55 minutes, or until firm and golden. Turn out and serve with the puréed fruit as an accompaniment.

Crunchy Gooseberry Crumble

Gooseberries are perfect for traditional family puddings like this one. When gooseberries are out of season, other fruits such as apples, plums or rhubarb could be used instead.

INGREDIENTS

Serves 4

500g/1¼lb/5 cups gooseberries
50g/2oz/4 tbsp caster (superfine) sugar
75g/3oz/scant 1 cup rolled oats
75g/3oz/⅔ cup wholemeal
   (whole-wheat) flour
60ml/4 tbsp sunflower oil
50g/2oz/4 tbsp demerara (raw) sugar
30ml/2 tbsp chopped walnuts
natural (plain) yogurt or custard, to serve

1 Preheat the oven to 200°C/ 400°F/Gas 6. Place the gooseberries in a pan with the caster sugar. Cover the pan and cook over a very low heat for about 10 minutes, until the gooseberries are just tender. Tip the contents of the pan into an ovenproof dish.

2 To make the crumble, place the oats, flour and oil in a bowl and stir with a fork until evenly mixed.

3 Stir in the demerara sugar and walnuts, then spread evenly over the gooseberries. Bake for 25–30 minutes, or until golden and bubbling. Serve hot with yogurt, or custard made with skimmed milk.

COOK'S TIP

~

The best gooseberries to use for cooking are the early, small, firm green ones.

Chocolate Amaretti Peaches

Quick and easy to prepare, this delicious dessert can also be made with fresh nectarines or apricots.

INGREDIENTS

Serves 4

115g/4oz amaretti, crushed

50g/2oz plain (semisweet) chocolate, chopped

grated rind of ½ orange

15ml/1 tbsp clear honey

1.5ml/¼ tsp ground cinnamon

1 egg white, lightly beaten

4 firm ripe peaches

150ml/¼ pint/⅔ cup white wine

15ml/1 tbsp caster (superfine) sugar

whipped cream, to serve

1 Preheat the oven to 190°C/ 375°F/Gas 5. Mix together the crushed amaretti, chocolate, orange rind, honey and cinnamon in a bowl. Add the beaten egg white and mix to bind the mixture together.

2 Halve and stone (pit) the peaches and fill the cavities with the chocolate mixture, mounding it up slightly.

3 Arrange the stuffed peaches in a lightly buttered, shallow ovenproof dish which will just hold the peaches comfortably. Pour the wine into a measuring jug (cup) and stir in the sugar.

4 Pour the wine mixture around the peaches. Bake for 30–40 minutes, until the peaches are tender. Serve immediately with a little of the cooking juices spooned over and the whipped cream.

Apple Fritters

Make sure you buy plenty of apples for this recipe. They taste so good you'll probably have to cook an extra batch.

INGREDIENTS

Serves 4–6

130g/4½oz/1⅓ cups plain (all-purpose) flour
10ml/2 tsp baking powder
1.5ml/¼ tsp salt
150ml/¼ pint/⅔ cup milk
1 egg, beaten
oil for deep-frying
150g/5oz/¾ cup granulated (white) sugar
5ml/1 tsp ground cinnamon
2 large tart-sweet apples, peeled, cored, and cut in 5mm/¼in slices
icing (confectioners') sugar, for dusting

1 Sift the flour, baking powder and salt into a bowl. Beat in the milk and egg with a wire whisk.

2 Heat at least 7.5cm/3in of oil in a heavy frying pan to 185°C/360°F or until a cube of bread browns in 1–2 minutes.

3 Mix the granulated sugar and cinnamon in a shallow bowl or plate. Toss the apple slices in the sugar mixture to coat all over.

4 Dip the apple slices in the batter, using a fork or slotted spoon. Drain off excess batter. Fry, in batches, in the hot oil until golden brown on both sides, about 4–5 minutes. Drain the fritters on kitchen paper.

5 Sprinkle with icing sugar, and serve hot.

Cherry Compote

Sweet cherries in syrup to serve with cream or ice cream.

INGREDIENTS

Serves 6

120ml/4fl oz/½ cup red wine
50g/2oz/¼ cup light brown sugar, firmly packed
50g/2oz/¼ cup granulated (white) sugar
15ml/1 tbsp honey
2 2.5cm/1in strips of orange rind
1.5ml/¼ tsp almond extract
675g/1½lb sweet fresh cherries, pitted
ice cream or whipped cream, for serving

1 Combine all the ingredients except the cherries in a pan with 120ml/4fl oz/½ cup of water. Stir over medium heat until the sugar dissolves. Raise the heat and boil until the liquid reduces slightly.

2 Add the cherries. Bring back to the boil. Reduce the heat slightly and simmer for 8–10 minutes. If necessary, skim off any foam.

3 Let cool to lukewarm. Spoon warm over vanilla ice cream, or chill and serve cold with whipped cream, if desired.

Ginger Baked Pears

*This simple French dessert is the
kind that would be served after
Sunday lunch or a family supper.
Try to find Comice or Anjou pears –
this recipe is especially useful for
slightly under-ripe fruit.*

INGREDIENTS

Serves 4

4 large pears
300ml/½ pint/1¼ cups whipping cream
50g/2oz/¼ cup caster (superfine) sugar
2.5ml/½ tsp vanilla extract
1.5ml/¼ tsp ground cinnamon
pinch of freshly grated nutmeg
5ml/1 tsp grated fresh root ginger

1 Preheat the oven to 190°C/
375°F/Gas 5. Lightly butter a
large shallow baking dish.

2 Peel the pears, cut in half
lengthways and remove the
cores. Arrange, cut-side down, in a
single layer in the baking dish.

3 Mix together the cream, sugar,
vanilla extract, cinnamon,
nutmeg and ginger and pour over
the pears.

4 Bake for 30–35 minutes,
basting from time to time,
until the pears are tender and
browned on top and the cream is
thick and bubbly. Cool slightly
before serving.

Prunes Poached in Red Wine

*Serve this simple dessert on its own,
or with crème fraîche or vanilla
ice cream.*

INGREDIENTS

Serves 8–10

1 unwaxed orange
1 unwaxed lemon
750ml/1¼ pints/3 cups fruity red wine
50g/2oz/¼ cup caster (superfine) sugar,
 or to taste
1 cinnamon stick
pinch of freshly grated nutmeg
2 or 3 cloves
5ml/1 tsp black peppercorns
1 bay leaf
900g/2lb large pitted prunes, soaked in
 cold water
strips of orange rind, to decorate
crème fraîche or vanilla ice cream, to
 serve

1 Using a vegetable peeler, peel
two or three strips of rind from
both the orange and lemon.
Squeeze the juice from both and
put in a large pan.

2 Add the wine, sugar, spices,
peppercorns, bay leaf, strips of
rind to the pan and 475ml/16fl oz/
2 cups of water.

3 Bring to the boil over a
medium heat, stirring
occasionally to dissolve the
sugar. Drain the prunes and
add to the pan, reduce the heat
to low and simmer, covered, for
10–15 minutes until the prunes
are tender. Remove from the heat
and set aside until cool.

4 Using a slotted spoon, transfer
the prunes to a serving dish.
Return the cooking liquid to a
medium-high heat and bring to
the boil. Boil for 5–10 minutes
until slightly reduced and syrupy,
then pour or strain over the
prunes. Cool, then chill before
serving with cream, decorated with
strips of orange rind, if you like.

Apple Strudel

*This Austrian pudding is tradition-
ally made with paper-thin layers of
buttered strudel pastry, filled with
spiced apples and nuts. Ready-made
filo pastry makes an easy substitute.*

INGREDIENTS

Serves 4–6

75g/3oz/¾ cup hazelnuts, chopped
    and roasted
30ml/2 tbsp nibbed almonds, roasted
50g/2oz/4 tbsp demerara (raw) sugar
2.5ml/½ tsp ground cinnamon
grated rind and juice of ½ lemon
2 large Bramley cooking apples, peeled,
    cored and chopped
50g/2oz/⅓ cup sultanas (golden raisins)
4 large sheet filo pastry
50g/2oz/4 tbsp unsalted butter, melted
icing (confectioners') sugar, for dusting
cream, custard or yogurt, to serve

1 Preheat the oven to 190°C/
375°F/Gas 5. In a bowl mix
together the hazelnuts, almonds,
sugar, cinnamon, lemon rind
and juice, apples and sultanas.
Set aside.

2 Lay one sheet of filo pastry on
a clean dish towel and brush
with melted butter. Lay a second
sheet on top and brush again with
melted butter. Repeat with the
remaining two sheets.

3 Spread the fruit and nut
mixture over the pastry,
leaving a 7.5cm/3in border at the
shorter ends. Fold the ends in
over the filling. Roll up from one
long edge, using the dish towel.

4 Transfer the strudel to a
greased baking sheet, placing
it seam side down. Brush with
butter and bake for 30–35 minutes,
until golden and crisp. Dust with
icing sugar and serve hot with
cream, custard or yogurt.

Chocolate Fruit Fondue

*Fondues originated in Switzerland
and this sweet treat is the perfect
ending to any meal.*

INGREDIENTS

Serves 6–8

16 fresh strawberries
4 rings fresh pineapple, cut into wedges
2 small nectarines, stoned (pitted) and
    cut into wedges
1 kiwi fruit, halved and thickly sliced
small bunch of black seedless grapes
2 bananas, chopped
1 small eating apple, cored and cut
    into wedges
lemon juice, for brushing
225g/8oz plain (semisweet) chocolate
15g/½oz/1 tbsp butter
150ml/¼ pint/⅔ cup single (light) cream
45ml/3 tbsp Irish cream liqueur
15ml/1 tbsp pistachio nuts, chopped

1 Arrange the fruit on a serving
platter and brush the banana
and apple pieces with a little lemon
juice. Cover and place in the
refrigerator until ready to serve.

2 Place the chocolate, butter,
cream and liqueur in a
bowl over a pan of simmering
water. Stir until melted and
completely smooth.

3 Pour the mixture into a
warmed serving bowl; sprinkle
with pistachios. Guests help
themselves by skewering fruits on to
forks and dipping in the hot sauce.

Crêpes Suzette

This is one of the best-known French desserts and is easy to do at home. You can make the crêpes in advance, then you will be able to put the dish together quickly at the last minute.

INGREDIENTS

Serves 6

115g/4oz/1 cup plain (all-purpose) flour
1.5ml/¼ tsp salt
25g/1oz/2 tbsp caster (superfine) sugar
2 eggs, lightly beaten
250ml/8fl oz/1 cup milk
30ml/2 tbsp orange flower water or
    orange liqueur (optional)
25g/1oz/2 tbsp unsalted butter, melted,
    plus more for frying

For the orange sauce

75g/3oz/6 tbsp unsalted butter
50g/2oz/¼ cup caster (superfine) sugar
grated rind and juice of 1 large
    unwaxed orange
grated rind and juice of 1 unwaxed lemon
150ml/¼ pint/⅔ cup fresh orange juice
60ml/4 tbsp orange liqueur, plus more for
    flaming (optional)
brandy, for flaming (optional)
orange segments, to decorate

1 In a medium bowl, sift together the flour, salt and sugar. Make a well in the centre and pour in the beaten eggs. Using a whisk, beat the eggs, bringing in a little flour until it is all incorporated. Slowly whisk in the milk and 60ml/4 tbsp water to make a smooth batter.

2 Whisk in the orange flower water or liqueur, if using, then strain the batter into a large jug (pitcher) and set aside for 20–30 minutes. If the batter thickens, add a little milk or water to thin.

3 Heat an 18–20cm/7–8in crêpe pan over a medium heat. Stir the melted butter into the crêpe batter. Brush the hot pan with a little extra melted butter and pour in about 30ml/2 tbsp of batter. Quickly tilt and rotate the pan to cover the base with a thin layer of batter. Cook for about 1 minute until the top is set and the base is golden. With a palette knife, carefully turn over the crêpe and cook for 20–30 seconds, just to set. Tip out on to a plate.

4 Continue cooking the crêpes, stirring the batter occasionally and brushing the pan with a little melted butter as and when necessary. Place a sheet of clear film (plastic wrap) between each crêpe as they are stacked.

5 To make the sauce, melt the butter in a large frying pan over a medium-low heat, then stir in the sugar, orange and lemon rind and juice, the additional orange juice and the orange liqueur, if using.

6 Place a crêpe in the pan browned-side down, swirling gently to coat with the sauce. Fold it in half, then in half again to form a triangle and push to the side of the pan. Continue heating and folding the crêpes until all are warm and covered with the sauce.

7 To flame the crêpes, heat 30–45ml/2–3 tbsp each of orange liqueur and brandy in a small pan over a medium heat. Remove the pan from the heat, carefully ignite the liquid with a match then gently pour over the crêpes. Scatter over the orange segments and serve immediately.

Spiced Mexican Fritters

Hot, sweet and spicy fritters are popular in both Spain and Mexico for either breakfast or a snack.

INGREDIENTS

Makes 16 (serves 4)

175g/6oz/1 cup raspberries

45ml/3 tbsp icing (confectioners') sugar,
    plus 15ml/1 tbsp for dusting

45ml/3 tbsp orange juice

For the fritters

50g/2oz/4 tbsp butter

65g/2½oz/⅔ cup plain (all-purpose)
    flour, sifted

2 eggs, lightly beaten

15ml/1 tbsp ground almonds

corn oil, for frying

2.5ml/½ tsp ground cinnamon, for dusting

8 fresh raspberries, to decorate

1 Mash the raspberries with the icing sugar, push through a sieve (strainer) into a bowl. Stir in the orange juice and chill until ready to serve.

2 To make the fritters, place the butter and 150ml/¼ pint/⅔ cup water in a pan and heat gently until the butter has melted. Bring to the boil and, when boiling, add the sifted flour all immediately and turn off the heat.

3 Beat until the mixture leaves the sides of the pan and forms a ball. Cool slightly then beat in the eggs a little at a time, then add the almonds.

4 Spoon the mixture into a piping (pastry) bag fitted with a large star nozzle. Half-fill a pan or deep-fat fryer with the oil and heat to 190°C/375°F.

5 Pipe about four 5cm/2in lengths at a time into the hot oil, cutting off the raw mixture with a knife as you go. Deep-fry for about 3–4 minutes, turning occasionally, until puffed up and golden. Drain on kitchen paper and keep warm in the oven while frying the remainder.

6 When you have fried all the mixture, dust the hot fritters with icing sugar and cinnamon. Serve three or four per person on serving plates drizzled with a little of the raspberry sauce, dust again with sifted icing sugar and decorate with fresh raspberries.

Thai Fried Bananas

A very simple and quick Thai pudding – bananas fried in butter, brown sugar and lime juice, and sprinkled with toasted coconut.

INGREDIENTS

Serves 4

40g/1½oz/3 tbsp butter

4 large slightly under-ripe bananas

15ml/1 tbsp desiccated (dry unsweetened
    shredded) coconut

60ml/4 tbsp soft light brown sugar

60ml/4 tbsp lime juice

2 fresh lime slices, to decorate

thick and creamy natural (plain) yogurt,
    to serve

1 Heat the butter in a large frying pan or wok and fry the bananas for 1–2 minutes on each side, or until they are lightly golden in colour.

2 Meanwhile, dry-fry the coconut in a small frying pan until lightly browned, and reserve.

3 Sprinkle the sugar into the pan with the bananas, add the lime juice and cook, stirring until dissolved. Arrange bananas on a serving dish. Sprinkle the coconut over the bananas, decorate with lime slices and serve with the thick and creamy yogurt.

Apple and Lemon Risotto with Poached Plums

*Although it's entirely possible to
cook this by the conventional
risotto method – that is by adding
the liquid gradually – it makes
more sense to cook the rice with
the milk in the same way as for a
rice pudding.*

INGREDIENTS

Serves 4

1 cooking apple
15g/½oz/1 tbsp butter
175g/6oz/scant 1 cup risotto rice
600ml/1 pint/2½ cups creamy milk
about 50g/2oz/¼ cup caster
   (superfine) sugar
1.5ml/¼ tsp ground cinnamon
30ml/2 tsp lemon juice
45ml/3 tbsp double (heavy) cream
grated rind of 1 lemon, to decorate
For the poached plums
50g/2oz/¼ cup light muscovado
   (brown) sugar
200ml/7fl oz/scant 1 cup apple juice
3 star anise
cinnamon stick
6 plums, halved, stoned (pitted) and sliced

1 Peel and core the apple and cut
it into large chunks. Put the
chunks in a large, non-stick pan
and add the butter. Heat gently
until the butter melts.

2 Add the rice and milk and stir
well to mix. Bring to the boil
over a medium heat, then simmer
very gently for 20–25 minutes,
stirring occasionally.

3 To make the poached plums,
dissolve the sugar in 150ml/
¼ pint/⅔ cup apple juice in a pan.
Add the spices and bring to the
boil. Boil for 2 minutes. Add the
plums and simmer for 2 minutes.
Set aside until ready to serve.

4 Stir the sugar, cinnamon and
lemon juice into the risotto.
Cook for 2 minutes, stirring all the
time, then stir in the cream. Taste
and add more sugar if necessary.
Decorate with the lemon rind and
serve hot with the poached plums.

Chocolate Risotto

If you've never tasted a sweet risotto, there's a treat in store, children of all ages love it.

Serves 4–6

175g/6oz/scant 1 cup risotto rice
600ml/1 pint/2½ cups creamy milk
75g/3oz plain (semisweet) chocolate, chopped
25g/1oz/2 tbsp butter
about 50g/2oz/¼ cup caster
    (superfine) sugar
pinch of ground cinnamon
60ml/4 tbsp double (heavy) cream
fresh raspberries and chocolate caraque,
    to decorate
chocolate sauce, to serve

1 Put the rice in a non-stick pan. Pour in the milk and bring to the boil over a low heat. Reduce the heat to the lowest setting and simmer for 20 minutes, stirring.

2 Stir in the chocolate, butter and sugar. Cook, stirring all the time over a very gentle heat for 1–2 minutes, until the chocolate has melted.

3 Remove the pan from the heat and stir in the ground cinnamon and double cream. Cover the pan and leave to stand for a few minutes.

4 Spoon the risotto into individual dishes or dessert plates, and decorate with fresh raspberries and chocolate caraque. Serve with chocolate sauce.

Caramel Rice Pudding

This rice pudding is delicious served with crunchy fresh fruit.

Serves 4

15g/½oz/1 tbsp butter

50g/2oz/¼ cup short grain rice

75ml/5 tbsp demerara (raw) sugar

400g/14oz can evaporated milk made up
   to 600ml/1 pint/2½ cups with water

2 fresh baby pineapples

2 figs

1 crisp eating apple

10ml/2 tsp lemon juice

salt

1 Preheat the oven to 150°C/ 300°F/Gas 2. Grease a soufflé dish lightly with butter. Put the rice in a sieve (strainer), wash under cold running water. Drain well and put into the soufflé dish.

2 Add 30ml/2 tbsp of the sugar to the dish, with a pinch of salt. Pour over the diluted evaporated milk and stir gently.

3 Dot the surface of the rice with butter. Bake for 2 hours, then leave to cool for 30 minutes.

4 Meanwhile, quarter the pineapple and the figs. Cut the apple into segments and toss in the lemon juice. Preheat the grill (broiler).

5 Sprinkle the remaining sugar evenly over the rice. Grill (broil) for 5 minutes or until the sugar has caramelized. Leave the rice to stand for 5 minutes to allow the caramel to harden, then serve warm with the fresh fruit.

Orange Rice Pudding

In Morocco, as in Spain, Greece and Italy, thick, creamy rice puddings are very popular, especially when sweetened with honey and flavoured with orange.

Serves 4

50g/2oz/generous ¼ cup short grain rice
600ml/1 pint/2½ cups milk
finely grated rind of ½ small orange
30–45ml/2–3 tbsp clear honey
150ml/¼ pint/⅔ cup double
   (heavy) cream
15ml/1 tbsp chopped pistachio nuts,
   toasted (optional)
grated orange rind, to garnish

1 Mix the rice with the milk and orange rind in a pan. Pour in the honey and stir well.

2 Bring to the boil, then lower the heat, cover and simmer very gently for about 1¼ hours, stirring frequently.

3 Remove the lid and continue cooking and stirring for 15–20 minutes, until the rice is creamy.

4 Pour in the cream, stirring constantly, then simmer for 5–8 minutes more. Spoon the rice pudding into warmed individual bowls. Sprinkle with the pistachio nuts, if wished, garnish with the orange rind and serve hot.

COLD PUDDINGS & DESSERTS

✦ ✦ ✦

Boodles Orange Fool

*This fool became the speciality of
Boodles Club, a gentlemen's club in
London's St James's.*

INGREDIENTS

Serves 4

4 trifle sponge cakes, cubed

300ml/½ pint/1¼ cups double
(heavy) cream

30–60ml/2–4 tbsp caster (superfine) sugar

grated rind and juice of 2 oranges

grated rind and juice of 1 lemon

orange and lemon slices and rind,
to decorate

1 Line the base and halfway up
the sides of a large glass serving
bowl or china dish with the cubed
trifle sponge cakes.

2 Whip the cream with the sugar
until it starts to thicken, then
gradually whip in the fruit juices,
adding the fruit rinds once most of
the juices have been incorporated.

3 Carefully pour the cream
mixture into the bowl or dish,
taking care not to dislodge the
sponge. Cover and chill for
3–4 hours. Serve decorated with
orange and lemon slices and rind.

Apricot and Orange Jelly

*A light and refreshing dessert for a
summer's day.*

INGREDIENTS

Serves 4

350g/12oz well-flavoured fresh ripe
apricots, stoned (pitted)

50–75g/2–3oz/about ⅓ cup granulated
(white) sugar

about 300ml/½ pint/1¼ cups freshly
squeezed orange juice

15ml/1 tbsp powdered gelatine

single (light) cream, to serve

finely chopped candied orange peel,
to decorate

1 Heat the apricots, sugar and
120ml/4fl oz/½ cup of the
orange juice, stirring until the
sugar has dissolved. Simmer gently
until the apricots are tender.

2 Press the apricot mixture
through a nylon sieve
(strainer) into a small measuring
jug (cup) using a spoon.

3 Pour 45ml/3 tbsp of the orange
juice into a small heatproof
bowl, sprinkle over the gelatine
and leave for about 5 minutes,
until softened.

4 Place the bowl over a pan of
hot water and heat until the
gelatine has dissolved. Slowly pour
into the apricot mixture, stirring
all the time. Make up to 600ml/
1 pint/2½ cups with the remaining
orange juice.

5 Pour the apricot mixture into
four individual dishes and chill
until set. To serve, pour a thin layer
of cream over the surface, and
decorate with candied orange peel.

Peach Melba

The story goes that one of the great French chefs, Auguste Escoffier, created this dessert in honour of the opera singer Nellie Melba, now forever enshrined in culinary, if not musical, history.

INGREDIENTS

Serves 6

50g/2oz/¼ cup caster (superfine) sugar

1 vanilla pod (bean), split lengthways

3 large peaches

For the sauce

450g/1lb/2⅔ cups fresh or frozen
    raspberries

15ml/1 tbsp lemon juice

25–40g/1–1½oz/2–3 tbsp caster
    (superfine) sugar

30–45ml/2–3 tbsp raspberry liqueur
    (optional)

vanilla ice cream, to serve

mint leaves and fresh raspberries, to
    decorate (optional)

1 In a pan large enough to hold the peach halves in a single layer, combine 1 litre/1¾ pints/ 4 cups of water with the sugar and vanilla pod. Bring to the boil over a medium heat, stirring occasionally to dissolve the sugar.

2 Cut the peaches in half and twist the halves to separate them. Using a small teaspoon, remove the peach stones (pits). Add the peach halves to the poaching syrup, cut-sides down, adding more water, if needed, to cover the fruit. Press a piece of baking parchment against the surface, reduce the heat to medium-low, then cover and simmer for 12–15 minutes until tender – the time will depend on the ripeness of the fruit. Remove the pan from the heat and leave the peaches to cool in the syrup.

3 Remove the peaches from the syrup and peel off the skins. Place on several thicknesses of kitchen paper to drain (reserve the syrup for another use), then cover and chill.

4 Put the raspberries, lemon juice and sugar in a blender or food processor fitted with the metal blade. Process for 1 minute, scraping down the sides once. Press through a fine sieve (strainer) into a small bowl, then stir in the raspberry liqueur, if using, and put in the refrigerator to chill.

5 To serve, place a peach half, cut-side up, on a dessert plate, fill with a scoop of vanilla ice cream and spoon the raspberry sauce over the ice cream. Decorate with mint leaves and a few fresh raspberries, if using.

Gooseberry and Elderflower Cream

When elderflowers are in season, instead of using the cordial, cook two to three elderflower heads with the gooseberries.

INGREDIENTS

Serves 4

500g/1¼lb gooseberries, topped and tailed

300ml/½ pint/1¼ cups double (heavy) cream

about 115g/4oz/1 cup icing (confectioners') sugar, to taste

30ml/2 tbsp elderflower cordial or orange flower water (optional)

mint sprigs, to decorate

almond biscuits (cookies), to serve

2 Beat the cream until soft peaks form, then fold in half the gooseberries. Sweeten and add elderflower cordial or orange flower water, if using. Sweeten the remaining gooseberries.

3 Layer the cream mixture and the crushed gooseberries in four dessert dishes or tall glasses, then cover and chill. Decorate with mint sprigs and serve accompanied by almond biscuits.

1 Place the gooseberries in a heavy pan, cover and cook over a low heat, shaking the pan occasionally, until the gooseberries are tender. Tip the gooseberries into a bowl, crush them, then leave to cool completely.

COOK'S TIP

If preferred, the cooked gooseberries can be puréed and strained. An equivalent quantity of real custard can replace the cream.

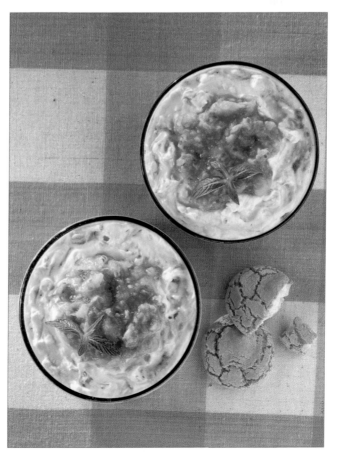

Apricots with Orange Cream

Mascarpone is a very rich cream cheese made from thick Lombardy cream. It is delicious flavoured with orange as a topping for these poached, chilled apricots.

INGREDIENTS

Serves 4

450g/1lb/2 cups ready-to-eat
   dried apricots

strip of lemon peel

1 cinnamon stick

45ml/3 tbsp caster (superfine) sugar

150ml/¼ pint/⅔ cup sweet dessert wine
   (such as Muscat de Beaumes de Venise)

115g/4oz/½ cup mascarpone cheese

45ml/3 tbsp orange juice

pinch of ground cinnamon and fresh mint
   sprig, to decorate

1 Place the apricots, lemon peel, cinnamon stick and 15ml/ 1 tbsp of the sugar in a pan and cover with 450ml/¼ pint/1⅞ cups cold water. Bring to the boil, cover and simmer gently for 25 minutes, until the fruit is tender.

2 Remove from the heat and stir in the dessert wine. Leave until cold, then chill for at least 3–4 hours or overnight.

3 Mix together the mascarpone cheese, orange juice and the remaining sugar in a bowl and beat well until smooth, then chill.

4 Just before serving remove the cinnamon stick and lemon peel and serve with a spoonful of the orange cream sprinkled with cinnamon and decorated with a sprig of fresh mint.

Rhubarb and Orange Fool

Perhaps this traditional English pudding got its name because it is so easy to make that even a "fool" can attempt it.

INGREDIENTS

Serves 4

30ml/2 tbsp orange juice

5ml/1 tsp finely shredded orange rind

1kg/2lb (about 10–12 stems) rhubarb,
   chopped

15ml/1 tbsp redcurrant jelly

45ml/3 tbsp caster (superfine) sugar

150g/5oz/⅔ cup ready-to-serve thick and
   creamy custard

150ml/¼ pint/⅔ cup double (heavy)
   cream, whipped

sweet biscuits (cookies), to serve

1 Place the orange juice and rind, the rhubarb, redcurrant jelly and sugar in a pan. Cover and simmer gently for about 8 minutes, stirring occasionally, until the rhubarb is just tender but not mushy.

2 Remove the pan from the heat, transfer the rhubarb to a bowl and leave to cool completely.

3 Drain the cooled rhubarb to remove some of the liquid. Reserve a few pieces of the rhubarb and a little orange rind for decoration. Purée the remaining rhubarb in a food processor or blender, or push through a sieve (strainer).

4 Stir the custard into the purée, then fold in the whipped cream. Spoon the fool into individual bowls, cover and chill. Just before serving, top with the reserved fruit and rind. Serve with crisp, sweet biscuits.

Cherry Syllabub

This recipe follows the style of the earliest syllabubs from the sixteenth and seventeenth centuries, producing a frothy, creamy layer over a liquid one.

Serves 4

225g/8oz ripe dark cherries, pitted
  and chopped
30ml/2 tbsp kirsch
2 egg whites
75g/3oz/scant ½ cup caster
  (superfine) sugar
30ml/2 tbsp lemon juice
150ml/¼ pint/⅔ cup sweet white wine
300ml/½ pint/1¼ cups double
  (heavy) cream

1 Divide the chopped cherries among six tall dessert glasses and sprinkle over the kirsch.

2 In a clean bowl, whisk the egg whites until stiff. Gently fold in the sugar, lemon juice and wine.

3 In a separate bowl (but using the same whisk), lightly beat the cream, then fold into the egg white mixture.

4 Spoon the cream mixture over the cherries and chill overnight.

Rose Petal Cream

This is an old-fashioned junket which is set with rennet – don't move it while it is setting, otherwise it will separate.

Serves 4

600ml/1 pint/2½ cups milk
45ml/3 tbsp caster (superfine) sugar
several drops triple-strength rosewater
10ml/2 tsp rennet
60ml/4 tbsp double (heavy) cream
sugared rose petals, to decorate (optional)

1 Gently heat the milk and 30ml/ 2 tbsp of the sugar, stirring continuously, until the sugar has melted and the temperature reaches 36.9°C/98.4°F, or the milk feels lukewarm.

2 Stir rosewater to taste into the milk, then remove the pan from the heat before stirring in the rennet.

3 Pour the milk into a serving dish and leave undisturbed for 2–3 hours, until the junket has set.

4 Stir the remaining sugar into the cream, then carefully spoon over the junket. Decorate with sugared rose petals, if wished.

COOK'S TIP

Only use rose petals taken from bushes which have not been sprayed with chemicals of any kind.

Creole Ambrosia

A refreshing cold fruity pudding that can be made at any time of the year.

Serves 6

6 oranges

1 coconut

25g/1oz/2 tbsp caster (superfine) sugar

1 Peel the oranges removing all white pith, then slice thinly, picking out seeds with the point of a knife. Do this on a plate to catch the juice.

2 Pierce the "eyes" of the coconut and pour away the milk, then crack open the coconut with a hammer. (This is best done outside on a stone surface.)

COOK'S TIP

Mangoes instead of oranges make the dessert more exotic but less authentically Creole.

3 Peel the coconut with a sharp knife, then grate half the flesh coarsely, either on a hand grater or on the grating blade of a blender or food processor.

4 Layer the coconut and orange slices in a glass bowl, starting and finishing with the coconut. After each orange layer, sprinkle on a little sugar and pour over some of the reserved orange juice.

5 Let the dessert stand for 2 hours before serving, either at room temperature or, in hot weather, keep it chilled.

Chocolate and Chestnut Pots

Prepared in advance, these are the perfect ending for a dinner party. Remove them from the refrigerator about 30 minutes before serving, to allow them to "ripen".

INGREDIENTS

Serves 6

250g/9oz plain (semisweet) chocolate
60ml/4 tbsp Madeira
25g/1oz/2 tbsp butter, diced
2 eggs, separated
225g/8oz/scant 1 cup unsweetened
 chestnut purée
crème fraîche or whipped double (heavy)
 cream, to decorate

1 Make a few chocolate curls for decoration, then break the rest of the chocolate into squares and melt it with the Madeira in a pan over a gentle heat. Remove from the heat and add the butter, a few pieces at a time, stirring until melted and smooth.

> ### COOK'S TIP
>
>
> If Madeira is not available, use brandy or rum instead. These chocolate pots can be frozen successfully for up to 2 months.

2 Beat the egg yolks quickly into the mixture, then beat in the chestnut purée, mixing until smooth.

3 Whisk the egg whites in a clean, grease-free bowl until stiff. Stir about 15ml/1 tbsp of the whites into the chestnut mixture to lighten it, then fold in the rest smoothly and evenly.

4 Spoon the mixture into six small ramekin dishes and chill until set. Serve the pots topped with a generous spoonful of crème fraîche or whipped double cream and decorated with the plain chocolate curls.

Coffee, Vanilla and Chocolate Stripe

This looks really special served in elegant wine glasses and tastes appropriately exquisite.

Serves 6

285g/10½oz/1½ cups caster
  (superfine) sugar
90ml/6 tbsp cornflour (cornstarch)
900ml/1½ pints/3¾ cups milk
3 egg yolks
75g/3oz/6 tbsp unsalted butter, at
  room temperature
20ml/4 tsp instant coffee powder
10ml/2 tsp vanilla extract
30ml/2 tbsp cocoa powder
whipped cream, to serve

1 To make the coffee layer, place 90g/3½oz/½ cup of the sugar and 30ml/2 tbsp of the cornflour in a heavy pan. Gradually add one-third of the milk, whisking until well blended. Over a medium heat, whisk in one of the egg yolks and bring to the boil, whisking. Boil for 1 minute.

2 Remove the pan from the heat. Stir in 25g/1oz/2 tbsp of the butter and the instant coffee powder. Set aside in the pan to cool slightly.

3 Divide the coffee mixture among six wine glasses. Smooth the tops before the mixture sets.

4 Wipe any dribbles on the insides and outsides of the glasses with damp kitchen paper.

5 To make the vanilla layer, place half of the remaining sugar and cornflour in a heavy pan. Whisk in 300ml/½ pint/1¼ cups of the milk. Over a medium heat, whisk in another egg yolk and bring to the boil, whisking. Boil for 1 minute.

6 Remove the pan from the heat and stir in 25g/1oz/2 tbsp of the butter and the vanilla. Leave to cool slightly, then spoon into the glasses on top of the coffee layer. Smooth the tops and wipe the glasses with kitchen paper.

7 To make the chocolate layer, place the remaining sugar and cornflour in a heavy pan. Gradually whisk in the remaining milk and continue whisking until blended. Over a medium heat, whisk in the last egg yolk and bring to the boil, whisking constantly. Boil for 1 minute. Remove from the heat, stir in the remaining butter and the cocoa. Leave to cool slightly, then spoon into the glasses on top of the vanilla layer. Chill until set.

8 Pipe swirls of whipped cream on top of each dessert just before serving.

C O O K ' S   T I P

For a special occasion, prepare the vanilla layer using a fresh vanilla pod (bean). Choose a plump, supple pod and split it down the centre with a sharp knife. Add to the mixture with the milk and discard the pod before spooning the mixture into the glasses. The flavour will be more pronounced and the pudding will have pretty brown speckles from the vanilla seeds.

Chocolate Hazelnut Galettes

Chocolate rounds sandwiched with fromage frais. If only all sandwiches looked and tasted this good.

INGREDIENTS

Serves 4

175g/6oz plain (semisweet) chocolate, broken into squares
45ml/3 tbsp single (light) cream
30ml/2 tbsp flaked hazelnuts
115g/4oz white chocolate, broken into squares
175g/6oz/¾ cup fromage frais (8% fat)
15ml/1 tbsp dry sherry
60ml/4 tbsp finely chopped hazelnuts, toasted
physalis, dipped in white chocolate, to decorate

1 Melt the plain chocolate in a heatproof bowl over hot water, then remove from the heat and stir in the cream.

2 Draw 12 x 7.5cm/3in circles on sheets of baking parchment. Turn the paper over and spread the plain chocolate over each marked circle, covering in a thin, even layer. Scatter flaked hazelnuts over four of the circles, then leave to set.

3 Melt the white chocolate in a heatproof bowl over hot water, then stir in the fromage frais and dry sherry. Fold in the chopped, toasted hazelnuts. Leave to cool until the mixture holds its shape.

4 Remove the chocolate rounds carefully from the paper and sandwich them together in stacks of three, spooning the hazelnut cream between each layer and using the hazelnut-covered rounds on top. Chill before serving.

5 To serve, place the galettes on individual plates and decorate with chocolate-dipped physalis.

COOK'S TIP

The chocolate could be spread over heart shapes instead, for a special Valentine's Day dessert.

Double Chocolate Snowball

This is an ideal party dessert as it can be made at least one day ahead.

INGREDIENTS

Serves 12–14

350g/12oz plain (semisweet)
  chocolate, chopped

285g/10½oz/1½ cups caster
  (superfine) sugar

275g/10oz/1¼ cups unsalted butter, cut
  into small pieces

8 eggs

50ml/2fl oz/¼ cup orange-flavoured
  liqueur or brandy (optional)

cocoa for dusting

For the white chocolate cream

200g/7oz fine quality white chocolate,
  broken into pieces

475ml/16fl oz/2 cups double (heavy) or
  whipping cream

30ml/2 tbsp orange-flavour
  liqueur (optional)

1 Preheat the oven to 180°C/
350°F/Gas 4. Line a 1.75 litre/
3 pint/7½ cup round ovenproof
bowl with foil, smoothing the
sides. In a bowl over a pan of
simmering water, melt the plain
chocolate. Add the sugar and stir
until it dissolves. Strain into a
medium bowl. With an electric
mixer at low speed, beat in the
butter, then the eggs, one at a time,
beating well after each addition.
Stir in the liqueur or brandy, if
using, and pour into the prepared
bowl. Tap gently to release any
large air bubbles.

2 Bake for 1¼–1½ hours until
the surface is firm and slightly
risen, but cracked. The centre will
still be wobbly: this will set on
cooling. Remove to a rack to cool
to room temperature. Cover with a
plate, then cover completely with
clear film (plastic wrap) or foil and
chill overnight. To unmould,
remove plate and film or foil and
invert mould on to a plate; shake
firmly to release. Peel off foil.
Cover until ready to decorate.

3 Process the white chocolate in
a blender or food processor
until fine crumbs form. In a small
pan, heat 120ml/4fl oz/½ cup of
the cream until just beginning to
simmer. With the food processor
running, pour cream through the
feed tube and process until the
chocolate is completely melted.
Strain into a medium bowl and
cool to room temperature,
stirring occasionally.

4 Beat the remaining cream until
soft peaks form, add the liqueur,
if using, and beat for 30 seconds or
until the cream just holds its shape.
Fold a spoonful of cream into the
chocolate then fold in remaining
cream. Spoon into an icing (pastry)
bag fitted with a star nozzle and
pipe rosettes over the surface. If you
wish, dust with cocoa.

White Chocolate Parfait

Everything you could wish for in a dessert; white and dark chocolate in one mouthwatering slice.

Serves 10

225g/8oz white chocolate, chopped
600ml/1 pint/2½ cups whipping cream
120ml/4fl oz/½ cup milk
10 egg yolks
15ml/1 tbsp caster (superfine) sugar
25g/1oz/scant ½ cup desiccated (dry unsweetened shredded) coconut
120ml/4fl oz/½ cup canned sweetened coconut milk
150g/5oz/1¼ cups unsalted macadamia nuts
For the chocolate icing
225g/8oz plain (semisweet) chocolate
75g/3oz/6 tbsp butter
20ml/4 tsp golden (light corn) syrup
175ml/6fl oz/¾ cup whipping cream
curls of fresh coconut, to decorate

1 Line the base and sides of a 1.4 litre/2⅓ pint/6 cup terrine mould (25 x 10cm/10 x 4in) with clear film (plastic wrap).

2 Place the chopped white chocolate and 50ml/2fl oz/½ cup of the cream in the top of a double boiler or in a heatproof bowl set over hot water. Stir until melted and smooth. Set aside.

3 Put 250ml/8fl oz/1 cup of the cream and the milk in a pan and bring to boiling point.

4 Meanwhile, whisk the egg yolks and caster sugar together in a large bowl, until thick and pale.

5 Add the hot cream mixture to the yolks, beating constantly. Pour back into the pan and cook over a low heat for 2–3 minutes, until thickened. Stir constantly and do not boil. Remove the pan from the heat.

6 Add the melted chocolate, desiccated coconut and coconut milk, then stir well and leave to cool.

7 Whip the remaining cream until thick, then fold into the chocolate and coconut mixture.

8 Put 475ml/16fl oz/2 cups of the parfait mixture in the prepared mould and spread evenly. Cover and freeze for about 2 hours, until just firm. Cover the remaining mixture and chill.

9 Scatter the macadamia nuts evenly over the frozen parfait. Pour in the remaining parfait mixture. Cover the terrine and freeze for 6–8 hours or overnight, until the parfait is firm.

10 To make the icing, melt the chocolate with the butter and syrup in the top of a double boiler set over hot water. Stir occasionally.

11 Heat the cream in a pan, until just simmering, then stir into the chocolate mixture. Remove the pan from the heat and leave to cool until lukewarm.

12 To turn out the parfait, wrap the terrine in a hot towel and set it upside-down on a plate. Lift off the terrine mould, then peel off the clear film. Place the parfait on a rack over a baking sheet and pour the chocolate icing evenly over the top. Working quickly, smooth the icing down the sides with a palette knife. Leave to set slightly, then freeze for a further 3–4 hours. Cut into slices using a knife dipped in hot water. Serve, decorated with curls of fresh coconut.

White Chocolate Mousse with Dark Sauce

Creamy vanilla-flavoured white chocolate mousse is served with a dark rum and chocolate sauce.

Serves 6–8

200g/7oz white chocolate, broken
    into squares
2 eggs, separated
60ml/4 tbsp caster (superfine) sugar
300ml/½ pint/1¼ cups double
    (heavy) cream
1 sachet powdered gelatine or alternative
150ml/¼ pint/⅔ cup Greek (US strained
    plain) yogurt
10ml/2 tsp vanilla extract
For the sauce
50g/2oz plain (semisweet) chocolate,
    broken into squares
30ml/2 tbsp dark rum
60ml/4 tbsp single (light) cream

1 Line a 1 litre/1¾ pint/4 cup loaf tin (pan) with baking parchment or clear film (plastic wrap). Melt the chocolate in a heatproof bowl over hot water, then remove from the heat.

2 Whisk the egg yolks and sugar in a bowl until pale and thick, then beat in the melted chocolate.

3 Heat the cream in a small pan until almost boiling, then remove from the heat. Sprinkle the powdered gelatine over, stirring gently until until it is completely dissolved.

4 Then pour on to the chocolate mixture, whisking vigorously to mix until smooth.

5 Whisk the yogurt and vanilla extract into the mixture. In a clean, grease-free bowl, whisk the egg whites until stiff, then fold them into the mixture. Tip into the prepared loaf tin, level the surface and chill until set.

6 Make the sauce. Melt the chocolate with the rum and cream in a heatproof bowl over barely simmering water, stirring occasionally, then leave to cool.

7 When the mousse is set, remove it from the tin with the aid of the paper or clear film. Serve in thick slices with the cooled chocolate sauce poured around.

COOK'S TIP

Make sure the gelatine is completely dissolved in the cream before adding to the other ingredients.

Fluffy Banana and Pineapple Mousse

This light, low-fat mousse looks very impressive but is really very easy to make, especially with a food processor. To make it even simpler, use a 1 litre/1¾ pint/4 cup serving dish which will hold all the mixture without a paper "collar".

Serves 6

2 ripe bananas

225g/8oz/1 cup cottage cheese

425g/15oz can pineapple chunks or pieces
    in juice

15ml/1 tbsp/1 sachet powdered gelatine,
    or alternative

2 egg whites

1 Tie a double band of baking parchment around a 600ml/1 pint/2½ cup soufflé dish, to come 5cm/2in above the rim.

2 Peel and chop one banana and place it in a blender or food processor with the cottage cheese. Process them until smooth.

3 Drain the pineapple, reserving the juice, and reserve a few pieces or chunks for decoration. Add the rest to the mixture in the blender or food processor and process for a few seconds until finely chopped.

4 Dissolve the gelatine in 60ml/4 tbsp of the reserved pineapple juice. Stir the gelatine quickly into the fruit mixture.

5 Whisk the egg whites until they hold soft peaks and fold them into the mixture. Tip the mousse mixture into the prepared dish, smooth the surface and chill, until set.

6 When the mousse is set, carefully remove the paper collar and decorate with the reserved banana and pineapple.

Portuguese Rice Pudding

This pudding is popular all over Portugal, and if you visit you're likely to find it on most menus. Traditionally it is served cold, but is actually delicious warm as well.

INGREDIENTS

Serves 4–6

175g/6oz/scant 1 cup short grain rice
600ml/1 pint/2½ cups creamy milk
2 or 3 strips pared lemon rind
65g/2½oz/5 tbsp butter, in pieces
115g/4oz/½ cup caster (superfine) sugar
4 egg yolks
salt
ground cinnamon, for dusting
lemon wedges, to serve

1 Cook the rice in plenty of lightly salted water for about 5 minutes, by which time it will have lost its brittleness.

2 Drain well, then return to the clean pan. Add the milk, lemon rind and butter. Bring to the boil over a moderately low heat, then cover, reduce the heat to the lowest setting and simmer for about 20 minutes or until the rice is thick and creamy.

3 Remove the pan from the heat and allow the rice to cool a little. Remove and discard the lemon rind, then stir in the sugar and the egg yolks. Mix well.

4 Divide among four to six serving bowls and dust with ground cinnamon. Serve cold, with lemon wedges for squeezing.

Rice Conde Sundae

Cooking rice pudding on top of the hob instead of in the oven gives it a light, creamy texture, especially if you remember to stir it frequently. It is particularly good served cold with a topping of fruit and toasted nuts or a trickle of hot chocolate sauce.

INGREDIENTS

Serves 4

50g/2oz/generous ¼ cup short grain rice

5ml/1 tsp vanilla extract

2.5ml/½ tsp ground cinnamon

45ml/3 tbsp granulated (white) sugar

600ml/1 pint/2½ cups milk

For the topping

soft berry fruits such as strawberries, raspberries and cherries

chocolate sauce and flaked (sliced) toasted almonds (optional)

1 Mix the rice, vanilla extract, cinnamon and sugar in a pan. Pour in the milk. Bring to the boil, stirring constantly, then reduce the heat so that the mixture barely simmers.

2 Cook the rice over a low heat for 30–40 minutes, stirring frequently. Add extra milk to the rice if it begins to dry out.

3 When the grains are soft, remove the pan from the heat. Allow the rice to cool, stirring occasionally, then chill.

4 Before serving, stir the rice pudding and spoon it into four sundae dishes. Top with fresh fruits, and with chocolate sauce and almonds, if using.

VARIATION

For a special occasion, use single (light) cream instead of milk, and glaze the fruit with a little melted redcurrant jelly. (Add a splash of port if you like.)

Cherries Jubilee

Fresh cherries are wonderful cooked lightly to serve hot over ice cream. Children will love this dessert.

INGREDIENTS

Serves 4

450g/1lb red or black cherries

115g/4oz/generous ½ cup granulated (white) sugar

pared rind of 1 lemon

15ml/1 tbsp arrowroot

60ml/4 tbsp Kirsch

vanilla ice cream, to serve

COOK'S TIP

ᘒ

If you don't have a cherry pitter, simply push the pits through with a skewer. Remember to save the juice to use in the recipe.

---

1 Pit the cherries over a pan to catch the juice. Drop the pits into the pan as you work.

2 Add the sugar, lemon rind and 300ml/½ pint/1¼ cups water to the pan. Stir over a low heat until the sugar dissolves, then bring to the boil and simmer for 10 minutes. Strain the syrup, then return to the pan. Add the cherries and cook for 3–4 minutes.

3 Blend the arrowroot to a paste with 15ml/1 tbsp cold water and stir into the cherries, after removing them from the heat.

4 Return the pan to the heat and bring to the boil, stirring all the time. Cook the sauce for a minute or two, stirring until it is thick and smooth. Heat the Kirsch in a ladle over a flame, ignite and pour over the cherries. Spoon the cherries and hot sauce over scoops of ice cream and serve immediately.

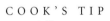

Apricots in Marsala

Make sure the apricots are completely covered by the syrup.

INGREDIENTS

Serves 4

12 apricots

50g/2oz/4 tbsp caster (superfine) sugar

300ml/½ pint/1¼ cups Marsala

2 strips pared orange rind

1 vanilla pod (bean), split

150ml/¼ pint/⅔ cup double (heavy) or whipping cream

15ml/1 tbsp icing (confectioners') sugar

1.5ml/¼ tsp ground cinnamon

150ml/¼ pint/⅔ cup Greek (US strained plain) yogurt

1 Halve and stone (pit) the apricots, then place in a bowl of boiling water for about 30 seconds. Drain well, then slip off their skins.

2 Place the caster sugar, Marsala, orange rind, vanilla pod and 250ml/8fl oz/1 cup water in a pan. Heat gently until the sugar dissolves. Bring to the boil, without stirring, then simmer for 2–3 minutes.

3 Add the apricot halves to the pan and poach for 5–6 minutes, or until just tender. Using a slotted spoon, transfer the apricots to a serving dish.

4 Boil the syrup rapidly until reduced by half, then pour over the apricots and leave to cool. Cover and chill. Remove the orange rind and vanilla pod.

5 Whip the cream with the icing sugar and cinnamon until it forms soft peaks. Gently fold in the yogurt. Spoon into a serving bowl and chill. Serve with the apricots.

Poached Pears in Red Wine

This makes a very pretty dessert, as the pears take on a red blush from the wine.

INGREDIENTS

Serves 4

1 bottle red wine
150g/5oz/¾ cup caster (superfine) sugar
45ml/3 tbsp honey
juice of ½ lemon
1 cinnamon stick
1 vanilla pod (bean), split open lengthways
5cm/2in piece of orange rind
1 clove
1 black peppercorn
4 firm, ripe pears
whipped cream or sour cream,
    to serve

1 Place the wine, sugar, honey, lemon juice, cinnamon stick, vanilla pod, orange rind, clove and peppercorn in a pan just large enough to hold the pears standing upright. Heat gently, stirring occasionally until the sugar has completely dissolved.

2 Meanwhile, peel the pears, leaving the stem intact. Take a thin slice off the base of each pear so that it will stand square and upright in the pan.

3 Place the pears in the wine mixture, then simmer, uncovered, for 20–35 minutes depending on size and ripeness, until the pears are just tender; be careful not to overcook.

4 Carefully transfer the pears to a bowl using a slotted spoon. Continue to boil the poaching liquid until reduced by about half. Leave to cool, then strain the cooled liquid over the pears and chill for at least 3 hours.

5 Place the pears in four individual serving dishes and spoon over a little of the red wine syrup. Serve with whipped cream or sour cream.

Coffee Crêpes with Peaches and Cream

*Juicy golden peaches and cream
conjure up the sweet taste
of summer.*

INGREDIENTS

Serves 6

75g/3oz/⅔ cup plain (all-purpose) flour

25g/1oz/¼ cup buckwheat flour

1.5ml/¼ tsp salt

1 egg, beaten

200ml/7fl oz/scant 1 cup milk

15g/½oz/1 tbsp butter, melted

100ml/3½ oz/scant ½ cup strong coffee

sunflower oil, for frying

For the filling

6 ripe peaches

300ml/½ pint/1¼ cups double
     (heavy) cream

15ml/1 tbsp Amaretto liqueur

225g/8oz/1 cup mascarpone

65g/2½oz/generous ¼ cup caster
     (superfine) sugar

30ml/2 tbsp icing (confectioners') sugar,
     for dusting

1 Sift the flours and salt into a
bowl. Make a well and add the
egg, half the milk and the melted
butter. Beat into the flour until
smooth, then beat in the remaining
milk and coffee.

2 Heat a drizzle of oil in a
15–20cm/6–8in crêpe pan.
Pour in just enough batter to thinly
cover the base of the pan. Cook for
2–3 minutes, until the underneath
is golden brown, then flip over and
cook the other side.

3 Slide the crêpe out of the pan
on to a plate. Continue making
crêpes until all the mixture is used,
stacking and interleaving with
baking parchment. Keep the crêpes
warm while you make the filling.

4 To make the filling, halve the
peaches and remove the stones
(pits). Cut into thick slices. Whip
the cream and Amaretto liqueur
until they form into soft peaks.
Beat the mascarpone with the
sugar until smooth. Beat 30ml/
2 tbsp of the cream into the
mascarpone, then fold in the rest.

5 Spoon a little of the Amaretto
cream on to one half of each
pancake and top with peach slices.
Gently fold the pancake over
and dust with icing sugar. Serve
immediately while still warm.

Fruit Kebabs with Mango and Yogurt Sauce

These mixed fresh fruit kebabs make an attractive and healthy dessert.

INGREDIENTS

Serves 4

½ pineapple, peeled, cored and cubed

2 kiwi fruit, peeled and cubed

175g/6oz/1½ cups strawberries, hulled
   and cut in half, if large

½ mango, peeled, stoned (pitted)
   and cubed

For the sauce

120ml/4fl oz/½ cup fresh mango purée,
   from 1–1½ peeled and stoned mangoes

120ml/4fl oz/½ cup thick natural
   (plain) yogurt

5ml/1 tsp caster (superfine) sugar

few drops vanilla extract

15ml/1 tbsp finely chopped mint leaves

1 To make the sauce, beat together the mango purée, yogurt, sugar and vanilla with an electric mixer.

2 Stir in the chopped mint. Cover the sauce and place in the refrigerator until required.

3 Thread the prepared fruit on to twelve 15cm/6in wooden skewers, alternating the pineapple, kiwi fruit, strawberries and mango cubes.

4 Arrange the kebabs on a large serving tray with the mango and yogurt sauce in the centre.

Tropical Fruits in Cinnamon Syrup

An exotic glazed fruit salad, a simply prepared but satisfying end to any meal.

INGREDIENTS

Serves 6

450g/1lb/2¼ cups caster (superfine) sugar

1 cinnamon stick

1 large or 2 medium papaya (about
   675g/1½lb), peeled, seeded and cut
   lengthways into thin pieces

1 large or 2 medium mangoes (about
   675g/1½lb), peeled, stoned (pitted) and
   cut lengthways into thin pieces

1 large or 2 small star fruit (carambola)
   (about 225g/8oz), thinly sliced

yogurt or crème fraîche, to serve

1 Sprinkle one-third of the sugar over the base of a large pan. Add the cinnamon stick and half the papaya, mango and star fruit pieces.

2 Sprinkle half of the remaining sugar over the fruit pieces in the pan. Add all the remaining fruit and sprinkle with the rest of the sugar.

3 Cover the pan and cook the fruit over a medium-low heat for 35–45 minutes, until the sugar melts completely. Shake the pan occasionally, but do not stir or the fruit will collapse.

4 Uncover the pan and simmer until the fruit begins to appear translucent, about 10 minutes. Remove the pan from the heat and leave to cool.

5 Transfer the fruit and syrup to a bowl, cover and chill overnight. Serve with yogurt or crème fraîche.

Greek Fig and Honey Pudding

A quick and easy pudding made from fresh or canned figs topped with thick and creamy Greek yogurt, drizzled with honey and sprinkled with pistachio nuts.

INGREDIENTS

Serves 4

4 fresh or canned figs

2 x 225g/8oz tubs/2 cups Greek (US strained plain) yogurt

60ml/4 tbsp clear honey

30ml/2 tbsp chopped pistachio nuts

1 Chop the figs and place in the bottom of four stemmed wine glasses or deep, individual dessert bowls.

2 Top each glass or bowl of figs with half a tub (½ cup) of the Greek yogurt. Chill until ready to serve.

3 Just before serving drizzle 15ml/1 tbsp of honey over each one and sprinkle with the pistachio nuts.

COOK'S TIP
~
Try specialist honeys made from, clover, acacia or thyme.

Russian Fruit Compote

This fruit pudding is traditionally called "Kissel" and is made from the thickened juice of stewed red or blackcurrants. This recipe uses the whole fruit with an added dash of blackberry liqueur.

INGREDIENTS

Serves 4

225g/8oz/2 cups red or blackcurrants or a mixture of both

225g/8oz/1⅓ cups raspberries

50g/2oz/4 tbsp caster (superfine) sugar

25ml/1½ tbsp arrowroot

15–30ml/1–2 tbsp Crème de Mûre

Greek (US strained plain) yogurt, to serve

COOK'S TIP
~
Use Crème de Cassis instead of Crème de Mûre.

1 Place the red or blackcurrants, raspberries and sugar in a pan with 150ml/¼ pint/⅔ cup of water. Cover the pan and cook gently over a low heat for 12–15 minutes, until the fruit is soft.

2 Blend the arrowroot with a little water in a bowl and stir into the fruit. Bring back to the boil, stirring until thickened.

3 Remove from the heat and cool slightly, then gently stir in the Crème de Mûre.

4 Pour into four serving bowls and leave until cold, then chill. Serve topped with spoonfuls of Greek yogurt.

Floating Islands

Originally these oval-shaped meringues were poached in milk and this was then used to make the rich custard sauce.

INGREDIENTS

Serves 4–6

1 vanilla pod (bean)
600ml/1 pint/2½ cups milk
8 egg yolks
50g/2oz/¼ cup granulated (white) sugar
For the meringues
4 size 1 egg whites
1.5ml/¼ tsp cream of tartar
225g/8oz/1¼ cups caster (superfine) sugar
For the caramel
150g/5oz/¾ cup granulated (white) sugar

1 Split the vanilla pod lengthways and scrape the seeds into a pan. Add the milk and bring just to the boil over a medium heat, stirring frequently. Cover and set aside for 15–20 minutes.

2 In a medium bowl, whisk the egg yolks and sugar for 2–3 minutes until thick and creamy. Whisk in the hot milk and return the mixture to the pan. With a wooden spoon, stir over a medium-low heat until the sauce begins to thicken and coat the back of the spoon (do not allow to boil). Immediately strain into a chilled bowl, allow to cool, stirring occasionally and then chill.

3 Half-fill a large wide frying pan with water and bring just to simmering point. In a clean, grease-free bowl, whisk the egg whites until frothy. Add the cream of tartar and continue whisking until they form soft peaks. Sprinkle over the caster sugar, about 30ml/2 tbsp at a time, and whisk until the whites are stiff and glossy.

4 Using two tablespoons, form egg-shaped meringues and slide them into the water (you may need to work in batches). Poach them for 2–3 minutes, turning once until just firm. Using a large slotted spoon, transfer the cooked meringues to a baking sheet lined with kitchen paper to drain.

5 Pour the cold custard into individual serving dishes and arrange the meringues on top.

6 To make the caramel, put the sugar into a small pan with 45ml/3 tbsp of water to moisten. Bring to the boil over a high heat, swirling the pan to dissolve the sugar. Boil, without stirring, until the syrup turns a dark caramel colour. Immediately drizzle the caramel over the meringues and custard sauce in a zig-zag pattern. Serve cold. (The caramel will soften if made too far ahead.)

Chestnut Pudding

This is an Italian speciality, made during October and November, when chestnuts are gathered.

Serves 4–5

450g/1lb fresh sweet chestnuts
300ml/½ pint/1¼ cups milk
115g/4oz/½ cup caster (superfine) sugar
2 eggs, separated, at room temperature
25g/1oz/¼ cup unsweetened
   cocoa powder
2.5ml/½ tsp pure vanilla extract
50g/2oz/½ cup icing (confectioners')
   sugar, sifted
fresh whipped cream, to garnish
marrons glacés, to garnish

1 Cut a cross in the side of the chestnuts, and drop them into a pan of boiling water. Cook for 5–6 minutes. Remove with a slotted spoon, and peel while still warm.

2 Place the peeled chestnuts in a heavy or non-stick pan with the milk and half of the caster sugar. Cook over low heat, stirring occasionally, until soft. Remove from the heat and allow to cool. Press the contents of the pan through a sieve (strainer).

3 Preheat the oven to 180°C/ 350°F/Gas 4. Beat the egg yolks with the remaining caster sugar until the mixture is pale yellow and fluffy. Beat in the cocoa powder and the vanilla.

4 In a separate bowl, whisk the egg whites with a wire whisk or electric beater until they form soft peaks. Gradually beat in the sifted icing sugar and continue beating until the mixture forms stiff peaks.

5 Fold the chestnut and egg yolk mixtures together. Fold in the egg whites. Turn the mixture into one large or several individual buttered pudding moulds. Place on a baking sheet, and bake in the oven for 12–20 minutes, depending on the size. Remove from the oven, and allow to cool for 10 minutes before unmoulding. Serve garnished with whipped cream and marrons glacés.

Bitter Chocolate Mousse

This is the quintessential French dessert – rich and extremely delicious. Use the darkest chocolate you can find for the most authentic and intense chocolate flavour.

INGREDIENTS

Serves 8

225g/8oz plain (semisweet)
   chocolate, chopped
30ml/2 tbsp orange liqueur or brandy
25g/1oz/2 tbsp unsalted butter, cut into
   small pieces
4 eggs, separated
90ml/6 tbsp whipping cream
1.5ml/¼ tsp cream of tartar
45ml/3 tbsp caster (superfine) sugar
crème fraîche or sour cream and chocolate
   curls, to decorate

1 Place the chocolate and 60ml/ 4 tbsp of water in a heavy pan. Melt over a low heat, stirring until smooth. Remove the pan from the heat and whisk in the liqueur and butter.

2 With an electric mixer, beat the egg yolks for 2–3 minutes until thick and creamy, then slowly beat into the melted chocolate until well blended. Set aside.

3 Whip the cream until soft peaks form and stir a spoonful into the chocolate to lighten it. Fold in the remaining cream.

4 In a clean, grease-free bowl, using an electric mixer, beat the egg whites until frothy. Add the cream of tartar and continue beating until they form soft peaks. Gradually sprinkle over the sugar and continue beating until the whites are stiff and glossy.

5 Using a rubber spatula or large metal spoon, stir quarter of the egg whites into the chocolate mixture, then gently fold in the remaining whites, cutting down to the bottom, along the sides and up to the top in a semicircular motion until they are just combined. (Don't worry about a few white streaks.) Gently spoon into a 2 litre/3½ pint/8 cup dish or into eight individual dishes. Chill for at least 2 hours until set.

6 Spoon a little crème fraîche or sour cream over the mousse and decorate with chocolate curls.

Brazilian Coffee Bananas

Rich, lavish and sinful-looking, this dessert takes only about two minutes to make!

INGREDIENTS

Serves 4

4 small ripe bananas

15ml/1 tbsp instant coffee granules
    or powder

30ml/2 tbsp dark muscovado
    (molasses) sugar

250g/9oz/1⅛ cups Greek (US strained
    plain) yogurt

15ml/1 tbsp toasted flaked
    (sliced) almonds

1 Peel and slice one banana and
mash the remaining three with
a fork.

2 Dissolve the coffee in 15ml/
1 tbsp of hot water and stir
into the mashed bananas.

3 Spoon a little of the mashed
banana mixture into four
serving dishes and sprinkle with
sugar. Top with a spoonful of
yogurt, then repeat until all the
ingredients are used up.

4 Swirl the last layer of yogurt
for a marbled effect. Finish
with a few banana slices and flaked
almonds. Serve cold. Best eaten
within about an hour of making.

VARIATION

For a special occasion, add a dash
of dark rum or brandy to the
bananas for extra richness.

CAKES
&
GÂTEAUX

◆ ◆ ◆

Raspberry Meringue Gâteau

A rich, hazelnut meringue sandwiched with whipped cream and raspberries makes an irresistible dessert for a special occasion.

INGREDIENTS

Serves 6

4 egg whites

225g/8oz/1 cup caster (superfine) sugar

a few drops of vanilla extract

5ml/1 tsp distilled malt vinegar

115g/4oz/1 cup roasted and chopped
hazelnuts, ground

300ml/½ pint/1¼ cups double
(heavy) cream

350g/12oz/2 cups raspberries

icing (confectioners') sugar, for dusting

raspberries and mint sprigs, to decorate

For the sauce

225g/8oz/1⅓ cups raspberries

45–60ml/3–4 tbsp icing (confectioners')
sugar, sifted

15ml/1 tbsp orange liqueur

1 Preheat the oven to 180°C/
350°F/Gas 4. Grease two 20cm/
8in sandwich tins (pans) and line
the bases with baking parchment.

2 Whisk the egg whites in a large
bowl until they hold stiff
peaks, then gradually whisk in the
caster sugar a tablespoon at a time,
whisking well after each addition.

3 Continue whisking the
meringue mixture for a
minute of two until very stiff, then
fold in the vanilla extract, vinegar
and ground hazelnuts.

4 Divide the meringue mixture
between the prepared
sandwich tins and spread level.
Bake for 50–60 minutes, until crisp.
Remove the meringues from the
tins and leave them to cool on a
wire rack.

5 While the meringues are
cooling, make the sauce.
Process the raspberries with the
icing sugar and orange liqueur in a
blender or food processor, then
press the purée through a fine
nylon sieve (strainer) to remove
any pips. Chill the sauce until
ready to serve.

6 Whip the cream until it forms
soft peaks, then gently fold in
the raspberries. Sandwich the
meringue rounds together with the
raspberry cream.

7 Dust the top of the gâteau with
icing sugar. Decorate with
mint sprigs and serve with the
raspberry sauce.

VARIATION

Fresh redcurrants make a good
alternative to raspberries. Pick over
the fruit, then pull each sprig
gently through the prongs of a fork
to release the redcurrants. Add
them to the whipped cream with a
little icing (confectioners') sugar,
to taste.

COOK'S TIP

You can buy roasted chopped
hazelnuts in supermarkets.
Otherwise toast whole hazelnuts
under the grill (broiler) and rub
off the flaky skins using a clean
dish towel. To chop finely,
process in a blender or food
processor for a few moments.

Chocolate Layer Cake

The cake layers can be made ahead, wrapped and frozen for future use. Always defrost cakes completely before icing.

Serves 10–12

unsweetened cocoa, for dusting

225g/8oz can cooked whole beetroot (beet), drained and juice reserved

115g/4oz/½ cup unsalted butter, softened

500g/1¼lb/2½ cups light brown sugar, firmly packed

3 eggs

15ml/1 tbsp vanilla extract

75g/3oz unsweetened chocolate, melted

275g/10oz/2¼ cups plain (all-purpose) flour

10ml/2 tsp baking powder

2.5ml/½ tsp salt

120ml/4fl oz/½ cup buttermilk

chocolate curls (optional)

For the chocolate ganache frosting

475ml/16fl oz/2 cups whipping or double (heavy) cream

500g/1¼lb fine quality, dark (bittersweet) or plain (semisweet) chocolate, chopped

15ml/1 tbsp vanilla extract

1 Preheat oven to 180°C/350°F/ Gas 4. Grease two 23cm/9in cake tins (pans) and dust bottom and sides with cocoa. Grate beetroot and add to beetroot juice. With electric mixer, beat the butter, brown sugar, eggs and vanilla until pale and fluffy (3–5 minutes). Reduce speed and beat in chocolate.

2 In a bowl, sift flour, baking powder and salt. With mixer on low speed, alternately beat in flour mixture in fourths and buttermilk in thirds. Add beetroot and juice and beat for 1 minute. Divide between tins and bake for 30–35 minutes or until a cake tester inserted in the centre comes out clean. Cool for 10 minutes, then unmould and cool completely.

3 To make the frosting, in a heavy pan over medium heat, heat cream until it just begins to boil, stirring occasionally to prevent it from scorching.

4 Remove from heat and stir in chocolate, stirring constantly until melted and smooth. Stir in vanilla. Strain into a bowl and chill, stirring every 10 minutes, until spreadable, about 1 hour.

5 Assemble the cake. Place one layer on a serving plate and spread with one-third of the ganache. Turn cake layer bottom side up and spread remaining ganache over top and side of cake. If using, top with the chocolate curls. Allow ganache to set for 20–30 minutes, then chill before serving.

Spiced Date and Walnut Cake

A classic flavour combination, which makes a very easy low fat, high-fibre cake.

INGREDIENTS

Makes 1 cake

300g/11oz/2¾ cups wholemeal (whole-wheat) self-raising (self-rising) (self-rising) flour
10ml/2 tsp mixed spice
150g/5oz/1 cup chopped dates
50g/2oz/½ cup chopped walnuts
60ml/4 tbsp sunflower oil
115g/4oz/½ cup dark muscovado (molasses) sugar
300ml/½ pint/1¼ cups skimmed milk
walnut halves, to decorate

1 Preheat the oven to 180°C/ 350°F/Gas 4. Grease and then line a 900g/2lb loaf tin (pan) with baking parchment.

2 Sift together the flour and spice, adding back any bran from the sieve (strainer). Stir in the dates and walnuts.

3 Mix the oil, sugar and milk, then stir evenly into the dry ingredients. Spoon into the prepared tin and arrange the walnut halves on top.

4 Bake the cake in the oven for about 45–50 minutes, or until golden brown and firm. Turn out the cake, remove the lining paper and leave to cool on a wire rack.

VARIATION

Pecan nuts can be used in place of the walnuts in this cake.

Banana Orange Loaf

*For the best banana flavour and a
really good, moist texture, make sure
the bananas are very ripe.*

INGREDIENTS

Makes 1 loaf

90g/3½oz/generous ¾ cup wholemeal
(whole-wheat) plain (all-purpose) flour

90g/3½oz/generous ¾ cup plain (all-
purpose) flour

5ml/1 tsp baking powder

5ml/1 tsp ground mixed spice

45ml/3 tbsp flaked (sliced) hazelnuts, toasted

2 large ripe bananas

1 egg

30ml/2 tbsp sunflower oil

30ml/2 tbsp clear honey

grated rind and juice of 1 small orange

4 orange slices, halved

10ml/2 tsp icing (confectioners') sugar

1 Preheat the oven to 180°C/
350°F/Gas 4. Brush a 1 litre/
1¾ pint/4 cup loaf tin (pan) with
sunflower oil and line the base
with baking parchment.

2 Sift the flours with the baking
powder and spice into a bowl.

3 Stir the hazelnuts into the dry
ingredients. Peel and mash the
bananas. Beat in the egg, oil, honey
and the orange rind and juice. Stir
evenly into the dry ingredients.

4 Spoon into the prepared tin
and smooth the top. Bake for
40–45 minutes, or until firm and
golden brown. Turn out and cool
on a wire rack.

5 Sprinkle the orange slices with
the icing sugar and grill (broil)
until golden. Use to decorate
the cake.

COOK'S TIP

If you plan to keep the loaf for
more than two or three days,
omit the orange slices. Brush the
cake with honey and sprinkle
with flaked (sliced) hazelnuts.

Banana Ginger Parkin

Parkin improves with keeping. Store it in a covered container for up to two months.

INGREDIENTS

Makes 12 squares

200g/7oz/1¾ cups plain (all-purpose) flour
10ml/2 tsp bicarbonate of soda (baking soda)
10ml/2 tsp ground ginger
150g/5oz/1¼ cups medium oatmeal
60ml/4 tbsp dark muscovado
   (molasses) sugar
75g/3oz/6 tbsp sunflower margarine
150g/5oz/⅔ cup golden (light corn) syrup
1 egg, beaten
3 ripe bananas, mashed
75g/3oz/¾ cup icing (confectioners') sugar
stem ginger, to decorate

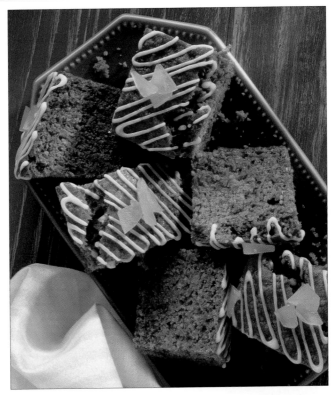

1 Preheat the oven to 160°C/ 325°F/Gas 3. Grease and line an 18 x 28cm/7 x 11in cake tin (pan).

2 Sift together the flour, bicarbonate of soda and ginger, then stir in the oatmeal. Melt the sugar, margarine and syrup in a pan, then stir into the flour mixture. Beat in the egg and mashed bananas.

3 Spoon into the tin and bake for about 1 hour, or until firm to the touch. Allow to cool in the tin, then turn out and cut into even-sized squares.

4 Sift the icing sugar into a bowl and stir in just enough water to make a smooth, runny icing. Drizzle the icing over each square and top with pieces of stem ginger, if you like.

COOK'S TIP
～

This is a nutritious cake, ideal for packed lunches as it doesn't break up too easily.

Greek Honey and Lemon Cake

The semolina in this recipe gives the cake an excellent texture.

INGREDIENTS

Makes 16 slices

40g/1½oz/3 tbsp sunflower margarine
60ml/4 tbsp clear honey
finely grated rind and juice of 1 lemon
150ml/¼ pint/⅔ cup skimmed milk
150g/5oz/1¼ cups plain (all-purpose) flour
7.5ml/1½ tsp baking powder
2.5ml/½ tsp grated nutmeg
50g/2oz/⅓ cup semolina
2 egg whites
10ml/2 tsp sesame seeds

1 Preheat the oven to 200°C/ 400°F/Gas 6. Lightly oil a 19cm/7½in square deep cake tin (pan) and line the base with baking parchment.

2 Place the margarine and 45ml/3 tbsp of the honey in a pan and heat gently until melted. Reserve 15ml/1 tbsp lemon juice, then stir in the rest with the lemon rind and milk.

3 Stir together the flour, baking powder and nutmeg, then beat in with the semolina. Whisk the egg whites until they form soft peaks, then fold evenly into the semolina mixture.

4 Spoon into the tin and sprinkle with sesame seeds. Bake for 25–30 minutes, until golden brown.

5 Mix the reserved honey and lemon juice and drizzle over the cake while warm. Cool in the tin, then cut into fingers to serve.

Strawberry Roulade

An attractive and delicious cake, perfect for a family supper.

INGREDIENTS

Serves 6

4 egg whites
115g/4oz/scant ⅔ cup golden caster
    (superfine) sugar
75g/3oz/⅔ cup plain (all-purpose)
    flour, sifted
30ml/2 tbsp orange juice
caster (superfine) sugar, for sprinkling
115g/4oz/1 cup strawberries, chopped
150g/5oz/¾ cup low-fat fromage frais
strawberries, to decorate

1 Preheat the oven to 200°C/ 400°F/Gas 6. Oil a 23 x 33cm/ 9 x 13in Swiss roll tin (jelly roll pan) and line with baking parchment.

2 Place the egg whites in a large clean bowl and whisk until they form soft peaks. Gradually whisk in the sugar. Fold in half of the sifted flour, then fold in the rest with the orange juice.

3 Spoon the mixture into the prepared tin, spreading evenly. Bake for 15–18 minutes, or until it is golden brown and firm to the touch.

4 Meanwhile, spread out a sheet of baking parchment and sprinkle with caster sugar. Turn out the cake on to this and remove the lining paper. Roll up the sponge loosely from one short side, with the paper inside. Cool.

5 Unroll and remove the paper. Stir the strawberries into the fromage frais and spread over the sponge. Roll up and serve decorated with strawberries.

Classic Cheesecake

You can decorate this with fruit and serve it with cream, if you like, but it tastes delicious just as it is.

INGREDIENTS

Serves 8
25g/1oz/½ cup digestive biscuit (graham cracker) crumbs
900g/2lb cream cheese
250g/9oz/1¼ cups caster (superfine) sugar
grated rind of 1 lemon
45ml/3 tbsp fresh lemon juice
5ml/1 tsp vanilla extract
4 eggs, at room temperature

1 Preheat the oven to 160°C/ 325°F/Gas 3. Grease a 23cm/ 8in springform cake tin (pan). Place on a round of foil 13cm/5in larger than the diameter of the tin. Press it up the sides to seal tightly.

2 Sprinkle the crumbs in the base of the tin. Press to form an even layer.

3 With an electric mixer, beat the cream cheese until smooth. Add the sugar, lemon rind and juice and vanilla extract, and beat until blended. Beat in the eggs, one at a time. Beat just enough to blend thoroughly.

4 Pour into the prepared tin. Set the tin in a larger roasting pan and place in the oven. Pour enough hot water in the outer pan to come 2.5cm/1in up the side of the tin.

5 Bake until the top of the cake is golden brown, about 1½ hours. Let cool in the tin.

6 Run a knife around the edge to loosen, then remove the rim of the tin. Chill for at least 4 hours before serving.

Chocolate Cheesecake

This popular variation of the classic dessert is made with a cinnamon and chocolate base.

INGREDIENTS

Serves 10–12
175g/6oz plain (semisweet) chocolate and 115g/4oz dark (bittersweet) chocolate, chopped into squares
1.15kg/2½lb cream cheese, at room temperature
200g/7oz/1 cup caster (superfine) sugar
10ml/2 tsp vanilla extract
4 eggs, at room temperature
175ml/6fl oz/¾ cup sour cream
For the base
75g/3oz/1½ cups chocolate wafer crumbs
75g/3oz/6 tbsp butter, melted
2.5ml/½ tsp ground cinnamon

1 Preheat the oven to 180°C/ 350°F/Gas 4. Grease a 23cm/ 9in springform cake tin (pan).

2 For the base, mix the chocolate wafer crumbs with the butter and cinnamon. Press evenly in the bottom of the tin.

3 Melt the plain and dark chocolate in the top of a double boiler, or in a heatproof bowl set over hot water. Set aside.

4 With an electric mixer, beat the cream cheese until smooth, then beat in the sugar and vanilla extract. Add the eggs, one at a time, scraping the bowl with a spatula when necessary.

5 Add the sour cream. Stir in the melted chocolate.

6 Pour into the tin. Bake for 1 hour. Let cool in the tin; remove rim. Chill before serving.

Blueberry-hazelnut Cheesecake

The base for this cheesecake is made with ground hazelnuts – a tasty and unusual alternative to a biscuit base.

Serves 6–8

350g/12oz blueberries

15ml/1 tbsp clear honey

75g/3oz/6 tbsp granulated (white) sugar

juice of 1 lemon

175g/6oz/¾ cup cream cheese, at
   room temperature

1 egg

5ml/1 tsp hazelnut liqueur (optional)

120ml/4fl oz/½ cup whipping cream

For the base

175g/6oz/1⅓ cups ground hazelnuts

75g/3oz/⅔ cup plain (all-purpose) flour

pinch of salt

50g/2oz/4 tbsp butter, at
   room temperature

65g/2½oz/⅓ cup light brown sugar,
   firmly packed

1 egg yolk

1 For the base, put the hazelnuts in a large bowl. Sift in the flour and salt, and stir to mix. Set aside.

2 Beat the butter with the brown sugar until light and fluffy. Beat in the egg yolk. Gradually fold in the nut mixture, in three batches, until well combined.

3 Press the dough into a greased 23cm/9in pie tin (pan), spreading it evenly against the sides. Form a rim around the top edge that is slightly thicker than the sides. Cover and chill for at least 30 minutes.

4 Preheat the oven to 180°C/ 350°F/Gas 4. Meanwhile, for the topping, combine the blueberries, honey, 15ml/1 tbsp of the granulated sugar and 5ml/1 tsp lemon juice in a heavy pan. Cook the mixture over low heat, stirring occasionally, until the berries have given off some liquid but still retain their shape, 5–7 minutes. Remove from the heat and set aside.

5 Place the pastry base in the oven and bake for 15 minutes. Remove and let cool while making the filling.

6 Beat together the cream cheese and remaining granulated sugar until light and fluffy. Add the egg, 15ml/1 tbsp lemon juice, the liqueur, if using, and the cream and beat until thoroughly blended.

7 Pour the cheese mixture into the pastry base and spread evenly. Bake until just set, 20–25 minutes.

8 Let the cheesecake cool completely on a wire rack, then cover and chill for at least 1 hour.

9 Spread the blueberry mixture evenly over the top of the cheesecake. Serve at cool room temperature.

COOK'S TIP

The cheesecake can be prepared 1 day in advance, but add the fruit shortly before serving.

Sponge Cake with Fruit and Cream

Called Génoise, this is the French cake used as the base for both simple and elaborate creations. You could simply dust it with icing sugar, or layer it with seasonal fruits to serve as a seasonal dessert.

INGREDIENTS

Serves 6

115g/4oz/1 cup plain (all-purpose) flour

pinch of salt

4 eggs, at room temperature

115g/4oz/scant ⅔ cup caster
  (superfine) sugar

2.5ml/½ tsp vanilla extract

50g/2oz/4 tbsp butter, melted or clarified
  and cooled

For the filling

450g/1lb fresh strawberries or raspberries

30–60ml/2–4 tbsp caster (superfine) sugar

475ml/16fl oz/2 cups whipping cream

5ml/1 tsp vanilla extract

1 Preheat the oven to 180°C/ 350°F/Gas 4. Lightly butter a 23cm/9in springform tin (pan) or deep cake tin. Line the base with baking parchment, and dust lightly with flour. Sift the flour and salt together twice.

2 Half-fill a medium pan with hot water and set over a low heat (do not allow the water to boil). Put the eggs in a heatproof bowl which just fits into the pan without touching the water. Using an electric mixer, beat the eggs at medium-high speed, gradually adding the sugar, for 8–10 minutes until the mixture is very thick and pale and leaves a ribbon trail when the beaters are lifted. Remove the bowl from the pan, add the vanilla extract and continue beating until the mixture is cool.

3 Fold in the flour mixture in three batches, using a balloon whisk or metal spoon. Before the third addition of flour, stir a large spoonful of the mixture into the melted or clarified butter to lighten it, then fold the butter into the remaining mixture with the last addition of flour. Work quickly, but gently, so the mixture does not deflate. Pour into the prepared tin, smoothing the top so the sides are slightly higher than the centre.

4 Bake in the oven for about 25–30 minutes until the top of the cake springs back when touched and the edge begins to shrink away from the sides of the tin. Place the cake in its tin on a wire rack to cool for 5–10 minutes, then invert the cake on to the rack to cool completely. Peel off the baking parchment.

5 To make the filling, slice the strawberries, place in a bowl, sprinkle with 15–30ml/1–2 tbsp of the sugar and set aside. Beat the cream with 15–30ml/1–2 tbsp of the sugar and the vanilla extract until it holds soft peaks.

6 To assemble the cake (up to 4 hours before serving), split the cake horizontally, using a serrated knife. Place the top, cut side up, on a serving plate. Spread with a third of the cream and cover with an even layer of sliced strawberries.

7 Place the bottom half of the cake, cut side down, on top of the filling and press lightly. Spread the remaining cream over the top and sides of the cake. Chill until ready to serve. Serve the remaining strawberries with the cake.

Devil's Food Cake with Orange Frosting

Chocolate and orange are the ultimate combination. Can you resist the temptation?

INGREDIENTS

Serves 8–10

50g/2oz/½ cup unsweetened
  cocoa powder
175g/6oz/¾ cup butter,
  at room temperature
350g/12oz/1½ cups dark brown sugar,
  firmly packed
3 eggs, at room temperature
225g/8oz/2 cups plain (all-purpose) flour
25ml/1½ tsp bicarbonate of soda
  (baking soda)
1.5ml/¼ tsp baking powder
175ml/6fl oz/¾ cup sour cream
orange rind strips, for decoration
For the frosting
285g/10½oz/1½ cups granulated
  (white) sugar
2 egg whites
60ml/4 tbsp frozen orange
  juice concentrate
15ml/1 tbsp fresh lemon juice
grated rind of 1 orange

1 Preheat the oven to 180°C/
350°F/Gas 4. Line two 23cm/
9in cake tins (pans) with baking
parchment and grease. In a bowl,
mix the cocoa and 175ml/6fl oz/
¾ cup of boiling water until
smooth. Set aside.

2 With an electric mixer, cream
the butter and sugar until light
and fluffy. Add the eggs, one at a
time, beating well.

3 When the cocoa mixture is
cooked to lukewarm, stir into
the butter mixture.

4 Sift together the flour,
bicarbonate of soda and
baking powder twice. Fold into the
cocoa mixture in three batches,
alternating with the sour cream.

5 Pour into the tins. Bake until
the cakes pull away from the
tin, 30–35 minutes. Stand for
15 minutes before unmoulding.

6 Thinly slice the orange rind
strips. Blanch in boiling water
for 1 minute.

7 For the frosting, place all the
ingredients in the top of a
double boiler or in a bowl set over
hot water. With an electric mixer,
beat until the mixture holds soft
peaks. Continue beating off the
heat until thick enough to spread.

8 Sandwich the cake with frosting, then spread over the top
and sides. Arrange the rind on top.

Black Forest Gâteau

This light chocolate sponge, moistened with Kirsch and layered with cherries and cream, is still one of the most popular of all the chocolate gâteaux.

INGREDIENTS

Serves 8–10

6 eggs

200g/7oz/scant 1 cup caster
  (superfine) sugar

5ml/1 tsp vanilla extract

50g/2oz/½ cup plain (all-purpose) flour

50g/2oz/½ cup cocoa powder

115g/4oz/½ cup unsalted butter, melted

For the filling and topping

60ml/4 tbsp Kirsch

600ml/1 pint/2½ cups double (heavy) or
  whipping cream

30ml/2 tbsp icing (confectioners') sugar

2.5ml/½ tsp vanilla extract

675g/1½lb jar pitted morello
  cherries, drained

To decorate

icing (confectioners') sugar, for dusting

grated chocolate

chocolate curls

fresh or drained canned morello cherries

1 Preheat the oven to 180°C/ 350°F/Gas 4. Grease three 19cm/7½in sandwich cake tins (pans) and line the base of each with baking parchment. Whisk the eggs with the sugar and vanilla extract in a large bowl until pale and very thick – the mixture should hold a firm trail when the whisk is lifted.

2 Sift the flour and cocoa over the mixture and fold in lightly and evenly. Stir in the melted butter. Divide the mixture among the prepared cake tins, smoothing them level.

3 Bake for 15–18 minutes, until risen and springy to the touch. Leave to cool in the tins for about 5 minutes, then turn out on to wire racks and leave to cool completely.

4 Prick each layer all over with a skewer or fork, then sprinkle with Kirsch. Whip the cream in a bowl until it starts to thicken, then beat in the icing sugar and vanilla extract until the mixture begins to hold its shape.

5 To assemble, spread one cake layer with a thick layer of flavoured cream and top with a quarter of the cherries. Spread a second cake layer with cream and cherries, then place it on top of the first layer. Top with the final layer.

6 Spread the remaining cream all over the cake. Dust a plate with icing sugar; position the cake. Press grated chocolate over the sides and decorate with the chocolate curls and cherries.

Angel Food Cake

This cake is beautifully light. The secret? Sifting the flour over and over again to let plenty of air into it.

INGREDIENTS

Serves 12–14

115g/4oz/1 cup sifted cake flour

285g/10½oz/1½ cups caster (superfine) sugar

300ml/½ pint/1¼ cups egg whites (about 10–11 eggs)

6.5ml/1¼ tsp cream of tartar

1.5ml/¼ tsp salt

5ml/1 tsp vanilla extract

1.5ml/¼ tsp almond extract

icing (confectioners') sugar, for dusting

1 Preheat the oven to 160°C/ 325°F/Gas 3. Sift the flour before measuring, then sift it four times with 90g/3½oz/½ cup of the sugar. Transfer to a bowl.

2 With an electric mixer, beat the egg whites until foamy. Sift over the cream of tartar and salt and continue to beat until they hold soft peaks when the beaters are lifted.

3 Add the remaining sugar in three batches, beating well after each addition. Stir in the vanilla and almond extract.

4 Add the flour mixture, ½ cup at a time, and fold in gently with a large metal spoon after each addition.

5 Transfer to an ungreased 25cm/10in straight-sided ring mould and bake until delicately browned on top, about 1 hour.

6 Turn the ring mould upside down on to a cake rack and let cool for 1 hour. If the cake does not unmould, run a spatula around the edge to loosen it. Invert on to a serving plate.

7 When cool, lay a star-shaped template on top of the cake, sift with icing sugar, and lift off.

Chocolate and Cherry Polenta Cake

*Polenta and almonds add an
unusual nutty texture.*

INGREDIENTS

Serves 8

50g/2oz/⅓ cup quick-cook polenta

200g/7oz plain (semisweet) chocolate,
  broken into squares

5 eggs, separated

175g/6oz/¾ cup caster (superfine) sugar

115g/4oz/1 cup ground almonds

60ml/4 tbsp plain (all-purpose) flour

finely grated rind of 1 orange

115g/4oz/½ cup glacé (candied)
  cherries, halved

icing (confectioners') sugar, for dusting

1 Place the polenta in a
heatproof bowl and pour over
just enough boiling water to cover,
about 120ml/4fl oz/½ cup. Stir
well, then cover the bowl and leave
to stand for about 30 minutes,
until the polenta has absorbed all
the excess moisture.

2 Preheat the oven to 190°C/
375°F/Gas 5. Grease a deep
22cm/8½in round cake tin (pan)
and line the base with baking
parchment. Melt the chocolate in a
heatproof bowl over hot water.

3 Whisk the egg yolks with the
sugar in a bowl until thick and
pale. Beat in the chocolate, then
fold in the polenta, ground
almonds, flour and orange rind.

4 Whisk the egg whites in a
clean bowl until stiff. Stir
15ml/1 tbsp of the whites into the
chocolate mixture, then fold in the
rest. Finally, fold in the cherries.

5 Scrape the mixture into the
prepared tin and bake for
45–55 minutes or until well risen
and firm to the touch. Cool on a
rack. Dust with icing sugar to serve.

Lemon Coconut Layer Cake

*The flavours of lemon and coconut
complement each other beautifully
in this light dessert cake.*

INGREDIENTS

Serves 8–10

175g/6oz/1½ cups plain (all-purpose) flour

pinch of salt

7 eggs

350g/12oz/1¾ cups granulated (white) sugar

15ml/1 tbsp grated orange rind

grated rind of 1½ lemons

juice of 1 lemon

65g/2½oz/scant 1 cup desiccated (dry
    unsweetened shredded) coconut

15ml/1 tbsp cornflour (cornstarch)

40g/1½oz/3 tbsp butter

For the frosting

75g/3oz/6 tbsp unsalted butter,
    at room temperature

175g/6oz/1½ cups icing (confectioners')
    sugar

grated rind of 1½ lemons

30ml/2 tbsp fresh lemon juice

200g/7oz/2½ cups desiccated (dry
    unsweetened shredded) coconut

1 Preheat the oven to 180°C/
350°F/Gas 4. Line three
20cm/8in cake tins (pans) with
baking parchment and grease. In a
bowl, sift together the flour and
salt and set aside.

2 Place six of the eggs in a large
heatproof bowl set over hot
water. With an electric mixer, beat
until frothy. Gradually beat in
225g/8oz/generous 1 cup of the
granulated sugar until the mixture
doubles in volume and is thick
enough to leave a ribbon trail
when the beaters are lifted, which
takes about 10 minutes.

3 Remove the bowl from the hot
water. Fold in the orange rind,
half the grated lemon rind and
15ml/1 tbsp of the lemon juice
until blended. Fold in the coconut.

4 Sift over the flour mixture
in three batches, gently folding
in thoroughly after each addition.

5 Divide the mixture between
the prepared tins.

6 Bake until the cakes pull
away from the sides of the
tin, 20–25 minutes. Leave to stand
for 5 minutes, then turn out and
transfer to a cooling rack.

7 In a bowl, blend the cornflour
with a little cold water to
dissolve. Whisk in the remaining
egg until just blended. Set aside.

8 In a pan, combine the
remaining lemon rind and
juice, the remaining sugar, butter
and 120ml/4fl oz/½ cup of water.

9 Over a moderate heat, bring
the mixture to the boil. Whisk
in the egg and cornflour, and return
to the boil. Whisk continuously until
thick, about 5 minutes. Remove
from the heat and pour into a bowl.
Cover with baking parchment and
set aside until cool.

10 For the frosting, cream the
butter and icing sugar until
smooth. Stir in the lemon rind and
enough lemon juice to obtain a
thick, spreadable consistency.

11 Sandwich the three cake
layers with the lemon
custard mixture. Spread the
frosting over the top and sides.
Cover the cake with the coconut,
pressing it in gently.

Carrot Cake with Maple Butter Frosting

A good, quick dessert cake for a family supper.

INGREDIENTS

Serves 12

450g/1lb carrots, peeled

175g/6oz/1½ cups plain
    (all-purpose) flour

10ml/2 tsp baking powder

2.5ml/½ tsp bicarbonate of soda
    (baking soda)

5ml/1 tsp salt

10ml/2 tsp ground cinnamon

4 eggs

10ml/2 tsp vanilla extract

225g/8oz/1 cup dark brown sugar,
    firmly packed

90g/3½oz/½ cup granulated (white) sugar

300ml/½ pint/1¼ cups sunflower oil

115g/4oz/1 cup walnuts, finely chopped

65g/2½oz/½ cup raisins

walnut halves, for decorating (optional)

For the frosting

75g/3oz/6 tbsp unsalted butter,
    at room temperature

375g/12oz/3 cups icing
    (confectioners') sugar

50ml/2fl oz/¼ cup maple syrup

1 Preheat the oven to 180°C/
350°F/Gas 4. Line a 28 x 20cm/
11 x 8in rectangular cake tin (pan)
with baking parchment and grease.
Grate the carrots and set aside.

2 Sift the flour, baking powder,
bicarbonate of soda, salt and
cinnamon into a bowl. Set aside.

3 With an electric mixer, beat
the eggs until blended. Add the
vanilla, sugars and oil and beat
well to incorporate.

4 Add the carrots, walnuts and
raisins to the mixture, and
fold in thoroughly.

5 Pour the batter into the
prepared tin and bake until the
cake springs back when touched
lightly, 40–45 minutes. Let stand
10 minutes, then unmould and
transfer to a rack.

6 For the frosting, cream the
butter with half the sugar until
soft. Add the syrup, then beat in
the remaining sugar until blended.

7 Spread the frosting over the
top of the cake. Using a metal
spatula, make decorative ridges in
the frosting. Cut into squares.
Decorate with walnut halves.

Black and White Pound Cake

A good cake for packed lunches and picnics as it cuts into neat slices with no messy filling, or serve with custard for dessert.

INGREDIENTS

Serves 16

115g/4oz plain (semisweet) chocolate,
    broken into squares
350g/12oz/3 cups plain (all-purpose) flour
5ml/1 tsp baking powder
450g/1lb/2 cups butter,
    at room temperature
650g/1lb 7oz/3⅓ cups sugar
15ml/1 tbsp vanilla extract
10 eggs, at room temperature
icing (confectioners') sugar, for dusting

1 Preheat the oven to 180°C/350°F/Gas 4. Line the bottom of a 25cm/10in straight-sided ring mould with baking parchment and grease. Dust with flour spread evenly with a brush.

2 Melt the chocolate in the top of a double boiler, or in a heatproof bowl set over a pan of hot water. Stir occasionally. Set aside.

3 In a bowl, sift together the flour and baking powder. In another bowl, cream the butter, sugar and vanilla extract with an electric mixer until light and fluffy. Add the eggs, two at a time, then gradually incorporate the flour mixture on low speed.

4 Spoon half of the batter into the prepared pan.

COOK'S TIP

∾

This is also known as Marbled Cake because of its distinctive appearance.

---

5 Stir the chocolate into the remaining batter, then spoon into the pan. With a metal spatula, swirl the two batters to create a marbled effect.

6 Bake until a cake tester inserted in the centre comes out clean, about 1¾ hours. Cover with foil halfway through baking. Let stand 15 minutes, then unmould and transfer to a cooling rack. To serve, dust with icing sugar.

Chocolate Mousse Strawberry Layer Cake

The strawberries used in this cake can be replaced by raspberries or blackberries and the appropriate flavour liqueur.

INGREDIENTS

Serves 10

115g/4oz fine quality white
   chocolate, chopped
120ml/4fl oz/½ cup whipping or double
   (heavy) cream
120ml/4fl oz/½ cup milk
15ml/1 tbsp rum or vanilla extract
115g/4oz/½ cup unsalted butter, softened
175g/6oz/generous ¾ cup granulated
   (white) sugar
3 eggs
275g/10oz/2½ cups plain
   (all-purpose) flour
5ml/1 tsp baking powder
pinch of salt
675g/1½lb fresh strawberries, sliced,
   plus extra for decoration
750ml/1¼ pints/3 cups whipping cream
30ml/2 tbsp rum or strawberry-
   flavour liqueur
For the white chocolate mousse
250g/9oz fine quality white
   chocolate, chopped
350ml/12fl oz/1½ cups whipping or
   double (heavy) cream
30ml/2 tbsp rum or strawberry-
   flavour liqueur

1 Preheat oven to 180°C/350°F/ Gas 4. Grease and flour two 23 x 5cm/9 x 2in cake tins (pans). Line the base of the tins with baking parchment. Melt chocolate and cream in a double boiler over a low heat, stirring until smooth. Stir in milk and rum or vanilla extract; set aside to cool.

2 In a large bowl with an electric mixer, beat the butter and sugar until light and creamy. Add the eggs one at a time, beating well.

3 In a small bowl, stir together the flour, baking powder and salt. Alternately add flour and melted chocolate to the eggs in batches, just until blended. Pour the batter evenly into the tins.

4 Bake for 20–25 minutes until a cake tester inserted in centre comes out clean. Cool on a wire rack for 10 minutes. Turn cakes out on to wire rack, peel off paper and cool completely.

5 Prepare the mousse. In a medium pan over low heat, melt the chocolate and cream until smooth, stirring frequently. Stir in rum or strawberry-flavour liqueur and pour into a bowl. Chill until just set. With a wire whisk, whip lightly until mixture has a "mousse" consistency.

6 Slice both cake layers in half crossways. Sandwich the four layers together with the mousse and strawberries.

7 Whip the cream with the rum or strawberry-flavour liqueur until firm peaks form. Spread half over top and sides of cake. Spoon remaining cream into a piping (pastry) bag with a star nozzle and pipe scrolls on top. Garnish with remaining strawberries.

Death by Chocolate

*One of the richest chocolate cakes
ever, so serve in thin slices.*

Serves 16–20

225g/8oz plain (semisweet) chocolate,
    broken into squares
115g/4oz/½ cup unsalted butter
150ml/¼ pint/⅔ cup milk
225g/8oz/1¼ cups light muscovado
    (brown) sugar
10ml/2 tsp vanilla extract
2 eggs, separated
150ml/¼ pint/⅔ cup sour cream
225g/8oz/2 cups self-raising
    (self-rising) flour
5ml/1 tsp baking powder
For the filling
60ml/4 tbsp seedless raspberry jam
60ml/4 tbsp brandy
400g/14oz plain (semisweet) chocolate,
    broken into squares
200g/7oz/scant 1 cup unsalted butter
For the topping
250ml/8fl oz/1 cup double (heavy) cream
225g/8oz plain (semisweet) chocolate,
    broken into squares
plain (semisweet) and white chocolate
    curls, to decorate
chocolate-dipped physalis,
    to decorate (optional)

1 Preheat the oven to 180°C/350°F/
Gas 4. Grease and base-line a
deep 23cm/9in springform cake tin
(pan). Place chocolate, butter and
milk in a pan. Heat gently until
smooth. Remove from heat, beat in
sugar and vanilla, then cool.

2 Beat the egg yolks and cream
in a bowl, then beat into the
chocolate mixture. Sift the flour
and baking powder over the
surface and fold in. Whisk the egg
whites in a grease-free bowl until
stiff; fold into the mixture.

3 Scrape into the prepared tin
and bake for 45–55 minutes,
or until firm to the touch. Cool in
the tin for 15 minutes, then invert
to a wire rack to cool.

4 Slice the cold cake across the
middle to make three even
layers. In a small pan, warm the
jam with 15ml/1 tbsp of the
brandy, then brush over two of the
layers. Heat the remaining brandy
in a pan with the chocolate and
butter, stirring, until smooth. Cool
until beginning to thicken.

5 Spread the bottom layer of the
cake with half the chocolate
filling, taking care not to disturb
the jam. Top with a second layer,
jam side up, and spread with the
remaining filling. Top with the
final layer and press lightly. Leave
to set.

6 To make the topping, heat the
cream and chocolate together
in a pan over a low heat, stirring
frequently until the chocolate has
melted. Pour into a bowl, leave to
cool, then whisk until the mixture
begins to hold its shape.

7 Spread the top and sides of
the cake with the chocolate
ganache. Decorate with plain and
white chocolate curls and, if liked,
chocolate-dipped physalis.

Simple Chocolate Cake

An easy, everyday chocolate cake which can be filled with buttercream, or with a rich chocolate ganache for a special occasion.

INGREDIENTS

Serves 6–8

115g/4oz plain (semisweet) chocolate,
   broken into squares
45ml/3 tbsp milk
150g/5oz/⅔ cup unsalted butter or
   margarine, softened
150g/5oz/scant 1 cup light muscovado
   (brown) sugar
3 eggs
200g/7oz/1¾ cups self-raising
   (self-rising) flour
15ml/1 tbsp cocoa powder
For the buttercream
75g/3oz/6 tbsp unsalted butter or
   margarine, softened
175g/6oz/1½ cups icing
   (confectioners') sugar
15ml/1 tbsp cocoa powder
2.5ml/½ tsp vanilla extract
icing (confectioners') sugar and cocoa
   powder, for dusting

1 Preheat the oven to 180°C/
350°F/Gas 4. Grease two 18cm/
7in round sandwich cake tins
(pans) and line the base of each
with baking parchment. Melt the
chocolate with the milk in a
heatproof bowl set over a pan of
simmering water.

2 Cream the butter or
margarine with the sugar in a
mixing bowl until pale and fluffy.
Add the eggs one at a time, beating
well after each addition. Stir in the
chocolate mixture until it is
well combined.

3 Sift the flour and cocoa over
the mixture and fold in with
a metal spoon until evenly mixed.
Scrape into the prepared tins,
smooth level and bake for
35–40 minutes or until well risen
and firm. Turn out on wire racks
and leave to cool.

4 To make the buttercream, beat
the butter or margarine, icing
sugar, cocoa powder and vanilla
extract together in a bowl until the
mixture is smooth.

5 Sandwich the cake layers
together with the buttercream.
Dust with a mixture of icing sugar
and cocoa just before serving.

Pineapple Upside-down Cake

This is a perennial favourite to serve in winter or summer.

Serves 8

115g/4oz/½ cup butter

225g/8oz/1 cup dark brown sugar, firmly packed

450g/16oz can pineapple slices, drained

4 eggs, separated

grated rind of 1 lemon

pinch of salt

90g/3½oz/½ cup granulated (white) sugar

85g/3¼oz/¾ cup plain (all-purpose) flour

5ml/1 tsp baking powder

1 Preheat the oven to 180°C/ 350°F/Gas 4. Melt the butter in an ovenproof cast-iron frying pan, about 25cm/10in in diameter. Remove 15ml/1 tbsp of the melted butter and set aside.

2 Add the brown sugar to the frying pan and stir until blended. Place the drained pineapple slices on top in one layer. Set aside.

3 In a bowl, whisk together the egg yolks, reserved butter and lemon rind until smooth and well blended. Set aside.

4 With an electric mixer, beat the egg whites with the salt until stiff. Fold in the granulated sugar, 30ml/2 tbsp at a time. Fold in the egg yolk mixture.

5 Sift the flour and baking powder together. Fold into the egg mixture in three batches.

6 Pour the batter over the pineapple and smooth level.

7 Bake until a cake tester inserted in the centre comes out clean, about 30 minutes.

8 While still hot, place a serving plate on top of the frying pan, bottom-side up. Holding them together with oven gloves, flip over. Serve hot or cold.

Raspberry and White Chocolate Cheesecake

Raspberries and white chocolate are
an irresistible combination,
especially when teamed with rich
mascarpone on a crunchy ginger
and pecan nut base.

INGREDIENTS

Serves 8

50g/2oz/4 tbsp unsalted butter
225g/8oz/2⅓ cups ginger nut biscuits
   (cookies), crushed
50g/2oz/½ cup chopped pecan nuts
   or walnuts
For the filling
275g/10oz/1¼ cups mascarpone cheese
175g/6oz/¾ cup fromage frais
2 eggs, beaten
45ml/3 tbsp caster (superfine) sugar
250g/9oz white chocolate, broken
   into squares
225g/8oz/1⅓ cups fresh or frozen
   raspberries
For the topping
115g/4oz/½ cup mascarpone cheese
75g/3oz/⅓ cup fromage frais
white chocolate curls and raspberries,
   to decorate

2 Make the filling. Beat the
mascarpone and fromage frais
in a bowl, then beat in the eggs and
caster sugar until evenly mixed.

3 Melt the white chocolate
gently in a heatproof bowl
over hot water.

4 Stir the chocolate into
the cheese mixture with
the raspberries.

5 Tip into the prepared tin and
spread evenly, then bake for
about 1 hour or until just set.
Switch off the oven, but do not
remove the cheesecake. Leave it
until cold and completely set.

6 Release the tin and lift the
cheesecake on to a plate.
Make the topping by mixing the
mascarpone and fromage frais
in a bowl and spread over the
cheesecake. Decorate with
chocolate curls and raspberries.

1 Preheat the oven to 150°C/
300°F/Gas 2. Melt the butter
in a pan, then stir in the crushed
biscuits and nuts. Press into the
base of a 23cm/9in springform
cake tin (pan).

Marbled Swiss Roll

The combination of light chocolate sponge and walnut chocolate buttercream is simply sensational.

INGREDIENTS

Serves 6–8

90g/3½oz/scant 1 cup plain
(all-purpose) flour

15ml/1 tbsp cocoa powder

25g/1oz plain (semisweet) chocolate, grated

25g/1oz white chocolate, grated

3 eggs

115g/4oz/generous ½ cup caster
(superfine) sugar

For the filling

75g/3oz/6 tbsp unsalted butter or
margarine, softened

175g/6oz/1½ cups icing
(confectioners') sugar

15ml/1 tbsp cocoa powder

2.5ml/½ tsp vanilla extract

45ml/3 tbsp chopped walnuts

plain (semisweet) and white chocolate
curls, to decorate (optional)

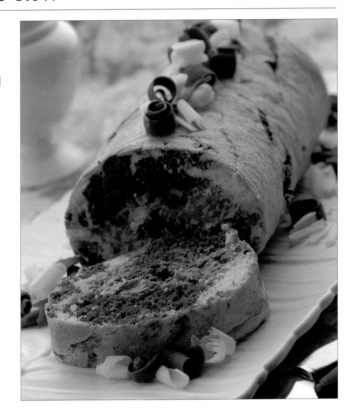

1 Preheat the oven to 200°C/ 400°F/Gas 6. Grease a 30 x 20cm/12 x 8in Swiss roll tin (jelly roll pan) and line with baking parchment. Sift half the flour with the cocoa into bowl. Stir in the grated plain chocolate. Sift the remaining flour into another bowl; stir in the grated white chocolate.

2 Whisk the eggs and sugar in a heatproof bowl; set over a pan of hot water until it holds its shape when the whisk is lifted.

3 Remove the bowl from the heat and tip half the mixture into a separate bowl. Fold the white chocolate mixture into one portion, then fold the plain chocolate mixture into the other. Stir 15ml/1 tbsp boiling water into each half to soften the mixtures.

4 Place alternate spoonfuls of mixture in the prepared tin and swirl lightly together for a marbled effect. Bake for about 12–15 minutes, or until firm. Turn out on to a sheet of baking parchment.

5 Trim the edges to neaten and cover with a damp, clean dish towel. Cool.

6 For the filling, beat the butter or margarine, icing sugar, cocoa powder and vanilla extract together in a bowl until smooth, then mix in the walnuts.

7 Uncover the sponge, lift off the baking parchment and spread the surface with the buttercream. Roll up carefully from a long side and place on a serving plate. Decorate with plain and white chocolate curls, if wished.

Sachertorte

This glorious gâteau was created in Vienna in 1832 by Franz Sacher, a chef in the royal household.

INGREDIENTS

Serves 10–12

225g/8oz plain (semisweet) chocolate, broken into squares
150g/5oz/⅔ cup unsalted butter, softened
115g/4oz/generous ½ cup caster (superfine) sugar
8 eggs, separated
115g/4oz/1 cup plain (all-purpose) flour
For the glaze
225g/8oz/scant 1 cup apricot jam
15ml/1 tbsp lemon juice
For the icing
225g/8oz plain (semisweet) chocolate, broken into squares
200g/7oz/1 cup caster (superfine) sugar
15ml/1 tbsp golden (light corn) syrup
250ml/8fl oz/1 cup double (heavy) cream
5ml/1 tsp vanilla extract
plain (semisweet) chocolate curls, to decorate

1 Preheat the oven to 180°C/ 350°F/Gas 4. Grease a 23cm/ 9in round springform cake tin (pan) and line with baking parchment. Melt the chocolate in a heatproof bowl over hot water, then remove from the heat.

2 Cream the butter with the sugar in a mixing bowl until pale and fluffy, then add the egg yolks, one at a time, beating after each addition. Beat in the melted chocolate, then sift the flour over the mixture and fold it in evenly.

3 Whisk the egg whites in a clean, grease-free bowl until stiff, then stir about a quarter of the whites into the chocolate mixture to lighten it. Fold in the remaining whites.

4 Tip the mixture into the prepared cake tin and smooth level. Place in the oven and bake for about 50–55 minutes, or until firm. Turn out carefully on to a wire rack to cool.

5 Heat the apricot jam with the lemon juice in a small pan until melted, then strain through a sieve (strainer) into a bowl. Once the cake is cold, slice in half across the middle to make two equal-size layers.

6 Brush the top and sides of each layer with the apricot glaze, then sandwich them together. Place on a wire rack.

7 Mix the icing ingredients in a heavy pan. Heat gently, stirring until thick. Simmer for 3–4 minutes, without stirring, until the mixture registers 95°C/ 200°F on a sugar thermometer. Pour quickly over the cake and spread evenly. Leave to set, then decorate with chocolate curls.

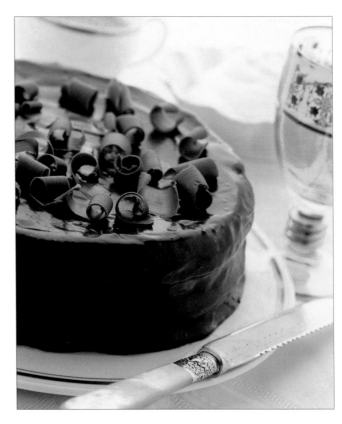

Australian Hazelnut Pavlova

*Meringue topped with fresh fruit
and cream – perfect for summer
dinner parties.*

INGREDIENTS

Serves 4–6

3 egg whites

175g/6oz/generous ¾ cup caster
   (superfine) sugar

5ml/1 tsp cornflour (cornstarch)

5ml/1 tsp white wine vinegar

40g/1½oz/5 tbsp chopped
   roasted hazelnuts

250ml/8fl oz/1 cup double (heavy) cream

15ml/1 tbsp orange juice

30ml/2 tbsp natural (plain) thick and
   creamy yogurt

2 ripe nectarines, stoned (pitted)
   and sliced

225g/8oz/1⅓ cups raspberries

15–30ml/1–2 tbsp redcurrant
   jelly, warmed

1 Preheat the oven to 140°C/
275°F/Gas 1. Lightly grease a
baking sheet. Draw a 20cm/8in
circle on a sheet of baking
parchment. Place pencil-side
down on the baking sheet.

2 Place the egg whites in a large,
clean, grease-free bowl and
whisk with an electric mixer until
stiff. Whisk in the sugar 15ml/
1 tbsp at a time, whisking well after
each addition.

3 Add the cornflour, vinegar and
hazelnuts and fold in carefully
with a large metal spoon.

4 Spoon the meringue on to the
marked circle and spread out,
making a dip in the centre.

5 Bake for about 1¼–1½ hours,
until crisp. Leave to cool, then
transfer to a serving platter.

6 Whip the cream and orange
juice until just thick, stir in the
yogurt and spoon on to the
meringue. Top with the fruit and
drizzle over the redcurrant jelly.
Serve immediately.

PASTRIES
&
PIES

◆ ◆ ◆

Chocolate Almond Meringue Pie

This dream dessert combines three very popular flavours: velvety chocolate filling on a light orange pastry case, topped with fluffy white meringue.

Serves 6

175g/6oz/1½ cups plain
   (all-purpose) flour
50g/2oz/⅓ cup ground rice
150g/5oz/⅔ cup unsalted butter
finely grated rind of 1 orange
1 egg yolk
flaked (sliced) almonds and melted plain
   (semisweet) chocolate, to decorate
For the filling
150g/5oz plain (semisweet) chocolate,
   broken into squares
50g/2oz/4 tbsp unsalted butter, softened
75g/3oz/⅓ cup caster (superfine) sugar
10ml/2 tsp cornflour (cornstarch)
4 egg yolks
75g/3oz/¾ cup ground almonds
For the meringue
3 egg whites
150g/5oz/¾ cup caster (superfine) sugar

2 Preheat the oven to 190°C/ 375°F/Gas 5. Prick the pastry base all over with a fork, cover with baking parchment weighed down with baking beans and bake blind for 10 minutes. Remove the pastry case (pie shell); take out the baking beans and paper.

3 Make the filling. Melt the chocolate in a heatproof bowl over hot water. Cream the butter with the sugar in a bowl, then beat in the cornflour and egg yolks. Fold in the almonds, then the chocolate. Spread in the pastry case. Bake for a further 10 minutes.

4 Make the meringue. Whisk the egg whites until stiff, then gradually add half the caster sugar. Fold in remaining sugar.

5 Spoon the meringue over the chocolate filling, lifting if up with the back of the spoon to form peaks. Reduce the oven temperature to 180°C/350°F/Gas 4 and bake the pie for 15–20 minutes or until the topping is pale gold. Serve warm, scattered with almonds and drizzled with melted chocolate.

1 Sift the flour and ground rice into a bowl. Rub in the butter until the mixture resembles breadcrumbs. Stir in the orange rind. Add the egg yolk; bring the dough together. Roll out and use to line a 23cm/9in round flan tin (pan). Chill for 30 minutes.

Red Berry Tart with Lemon Cream Filling

This tart is best filled just before serving so the pastry remains mouthwatering crisp. Select red summer berry fruits.

INGREDIENTS

Serves 6–8

150g/5oz/1¼ cups plain (all-purpose) flour

25g/1oz/¼ cup cornflour (cornstarch)

40g/1½oz/5 tbsp icing
   (confectioners') sugar

90g/3½oz/7 tbsp butter

5ml/1 tsp vanilla extract

2 egg yolks, beaten

sprig of mint, to decorate

For the filling

200g/7oz/scant 1 cup cream cheese

45ml/3 tbsp lemon curd

grated rind and juice of 1 lemon

icing (confectioners') sugar,
   to sweeten (optional)

225g/8oz/2 cups mixed red berry fruits

45ml/3 tbsp redcurrant jelly

1 Sift the flour, cornflour and icing sugar together, then rub in the butter until the mixture resembles breadcrumbs.

2 Beat the vanilla into the egg yolks, then mix into the crumbs to make a firm dough, adding cold water if necessary.

3 Roll out the pastry and line a 23cm/9in round flan tin (pan). Prick the base of the flan with a fork and allow it to rest in the refrigerator for 30 minutes.

4 Preheat the oven to 200°C/ 400°F/Gas 6. Line the flan with baking parchment and baking beans. Place the tin on a baking sheet and bake for 20 minutes, removing the paper and beans for the last 5 minutes. When cooked, cool and remove the pastry case from the flan tin.

5 Cream the cheese, lemon curd and lemon rind and juice, adding icing sugar to sweeten, if you wish. Spread the mixture into the base of the flan.

6 Top the flan with the fruits. Gently warm the redcurrant jelly and trickle it over the fruits just before serving the flan decorated with a sprig of mint.

VARIATION

There are all sorts of delightful variations to this recipe. For instance, leave out the redcurrant jelly and sprinkle lightly with icing sugar or decorate with fresh strawberry leaves. Alternatively, top with sliced kiwi fruits or bananas slices sprinkled with lemon juice.

Peach and Blueberry Pie

The unusual combination of fruits in this pie looks especially good with a lattice pastry topping.

INGREDIENTS

Serves 8

225g/8oz/2 cups plain (all-purpose) flour

pinch of salt

10ml/2 tsp sugar

150g/5oz/10 tbsp cold butter or margarine

1 egg yolk

30ml/2 tbsp milk, to glaze

For the filling

450g/1lb fresh peaches, peeled, stoned (pitted) and sliced

275g/10oz/2 cups fresh blueberries

150g/5oz/¾ cup caster (superfine) sugar

30ml/2 tbsp fresh lemon juice

40g/1½oz/⅓ cup plain (all-purpose) flour

large pinch of grated nutmeg

25g/1oz/2 tbsp butter or margarine, cut into tiny pieces

1 To make the pastry, sift the flour, salt and sugar into a bowl. Rub the butter or margarine into the dry ingredients as quickly as possible until the mixture resembles coarse breadcrumbs.

2 Mix the egg yolk with 50ml/ 2fl oz/¼ cup of iced water and sprinkle over the flour mixture. Combine with a fork until the dough holds together. If the dough is too crumbly, add a little more water, 15ml/1 tbsp at a time. Gather the dough into a ball and flatten into a round. Place in a sealed polythene bag and chill for at least 20 minutes.

3 Roll out two-thirds of the pastry between two sheets of baking parchment to a thickness of about 3mm/⅛in. Use to line a 23cm/9in pie dish.

4 Trim the pastry all around, leaving a 1cm/½in overhang. Fold the overhang under to form the edge. Using a fork, press the edge to the rim of the pie dish.

5 Gather the trimmings and remaining pastry into a ball, and roll out to a thickness of about 5mm/¼in. Using a pastry wheel or sharp knife, cut into long, 1cm/½in wide strips. Chill both the pastry case and the strips of pastry for 20 minutes. Meanwhile, preheat the oven to 200°C/400°F/Gas 6.

6 Line the pastry case with baking parchment and fill with dried beans. Bake for 7–10 minutes, until the pastry is just set. Remove from the oven and carefully lift out the paper with the beans. Prick the base of the pastry case with a fork, then return to the oven and bake for a further 5 minutes. Leave to cool slightly before filling. Leave the oven on.

7 For the filling, place the peach slices and blueberries in a bowl and stir in the sugar, lemon juice, flour and nutmeg. Spoon the fruit mixture into the pastry case. Dot the top with the pieces of butter or margarine.

8 Weave a lattice top with the chilled pastry strips, pressing the ends to the edge of the baked pastry case. Brush the strips with the milk.

9 Bake the pie for 15 minutes. Reduce the oven temperature to 180°C/350°F/Gas 4, and continue baking for another 30 minutes, until the filling is tender and bubbling and the pastry lattice is golden. If the pastry becomes too brown, cover loosely with a piece of foil. Serve the pie warm or at room temperature.

COOK'S TIP

Don't over-chill the pastry strips. If they become too firm, they may crack and break as you weave them into a lattice.

Rhubarb Pie

Use a cutter to cut out decorative pastry shapes and make it special.

INGREDIENTS

Serves 6

175g/6oz/1½ cups plain (all-purpose) flour
2.5ml/½ tsp salt
10ml/2 tsp caster (superfine) sugar
75g/3oz/6 tbsp cold butter or margarine
30ml/2 tbsp single (light) cream
single (light) or double (heavy) cream,
    to serve
For the filling
1kg/2¼lb fresh rhubarb, cut into 2.5cm/
    1in slices
30ml/2 tbsp cornflour (cornstarch)
1 egg
275g/10oz/1½ cups caster (superfine) sugar
15ml/1 tbsp grated orange rind

1 To make the pastry, sift the flour, salt and sugar into a bowl. Using a pastry blender or two knives, cut the butter or margarine into the dry ingredients as quickly as possible until the mixture resembles breadcrumbs.

2 Sprinkle the flour mixture with about 50ml/2fl oz/¼ cup of iced water and mix until the dough just holds together. If the dough is too crumbly, add a little more water, 15ml/1 tbsp at a time.

3 Gather the dough into a ball, flatten into a round, place in a polythene bag and put in the refrigerator for 20 minutes.

4 Roll out the pastry between two sheets of baking parchment to a 3mm/⅛in thickness. Use to line a 23cm/9in pie dish or tin (pan). Trim all around, leaving a 1cm/½in overhang. Fold the overhang under the edge and flute. Chill the case and trimmings for 30 minutes.

5 To make the filling, put the rhubarb in a bowl, sprinkle with the cornflour and toss to coat.

6 Preheat the oven to 220°C/425°F/Gas 7. Beat the egg with the sugar in a bowl until thoroughly blended, then mix in the orange rind.

7 Stir the sugar mixture into the rhubarb and mix well together, then spoon the fruit into the prepared pastry case.

8 Roll out the pastry trimmings. Stamp out decorative shapes with a biscuit (cookie) cutter.

9 Arrange the pastry shapes on top of the pie. Brush the shapes and the edge of the pastry case with cream.

10 Bake the pie for 30 minutes. Reduce the oven temperature to 160°C/325°F/Gas 3 and continue baking for a further 15–20 minutes, until the pastry is golden brown and the rhubarb is tender. Serve the pie hot with cream.

Chocolate Pecan Torte

This torte uses finely ground nuts instead of flour. Toast then cool the nuts before grinding finely in a blender or food processor. Do not over-grind the nuts, as the oils will form a paste.

INGREDIENTS

Serves 16

200g/7oz dark (bittersweet) or plain
   (semisweet) chocolate, chopped
150g/5oz/10 tbsp unsalted butter, cut
   into pieces
4 eggs
90g/3½oz/½ cup caster (superfine) sugar
10ml/2 tsp vanilla extract
115g/4oz/1 cup ground pecans
10ml/2 tsp ground cinnamon
24 toasted pecan halves,
   to decorate (optional)
For the chocolate honey glaze
115g/4oz dark (bittersweet) or plain
   (semisweet) chocolate, chopped
60g/2oz/¼ cup unsalted butter, cut
   into pieces
30ml/2 tbsp clear honey
pinch of ground cinnamon

1 Preheat oven to 180°C/350°F/ Gas 4. Grease a 20 x 5cm/ 8 x 2in springform tin (pan); line with baking parchment then grease the paper. Wrap bottom and side of tin with foil to prevent water seeping in. In a pan over a low heat, melt the chocolate and butter, stirring until smooth. Remove from the heat. In a mixing bowl with the electric mixer, beat the eggs, sugar and vanilla extract until frothy, 1–2 minutes. Stir in the melted chocolate, ground nuts and cinnamon. Pour into the prepared tin.

2 Place the foil-wrapped tin in a large roasting pan and pour boiling water into the roasting pan, to come 2cm/¾in up the side of the springform tin. Bake for 25–30 minutes until the edge of the cake is set, but centre is soft. Remove from the water bath and remove foil. Cool on a rack.

3 Prepare glaze. In a small pan over low heat, melt the chocolate, butter, honey and cinnamon, stirring until smooth; remove from the heat. Carefully dip toasted pecan halves halfway into glaze and place on a baking parchment-lined baking sheet until it is set.

4 Remove side from springform tin and invert the cake on to wire rack. Remove the tin bottom and paper, so the bottom of the cake is now the top. Pour the thickened glaze over cake, tilting rack slightly to spread glaze. Use a metal palette knife to smooth the sides. Arrange the glazed nuts around outside edge of the torte and allow the glaze to set.

Key Lime Pie

Key limes come from Florida but if they are not available, ordinary limes will do just as well.

INGREDIENTS

Serves 8

3 large egg yolks

400g/14oz can sweetened condensed milk

15ml/1 tbsp grated Key lime rind

120ml/4fl oz/½ cup fresh Key lime juice

green food colouring (optional)

120ml/4fl oz/½ cup whipping cream

For the crust

115g/4oz/1¼ cups digestive biscuit (graham cracker) crumbs

75ml/5 tbsp butter or margarine, melted

1 Preheat the oven to 180°C/ 350°F/Gas 4. For the crust, place the biscuit crumbs in a bowl and add the butter or margarine. Mix to combine.

2 Press the crumbs evenly over the bottom and sides of a 23cm/9in pie dish or tin (pan). Bake for 8 minutes. Let cool.

3 Beat the yolks until thick. Beat in the milk, lime rind and juice, and colouring, if using. Pour into the prebaked pie crust and chill until set, about 4 hours. To serve, whip the cream. Pipe a lattice pattern on top, or spoon dollops around the edge.

Fruit Tartlets

The chocolate pastry cases make a dramatic base to these tartlets.

INGREDIENTS

Makes 8

215g/7½oz/¾ cup redcurrant or grape jelly

15ml/1 tbsp fresh lemon juice

175ml/6fl oz/¾ cup whipping cream

675g/1½lb fresh fruit, such as strawberries, raspberries, kiwi fruit, peaches, grapes or blueberries, peeled and sliced as necessary

For the pastry

150g/5oz/⅔ cup cold butter, cut in pieces

65g/2½oz/⅓ cup dark brown sugar, firmly packed

45ml/3 tbsp unsweetened cocoa powder

175g/6oz/1½ cups plain (all-purpose) flour

1 egg white

1 For the pastry, combine the butter, brown sugar and cocoa over low heat. When the butter is melted, remove from the heat and sift over the flour. Stir, then add just enough egg white to bind the mixture. Gather into a ball, wrap in baking parchment, and chill for at least 30 minutes.

2 Preheat the oven to 180°C/ 350°F/Gas 4. Grease eight 7.5cm/3in tartlet tins (pans). Roll out the dough between two sheets of baking parchment and stamp out eight 10cm/4in rounds with a fluted cutter.

3 Line the tartlet tins with dough. Prick the bottoms. Chill for 15 minutes.

4 Bake until firm, 20–25 minutes. Leave to cool, then remove from the tins.

5 Melt the jelly with the lemon juice. Brush a thin layer in the bottom of the tartlets. Whip the cream and spread a thin layer in the tartlet shells. Arrange the fruit on top. Brush evenly with the glaze and serve.

Cherry Pie

The woven lattice is the perfect finishing touch, although you can cheat and use a lattice pastry roller if you prefer.

Serves 8

900g/2lb fresh Morello cherries, pitted, or 2 x 450g /1lb cans or jars, drained and pitted
65g/2½oz/generous ¾ cup caster (superfine) sugar
25g/1oz/¼ cup plain (all-purpose) flour
25ml/1½ tbsp fresh lemon juice
1.5ml/¼ tsp almond extract
25g/1oz/2 tbsp butter or margarine
For the pastry
225g/8oz/2 cups plain (all-purpose) flour
5ml/1 tsp salt
175g/6oz/¾ cup lard or vegetable fat

1 For the pastry, sift the flour and salt into a mixing bowl. Using a pastry blender, cut in the fat until the mixture resembles coarse breadcrumbs.

2 Sprinkle in 60–75ml/4–5 tbsp iced water, a tablespoon at a time, tossing lightly with your fingertips or a fork until the pastry forms a ball.

3 Preheat the oven to 220°C/ 425°F/Gas 7. Divide the pastry in half and shape each half into a ball. On a lightly floured surface, roll out one of the balls to a circle about 30cm/12in in diameter.

4 Use it to line a 23cm/9in pie tin (pan), easing the pastry in and being careful not to stretch it. With scissors, trim off excess pastry, leaving a 1cm/½in overhang around the pie tin.

5 Roll out the remaining pastry to 3mm/⅛in thick. Cut out eleven strips 1cm/½in wide.

6 In a mixing bowl, combine the cherries, sugar, flour, lemon juice and almond extract. Spoon the mixture into the pastry case and dot the top with the butter or margarine.

7 To make the lattice, place five of the pastry strips evenly across the filling. Fold every other strip back. Lay the first strip across in the opposite direction. Continue in this pattern, folding back every other strip each time you add a cross strip.

8 Trim the ends of the lattice strips even with the case overhang. Press together so that the edge rests on the pie-tin rim. With your thumbs, flute the edge. Chill for 15 minutes.

9 Bake the pie for 30 minutes, covering the edge of the pastry case with foil, if necessary, to prevent over-browning. Let cool, in the tin, on a wire rack.

Mince Pies with Orange Cinnamon Pastry

Home-made mince pies are so much nicer than shop bought, especially with this tasty pastry.

INGREDIENTS

Makes 18

225g/8oz/2 cups plain (all-purpose) flour
40g/1½oz icing (confectioners') sugar
10ml/2 tsp ground cinnamon
150g/5oz/10 tbsp butter
grated rind of 1 orange
225g/8oz/⅔ cup mincemeat
1 beaten egg, to glaze
icing (confectioners') sugar, to dust

1 Sift together the flour, icing sugar and cinnamon then rub in the butter until it forms crumbs. (This can be done in a food processor.) Stir in the grated orange rind.

2 Mix to a firm dough with about 60ml/4 tbsp ice cold water. Knead lightly, then roll out to a 5mm/¼in thickness.

3 Using a 6cm/2½in round cutter, cut out 18 circles, re-rolling as necessary. Then cut out 18 smaller 5cm/2in circles.

4 Line two bun tins (muffin pans) with the 18 larger circles – they will fill one and a half tins. Spoon a small spoonful of mincemeat into each pastry case and top with the smaller pastry circles, pressing the edges lightly together to seal.

5 Glaze the tops of the pies with egg and leave to rest in the refrigerator for 30 minutes. Preheat the oven to 200°C/400°F/Gas 6.

6 Bake the pies for 15–20 minutes until they are golden brown. Remove them to wire racks to cool. Serve just warm, dusted with icing sugar.

Apple-cranberry Lattice Pie

*Use fresh or frozen cranberries for
this classic American pie.*

INGREDIENTS

Serves 8

grated rind of 1 orange

45ml/3 tbsp fresh orange juice

2 large, tart cooking apples

115g/4oz/1 cup cranberries

65g/2½oz/½ cup raisins

25g/1oz/¼ cup walnuts, chopped

225g/8oz/1 cup granulated (white) sugar

115g/4oz/½ cup dark brown sugar

15ml/1 tbsp quick-cooking tapioca

For the pastry

225g/8oz/2 cups plain (all-purpose) flour

2.5ml/½ tsp salt

90ml/6 tbsp cold butter, cut in pieces

60ml/4 tbsp cold lard, cut in pieces

15ml/1 tbsp granulated (white) sugar,
   for sprinkling

1 For the pastry, sift the flour
and salt into a bowl. Add the
butter and lard and rub in until the
mixture resembles coarse crumbs.
With a fork, stir in just enough
iced water to bind the dough.
Gather into two equal balls, wrap
in baking parchment, and chill for
at least 20 minutes.

2 Put the orange rind and juice
into a mixing bowl. Peel and
core the apples and grate them into
the bowl. Stir in the cranberries,
raisins, walnuts, granulated sugar,
brown sugar and tapioca.

3 Place a baking sheet in the
oven and preheat to 200°C/
400°F/Gas 6.

4 On a lightly floured surface,
roll out one ball of dough
about 3mm/⅛in thick. Transfer to
a 23cm/9in pie tin (pan) and trim
the edge. Spoon the cranberry and
apple mixture into the shell.

5 Roll out the remaining dough
to a circle about 28cm/11in in
diameter. With a serrated pastry
wheel, cut the dough into ten
strips, 2cm/¾in wide. Place five
strips horizontally across the top of
the tart at 1-inch intervals. Weave
in six vertical strips. Trim the
edges. Sprinkle the top with 15ml/
1 tbsp of sugar.

6 Bake for 20 minutes. Reduce
the heat to 180°C/350°F/Gas
4 and bake until the crust is golden
and the filling is bubbling, about
15 minutes more.

Lemon Meringue Pie

*Serve this exactly as it is, hot,
warm or cold. It doesn't need any
accompaniment.*

INGREDIENTS

Serves 8

grated rind and juice of 1 large lemon

200g/7oz/1 cup caster (superfine) sugar

25g/1oz/2 tbsp butter

45ml/3 tbsp cornflour (cornstarch)

3 eggs, separated

pinch of salt

0.75ml/⅛ tsp cream of tartar

For the pastry

115g/4oz/1 cup plain (all-purpose) flour

2.5ml/½ tsp salt

65g/2½oz/⅓ cup cold lard, cut in pieces

1 For the pastry, sift the flour
and salt into a bowl. Add the
lard and cut in with a pastry
blender until the mixture
resembles coarse crumbs. With a
fork, stir in just enough iced water
to bind the dough (about 30ml/
2 tbsp). Gather the dough into a ball.

2 On a lightly floured surface,
roll out the dough to 3mm/
⅛in thick. Transfer to a 23cm/9in
pie tin (pan) and trim the edge to
leave a 1cm/½in overhang.

3 Fold the overhang under and
crimp the edge. Chill the pastry
case (pie shell) in the refrigerator
for at least 20 minutes. Preheat the
oven to 200°C/400°F/Gas 6.

4 Prick the dough all over with a
fork. Line with baking
parchment and fill with baking
beans. Bake for 12 minutes.
Remove the paper and beans and
continue baking until golden,
about 6–8 minutes more.

5 In a pan, combine the lemon
rind and juice, 90g/ 3½oz/
½ cup of the sugar, butter and
250ml/8fl oz/1 cup of water. Bring
the mixture to the boil.

6 Meanwhile, in a mixing bowl,
dissolve the cornflour in
15ml/1 tbsp of cold water. Add the
egg yolks.

7 Add the egg yolks to the lemon
mixture and return to the boil,
whisking continuously until the
mixture thickens, about 5 minutes.

8 Cover the surface with baking
parchment to prevent a skin
forming and let cool.

9 For the meringue, using an
electric mixer beat the egg
whites with the salt and cream of
tartar until they hold stiff peaks.
Add the remaining sugar and beat
until glossy.

10 Spoon the lemon mixture
into the pastry case and
spread level. Spoon the meringue
on top, smoothing it up to the edge
of the crust to seal. Bake until
golden, 12–15 minutes.

Chocolate Chiffon Pie

This light and creamy dessert is as luxurious as its name suggests.

INGREDIENTS

Serves 8

175g/6oz plain (semisweet) chocolate and
   25g/1oz dark (bittersweet) chocolate,
   broken into squares
250ml/8fl oz/1 cup milk
15ml/1 tbsp gelatine, or alternative
130g/4½oz/⅔ cup granulated (white) sugar
2 size 1 eggs, separated
5ml/1 tsp vanilla extract
350ml/12fl oz/1½ cups whipping cream
pinch of salt
whipped cream and chocolate curls

For the crust

75g/3oz/1½ cups digestive biscuit
   (graham crackers) crumbs
75g/3oz/6 tbsp butter, melted

1 Place a baking sheet in the oven and preheat to 180°C/350°F/Gas 4. For the crust, mix the digestive biscuit crumbs and butter in a bowl. Press the crumbs evenly over the bottom and sides of a 23cm/9in pie tin (pan). Bake for 8 minutes. Let cool.

2 Chop the chocolate, then grind in a food processor or blender. Set aside.

3 Place the milk in the top of a double boiler or in a heatproof bowl. Sprinkle over the gelatine. Let stand 5 minutes to soften.

4 Set the top of the double boiler or heatproof bowl over hot water. Add 50g/2oz/⅓ cup of the sugar, the chocolate and egg yolks. Stir until dissolved. Add the vanilla extract.

5 Set the top of the double boiler in a bowl of ice and stir until the mixture reaches room temperature. Remove from the ice and set aside.

6 Whip the cream lightly. Set aside. With an electric mixer, beat the egg whites and salt until they hold soft peaks. Add the remaining sugar and beat only enough to blend.

7 Fold a dollop of egg whites into the chocolate mixture, then pour back into the whites and gently fold in.

8 Fold in the whipped cream and pour into the pastry case (pie shell). Put in the freezer until just set, about 5 minutes. If the centre sinks, fill with any remaining mixture. Chill for 3–4 hours. Decorate with whipped cream and chocolate curls. Serve cold.

Coconut Cream Pie

Once you have made the pastry, the delicious filling can be put together in moments.

Serves 8
200g/7oz/2½ cups shredded coconut
115g/4oz/⅔ cup caster (superfine) sugar
60ml/4 tbsp cornflour (cornstarch)
pinch of salt
600ml/1 pint/2½ cups milk
50ml/2fl oz/¼ cup whipping cream
2 egg yolks
25g/1oz/2 tbsp unsalted butter
10ml/2 tsp vanilla extract
For the pastry
115g/4oz/1 cup plain (all-purpose) flour
1.5ml/¼ tsp salt
40g/1½oz/3 tbsp cold butter, cut in pieces
25g/1oz/2 tbsp cold lard

1 For the pastry, sift the flour and salt into a bowl. Add the butter and lard and cut in with a pastry blender or two knives until the mixture resembles coarse breadcrumbs.

2 With a fork, stir in just enough iced water to bind the dough (30–45ml/2–3 tbsp). Gather into a ball, wrap in baking parchment and chill for at least 20 minutes.

3 Preheat the oven to 220°C/425°F/Gas 7. Roll out the dough 3mm/⅛in thick. Transfer to a 23cm/9in flan tin (pan). Trim and flute the edges. Prick the bottom. Line with baking parchment and fill with baking beans. Bake for 10–12 minutes. Remove the paper and beans, reduce the heat to 180°C/350°F/Gas 4 and bake until brown, about 10–15 minutes more.

4 Spread 75g/3oz/1 cup of the coconut on a baking sheet and toast in the oven until golden, 6–8 minutes, stirring often. Set aside for decorating.

5 Put the sugar, cornflour and salt in a pan. In a bowl, whisk together the milk, cream and egg yolks. Add the egg mixture to the pan.

6 Cook over low heat, stirring constantly, until the mixture comes to the boil. Boil for 1 minute, then remove from the heat. Add the butter, vanilla extract and remaining coconut.

7 Pour into the prebaked pastry case (pie shell). When the filling is cool, sprinkle toasted coconut in a ring in the centre.

Peach Tart with Almond Cream

The almond cream filling should be baked until it is just turning brown. Take care not to overbake it or the delicate flavours will be spoilt.

INGREDIENTS

Serves 8–10

4 large ripe peaches

115g/4oz/⅔ cup blanched almonds

30ml/2 tbsp plain (all-purpose) flour

90g/3½oz/7 tbsp unsalted butter,
    at room temperature

130g/4½oz/scant ¾ cup granulated
    (white) sugar

1 egg

1 egg yolk

2.5ml/½ tsp vanilla extract, or 10ml/
    2 tsp rum

For the pastry

150g/5oz/1¼ cups flour

4ml/¾ tsp salt

90g/3½oz/7 tbsp cold unsalted butter,
    cut in pieces

1 egg yolk

1 For the pastry, sift the flour and salt into a bowl.

2 Add the butter and cut in with a pastry blender until the mixture resembles coarse crumbs. With a fork, stir in the egg yolk and just enough iced water (30–45ml/ 2–3 tbsp) to bind the dough. Gather into a ball, wrap in baking parchment and chill for at least 20 minutes. Place a baking sheet in the oven and preheat to 200°C/ 400°F/Gas 6.

3 On a lightly floured surface, roll out the pastry 3mm/⅛in thick. Transfer to a 25cm/10in flan tin (pan). Trim the edge, prick the bottom and chill.

4 Score the bottoms of the peaches. Drop the peaches, one at a time, into boiling water. Leave for 20 seconds, then dip in cold water. Peel off the skins using a sharp knife.

5 Grind the almonds finely with the flour in a food processor, blender or nut grinder. With an electric mixer, cream the butter and 90g/3½oz/½ cup of the sugar until light and fluffy. Gradually beat in the egg and yolk. Stir in the almonds and vanilla or rum. Spread in the pastry case (pie shell).

6 Halve the peaches and remove the stones (pits). Cut crosswise in thin slices and arrange on top of the almond cream like the spokes of a wheel; keep the slices of each peach-half together. Fan them out by pressing down gently at a slight angle.

7 Bake until the pastry begins to brown, 10–15 minutes. Lower the heat to 180°C/350°F/Gas 4 and continue baking until the almond cream sets, about 15 minutes more. Ten minutes before the end of the cooking time, sprinkle with the remaining sugar.

VARIATION

For a Nectarine and Apricot Tart with Almond Cream, replace the peaches with nectarines, prepared and arranged the same way. Peel and chop three fresh apricots. Fill the spaces between the fanned-out nectarines with chopped apricots. Bake as above.

Raspberry Tart

This glazed fruit tart really does taste as good as it looks.

INGREDIENTS

Serves 8

4 egg yolks

65g/2½ oz/⅓ cup granulated (white) sugar

45ml/3 tbsp plain (all-purpose) flour

300ml/½ pint/1¼ cups milk

pinch of salt

2.5ml/½ tsp vanilla extract

450g/1lb fresh raspberries

75ml/5 tbsp grape or redcurrant jelly

15ml/1 tbsp fresh orange juice

For the pastry

150g/5oz/1¼ cups plain
   (all-purpose) flour

2.5ml/½ tsp baking powder

1.5ml/¼ tsp salt

15ml/1 tbsp sugar

grated rind of ½ orange

90ml/6 tbsp cold butter, cut in pieces

1 egg yolk

45–60ml/3–4 tbsp whipping cream

1 For the pastry, sift the flour, baking powder and salt into a bowl. Stir in the sugar and orange rind. Add the butter and mix until the mixture resembles coarse crumbs. With a fork, stir in the egg yolk and just enough cream to bind the dough. Gather into a ball, wrap in baking parchment and chill.

2 For the custard filling, beat the egg yolks and sugar until thick and lemon-coloured. Gradually stir in the flour.

3 In a pan, bring the milk and salt just to the boil, and remove from the heat. Whisk into the egg yolk mixture, return to the pan, and continue whisking over moderately high heat until just bubbling. Cook for 3 minutes to thicken. Transfer immediately to a bowl. Stir in the vanilla to blend.

4 Cover with baking parchment to prevent a skin from forming.

5 Preheat the oven to 200°C/ 400°F/Gas 6. On a lightly floured surface, roll out the dough about 3mm/⅛in thick, transfer to a 25cm/10in flan tin (pan) and trim the edge. Prick the bottom all over with a fork and line with baking parchment. Fill with baking beans and bake for 15 minutes. Remove the paper and baking beans. Continue baking until golden, 6–8 minutes more. Let cool.

6 Spread an even layer of the pastry cream filling in the tart shell and arrange the raspberries on top. Melt the jelly and orange juice in a pan over a low heat and brush on top to glaze.

Kiwi Ricotta Cheese Tart

It is well worth taking your time arranging the kiwi fruit topping in neat rows for this exotic and impressive-looking tart.

INGREDIENTS

Serves 8

50g/2oz/½ cup blanched almonds
90g/3½oz/½ cup plus 15ml/1 tbsp caster (superfine) sugar
900g/2lb/4 cups ricotta cheese
250ml/8fl oz/1 cup whipping cream
1 egg
3 egg yolks
15ml/1 tbsp plain (all-purpose) flour
pinch of salt
30ml/2 tbsp rum
grated rind of 1 lemon
40ml/2½ tbsp lemon juice
50ml/2fl oz/¼ cup clear honey
5 kiwi fruit
For the pastry
150g/5oz/1¼ cups plain (all-purpose) flour
15ml/1 tbsp granulated (white) sugar
2.5ml/½ tsp salt
2.5ml/½ tsp baking powder
75g/3oz/6 tbsp cold butter, cut in pieces
1 egg yolk
45–60ml/3–4 tbsp whipping cream

1 For the pastry, sift the flour, sugar, salt and baking powder into a bowl. Cut in the butter until the mixture resembles coarse crumbs. Mix the egg yolk and cream. Stir in just enough to bind the dough.

2 Transfer to a lightly floured surface, flatten slightly, wrap in baking parchment and chill for 30 minutes. Preheat the oven to 220°C/425°F/Gas 7.

3 On a lightly floured surface, roll out the dough 3mm/⅛in thick and transfer to a 23cm/9in spring-form tin (pan). Crimp the edge.

4 Prick the bottom of the dough all over with a fork. Line with baking parchment and fill with baking beans. Bake for 10 minutes. Remove the paper and beans and bake until golden, 6–8 minutes more. Let cool. Reduce the heat to 180°C/350°F/Gas 4.

5 Grind the almonds finely with 15ml/1 tbsp of the sugar in a food processor or blender.

6 With an electric mixer, beat the ricotta until creamy. Add the cream, egg, yolks, remaining sugar, flour, salt, rum, lemon rind and 30ml/2 tbsp of the lemon juice. Beat to combine.

7 Stir in the ground almonds until well blended.

8 Pour into the shell and bake until golden, about 1 hour. Let cool, then chill, loosely covered, for 2–3 hours. Unmould and place on a serving plate.

9 Combine the honey and remaining lemon juice for the glaze. Set aside.

10 Peel the kiwis. Halve them lengthways, then cut crosswise into 5mm/¼in slices. Arrange the slices in rows across the top of the tart. Just before serving, brush with the glaze.

Lemon and Orange Tart

Citrus fruits in a nutty pastry case.

INGREDIENTS

Serves 8–10

115g/4oz/1 cup plain (all-purpose)
    flour, sifted
115g/4oz/1 cup wholemeal
    (whole-wheat) flour
25g/1oz/3 tbsp ground hazelnuts
25g/1oz/3 tbsp icing (confectioners')
    sugar, sifted
pinch of salt
115g/4oz/½ cup unsalted butter
60ml/4 tbsp lemon curd
300ml/½ pint/1¼ cups whipped cream or
    fromage frais
4 oranges, peeled and thinly sliced

1 Place the flours, hazelnuts, sugar, salt and butter in a food processor and process in short bursts until the mixture resembles breadcrumbs. Add 30–45ml/ 2–3 tbsp cold water and process until the dough comes together.

2 Turn out on to a lightly floured surface and knead gently until smooth. Roll out and line a 25cm/10in flan tin (pan). Ease the pastry gently into the corners without stretching it. Chill for 20 minutes. Preheat the oven to 190°C/375°F/Gas 5.

3 Line the pastry with baking parchment and fill with baking beans. Bake blind for 15 minutes, remove the paper and beans and continue for a further 5–10 minutes, until the pastry is crisp. Allow to cool.

4 Whisk the lemon curd into the cream or fromage frais and spread over the base of the pastry. Arrange the orange slices on top and serve at room temperature.

Chocolate Pear Tart

*Serve slices of this drizzled with
single cream or with a scoop of
vanilla ice cream for a special treat.*

INGREDIENTS

Serves 8

115g/4oz plain (semisweet)
    chocolate, grated
3 large firm, ripe pears
1 egg
1 egg yolk
120ml/4fl oz/½ cup single (light) cream
2.5ml/½ tsp vanilla extract
45ml/3 tbsp caster (superfine) sugar
For the pastry
115g/4oz/1 cup plain (all-purpose) flour
pinch of salt
30ml/2 tbsp caster (superfine) sugar
115g/4oz/½ cup cold unsalted butter,
    cut into pieces
1 egg yolk
15ml/1 tbsp fresh lemon juice

1 For the pastry, sift the flour
and salt into a bowl. Add the
sugar and butter. Cut in with a
pastry blender until the mixture
resembles coarse crumbs. With a
fork, stir in the egg yolk and lemon
juice until the mixture forms a
dough. Gather into a ball, wrap in
baking parchment, and chill for at
least 20 minutes.

2 Place a baking sheet in the
oven and preheat to 200°C/
400°F/Gas 6. On a lightly floured
surface, roll out the dough to
3mm/⅛in thick and trim the
edge. Transfer to a 25cm/10in
flan tin (pan).

3 Sprinkle the bottom of the tart
shell with the grated chocolate.

4 Peel, halve and core the pears.
Cut in thin slices crosswise,
then fan them out slightly.

5 Transfer the pear halves to the
tart with the help of a metal
spatula and arrange on top of the
chocolate to resemble the spokes
of a wheel.

6 Whisk together the egg and
egg yolk, cream and vanilla
extract. Ladle over the pears, then
sprinkle with sugar.

7 Bake for 10 minutes. Reduce
the heat to 180°C/350°F/
Gas 4 and cook until the custard
is set and the pears begin to
caramelize, about 20 minutes
more. Serve at room temperature.

Tarte au Citron

You can find this classic lemon tart in bistros all over France.

INGREDIENTS

Serves 8–10

350g/12oz shortcrust or sweet
 shortcrust pastry
grated rind of 2 or 3 lemons
150ml/¼ pint/⅔ cup freshly squeezed
 lemon juice
90g/3½oz/½ cup caster (superfine) sugar
60ml/4 tbsp crème fraîche or double
 (heavy) cream
4 eggs, plus 3 egg yolks
icing (confectioners') sugar, for dusting

1 Preheat the oven to 190°C/ 375°F/Gas 5. Roll out the pastry thinly and use to line a 23cm/9in flan tin (pan). Prick the base of the pastry.

2 Line the pastry case (pie shell) with foil and fill with baking beans. Bake for about 15 minutes until the edges are set and dry. Remove the foil and beans and continue baking for a further 5–7 minutes until golden.

3 Place the lemon rind, juice and sugar in a bowl. Beat until combined and then gradually add the crème fraîche or double cream and beat until well blended.

4 Beat in the eggs, one at a time, then beat in the egg yolks and pour the filling into the pastry case. Bake for 15–20 minutes, until the filling is set. If the pastry begins to brown too much, cover the edges with foil. Leave to cool. Dust with a little icing sugar before serving.

Treacle Tart

Quite a filling tart, this, so best served after a light main course.

INGREDIENTS

Serves 4–6

175ml/6fl oz/¾ cup golden
  (light corn) syrup
75g/3oz/1½ cups fresh white breadcrumbs
grated rind of 1 lemon
30ml/2 tbsp fresh lemon juice
For the pastry
150g/5oz/1¼ cups flour
2.5ml/½ tsp salt
75g/3oz/6 tbsp cold butter, cut in pieces
75g/3oz/3 tbsp cold margarine,
  cut in pieces

1 For the pastry, combine the flour and salt in a bowl. Add the butter and margarine and cut in with a pastry blender until the mixture resembles coarse crumbs.

2 With a fork, stir in just enough iced water (about 45–60ml/ 3–4 tbsp) to bind the dough. Gather into a ball, wrap in baking parchment, and chill for at least 20 minutes.

3 On a lightly floured surface, roll out the dough 3mm/⅛in thick. Transfer to a 20cm/8in flan tin (pan) and trim off the overhang. Chill for at least 20 minutes. Reserve the trimmings for the lattice top.

4 Place a baking sheet above the centre of the oven and heat to 200°C/400°F/Gas 6.

5 In a pan, warm the syrup until thin and runny.

6 Remove from the heat and stir in the breadcrumbs and lemon rind. Let sit for 10 minutes so the bread can absorb the syrup. Add more breadcrumbs if the mixture is thin. Stir in the lemon juice and spread evenly in the pastry case (pie shell).

7 Roll out the pastry trimmings and cut into 10–12 thin strips.

8 Lay half the strips on the filling, then carefully arrange the remaining strips to form a lattice pattern.

9 Place on the hot sheet and bake for 10 minutes. Lower the heat to 190°C/375°F/Gas 5. Bake until golden, about 15 minutes more. Serve warm or cold.

Rich Chocolate-berry Tart

Use any berries you like to top this exotic tart.

INGREDIENTS

Serves 10

115g/4oz/½ cup unsalted butter, softened

90g/3½oz/½ cup caster (superfine) sugar

2.5ml/½ tsp salt

15ml/1 tbsp vanilla extract

50g/2oz/½ cup unsweetened cocoa

215g/7½oz/1¾ cups plain
(all-purpose) flour

450g/1lb fresh berries for topping

For the chocolate ganache filling

475ml/16fl oz/2 cups double (heavy) cream

150g/5oz/½ cup seedless
blackberry preserve

225g/8oz plain (semisweet)
chocolate, chopped

25g/1oz/2 tbsp unsalted butter

For the blackberry sauce

225g/8oz fresh or frozen blackberries
or raspberries

15ml/1 tbsp lemon juice

25g/1oz/2 tbsp caster (superfine) sugar

30ml/2 tbsp blackberry liqueur

1 Prepare the pastry. Place the butter, sugar, salt and vanilla in a food processor and process until creamy. Add cocoa and process for 1 minute. Add flour all at once and process for 10–15 seconds, until just blended. Place a piece of clear film (plastic wrap) on work surface. Turn out dough on to clear film. Use clear film to help shape dough into flat disc and wrap tightly. Chill for 1 hour.

2 Lightly grease a 23cm/9in tart tin (pan) with removable base. Roll out dough between two sheets of clear film to a 28cm/11in round, about 5 mm/¼in thick. Peel off top sheet of clear film and invert dough into prepared tin. Ease dough into tin. Remove clear film.

3 With floured fingers, press dough on to base and side of tin, then roll rolling pin over edge of tin to cut off any excess dough. Prick base of dough with fork. Chill for 1 hour. Preheat oven to 180°C/350°F/Gas 4. Line tart shell with foil or baking parchment; fill with dry beans or rice. Bake for 10 minutes; lift out foil with beans and bake for 5 minutes more, until just set (pastry may look underdone on the bottom, but will dry out). Remove to wire rack to cool completely.

4 Prepare filling. In a medium pan over medium heat, bring cream and blackberry preserve to the boil. Remove from heat and add chocolate, stirring until smooth. Stir in butter and strain into cooled tart, smoothing top. Cool tart completely.

5 Prepare sauce. In a food processor combine blackberries, lemon juice and sugar and process until smooth. Strain into a small bowl and add blackberry-flavour liqueur. If sauce is too thick, thin with a little water.

6 To serve, remove tart from tin. Place on serving plate and arrange the berries on the top of the tart. With a pastry brush, brush berries with a little of the blackberry sauce to glaze lightly. Serve remaining sauce separately.

Bakewell Tart

Although the pastry base makes this a tart, it was originally a pudding.

Serves 4

225g/8oz ready-made puff pastry
30ml/2 tbsp raspberry or apricot jam
2 eggs
2 egg yolks
115g/4oz/generous ½ cup caster
   (superfine) sugar
115g/4oz/½ cup butter, melted
50g/2oz/½ cup ground almonds
few drops of almond extract
icing (confectioners') sugar, for sifting

1 Preheat the oven to 200°C/
400°F/Gas 6. Roll out the
pastry on a lightly floured surface
and use it to line an 18cm/7in pie
plate or loose-based flan tin (pan).
Spread the jam over the bottom of
the pastry case (pie shell).

COOK'S TIP

Since this pastry case isn't baked
blind first, place a baking sheet
in the oven while it preheats,
then place the flan tin on the hot
sheet. This will ensure that the
bottom of the pastry case cooks
right through.

2 Whisk the eggs, egg yolks and
sugar together in a large bowl
until thick and pale.

3 Gently stir the butter, ground
almonds and almond extract
into the mixture.

4 Pour the mixture into the
pastry case and bake for
30 minutes, until the filling is just
set and browned. Sift icing sugar
over the top before serving the tart
hot, warm or cold.

VARIATION

Ground hazelnuts are increasingly
available and make an interesting
change to the almonds in this tart.
If you are going to grind shelled
hazelnuts yourself, first roast them
in the oven for 10–15 minutes to
bring out their flavour then rub in
a dish towel to remove skins.

Apple Pie

Delicious on its own, or with a dollop of double cream or ice cream.

INGREDIENTS

Serves 8

900g/2lb tart cooking apples
30ml/2 tbsp plain (all-purpose) flour
90g/3½oz/½ cup sugar
25ml/1½ tbsp fresh lemon juice
2.5ml/½ tsp ground cinnamon
2.5ml/½ tsp ground allspice
1.5ml/¼ tsp ground ginger
1.5ml/¼ tsp grated nutmeg
1.5ml/¼ tsp salt
50g/2oz/4 tbsp butter, diced
For the pastry
225g/8oz/2 cups plain (all-purpose) flour
5ml/1 tsp salt
75g/3oz/6 tbsp cold butter, cut in pieces
50g/2oz/4 tbsp cold lard, cut in pieces

1 For the pastry, sift the flour and salt into a bowl.

2 Add the butter and lard and cut in with a pastry blender or rub between your fingertips until the mixture resembles coarse crumbs. With a fork, stir in just enough iced water to bind the dough (60–120ml/4–8 tbsp).

3 Gather into two balls, wrap in baking parchment and chill for 20 minutes.

4 On a lightly floured surface, roll out one dough ball to 3mm/⅛in thick. Transfer to a 23cm/9in pie tin (pan) and trim the edge. Place a baking sheet in the centre of the oven and preheat to 220°C/425°F/Gas 7.

5 Peel, core and slice the apples into a bowl. Toss with the flour, sugar, lemon juice, spices and salt. Spoon into pastry case (pie shell); dot with butter.

6 Roll out the remaining dough. Place on top of the pie and trim to leave a 2cm/¾in overhang. Fold the overhang under the bottom dough and press to seal. Crimp the edge.

7 Roll out the scraps and cut out leaf shapes and roll balls. Arrange on top of the pie. Cut steam vents.

8 Bake for 10 minutes. Reduce the heat to 180°C/350°F/ Gas 4 and bake until golden, 40–45 minutes more. If the pie browns too quickly, protect with foil.

Mississippi Pecan Pie

This fabulous dessert started life in the United States but has become an international favourite.

INGREDIENTS

Serves 6–8

For the pastry

115g/4oz/1 cup plain (all-purpose) flour

50g/2oz/4 tbsp butter, cubed

25g/1oz/2 tbsp caster (superfine) sugar

1 egg yolk

For the filling

175g/6oz/½ cup golden (light corn) syrup

50g/2oz/⅓ cup dark muscovado
    (molasses) sugar

50g/2oz/4 tbsp butter

3 eggs, lightly beaten

2.5ml/½ tsp vanilla extract

150g/5oz/1¼ cups pecan nuts

fresh cream or ice cream, to serve

1 Place the flour in a bowl and add the butter. Rub in the butter with your fingertips until the mixture resembles bread-crumbs, then stir in the sugar, egg yolk and about 30ml/2 tbsp cold water. Mix to a dough and knead lightly on a floured surface until smooth and free of lumps.

2 Roll out the pastry and use to line a 20cm/8in loose-based fluted flan tin (pan). Prick the base, then line with baking parchment and fill with baking beans. Chill for 30 minutes. Preheat the oven to 200°C/400°F/Gas 6.

3 Bake the pastry case for 10 minutes. Remove the paper and beans and bake for 5 minutes. Reduce the oven temperature to 180°C/350°F/Gas 4.

4 Meanwhile, heat the syrup, sugar and butter in a pan until the sugar dissolves. Remove from the heat and cool slightly. Whisk in the eggs and vanilla extract and stir in the pecans.

5 Pour into the pastry case (pie shell) and bake for 35–40 minutes, until the filling is set. Serve with cream or ice cream.

Boston Banoffee Pie

*There are many variations of this
American treat; this one is easy to
make and tastes wonderful.*

INGREDIENTS

Serves 6–8

150g/5oz/1¼ cups plain (all-purpose) flour
225g/8oz/1 cup butter
50g/2oz/4 tbsp caster (superfine) sugar
½ x 405g/14oz can skimmed, sweetened
  condensed milk
115g/4oz/⅔ cup soft light brown sugar
30ml/2 tbsp golden (light corn) syrup
2 small bananas, sliced
a little lemon juice
whipped cream, to decorate
5ml/1 tsp grated plain (semisweet) chocolate

1 Preheat the oven to 160°C/
325°F/Gas 3. Place the flour
and 115g/4oz/½ cup of the butter
in a food processor and blend
until crumbed (or rub in with
your fingertips). Stir in the
caster sugar.

2 Squeeze the mixture together
until it forms a dough. Press
into the base of a 20cm/8in loose-
based fluted flan tin (pan). Bake
for 25–30 minutes.

3 Place the remaining 115g/
4oz/½ cup of butter with the
condensed milk, brown sugar and
golden syrup in a large non-stick
pan and heat gently, stirring, until
the butter has melted and the
sugar has dissolved.

4 Bring to a gentle boil and cook
for 7 minutes, stirring all the
time (to prevent burning), until
the mixture thickens and turns a
light caramel colour. Pour on to
the cooked pastry case (pie shell)
and leave until cold.

5 Sprinkle the bananas with
lemon juice and arrange in
overlapping circles on top of the
caramel filling, leaving a gap in the
centre. Pipe a swirl of whipped
cream in the centre and sprinkle
with the grated chocolate.

Chocolate Profiteroles

This mouth-watering dessert is served in cafés throughout France. Sometimes the profiteroles are filled with whipped cream instead of ice cream, but they are always drizzled with chocolate sauce.

INGREDIENTS

Serves 4–6

275g/10oz plain (semisweet) chocolate

750ml/1¼ pints/3 cups vanilla ice cream

For the profiteroles

110g/3¾oz/¾ cup plain
  (all-purpose) flour

1.5ml/¼ tsp salt

pinch of freshly grated nutmeg

75g/3oz/6 tbsp unsalted butter, cut into
  6 pieces

3 eggs

1 Preheat the oven to 200°C/
400°F/Gas 6 and butter a
baking sheet.

2 To make the profiteroles, sift
together the flour, salt and
nutmeg. In a medium pan, bring
the butter and 175ml/6fl oz/¾ cup
of water to the boil. Remove
from the heat and add the dry
ingredients all at once. Beat with a
wooden spoon for about 1 minute
until well blended and the mixture
starts to pull away from the sides
of the pan, then set the pan over
a low heat and cook the mixture
for about 2 minutes, beating
constantly. Remove from the heat.

3 Beat one egg in a small
bowl and set aside. Add the
remaining eggs, one at a time, to
the flour mixture, beating well.
Add the beaten egg gradually until
the dough is smooth and shiny; it
should fall slowly when dropped
from a spoon.

4 Using a tablespoon, drop
the dough on to the baking
sheet in 12 mounds. Bake for
25–30 minutes until the pastry is
well risen and browned. Turn off
the oven and leave the puffs to cool
with the oven door open.

5 To make the sauce, place the
chocolate and 120ml/4fl oz/
½ cup of warm water in a double
boiler or in a bowl and melt,
stirring occasionally over a pan of
hot water.

6 Split the profiteroles in half
and put a small scoop of ice
cream in each. Arrange on a
serving platter. Pour the sauce
over the top and serve at once.

Pear and Almond Cream Tart

This tart is equally successful made with other kinds of fruit, and some variation can be seen in almost every good French pâtisserie. Try making it with nectarines, peaches, apricots or apples.

INGREDIENTS

Serves 6

350g/12oz shortcrust or sweet
   shortcrust pastry
3 firm pears
lemon juice
15ml/1 tbsp peach brandy or water
60ml/4 tbsp peach preserve, strained
For the almond cream filling
115g/4oz/¾ cup blanched whole almonds
50g/2oz/¼ cup caster (superfine) sugar
65g/2½oz/5 tbsp butter
1 egg, plus 1 egg white
few drops almond extract

1 Roll out the pastry thinly and use to line a 23cm/9in flan tin (pan). Chill the pastry case (pie shell) while you make the filling. Put the almonds and sugar in a food processor and pulse until finely ground; they should not be pasty. Add the butter and process until creamy, then add the egg, egg white and almond extract and mix well.

2 Place a baking sheet in the oven and preheat to 190°C/375°F/Gas 5. Peel the pears, halve them, remove the cores and rub with lemon juice.

3 Put the pear halves cut-side down on a board and slice thinly crossways, keeping the slices together.

4 Pour the almond cream filling into the pastry case. Slide a palette knife under one pear half and press the top with your fingers to fan out the slices. Transfer to the tart, placing the fruit on the filling like spokes of a wheel. If you like, remove a few slices from each half before arranging and use to fill in any gaps in the centre.

5 Place on the baking sheet and bake for 50–55 minutes until the filling is set and well browned. Cool on a rack.

6 Meanwhile, heat the brandy or water and the preserve in a small pan, then brush over the top of the hot tart to glaze. Serve the tart warm.

Greek Chocolate Mousse Tartlets

*The combination of white chocolate
and Greek yogurt makes an
irresistibly light, but not too sweet,
filling for these little tarts.*

INGREDIENTS

Serves 6

175g/6oz/1½ cups plain
   (all-purpose) flour
30ml/2 tbsp cocoa powder
30ml/2 tbsp icing (confectioners') sugar
115g/4oz/½ cup butter
melted dark (bittersweet) chocolate,
   to decorate

For the filling

200g/7oz white chocolate, broken
   into squares
120ml/4fl oz/½ cup milk
10ml/2 tsp powdered gelatine
30ml/2 tbsp caster (superfine) sugar
5ml/1 tsp vanilla extract
2 eggs, separated
250g/9oz/generous 1 cup Greek
   (US strained plain) yogurt

1 Preheat the oven to 190°C/
375°F/Gas 5. Sift the flour,
cocoa and icing sugar into a
large bowl.

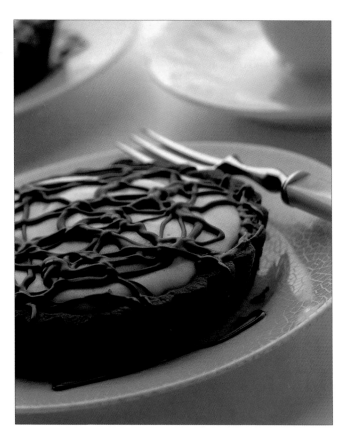

2 Place the butter in a pan with
60ml/4 tbsp water and heat
gently until just melted. Cool, then
stir into the flour to make a
smooth dough. Chill until firm.

3 Roll out the pastry and line six
deep 10cm/4in loose-based
flan tins (pans).

4 Prick the base of each pastry
case (pie shell) with a fork,
cover with baking parchment
weighed down with baking beans
and bake blind for 10 minutes.
Remove the beans and paper, return
to the oven and bake a further
15 minutes, or until the pastry is
firm. Leave to cool in the tins.

5 Make the filling. Melt the
chocolate in a heatproof bowl
over hot water. Pour the milk into
a pan, sprinkle over the gelatine
and heat gently, stirring, until the
gelatine has dissolved completely.
Remove from the heat and stir in
the chocolate.

6 Whisk the sugar, vanilla
extract and egg yolks in a large
bowl, then beat in the chocolate
mixture. Beat in the yogurt until
evenly mixed.

7 Whisk the egg whites in a
clean, grease-free bowl until
stiff, then fold into the mixture.
Divide among the pastry cases and
leave to set.

8 Drizzle the melted dark
chocolate over the tartlets
to decorate.

Tarte Tatin

This upside-down apple tart was first made by two sisters at their restaurant in the Loire Valley, France.

INGREDIENTS

Serves 8–10

225g/8oz puff or shortcrust pastry
10–12 large Golden Delicious apples
lemon juice
115g/4oz/½ cup butter, cut into pieces
90g/3½oz/½ cup caster (superfine) sugar
1.5ml/½ tsp ground cinnamon
crème fraîche or whipped cream, to serve

1 On a lightly floured surface, roll out the pastry into a 28cm/11in round less than 5mm/¼in thick. Transfer to a lightly floured baking sheet and chill.

2 Peel the apples, cut them in half lengthways and core. Sprinkle them generously with lemon juice.

3 Preheat the oven to 230°C/450°F/Gas 8. In a 25cm/10in tarte tatin tin (pan), cook the butter, sugar and cinnamon over medium heat until the butter has melted and sugar dissolved, stirring occasionally. Continue cooking for 6–8 minutes, until the mixture turns a medium caramel colour, then remove the pan from the heat and arrange the apple halves, standing on their edges, in the tin, fitting them in tightly since they shrink during cooking.

4 Return the apple-filled tin to the heat and bring to a simmer over a medium heat for 20–25 minutes until the apples are tender and coloured. Remove the tin from the heat and cool slightly.

5 Place the pastry on top of the apple-filled pan and tuck the edges of the pastry inside the edge of the tin around the apples.

6 Pierce the pastry in two or three places, then bake for 25–30 minutes until the pastry is golden and the filling is bubbling. Let the tart cool in the tin for 10–15 minutes.

7 To serve, run a sharp knife around edge of the tin to loosen the pastry. Cover with a serving plate and, holding them tightly, carefully invert the tin and plate together (do this over the sink in case any caramel drips). Lift off the tin and loosen any apples that stick with a spatula. Serve the tart warm with cream.

Jam Tart

Jam tarts are popular in Italy where they are traditionally decorated with pastry strips.

INGREDIENTS

Serves 6–8

200g/7oz/1¾ cups plain (all-purpose) flour

pinch of salt

50g/2oz/¼ cup granulated (white) sugar

115g/4oz/½ cup butter or
　　margarine, chilled

1 egg

1.5ml/¼ tsp grated lemon rind

350g/12oz/1¼ cups fruit jam, such as
　　raspberry, apricot or strawberry

1 egg, lightly beaten with 30ml/2 tbsp
　　whipping cream, for glazing

1 Make the pastry by placing the flour, salt and sugar in a mixing bowl. Using a pastry blender or two knives, cut the butter or margarine into the dry ingredients as quickly as possible until the mixture resembles coarse crumbs.

2 Beat the egg with the lemon rind in a cup, and pour it over the flour mixture. Combine with a fork until the dough holds together. If it is too crumbly, mix in 15–30ml/1–2 tbsp of water.

3 Gather the dough into two balls, one slightly larger than the other, and flatten into discs. Wrap in baking parchment, and put in the refrigerator for at least 40 minutes.

4 Lightly grease a shallow 23cm/9in tart or pie tin (pan), preferably with a removable bottom. Roll out the larger disc of pastry on a lightly floured surface to a thickness of about 3mm/⅛in.

5 Roll the pastry around the rolling pin and transfer to the prepared tin. Trim the edges evenly with a small knife. Prick the bottom with a fork. Chill for at least 30 minutes.

6 Preheat the oven to 190°C/ 375°F/Gas 5. Spread the jam thickly and evenly over the base of the pastry. Roll out the remaining pastry.

7 Cut the pastry into strips about 1cm/¼in wide using a ruler as a guide. Arrange them over the jam in a lattice pattern. Trim the edges of the strips even with the edge of the tin, pressing them lightly on to the pastry case (pie shell). Brush the pastry with the egg and cream glaze. Bake for about 35 minutes, or until the pastry is golden brown. Cool before serving.

American Spiced Pumpkin Pie

The unofficial national dish of the United States.

Serves 4–6

175g/6oz/1½ cups plain
  (all-purpose) flour
pinch of salt
75g/3oz/6 tbsp unsalted butter
15ml/1 tbsp caster (superfine) sugar
450g/1lb/4 cups peeled fresh pumpkin,
  cubed, or 400g/14oz/2 cups canned
  pumpkin, drained
115g/4oz/½ cup soft light brown sugar
1.5ml/¼ tsp salt
1.5ml/¼ ground allspice
2.5ml/½ tsp ground cinnamon
2.5ml/½ tsp ground ginger
2 eggs, lightly beaten
120ml/4fl oz/½ cup double (heavy) cream
whipped cream, to serve

1 Place the flour in a bowl with the salt and butter and rub with your fingertips until the mixture resembles breadcrumbs (or use a food processor).

2 Stir in the sugar and add about 30–45ml/2–3 tbsp water and mix to a soft dough. Knead the dough lightly on a floured surface. Flatten out into a round, wrap in a polythene bag and chill for 1 hour.

3 Preheat the oven to 200°C/ 400°F/Gas 6 with a baking sheet inside. If you are using raw pumpkin for the pie, steam for 15 minutes until quite tender, then leave to cool completely. Purée the steamed or canned pumpkin in a food processor or blender until it is very smooth.

4 Roll out the pastry quite thinly and use to line a 24cm/9½in (measured across the top) x 2.5cm/ 1in deep pie tin (pan). Trim off any excess pastry and reserve for the decoration. Prick the base of the pastry case (pie shell).

5 Cut as many leaf shapes as you can from the excess pastry and make vein markings with the back of a knife on each. Brush the edge of the pastry with water and stick the leaves all round the edge. Chill.

6 In a large bowl mix together the pumpkin purée, sugar, salt, spices, eggs and cream and pour into the prepared pastry case. Smooth the top with a knife.

7 Place on the preheated baking sheet and bake for 15 minutes. Then reduce the temperature to 180°C/350°F/Gas 4 and cook for a further 30 minutes, or until the filling is set and the pastry golden. Serve the pie warm with a generous dollop of whipped cream.

CUSTARDS, SOUFFLÉS & WHIPS

◆ ✦ ◆

Coffee Coeur à la Crème

These pretty heart-shaped creams, speckled with espresso-roasted coffee beans, are served with a fruit sauce.

INGREDIENTS

Serves 6

25g/1oz/generous ¼ cup espresso-roasted
   coffee beans
225g/8oz/1 cup ricotta or curd cheese
300ml/½ pint/1¼ cups crème fraîche
25g/1oz/2 tbsp caster (superfine) sugar
finely grated rind of ½ orange
2 egg whites
For the red fruit coulis
175g/6oz/1 cup raspberries
30ml/2 tbsp icing (confectioners')
   sugar, sifted
115g/4oz/⅔ cup small strawberries (or
   wild ones, if available), halved

1 Preheat the oven to 180°C/
350°F/Gas 4. Spread the coffee
beans on to a baking sheet and
toast for 10 minutes. Cool, put in a
large plastic bag and crush with a
rolling pin.

2 Rinse 12 pieces of muslin
(cheesecloth) in cold water and
squeeze dry. Line six coeur à la
crème moulds with a double layer,
allowing the muslin to overhang.

3 Press the ricotta or curd cheese
through a sieve (strainer) into a
bowl. Stir the crème fraîche, sugar,
orange rind and crushed roasted
coffee beans together. Add to the
cheese and mix well.

4 Whisk the egg whites until stiff
and fold into the mixture.
Spoon into the prepared moulds,
then bring the muslin up and over
the filling. Drain and chill in the
refrigerator overnight.

5 To make the red fruit coulis,
put the raspberries and icing
sugar in a food processor and blend
until smooth. Push through a fine
sieve to remove the pips. Stir in the
strawberries. Chill until you are
ready to serve.

6 Unmould the hearts on to
individual serving plates and
carefully remove the muslin. Spoon
the coulis over before serving.

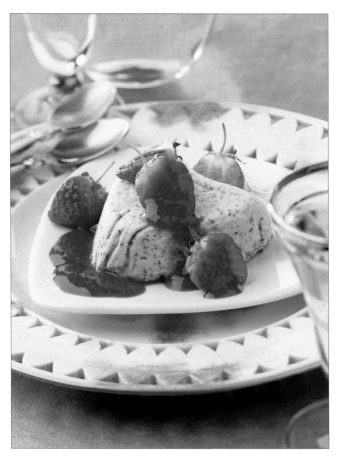

Tiramisù

The name of this classic dessert translates as "pick me up", and is said to derive from the fact that it is so good that it literally makes you swoon when you eat it.

Serves 4

225g/8oz/1 cup mascarpone

25g/1oz/¼ cup icing (confectioners')
  sugar, sifted

150ml/¼ pint/⅔ cup strong coffee, chilled

300ml/½ pint/1¼ cups double
  (heavy) cream

45ml/3 tbsp coffee liqueur such as Tia
  Maria, Kahlúa or Toussaint

115g/4oz Savoiardi (sponge finger)
  biscuits (cookies)

50g/2oz dark (bittersweet) or plain
  (semisweet) chocolate, coarsely grated

cocoa powder, for dusting

1 Lightly grease and line a 900g/2lb loaf tin (pan) with clear film (plastic wrap). In a large bowl, beat the mascarpone and icing sugar for 1 minute. Stir in 30ml/2 tbsp of the chilled coffee. Mix thoroughly.

2 Whip the cream and 15ml/ 1 tbsp of the liqueur to soft peaks. Stir a spoonful into the mascarpone, then fold in the rest. Spoon half the mixture into the tin and smooth the top.

COOK'S TIP

This dish also works well with a single layer of Savoiardi biscuits.

---

3 Put the remaining strong brewed coffee and liqueur in a shallow dish just wider than the Savoiardi biscuits. Using half the biscuits, dip one side of each biscuit into the coffee mixture, then arrange on top of the mascarpone mixture in a single layer.

4 Spoon the rest of the mascarpone mixture over the biscuit layer and smooth the top.

5 Dip the remaining biscuits in the coffee, arrange on top, and drizzle over any remaining coffee mixture. Cover with clear film and chill for 4 hours. Turn the tiramisù out of the tin and sprinkle with grated chocolate and cocoa powder; serve cut into slices.

Hot Chocolate Zabaglione

This is a delicious chocolate-flavoured variation of the classic Italian dessert.

Serves 6

6 egg yolks

150g/5oz/¾ cup caster (superfine) sugar

45ml/3 tbsp cocoa powder

200ml/7fl oz/scant 1 cup Marsala

cocoa powder or icing (confectioners') sugar, for dusting

almond biscuits (cookies), to serve

1 Half fill a medium pan with water and bring to simmering point.

2 Place the egg yolks and sugar in a heatproof bowl and whisk until the mixture is pale and all the sugar has dissolved.

3 Add the cocoa and Marsala, then place the bowl over the simmering water. Whisk until the consistency of the mixture is smooth, thick and foamy.

4 Pour quickly into tall heatproof glasses, dust lightly with cocoa or icing sugar and serve immediately with almond biscuits.

Crème Caramel

Crème caramel, or crème renversée, is one of the most popular French desserts and is wonderful when freshly made. This is a slightly lighter modern version of the recipe.

INGREDIENTS

Serves 6–8

250g/9oz/1¼ cups granulated
   (white) sugar
60ml/4 tbsp water
1 vanilla pod (bean) or 10ml/
   2 tsp vanilla extract
400ml/14fl oz/1⅔ cups milk
250ml/8fl oz/1 cup whipping cream
5 large eggs
2 egg yolks

1 Put 175g/6oz/scant 1 cup of the sugar in a small heavy pan with 60ml/4 tbsp of water to moisten. Bring to the boil over a high heat, swirling the pan to dissolve the sugar. Boil, without stirring, until the syrup turns a dark caramel colour (this will take about 4–5 minutes).

2 Immediately pour the caramel into a 1 litre/1¾ pint/4 cup soufflé dish. Holding the dish with oven gloves, quickly swirl the dish to coat the base and sides with the caramel and set aside. (The caramel will harden quickly as it cools.) Place the dish in a small roasting pan.

3 Preheat the oven to 160°C/ 325°F/Gas 3. With a small sharp knife, carefully split the vanilla pod lengthways and scrape the black seeds into a medium pan. Add the milk and cream and bring just to the boil over a medium-high heat, stirring frequently. Remove the pan from the heat, cover and set aside for 15–20 minutes.

4 In a bowl, whisk the eggs and egg yolks with the remaining sugar for 2–3 minutes until smooth and creamy. Whisk in the hot milk and carefully strain the mixture into the caramel-lined dish. Cover with foil.

5 Place the dish in a roasting pan and pour in enough boiling water to come halfway up the sides of the dish. Bake the custard for 40–45 minutes until just set and a knife inserted about 5cm/2in from the edge comes out clean. Remove from the roasting pan and cool for at least 30 minutes, then chill overnight.

6 To turn out, carefully run a sharp knife around the edge of the dish to loosen the custard. Cover the dish with a serving plate and, holding them tightly, invert the dish and plate together. Gently lift one edge of the dish, allowing the caramel to run over the sides, then slowly lift off the dish.

Classic Coffee Crème Caramel

These lightly set coffee custards are served in a pool of caramel sauce. For a richer flavour, make them with half single cream, half milk.

INGREDIENTS

Serves 6

600ml/1 pint/2½ cups milk

45ml/3 tbsp ground coffee

50g/2oz/¼ cup caster (superfine) sugar

4 eggs

4 egg yolks

spun sugar, to decorate (optional)

For the caramel sauce

150g/5oz/¾ cup caster (superfine) sugar

60ml/4 tbsp water

1 Preheat the oven to 160°C/ 325°F/Gas 3. To make the sauce, heat the sugar with the water in a heavy pan until it has dissolved.

2 Bring to the boil and boil rapidly until the syrup turns a rich golden brown. Quickly pour the hot syrup into six warmed 150ml/¼ pint/⅔ cup ramekins.

3 To make the coffee custard, heat the milk until almost boiling. Pour over the ground coffee and leave to infuse for about 5 minutes. Strain through a fine sieve (strainer) into a jug (pitcher).

4 In a bowl, whisk the caster sugar, eggs and yolks until light and creamy. Whisk the coffee-flavoured milk into the egg mixture. Pour into the ramekins.

5 Put the ramekins in a roasting pan and add hot water to come two-thirds of the way up the dishes. Bake for 30–35 minutes until just set. Remove the custards from the heat and cool, then chill for 3 hours. To serve, invert on to plates and decorate if you wish.

COOK'S TIP

To make spun sugar, gently heat 75g/3oz/scant ½ cup caster (superfine) sugar, 5ml/1 tsp liquid glucose and 30ml/2 tbsp water in a heavy pan until the sugar dissolves. Boil the syrup to 160°C/325°F, then dip the base of the pan into cold water. Place baking parchment on the work surface and, holding two forks together, dip them in the syrup and flick rapidly back and forth over an oiled rolling pin.

Crème Brûlée

*This dessert actually originated in
Cambridge, but has become linked
to France and is widely eaten there.
Add a little liqueur, if you like.*

INGREDIENTS

Serves 6

1 vanilla pod (bean)

1 litre/1¾ pints/4 cups double
   (heavy) cream

6 egg yolks

90g/3½oz/½ cup caster (superfine) sugar

30ml/2 tbsp almond or orange
   liqueur (optional)

75g/3oz/⅓ cup soft light brown sugar

1 Preheat the oven to 150°C/
300°F/Gas 2. Place six 120ml/
4fl oz/½ cup ramekins in a roasting
pan and set aside.

2 With a small sharp knife, split
the vanilla pod lengthways
and scrape the black seeds into a
medium pan. Add the cream and
bring just to the boil over a
medium heat, stirring. Remove
from the heat and cover. Set aside
for 15–20 minutes.

COOK'S TIP

To test if the custards are ready,
push the point of a knife into
centre of one – if it comes out
clean, the custards are cooked.

---

3 In a bowl, whisk the egg yolks,
caster sugar and liqueur, if
using, until well blended. Whisk in
the hot cream and strain into a
large jug. Divide the custard
equally among the ramekins.

4 Pour enough boiling water
into the roasting pan to come
halfway up the sides of the
ramekins. Cover the pan with foil
and bake for about 30 minutes
until the custards are just set.
Remove from the pan and leave to
cool. Return to the dry roasting
pan and chill.

5 Preheat the grill (broiler).
Sprinkle the sugar evenly over
the surface of each custard and
grill (broil) for 30–60 seconds until
the sugar melts and caramelizes.
(Do not let the sugar burn or the
custard curdle.) Place in the
refrigerator to set the crust and
chill completely before serving.

Coffee Cardamom Zabaglione

This warm Italian dessert is usually made with Marsala wine. In this recipe coffee liqueur is used.

INGREDIENTS

Serves 4

4 cardamom pods

8 egg yolks

50g/2oz/4 tbsp golden caster (superfine) sugar

30ml/2 tbsp strong brewed coffee

50ml/2fl oz/¼ cup coffee liqueur such as Tia Maria, Kahlúa or Toussaint

a few crushed roasted coffee beans, to decorate

1 Peel away the pale green outer husks from the cardamom pods and remove the black seeds. Crush these to a fine powder using a pestle and mortar.

2 Put the egg yolks, caster sugar and cardamom in a bowl and whisk until pale and creamy.

3 Gradually whisk the coffee and the liqueur into the egg yolk mixture until evenly combined.

4 Place the bowl over a pan of near-boiling water and continue whisking for about 10 minutes.

5 Continue whisking until the mixture is very thick and fluffy and has doubled in volume, making sure the water doesn't boil – if it does the mixture will curdle. Remove the bowl from the heat and carefully pour the zabaglione into four warmed glasses or dishes. Sprinkle with a few crushed roasted coffee beans and serve at once.

Petits Pots de Cappuccino

These rich coffee custards, with a cream topping and a light dusting of drinking chocolate, look wonderful presented in fine china coffee cups.

Serves 6–8

75g/3oz/1 cup roasted coffee beans

300ml/½ pint/1¼ cups milk

300ml/½ pint/1¼ cups single (light) cream

1 whole egg and 4 egg yolks

50g/2oz/4 tbsp caster (superfine) sugar

2.5ml/½ tsp vanilla extract

For the topping

120ml/4fl oz/½ cup whipping cream

45ml/3 tbsp iced water

10ml/2 tsp drinking chocolate

1 Preheat the oven to 160°C/ 325°F/Gas 3. Put the coffee beans in a pan over a low heat for 3 minutes, shaking frequently.

2 Pour the milk and cream over the beans. Heat until almost boiling; cover and infuse for 30 minutes. Whisk the egg and yolks, sugar and vanilla together. Return the milk to boiling and pour through a sieve (strainer) on to the egg mixture. Discard the beans.

3 Pour the mixture into eight 75ml/5 tbsp coffee cups or six 120ml/4fl oz/½ cup ramekins. Cover each with a piece of foil.

4 Put the coffee cups or ramekins in a roasting pan with hot water reaching about two-thirds of the way up the sides of the dishes. Bake for 30–35 minutes, or until lightly set. Leave to cool. Chill in the refrigerator for at least 2 hours.

5 Whisk the whipping cream and iced water until thick and frothy and spoon on top of the custards. Dust with drinking chocolate before serving.

Almost Instant Banana Pudding

Banana and ginger make a great combination in this very fast dessert.

INGREDIENTS

Serves 6–8

4 thick slices ginger cake
6 bananas
30ml/2 tbsp lemon juice
300ml/½ pint/1¼ cups whipping cream or
    fromage frais
60ml/4 tbsp fruit juice
30–45ml/3–4 tbsp soft brown sugar

1 Break up the cake into chunks and arrange in an ovenproof dish. Slice the bananas and toss in the lemon juice.

2 Whip the cream and, when firm, gently whip in the juice. (If using fromage frais, just gently stir in the juice.) Fold in the bananas and spoon the mixture over the ginger cake.

3 Top with the soft brown sugar and place under a hot grill (broiler) for 2–3 minutes to caramelize. Chill to set firm again if you wish, or serve when required.

Ginger and Orange Crème Brûlée

This is a useful way of cheating at crème brûlée! Most people would never know unless you overchill the custard, or keep it more than a day, but there's little risk of that!

INGREDIENTS

Serves 4–5

2 eggs, plus 2 egg yolks
300ml/½ pint/1¼ cups single (light) cream
30ml/2 tbsp caster (superfine) sugar
5ml/1 tsp powdered gelatine or alternative
finely grated rind and juice of ½ orange
1 large piece stem ginger, finely chopped
45–60ml/3–4 tbsp icing (confectioners')
    or caster (superfine) sugar
orange segments and sprig of mint,
    to decorate

COOK'S TIP
~

For a milder ginger flavour, just add up to 5ml/1 tsp ground ginger instead of the stem ginger.

---

1 Whisk the eggs and yolks together until pale. Bring the cream and sugar to the boil, remove from the heat and sprinkle on the gelatine. Stir until the gelatine has dissolved and then pour the cream mixture on to the eggs, whisking all the time.

2 Add the orange rind, a little juice to taste, and the chopped ginger to the mixture.

3 Pour into four or five ramekins and chill until set.

4 Some time before serving, sprinkle the sugar generously over the top of the custard and put under a very hot grill (broiler). Watch closely for the couple of moments it takes for the tops to caramelize. Allow to cool before serving. Decorate with a few segments of orange and a sprig of mint.

Chocolate Mandarin Trifle

Trifle is always a tempting treat, but when a rich chocolate and mascarpone custard is combined with amaretto and mandarin oranges, it becomes irresistible.

INGREDIENTS

Serves 6–8

4 trifle sponges

14 amaretti

60ml/4 tbsp Amaretto di Saronno or
   sweet sherry

8 mandarin oranges

For the custard

200g/7oz plain (semisweet) chocolate,
   broken into squares

30ml/2 tbsp cornflour (cornstarch) or
   custard powder

30ml/2 tbsp caster (superfine) sugar

2 egg yolks

200ml/7fl oz/scant 1 cup milk

250g/9oz/generous 1 cup mascarpone

For the topping

250g/9oz/generous 1 cup fromage frais

chocolate shapes

mandarin slices

1 Break up the trifle sponges and place them in a large glass serving dish. Crumble the amaretti over and then sprinkle with amaretto or sweet sherry.

2 Squeeze the juice from two of the mandarins and sprinkle into the dish. Segment the rest and put in the dish.

3 Make the custard. Melt the chocolate in a heatproof bowl over hot water. In a separate bowl, mix the cornflour or custard powder, sugar and egg yolks to a smooth paste.

4 Heat the milk in a small pan until almost boiling, then pour in a steady stream on to the egg yolk mixture, stirring constantly. Return to the clean pan and stir over a low heat until the custard has thickened slightly and is smooth.

5 Stir the mascarpone until melted, then add the melted chocolate, mixing it thoroughly. Spread evenly over the trifle, cool, then chill until set.

6 To finish, spread the fromage frais over the custard, then decorate with chocolate shapes and the remaining mandarin slices just before serving.

COOK'S TIP

Always use the best chocolate which has a high percentage of cocoa solids, and take care not to overheat the chocolate when melting as it will lose its gloss and look "grainy".

Tangerine Trifle

An unusual variation on a traditional trifle – of course, you can add a little alcohol if you wish.

INGREDIENTS

Serves 4

5 trifle sponges, halved lengthways

30ml/2 tbsp apricot jam

15–20 ratafia biscuits (almond macaroons)

142g/4¾oz packet tangerine jelly

300g/11oz can mandarin oranges, drained, reserving juice

600ml/1 pint/2½ cups ready-made (or home-made) custard

whipped cream and shreds of orange rind, to decorate

caster (superfine) sugar, for sprinkling

1 Spread the halved sponge cakes with apricot jam and arrange in the base of a deep serving bowl or glass dish. Sprinkle over the ratafia biscuits.

2 Break up the jelly into a heatproof measuring jug (cup), add the juice from the canned mandarins and dissolve in a pan of hot water or in the microwave. Stir until the liquid clears.

3 Make up to 600ml/1 pint/ 2½ cups with ice cold water, stir well and leave to cool for up to 30 minutes. Scatter the mandarin oranges over the cakes and ratafias.

4 Pour the jelly over the mandarin oranges, cake and ratafias and chill for 1 hour.

5 When the jelly has set, pour the custard smoothly over the top and chill again.

6 When ready to serve, pipe the whipped cream over the custard. Wash the orange rind shreds, sprinkle them with caster sugar and use to decorate the trifle.

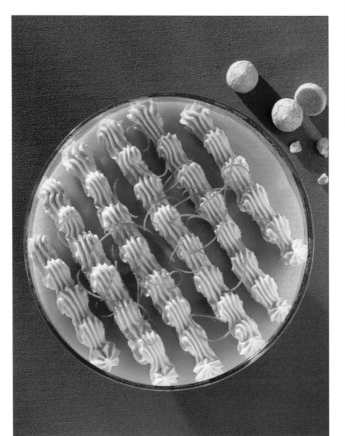

Raspberry Trifle

Use fresh or frozen raspberries for this ever-popular dessert.

INGREDIENTS

Serves 6 or more

175g/6oz trifle sponges, or 2.5cm/1in cubes of plain Victoria sponge or coarsely crumbled sponge fingers

60ml/4 tbsp medium sherry

115g/4oz raspberry jam

275g/10oz/1⅔ cups raspberries

450ml/¾ pint/scant 2 cups custard, flavoured with 30ml/2 tbsp medium or sweet sherry

300ml/½ pint/1¼ cups sweetened whipped cream

toasted flaked (sliced) almonds and mint leaves, to decorate

1 Spread half of the sponges, cake cubes or sponge fingers over the bottom of a large serving bowl. (A glass bowl is best for presentation.)

2 Sprinkle half of the sherry over the cake to moisten it. Spoon over half of the jam, dotting it evenly over the cake cubes.

3 Reserve a few raspberries for decoration. Make a layer of half of the remaining raspberries on top.

4 Pour over half of the custard, covering the fruit and cake. Repeat the layers of moistened cake, jam, fruit and custard. Cover and chill for at least 2 hours.

5 Before serving, spoon the sweetened whipped cream evenly over the top. To decorate, sprinkle with toasted flaked almonds and arrange the reserved raspberries and the mint leaves on the top.

VARIATION

You can use other ripe summer fruit in the trifle, such as apricots, nectarines, strawberries and peaches, with different jams and fruit liqueurs to suit.

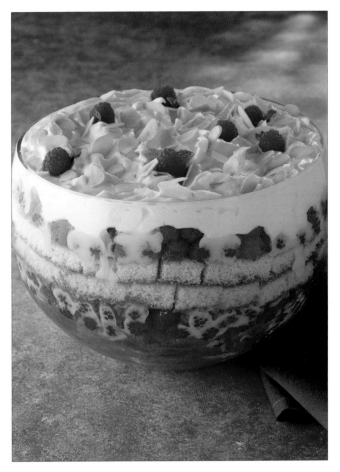

Coconut and Coffee Trifle

Dark coffee sponge, laced with liqueur, coconut custard and a coffee cream topping makes a rich dessert.

INGREDIENTS

Serves 6–8

For the coffee sponge

45ml/3 tbsp strong-flavoured
    ground coffee
45ml/3 tbsp near-boiling water
2 eggs
50g/2oz/¼ cup soft dark brown sugar
40g/1½oz/⅓ cup self-raising (self-rising)
    flour, sifted
25ml/1½ tbsp hazelnut or sunflower oil

For the coconut custard

400ml/14fl oz/1⅔ cup canned coconut milk
3 eggs
40g/1½oz/3 tbsp caster (superfine) sugar
10ml/2 tsp cornflour (cornstarch)

For the filling and topping

2 medium bananas
60ml/4 tbsp coffee liqueur, such as
    Tia Maria
300ml/½ pint/1¼ cups double (heavy) cream
30ml/2 tbsp icing (confectioners')
    sugar, sifted
ribbons of fresh coconut, to decorate

1 Preheat the oven to 160°C/ 325°F/Gas 3. Oil and line an 18cm/7in square tin (pan) with baking parchment.

2 Put the ground coffee in a small bowl. Pour the hot water over and leave to infuse for 4 minutes. Strain the coffee, discarding the grounds.

3 Whisk the eggs and soft dark brown sugar in a large bowl until the whisk leaves a trail when lifted from the mixture.

4 Gently fold in the flour, 15ml/ 1 tbsp of the coffee and the oil. Spoon the mixture into the tin and bake for 20 minutes. Turn out on a rack, remove the paper and cool.

5 To make the coconut custard, heat the coconut milk in a pan until it is almost boiling.

6 Whisk the eggs, sugar and cornflour until frothy, then whisk in the hot coconut milk. Add to the pan and heat gently, stirring for 1–2 minutes, until the custard thickens. Set aside to cool.

7 Cut the coffee sponge into 5cm/2in squares and arrange in a large glass bowl. Slice the bananas and arrange on the sponge. Drizzle the coffee liqueur on top. Pour the custard over and leave until cold.

8 Whip the cream with the remaining coffee and icing sugar until soft peaks form. Spoon the cream over the custard. Cover and chill for several hours. Sprinkle with ribbons of fresh coconut.

COOK'S TIP

If fresh coconut is not available, use shredded coconut and toast until pale golden.

Jamaican Fruit Trifle

This trifle is actually based on a Caribbean fool that consists of fruit stirred into thick vanilla-flavoured cream. This version is much less rich, redressing the balance with plenty of fruit, and with crème fraîche replacing some of the cream.

INGREDIENTS

Serves 8

1 large sweet pineapple, peeled and cored, about 350g/12oz

300ml/½ pint/1¼ cups double (heavy) cream

200ml/7fl oz/scant 1 cup crème fraîche

60ml/4 tbsp icing (confectioners') sugar, sifted

10ml/2 tsp pure vanilla extract

30ml/2 tbsp white or coconut rum

3 papayas, peeled, seeded and chopped

3 mangoes, peeled, stoned (pitted) and chopped

thinly pared rind and juice of 1 lime

25g/1oz/⅓ cup coarsely shredded or flaked coconut, toasted

1 Cut the pineapple into large chunks, place in a food processor or blender and process briefly until chopped. Tip into a sieve (strainer) placed over a bowl and leave for 5 minutes to drain the juices from the fruit.

2 Whip the double cream to soft peaks. Fold in the crème fraîche, icing sugar, vanilla extract and rum.

3 Fold the drained chopped pineapple into the cream mixture. Place the chopped papayas and mangoes in a large bowl and pour over the lime juice. Gently stir the fruit mixture to combine the ingredients. Shred the pared lime rind.

4 Divide the fruit mixture and the pineapple cream among eight dessert plates. Decorate with the lime shreds, toasted coconut and a few small pineapple leaves, if you like, and serve at once.

Pineapple with Rum Custard

*Ground black pepper may seem an
unusual ingredient to put with
pineapple, until you realise that
peppercorns are the fruit of a
tropical vine. If the idea does not
appeal, leave out the pepper.*

Serves 4

1 ripe pineapple

25g/1oz/2tbsp butter

fresh strawberries, sliced, to serve

a few pineapple leaves, to decorate

For the sauce

1 egg

2 egg yolks

30ml/2 tbsp caster (superfine) sugar

30ml/2 tbsp dark rum

2.5ml/½ tsp ground black pepper

1 Remove the top and bottom
from the pineapple with a
serrated knife. Pare away the outer
skin from top to bottom, remove
the core and cut into slices.

COOK'S TIP

The sweetest pineapples are
picked and exported when ripe.
Contrary to popular belief,
pineapples do not ripen well
after picking. Choose fruit that
smells sweet and yields to firm
pressure from your thumbs.

---

2 Preheat a moderate grill
(broiler). Dot the pineapple
slices with butter and grill (broil)
for about 5 minutes.

3 To make the sauce, place all
the ingredients in a bowl. Set
over a pan of simmering water
and whisk with a hand-held mixer
for about 3–4 minutes or until
foamy and cooked. Scatter the
strawberries over the pineapple,
decorate with a few pineapple
leaves and serve with the sauce.

Banana and Passion Fruit Whip

*This easy and quickly prepared
dessert is delicious with crisp biscuits.*

INGREDIENTS

Serves 4

2 ripe bananas

2 passion fruit

90ml/6 tbsp fromage frais

150ml/¼ pint/⅔ cup double (heavy) cream

10ml/2 tsp clear honey

shortcake or ginger biscuits (cookies),
   to serve

1 Peel the bananas, then mash
them with a fork in a bowl to a
smooth purée.

2 Halve the passion fruit and
scoop out the pulp. Mix the
pulp with the bananas and
fromage frais. In a separate bowl,
whip the cream with the honey
until it forms soft peaks.

3 Carefully fold the cream and
honey mixture into the fruit
mixture. Spoon the whip into
individual glass dishes and serve
immediately with shortcake or
ginger biscuits.

Cappuccino Coffee Cups

Coffee-lovers will love this one – and it tastes rich and creamy, even though it's very light.

INGREDIENTS

Serves 4

2 eggs

215g/7.7oz carton evaporated
   semi-skimmed (low-fat) milk

25ml/1½ tbsp instant coffee granules
   or powder

30ml/2 tbsp caster (superfine) sugar

10ml/2 tsp powdered gelatine,
   or alternative

60ml/4 tbsp light crème fraîche

cocoa powder or ground cinnamon,
   to decorate

1 Separate one egg and reserve the white. Beat the yolk with the whole of the remaining egg.

2 Put the evaporated milk, coffee granules, sugar and beaten eggs in a pan; whisk until evenly combined.

3 Put the pan over a low heat and stir constantly until the mixture is hot, but not boiling. Cook, stirring constantly, without boiling, until the mixture is slightly thickened and smooth.

4 Remove the pan from the heat. Sprinkle the gelatine over the pan and whisk until the gelatine has completely dissolved.

5 Spoon the coffee custard into four individual dishes or glasses and chill them until set.

6 Whisk the reserved egg white until stiff. Whisk in the crème fraîche and then spoon the mixture over the desserts. Sprinkle with cocoa or cinnamon and serve.

VARIATION

Greek (US strained plain) yogurt can be used instead of the crème fraîche, if you prefer.

Vermont Baked Maple Custard

Try to find pure maple syrup for this custard as it will really enhance the flavour.

INGREDIENTS

Serves 6

3 eggs

120ml/4fl oz/½ cup maple syrup

600ml/1 pint/2½ cups milk

pinch of salt

pinch of grated nutmeg

COOK'S TIP

Baking delicate mixtures such as custards in a water bath helps protect them from uneven heating which could make them rubbery.

1 Preheat the oven to 180°C/ 350°F/Gas 4. Combine all the ingredients in a large bowl and mix together thoroughly.

2 Set individual custard cups or ramekins in a roasting pan half filled with hot water. Pour the custard mixture into the cups. Bake until the custards are set, 45 minutes–1 hour. Test by inserting the blade of a knife in the centre: it should come out clean. Serve warm or chilled.

Mocha Cream Pots

The name of this rich baked custard, a classic French dessert, comes from the baking cups, called pots de crème. *The addition of coffee gives the dessert an exotic touch.*

INGREDIENTS

Serves 8

15ml/1 tbsp instant coffee powder

475ml/16fl oz/2 cups milk

75g/3oz/⅓ cup caster (superfine) sugar

225g/8oz plain (semisweet)
  chocolate, chopped

10ml/2 tsp vanilla extract

30ml/2 tbsp coffee liqueur (optional)

7 egg yolks

whipped cream and crystallized mimosa
  balls, to decorate (optional)

1 Preheat the oven to 160°C/
325°F/Gas 3. Place eight
120ml/4fl oz/½ cup *pots de crème*
cups or ramekins in a roasting pan.

2 Put the instant coffee into a
pan and stir in the milk, then
add the sugar and set the pan over
a medium-high heat. Bring
to the boil, stirring constantly,
until both the coffee and sugar
have dissolved.

3 Remove the pan from the heat
and add the chocolate. Stir
until the chocolate has melted and
the sauce is smooth. Stir in the
vanilla extract and coffee liqueur, if
using, until evenly combined.

4 In a bowl, whisk the egg yolks
to blend them lightly. Slowly
whisk in the chocolate mixture
until well blended, then strain
the mixture into a large jug and
divide equally among the cups or
ramekins. Place them in a roasting
pan and pour in enough boiling
water to come halfway up the sides
of the cups or ramekins. Cover the
pan with foil.

5 Bake for 30–35 minutes until
the custard is just set and a
knife inserted into a custard comes
out clean. Remove the cups or
ramekins from the roasting pan
and allow to cool. Place on a
baking sheet, cover and chill
completely. Decorate with the
whipped cream and crystallized
mimosa balls, if using.

Plum and Custard Creams

If you were reluctantly raised on stewed plums and custard, this sophisticated version, prettily layered in a glass, will bring a smile to your lips.

Serves 6

675g/1½lb red plums, stoned (pitted)
   and sliced
grated rind and juice of 1 orange
50g/2oz/¼ cup caster (superfine) sugar
400g/14oz carton ready-made custard
300ml/½ pint/1¼ cups double (heavy) cream
30ml/2 tbsp water
15ml/1 tbsp powdered gelatine
1 egg white
plum slices and fresh mint sprigs,
   to decorate

1 Put the plums in a pan with the orange rind and juice and caster sugar. Heat, stirring constantly, until the sugar has dissolved. Cook the plums until tender. Allow to cool slightly, then process the plums to a smooth purée. Pass through a sieve (strainer) into a bowl and cool.

2 Put the custard and half the cream in a pan, and heat until boiling. Pour the water into a heatproof bowl and sprinkle the gelatine on top; set aside for 5 minutes. Whisk the soaked gelatine into the hot custard until dissolved and allow to cool.

3 Whip the remaining cream and fold it into the custard mixture. In a grease-free bowl, whisk the egg white to form soft peaks and fold into the custard. Leave aside until just setting.

4 Quickly spoon alternate spoonfuls of the custard and plum purée into six tall dessert glasses. Marble the mixtures together. Chill for 2–3 hours or until the custard has set. Decorate each dessert with plum slices and fresh mint sprigs before serving.

Amaretto Soufflé

A mouthwatering soufflé with more than a hint of Amaretto liqueur.

INGREDIENTS

Serves 6

6 amaretti, coarsely crushed

90ml/4 tbsp Amaretto liqueur

4 eggs, separated, plus 1 egg white

130g/3½oz/½ cup caster (superfine) sugar

30ml/2 tbsp plain (all-purpose) flour

250ml/8fl oz/1 cup milk

pinch of cream of tartar (if needed)

icing (confectioners') sugar, for dusting

1 Preheat the oven to 200°C/ 400°F/Gas 6. Butter a 1.5 litre/ 2½ pint/6¼ cup soufflé dish and sprinkle it with a little of the caster sugar.

2 Put the biscuits in a bowl. Sprinkle them with 30ml/ 2 tbsp of the Amaretto liqueur and set aside.

3 In another bowl, carefully mix together the four egg yolks, 30ml/2 tbsp of the sugar and all of flour.

4 Heat the milk just to the boil in a heavy pan. Gradually add the hot milk to the egg mixture, stirring.

5 Pour the mixture back into the pan. Set over a low heat and simmer gently for 3–4 minutes or until thickened, stirring occasionally.

6 Add the remaining Amaretto liqueur. Remove from the heat.

7 In a scrupulously clean, grease-free bowl, whisk the five egg whites until they will hold soft peaks. (If not using a copper bowl, add the cream of tartar as soon as the whites are frothy.) Add the remaining sugar and continue whisking until stiff.

8 Add about one-quarter of the whites to the liqueur mixture and stir in with a rubber spatula. Add the remaining whites and fold in gently.

9 Spoon half of the mixture into the prepared soufflé dish. Cover with a layer of the moistened amaretti biscuits, then spoon the remaining soufflé mixture on top.

10 Bake for 20 minutes or until the soufflé is risen and lightly browned. Sprinkle with sifted icing sugar and serve immediately.

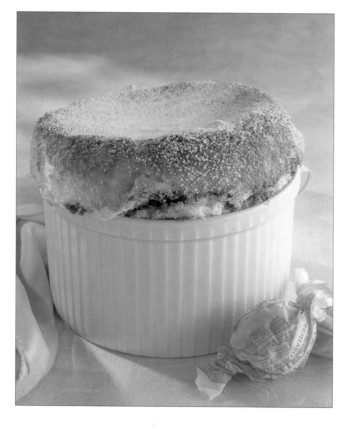

Hot Quince Soufflés

These delicious fruits are more often picked than purchased, as they are seldom found in shops or markets. You can use pears instead.

INGREDIENTS

Serves 6

2 quinces, peeled and cored

60ml/4 tbsp water

115g/4oz/½ cup caster (superfine) sugar

5 egg whites

melted butter, for greasing

icing (confectioners') sugar, for dusting

For the pastry cream

250ml/8fl oz/1 cup milk

1 vanilla pod (bean)

3 egg yolks

75g/3oz/⅓ cup caster (superfine) sugar

25g/1oz/¼ cup plain (all-purpose) flour

15ml/1 tbsp Poire William liqueur

1 Cut the quinces into cubes. Place in a pan with the water. Stir in half the sugar and bring to the boil. Lower the heat, cover and simmer until tender. Remove the lid and boil until the liquid has almost evaporated.

2 Cool slightly, then purée the fruit in a blender or food processor. Press through a sieve (strainer) into a bowl and set aside.

3 Make the pastry cream. Pour the milk into a small pan. Add the vanilla pod and bring to the boil over a low heat. Meanwhile, beat the egg yolks, caster sugar and flour in a bowl until smooth.

4 Gradually strain the hot milk on to the yolks, whisking frequently until the mixture is smooth and free of lumps.

5 Discard the vanilla pod. Return the mixture to a clean pan and heat gently, stirring until thickened. Cook for a further 2 minutes, whisking constantly, to ensure that the sauce is quite smooth and the flour is cooked.

6 Remove the pan from the heat and stir in the quince purée and liqueur. Cover the surface of the pastry cream with clear film (plastic wrap) to prevent it from forming a skin. Allow to cool slightly, while you prepare the ramekins.

7 Preheat the oven to 220°C/ 425°F/Gas 7. Place a baking sheet in the oven to heat. Butter six ramekins and sprinkle the insides with caster sugar. In a grease-free bowl, whisk the egg whites to stiff peaks. Slowly whisk in the remaining caster sugar, then carefully fold the egg whites into the pastry cream.

8 Divide the mixture among the prepared ramekins and level the surfaces. Carefully run a sharp knife around the sides of the ramekins, then place them on the hot baking sheet and bake for 8–10 minutes, until the tops of the soufflés are well risen and golden. Generously dust the tops with icing sugar and serve the soufflés at once.

COOK'S TIP

Kirsch, made from cherries, is a good alternative to Poire William.

Lemon Soufflé with Blackberries

The simple fresh taste of cold lemon mousse combines well with rich blackberry sauce, and the colour contrast looks wonderful, too. Blueberries or raspberries make equally delicious alternatives to blackberries.

INGREDIENTS

Serves 6

grated rind of 1 lemon and juice of
  2 lemons
15ml/1 tbsp/1 sachet powdered gelatine
5 eggs, separated
150g/5oz/¾ cup caster (superfine) sugar
few drops vanilla extract
400ml/14fl oz/1⅔ cups whipping cream
For the sauce
175g/6oz/¾ cup blackberries (fresh
  or frozen)
30–45ml/2–3 tbsp caster (superfine) sugar
few fresh blackberries and blackberry
  leaves, to decorate

1 Place the lemon juice in a small pan and heat through. Sprinkle on the gelatine and leave to dissolve or heat further until clear. Allow to cool.

2 Put the lemon rind, egg yolks, sugar and vanilla into a large bowl and whisk until the mixture is very thick, pale and creamy.

3 Whisk the egg whites until stiff and almost peaky. Whip the cream until stiff.

4 Stir the gelatine mixture into the yolks, then fold in the whipped cream and lastly the egg whites. Turn into a 1.5 litre/2½ pint/6 cup soufflé dish and freeze for about 2 hours.

5 To make the sauce, place the blackberries in a pan with the sugar and cook for 4–6 minutes, until the juices begin to run and all the sugar has dissolved. Pass through a sieve (strainer) to remove the seeds, then chill.

6 When the soufflé is almost frozen, but still spoonable, scoop or spoon out on to individual plates and serve with the blackberry sauce, decorated with fresh blackberries and blackberry leaves.

Apple Soufflé Omelette

*Apples sautéed until they are slightly
caramelized make a delicious
autumn filling – you could use fresh
raspberries or strawberries when
they are in seeason.*

INGREDIENTS

Serves 2

4 eggs, separated
30ml/2 tbsp single (light) cream
15ml/1 tbsp caster (superfine) sugar
15g/½oz/1 tbsp butter
icing (confectioners') sugar, for dredging
For the filling
1 eating apple, peeled, cored and sliced
25g/1oz/2 tbsp butter
30ml/2 tbsp soft light brown sugar
45ml/3 tbsp single (light) cream

1 To make the filling, sauté the apple slices in the butter and sugar until just tender. Stir in the cream and keep warm, while making the omelette.

2 Place the egg yolks in a bowl with the cream and sugar and beat well. Whisk the egg whites until they form stiff peaks, then fold into the yolk mixture.

3 Melt the butter in a large heavy frying pan, pour in the soufflé mixture and spread evenly. Cook for 1 minute until golden underneath, then cover the pan handle with foil and place under a hot grill (broiler) to brown the top.

4 Slide the omelette on to a plate, add the apple mixture, then fold over. Sift the icing sugar over thickly, then mark in a criss-cross pattern with a hot metal skewer. Serve immediately.

Hot Mocha Rum Soufflés

Serve these superb soufflés as soon as they are cooked for a dinner party.

INGREDIENTS

Serves 6

25g/1oz/2 tbsp unsalted butter, melted
65g/2½oz/generous ½ cup cocoa powder
75g/3oz/generous ⅓ cup caster
   (superfine) sugar
60ml/4 tbsp strong black coffee
30ml/2 tbsp dark rum
6 egg whites
icing (confectioners') sugar, for dusting

1 Preheat the oven with a baking sheet inside to 190°C/375°F/ Gas 5. Grease six 250ml/8fl oz/ 1 cup soufflé dishes with the melted butter.

2 Mix 15ml/1 tbsp of the cocoa with 15ml/1 tbsp of the caster sugar in a bowl. Tip the mixture into each of the dishes in turn, rotating them so that they are evenly coated.

3 Mix the remaining cocoa with the coffee and rum.

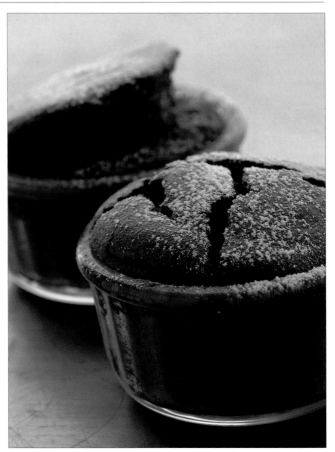

4 Whisk the egg whites in a clean, grease-free bowl until they form firm peaks. Whisk in the remaining caster sugar. Stir a generous spoonful of the whites into the cocoa mixture to lighten it, then gently fold in the remaining whites.

5 Spoon the mixture into the prepared dishes, smoothing the tops. Place on the hot baking sheet, and bake for 12–15 minutes or until well risen. Serve the soufflés immediately, lightly dusted with icing sugar.

COOK'S TIP

When serving the soufflés at the end of a dinner party, prepare them just before the meal is served. Pop in the oven as soon as the main course is finished and serve freshly baked.

Cold Mango Soufflés with Toasted Coconut

Fragrant, fresh mango is one of the most delicious exotic fruits around, whether it is simply served in slices or used as the basis for an ice cream or soufflé.

INGREDIENTS

Makes 4

4 small mangoes, peeled, stoned (pitted)
   and chopped

30ml/2 tbsp water

15ml/1 tbsp powdered gelatine

2 egg yolks

115g/4oz/½ cup caster (superfine) sugar

120ml/4fl oz/½ cup milk

grated rind of 1 orange

300ml/½ pint/1¼ cups double (heavy) cream

toasted flaked or coarsely shredded
   coconut, to decorate

1 Place a few pieces of mango in the base of four ramekins. Wrap a greased collar of baking parchment around the outside of each ramekin so that it stands about 5cm/2in above the rim the dish. Tape to secure, then tie with string.

2 Pour the water into a small heatproof bowl and sprinkle the gelatine over it. Leave for 5 minutes. Place the bowl in a pan of hot water. Stir until the gelatine has dissolved.

3 Whisk the egg yolks, caster sugar and milk in another heatproof bowl. Place the bowl over a pan of simmering water and whisk until the mixture is thick and frothy. Remove from the heat and whisk continuously until the mixture cools. Whisk in the liquid gelatine.

4 Process the remaining mango to a purée, then fold the purée into the egg yolk mixture with the orange rind. Set the mixture aside until it is starting to thicken.

5 Whip the double cream to form soft peaks. Reserve 60ml/ 4 tbsp and keep chilled. Fold the rest into the mango mixture. Spoon into the ramekins until the mixture is 2.5cm/1in above the rim of each dish. Chill for 3–4 hours.

6 Carefully remove the paper collars from the soufflés. Spoon a little of the reserved cream on top of each soufflé and decorate with the coconut before serving.

Chocolate Soufflé Crêpes

A non-stick pan is ideal as it does not need greasing between each crêpe. Serve two crêpes per person.

INGREDIENTS

Makes 12 crêpes

75g/3oz/⅔ cup plain (all-purpose) flour
10g/¼oz/1 tbsp unsweetened cocoa
5ml/1 tsp caster (superfine) sugar
pinch of salt
5ml/1 tsp ground cinnamon
2 eggs
175ml/6fl oz/¾ cup milk
5ml/1 tsp vanilla extract
50g/2oz/4 tbsp unsalted butter, melted
icing (confectioners') sugar, for dusting
raspberries, pineapple and mint sprigs,
    to decorate
For the pineapple syrup
½ medium pineapple, peeled, cored and
    finely chopped
30ml/2 tbsp natural maple syrup
5ml/1 tsp cornflour (cornstarch)
½ cinnamon stick
30ml/2 tbsp rum
For the soufflé filling
250g/9oz plain (semisweet) or dark
    (bittersweet) chocolate
85ml/3fl oz/⅓ cup double (heavy) cream
3 eggs, separated
25g/1oz/2 tbsp caster (superfine) sugar

1 Prepare syrup. In a pan over medium heat, bring pineapple, 125ml/4fl oz/½ cup of water, maple syrup, cornflour and cinnamon stick to the boil. Simmer for 2–3 minutes until sauce thickens, whisking frequently. Remove from heat; discard cinnamon. Pour into a bowl, stir in rum and chill.

2 Prepare crêpes. In a bowl, sift flour, cocoa, sugar, salt and cinnamon. Stir to blend, then make a well in the centre.

3 In a bowl, beat eggs, milk and vanilla and gradually add to the well, whisking in flour from the side to form a smooth batter. Stir in half the melted butter and pour batter into a jug (pitcher). Allow to stand 1 hour.

4 Heat an 18–20cm/7–8in crêpe pan. Brush with butter. Stir the batter. Pour 45ml/3 tbsp batter into the pan; swirl pan quickly to cover bottom with a thin layer. Cook over medium-high heat for 1–2 minutes until bottom is golden. Turn over and cook for 30–45 seconds, then turn on to a plate. Stack crêpes between baking parchment and set aside.

5 Prepare filling. In a small pan, over medium heat, melt chocolate and cream until smooth, stirring frequently.

6 In a bowl, beat yolks with half the sugar for 3–5 minutes, until light and creamy. Gradually beat in the chocolate mixture. Allow to cool. In a large bowl, beat egg whites until soft peaks form. Gradually beat in remaining sugar until stiff. Beat in a spoonful of egg whites to the chocolate mixture, then fold in remaining whites.

7 Preheat the oven to 200°C/ 400°F/Gas 6. Lay a crêpe on a plate. Spoon a little soufflé mixture on to crêpe, spreading it to the edge. Fold the bottom half over the soufflé mixture, then fold in half again to form a filled "triangle". Place on a buttered baking sheet. Repeat with remaining crêpes.

8 Brush the tops with melted butter and bake for 15–20 minutes until souffléd. Dust with icing sugar and garnish with raspberries, pineapple, mint and a spoonful of pineapple syrup.

Chocolate Soufflés

*These are easy to make and can be
prepared in advance – the filled
dishes can wait for up to one hour
before baking. For best results, use
good quality chocolate.*

INGREDIENTS

Serves 6

175g/6oz plain (semisweet)
   chocolate, chopped
150g/5oz/⅔ cup unsalted butter, cut in
   small pieces
4 large eggs, separated
30ml/2 tbsp orange liqueur (optional)
1.5ml/¼ tsp cream of tartar
45ml/3 tbsp caster (superfine) sugar
icing (confectioners') sugar, for dusting
sprigs of redcurrants and white chocolate
   roses, to decorate
For the white chocolate sauce
75g/3oz white chocolate, chopped
90ml/6 tbsp whipping cream
15–30ml/1–2 tbsp orange liqueur
grated rind of ½ orange

1 Generously butter six 150ml/
¼ pint/⅓ cup ramekins.
Sprinkle each with a little caster
sugar and tap out any excess. Place
the ramekins on a baking sheet.

2 In a heavy pan over a very low
heat, melt the chocolate and
butter, stirring until smooth.
Remove from the heat and cool
slightly, then beat in the egg yolks
and orange liqueur, if using. Set
aside, stirring occasionally.

3 Preheat the oven to 220°C/
425°F/Gas 7. In a clean,
grease-free bowl, whisk the egg
whites slowly until frothy. Add the
cream of tartar, increase the speed
and whisk until they form soft
peaks. Gradually sprinkle over
the sugar, 15ml/1 tbsp at a time,
whisking until the whites are stiff
and glossy.

4 Stir a third of the whites
into the cooled chocolate
mixture to lighten it, then pour
the chocolate mixture over the
remaining whites. Using a rubber
spatula or large metal spoon,
gently fold the sauce into the
whites. (Don't worry about a few
white streaks.) Spoon into the
prepared dishes.

5 To make the white chocolate
sauce, put the chopped white
chocolate and the cream into a
small pan. Place over a low heat
and cook, stirring constantly until
melted and smooth. Remove
from the heat and stir in the
liqueur and orange rind, then
pour into a serving jug (pitcher)
and keep warm.

6 Bake the soufflés for
10–12 minutes until risen
and set, but still slightly wobbly
in the centre. Dust with icing
sugar and decorate with a sprig of
redcurrants and a white chocolate
rose. Serve the sauce separately.

Iced Gin and Damson Soufflés

For an unforgettable taste sensation, use sloe gin for these delicious individual frozen soufflés.

INGREDIENTS

Makes 6

500g/1¼lb damsons
250ml/8fl oz/1 cup water
275g/10oz/1¼ cups caster (superfine) sugar
30ml/2 tbsp gin or sloe gin
4 large egg whites
300ml/½ pint/1¼ cups double (heavy) cream, whipped
fresh mint leaves, to decorate

4 Whisk the egg whites in a grease-free bowl until they form stiff peaks. Still whisking, slowly pour in the hot syrup until the meringue mixture is stiff and glossy. Fold in the whipped cream and fruit purée.

5 Spoon the mixture into the dishes to come 2.5cm/1in above the rim. Freeze until firm. Remove from the freezer 10 minutes before serving. Remove the collars, then decorate each with damson slices and mint leaves.

1 Wrap collars of greased baking parchment around the outside of six ramekins, so that they extend 5cm/2in above the rim. Tie in place with string.

2 Slice two damsons and reserve. Put the rest in a pan with half the water and 50g/2oz/¼ cup of the caster sugar. Cover and simmer for about 7 minutes, until the damsons are tender. Sieve (strainer) the pulp into a bowl to remove all the stones (pits) and skin, stir in the gin and set aside.

3 Combine the remaining sugar and water in the clean pan and heat gently until the sugar has dissolved. Bring to the boil and cook the syrup until it registers 119°C/238°F on a sugar thermometer, or until a small amount of the mixture dropped into a cup of cold water can be moulded into a soft ball.

Chilled Coffee and Praline Soufflé

A smooth coffee soufflé with a crushed praline topping that is spectacular and easy.

INGREDIENTS

Serves 6

150g/5oz/¼ cup caster (superfine) sugar

75ml/5 tbsp water

150g/5oz/generous 1 cup blanched
    almonds, plus extra, for decoration

120ml/4fl oz/½ cup strong brewed coffee

15ml/1 tbsp powdered gelatine

3 eggs, separated

75g/3oz/scant ½ cup soft light brown sugar

15ml/1 tbsp coffee liqueur, such as
    Tia Maria

150ml/¼ pint/⅔ cup double (heavy) cream

about 150ml/¼ pint/⅔ cup double (heavy)
    cream, for decoration (optional)

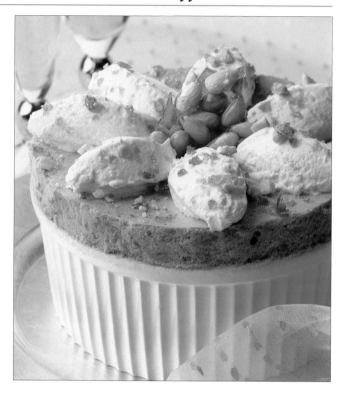

1 Make a collar of greased baking parchment, 5cm/2in deeper than a 900ml/1½ pint/3¾ cup soufflé dish. Wrap around the dish and tie in place with string. Chill.

2 Oil a baking sheet. Heat the caster sugar with the water in a heavy pan until dissolved. Boil rapidly until pale golden. Add the almonds and boil until golden.

3 Pour on to the baking sheet and leave to set hard. Break into pieces, reserving 50g/2oz/½ cup, transfer the remainder to a plastic bag and crush with a rolling pin.

4 Pour half the coffee into a bowl; sprinkle over the gelatine and soak for 5 minutes, then place the bowl over hot water and stir until completely dissolved.

5 Over a pan of simmering water whisk the egg yolks, light brown sugar, remaining coffee and liqueur, until thick, then whisk in the gelatine.

6 Whip the cream until thick, then whisk the egg whites until stiff. Fold the praline into the cream, then fold into the coffee mixture. Finally, fold in the egg whites, half at a time.

7 Spoon into the soufflé dish and smooth the top; chill for at least 2 hours. Put in the freezer for 15–20 minutes before serving. Remove the paper collar by running a warmed palette knife between the soufflé and the paper. Whisk the cream, if using, and place large spoonfuls on top. Decorate with the reserved praline pieces and blanched almonds.

Twice-baked Mocha Soufflé

*The perfect way to end a meal, these
mini mocha soufflés can be made up
to 3 hours ahead, then reheated.*

INGREDIENTS

Serves 6

75g/3oz/6 tbsp unsalted butter, softened
90g/3½oz dark (bittersweet) or plain
  (semisweet) chocolate, grated
30ml/2 tbsp ground coffee
400ml/14fl oz/1⅔ cups milk
40g/1½oz/⅓ cup plain (all-purpose)
  flour, sifted
15g/½ oz/2 tbsp cocoa, sifted
3 eggs, separated
50g/2oz/¼ cup caster (superfine) sugar
175ml/6fl oz/¾ cup creamy chocolate
  or coffee liqueur, such as Crème de
  Caçao, Sheridans

1 Preheat the oven to 200°C/
400°F/Gas 6. Brush six 150ml/
¼ pint/⅔ cup dariole moulds or
heatproof bowls with 25g/1oz/
2 tbsp of the butter. Coat with
50g/2oz of the grated chocolate.

2 Put the coffee in a small bowl.
Heat the milk until almost
boiling and pour over the coffee.
Infuse for 4 minutes and strain.

3 Melt the remaining butter in a
pan. Stir in the flour and cocoa
to make a roux. Cook for 1 minute,
then add the coffee milk, stirring all
the time to make a thick sauce.
Simmer for 2 minutes. Remove
from the heat and stir in the yolks.

4 Cool for 5 minutes, then stir in
the chocolate. Whisk the egg
whites until stiff, then gradually
whisk in the sugar. Stir half into the
sauce, then fold in the remainder.

5 Spoon the mixture into the
dariole moulds and place them
in a roasting pan. Pour in hot water
to come two-thirds of the way up
the sides of the pan.

6 Bake the soufflés for 15 minutes.
Turn them out on to a baking
sheet and leave to cool.

7 Before serving, spoon 15ml/
1 tbsp chocolate or coffee
liqueur over each pudding and
reheat in the oven for 6–7 minutes.
Serve the puddings on individual
plates with the remaining liqueur
poured over them.

Lemon Soufflé with Caramelized Almonds

This attractive and refreshing dessert soufflé is light and luscious, with a deliciously crunchy caramelized nut topping.

INGREDIENTS

Serves 6

oil, for greasing
grated rind and juice of 3 large lemons
5 large eggs, separated
115g/4oz/½ cup caster (superfine) sugar
25ml/1½ tbsp powdered gelatine
450ml/¾ pint/scant 2 cups double
  (heavy) cream
For the decoration
75g/3oz/¾ cup flaked (sliced) almonds
75g/3oz/¾ cup icing (confectioners') sugar
3 physalis

1 Make the soufflé collar. Cut a strip of baking parchment to fit around a 900ml/1½ pint/3¾ cup soufflé dish and extending 7.5cm/3in above the rim. Fit the strip around the dish, tape, then tie it around the top of the dish with string. Brush the inside of the paper lightly with oil.

2 Put the lemon rind and egg yolks in a bowl. Add 75g/3oz/6 tbsp of the caster sugar and whisk until light and creamy.

3 Place the lemon juice in a bowl and sprinkle the gelatine over it. Soak for 5 minutes, then place the bowl over a pan of simmering water. Stir until the gelatine has dissolved. Cool, then stir the gelatine into the egg yolk mixture. In a separate bowl, lightly whip the cream to soft peaks. Fold into the egg yolk mixture and set aside.

4 Whisk the egg whites in a grease-free bowl until stiff. Gradually whisk in the caster sugar, then lightly fold the whites into the yolk mixture. Pour into the prepared dish, smooth the surface and chill for 4–5 hours.

5 Preheat the grill (broiler). Lightly oil a baking sheet and scatter the almonds and icing sugar over it. Grill (broil) until the sugar has caramelized and the nuts are golden. Allow to cool, then remove from the sheet and break into pieces.

6 Carefully peel the paper off the soufflé and decorate with the caramelized almonds and physalis.

Fruit Salads, Ices & Sorbets

✦ ✦ ✦

Frudités with Honey Dip

*A colourful and tasty variation
on the popular savoury crudités.
Quick to prepare from ingredients
to hand, it's ideal for impromptu
entertaining.*

INGREDIENTS

Serves 4

225g/8oz/1 cup Greek (US strained
    plain) yogurt

45ml/3 tbsp clear honey

selection of fresh fruit for dipping such as
    apples, pears, tangerines, grapes, figs,
    cherries, strawberries and kiwi fruit

1 Place the yogurt in a dish, beat until smooth, then partially stir in the honey, leaving a little marbled effect.

2 Cut the various fruits into wedges or bite-sized pieces or leave whole.

3 Arrange the fruits on a platter with the bowl of dip in the centre. Serve chilled.

COOK'S TIP
Sprinkle the apple and pear
wedges with lemon juice to
prevent discolouring.

Watermelon, Ginger and Grapefruit Salad

*This pretty, pink combination is
very light and refreshing for any
summer meal.*

INGREDIENTS

Serves 4

450g/1lb/2 cups diced watermelon flesh
2 ruby or pink grapefruit
2 pieces stem ginger in syrup
30ml/2 tbsp stem ginger syrup
whipped cream, to serve

1 Remove any seeds from the
watermelon and cut into bite-
sized chunks.

2 Using a small sharp knife, cut
away all the peel and white
pith from the grapefruit and
carefully lift out the segments,
catching any juice in a bowl.

COOK'S TIP

Toss the fruits gently – grapefruit
segments will break up easily
and the appearance of the dish
will be spoiled.

3 Finely chop the stem ginger
and place in a serving bowl
with the melon cubes and
grapefruit segments, adding the
reserved juice.

4 Spoon over the ginger syrup
and toss the fruits lightly to
give them an equal coating. Chill
before serving with a bowl of
whipped cream.

Fruits of the Forest with Chocolate Creams

Colourful berries make a fantastic accompaniment to a delightfully creamy white chocolate mousse.

INGREDIENTS

Serves 4

75g/3oz white cooking chocolate
   (unsweetened), in squares
150ml/¼ pint/⅔ cup double (heavy) cream
30ml/2 tbsp crème fraîche
1 egg, separated
5ml/1 tsp powdered gelatine
30ml/2 tbsp cold water
a few drops of pure vanilla extract
115g/4oz/1 cup small strawberries, sliced
75g/3oz/½ cup raspberries
75g/3oz/¾ cup blueberries
45ml/3 tbsp caster (superfine) sugar
75ml/5 tbsp white coconut rum
strawberry leaves, to decorate (optional)

1 Melt the chocolate in a heatproof bowl set over a pan of hot water. Heat the cream in a separate pan until almost boiling, then stir into the chocolate with the crème fraîche. Cool slightly, then beat in the egg yolk.

2 Sprinkle the gelatine over the cold water in another heatproof bowl and set aside for a few minutes to swell.

3 Set the bowl in a pan of hot water until the gelatine has dissolved completely. Stir the dissolved gelatine into the chocolate mixture and add the vanilla extract. Set aside until starting to thicken and set.

4 Oil four dariole moulds or small soufflé dishes and line the base of each with baking parchment.

5 In a grease-free bowl, whisk the egg white to soft peaks, then fold into the chocolate mixture.

6 Spoon the mixture into the prepared moulds or soufflé dishes, then level the surface of each and chill for 2–3 hours or until firm.

7 Meanwhile, place the fruits in a bowl. Add the caster sugar and coconut rum and stir gently to mix. Cover and chill until required.

8 Ease the chocolate cream away from the rims of the moulds or dishes and turn out on to dessert plates. Spoon the fruits around the outside. Decorate with the strawberry leaves, if you like, then serve immediately.

Fruit Salad with Passion Fruit Dressing

Passion fruit juice makes a superb dressing for any fruit, but really brings out the flavour of exotic varieties in particular.

INGREDIENTS

Serves 6

1 mango

1 papaya

2 kiwi fruit

coconut or vanilla ice cream, to serve

For the dressing

3 passion fruit

thinly pared rind and juice of 1 lime

5ml/1 tsp hazelnut or walnut oil

15ml/1 tbsp clear honey

1 Peel the mango, cut it into three slices, then cut the flesh into chunks and place it in a large bowl. Peel the papaya and cut it in half. Scoop out the seeds, then chop the flesh.

2 Cut both ends off each kiwi fruit, then stand them on a board. Using a small sharp knife, cut off the skin from top to bottom. Cut each kiwi fruit in half lengthways, then cut into thick slices. Combine all the fruit in a large bowl.

3 Cut each passion fruit in half and scoop the seeds into a sieve (strainer), over a bowl. Press well to extract all the juices. Lightly whisk the remaining dressing ingredients into the juice, then pour over the fruit. Mix gently and chill for 1 hour before serving with coconut or vanilla ice cream.

Iced Pear Terrine with Chocolate Sauce

This terrine, based on a classic French dessert, makes a refreshing and impressive end to any meal.

INGREDIENTS

Serves 8

1.5kg/3–3½lb ripe Williams pears
juice of 1 lemon
115g/4oz/½ cup caster (superfine) sugar
10 whole cloves
90ml/6 tbsp water
julienne strips of orange rind, to decorate
For the sauce
200g/7oz plain (semisweet) chocolate
60ml/4 tbsp hot strong black coffee
200ml/7fl oz/scant 1 cup double
  (heavy) cream
30ml/2 tbsp Calvados or brandy

1 Peel, core and slice the pears. Put in a pan with the lemon juice, sugar, cloves and water. Cover and simmer for 10 minutes. Remove the cloves and cool.

2 Process the pears and juice in a processor or blender until smooth. Pour into a freezerproof bowl, cover and freeze until firm.

3 Meanwhile, line a 900g/2lb loaf tin (pan) with clear film (plastic wrap), allowing plenty of overlap. Spoon the frozen pear purée into a food processor or blender. Process until smooth. Pour into the prepared tin, cover and freeze until firm.

4 Break the chocolate into a large heatproof bowl and place over a pan of hot water. When the chocolate has melted, stir in the coffee until smooth. Gradually stir in the cream and then the Calvados or brandy. Set the sauce aside.

5 20 minutes before serving, remove the tin from the freezer. Invert the terrine on to a plate, lift off the clear film and place in the refrigerator to soften slightly. To serve, warm the sauce over hot water. Place a slice of terrine on each dessert plate and spoon over some sauce. Decorate with julienne strips of orange rind.

Chocolate Sorbet with Red Fruits

The chill that thrills – that's chocolate sorbet. For a really fine texture, it helps to have an ice cream maker, which churns the mixture as it freezes, but you can make it by hand quite easily.

Serves 6

475ml/16fl oz/2 cups water

45ml/3 tbsp clear honey

115g/4oz/½ cup caster (superfine) sugar

75g/3oz/¾ cup cocoa powder

50g/2oz plain (semisweet) chocolate, broken into squares

400g/14oz soft fruits, such as raspberries, redcurrants or strawberries

1 Place the water, honey, sugar and cocoa in a pan. Heat gently, stirring occasionally, until the sugar has completely dissolved.

2 Remove from the heat, add the chocolate and stir until melted. Leave to cool.

3 Tip into an ice cream maker and churn until frozen. Alternatively, pour into a freezer-proof container, freeze until slushy, whisk until smooth, then freeze again. Whisk for a second time before the mixture hardens.

4 Remove from the freezer 10–15 minutes before serving, so that the sorbet softens slightly. Serve in scoops, with a mixture of berries, or with just one variety.

COOK'S TIP

This sorbet looks attractive if served in small oval scoops – simply scoop out the sorbet with one tablespoon, then use another to smooth it off and transfer it to the plate.

Lemon Sorbet

This is probably the most classic sorbet of all. It is refreshingly tangy and yet deliciously smooth.

INGREDIENTS

Serves 6

200g/7oz/1 cup caster (superfine) sugar
300ml/¹/₂ pint/1¹/₄ cups water
4 lemons, well scrubbed
1 egg white
sugared lemon rind to decorate

1 Put the sugar and water into a pan and bring to the boil, stirring occasionally, until the sugar has just dissolved.

2 Using a swivel vegetable peeler, pare the rind thinly from two of the lemons so that it falls straight into the pan. Simmer for 2 minutes without stirring, then take the pan off the heat, leave to cool, then chill.

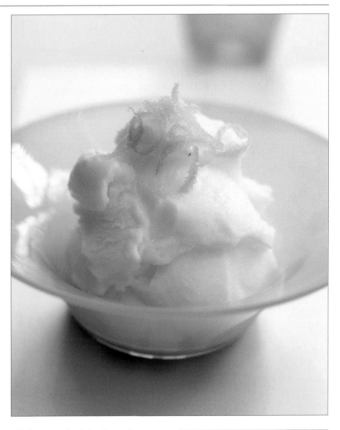

3 Squeeze the juice from the lemons and add to the syrup. Strain the syrup and lemon juice and churn in an ice cream maker until thick. Alternatively, freeze and whisk as in the previous recipe.

COOK'S TIP

Cut one third off the top of the lemon and retain as a lid. Squeeze the juice out of the larger portion. Remove any membrane and use the shell as a ready-made container. Scoop or pipe sorbet into the shell, top with the lid and add lemon leaves or small bay leaves.

---

5 Using an ice cream maker, add the egg white to the mixture and continue to churn for 10–15 minutes until firm enough to scoop.

4 In a small bowl, whisk the egg white lightly with a fork.

6 Scoop into bowls or glasses and decorate with sugared lemon rind to serve.

Mango Sorbet

A light and refreshing dessert that's surprisingly easy to make.

INGREDIENTS

Serves 6

150g/5oz/¾ cup caster (superfine) sugar

a large strip of orange rind

1 large mango, peeled, stoned (pitted) and cubed

60ml/4 tbsp orange juice

mint sprigs, to decorate

1 Combine the sugar, orange rind and 175ml/6fl oz/¾ cup of water in a pan. Bring to the boil, stirring to dissolve the sugar. Leave the syrup to cool.

2 Purée the mango cubes with the orange juice in a blender or food processor. There should be about 475ml/16fl oz/2 cups of purée.

3 Add the purée to the cooled sugar syrup and mix well. Strain, then chill.

4 When cold, tip into a freezer container and freeze until firm around the edges.

5 Spoon the semi-frozen mixture into the food processor and process until smooth. Return to the freezer and freeze until solid. Allow the sorbet to soften slightly at room temperature for 15–20 minutes before serving, decorated with mint sprigs.

VARIATIONS

For Banana Sorbet: peel and cube 4–5 large bananas. Purée with 30ml/2 tbsp lemon juice to make 475ml/16fl oz/2 cups. If liked, replace the orange rind in the sugar syrup with 2–3 whole cloves, or omit the rind.

For Papaya Sorbet: peel, seed and cube 675g/1½lb papaya. Purée with 45ml/3 tbsp lime juice to make 475ml/16fl oz/2 cups. Replace the orange rind with lime rind.

For Passion Fruit Sorbet: halve 16 or more passion fruit and scoop out the seeds and pulp (there should be about 475ml/16fl oz/2 cups). Work in a blender or food processor until the seeds are like coarse pepper. Omit the orange juice and rind. Add the passion fruit to the sugar syrup, then press through a wire sieve (strainer) before freezing.

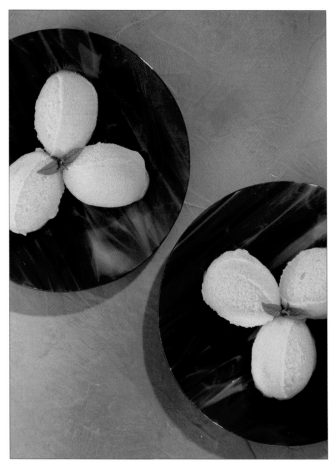

Lime Sherbet

This light, refreshing sherbet is a
good dessert to serve after a
substantial main course.

Serves 4

250g/9oz/1¼ cups granulated
    (white) sugar
grated rind of 1 lime
175ml/6fl oz/¾ cup freshly squeezed
    lime juice
15–30ml/1–2 tbsp fresh lemon juice
icing (confectioners') sugar, to taste
slivers of lime rind, to decorate

1 In a small heavy pan, dissolve
the granulated sugar in
600ml/1 pint/2½ cups of water,
without stirring, over medium
heat. When the sugar has
dissolved, boil for 5-6 minutes.
Remove from the heat and let cool.

2 Combine the cooled sugar
syrup and lime rind and juice
in a measuring jug (cup) or bowl.
Stir well. Taste and adjust the
flavour by adding lemon juice or
some icing sugar, if necessary. Do
not over-sweeten.

3 Freeze the mixture in an ice
cream maker, following the
manufacturer's instructions.

4 If you do not have an ice
cream maker, pour the
mixture into a metal or plastic
freezer container and freeze until
softly set, for about 3 hours.

5 Remove from the container
and chop roughly into
7.5cm/3in pieces. Place in a food
processor and process until
smooth. Return the mixture to the
freezer container and freeze again
until set. Repeat this freezing and
chopping process two or three
times, until a smooth consistency
is obtained.

6 Serve in scoops decorated with
slivers of lime rind.

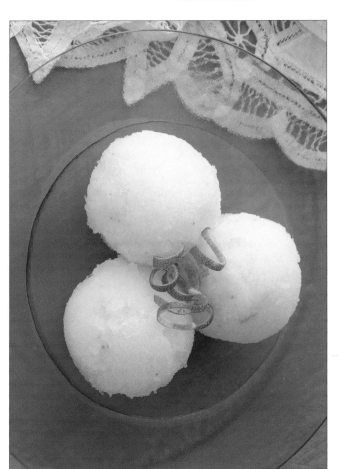

COOK'S TIP
〜

If using an ice cream maker
for these sherbets, check
the manufacturer's instructions
to find out the freezing
capacity. If necessary, halve
the recipe quantities.

Ruby Orange Sherbet in Ginger Baskets

This superb frozen dessert is perfect for people without ice cream makers who can't be bothered with the freezing and stirring that home-made ices normally require. It is also ideal for serving at a special dinner party as both the sherbet and ginger baskets can be made in advance, leaving you to simply assemble the dessert between courses.

Serves 6

grated rind and juice of 2 blood oranges
175g/6oz/1½ cups icing
   (confectioners') sugar
300ml/½ pint/1¼ cups double
   (heavy) cream
200g/7oz/scant 1 cup Greek (US strained
   plain) yogurt
blood orange segments,
   to decorate (optional)
For the ginger baskets
25g/1oz/2 tbsp unsalted butter
15ml/1 tbsp golden (light corn) syrup
30ml/2 tbsp caster (superfine) sugar
1.5ml/¼ tsp ground ginger
15ml/1 tbsp finely chopped mixed
   citrus peel
15ml/1 tbsp plain (all-purpose) flour

1 Place the orange rind and juice in a bowl. Sift the icing sugar over the top and set aside for 30 minutes, then stir until smooth.

2 Whisk the double cream in a large bowl until the mixture forms soft peaks, then carefully fold in the yogurt.

3 Gently stir in the orange juice, then pour into a freezerproof container. Cover, freeze until firm.

4 Make the baskets. Preheat the oven to 180°C/350°F/Gas 4. Place the butter, syrup and sugar in a heavy pan and heat gently until melted.

5 Add the ground ginger, mixed citrus peel and flour and stir until the mixture is smooth.

COOK'S TIP

It is essential to have the greased tins or cups ready and to work quickly. If the biscuits (cookies) firm up before you have made them all, a few seconds in the oven will soften them.

6 Lightly grease two baking sheets. Drop three portions of the ginger dough on to each baking sheet, using about 10ml/2 tsp of the mixture at a time; space well apart. Spread each one to a 5cm/2in circle, then bake for 12–14 minutes until dark golden.

7 Remove the biscuits from the oven and allow to stand on the baking sheets for 1 minute to firm slightly. Lift off with a fish slice and drape over six greased mini pudding tins (pan) or upturned cups; flatten the top (which will become the base) and flute the edges to form a basket shape.

8 When cool, lift the baskets off the tins or cups and place on individual dessert plates. Arrange scoops of the frozen sherbet in each basket. Decorate each portion with a few orange segments, if you like.

Apple and Cider Water Ice

This very English combination has a subtle apple flavour with just a hint of cider. As the apple purée is very pale, almost white, add a few drops of green food colouring to echo the pale green skin of the Granny Smith apples.

INGREDIENTS

Serves 6

500g/1¼lb Granny Smith apples
150g/5oz/¾ cup caster (superfine) sugar
300ml/½ pint/1¼ cups water
250ml/8fl oz/1 cup strong dry cider
few drops of green food colouring
   (optional)
strips of thinly pared lime rind,
   to decorate

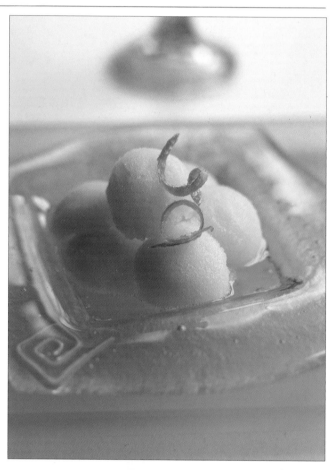

1 Quarter, core and roughly chop the apples. Put them into a pan. Add the caster sugar and half the water. Cover and simmer for 10 minutes or until the apples are soft.

COOK'S TIP

Add the food colouring gradually, making the mixture a little darker than you would like the finished sorbet to be as freezing lightens the colour slightly.

2 Press the mixture through a sieve (strainer) placed over a bowl. Discard the apple skins and seeds. Stir the cider and the remaining water into the apple purée and add a little colouring.

3 If making by hand, pour the mixture into a shallow plastic container and freeze for 6 hours, beating with a fork once or twice to break up the ice crystals. If you have an ice cream maker, churn the mixture until it is firm enough to scoop.

4 Scoop into the water ice into dishes and decorate with twists of thinly pared lime rind.

Gooseberry and Clotted Cream Ice Cream

The delicious, slightly tart flavour of gooseberries goes particularly well with melt-in-the-mouth meringues.

INGREDIENTS

Serves 4–6

500g/1¼lb/4 cups gooseberries, topped
    and tailed
60ml/4 tbsp water
75g/3oz/6 tbsp caster (superfine) sugar
150ml/¼ pint/⅔ cup whipping cream
a few drops of green food colouring
    (optional)
120ml/4fl oz/½ cup clotted cream
fresh mint sprigs, to decorate
meringues, to serve

1 Put the gooseberries in a pan and add the water and sugar. Cover and simmer for 10 minutes or until soft.

2 Tip into a food processor or blender and process to a smooth purée. Press through a sieve (strainer) placed over a bowl. Cool, then chill.

3 Chill the purée in a plastic tub or similar container. Whip the cream until it is thick but still falls from a spoon. Fold into the purée with the green food colouring, if using. Freeze for 2 hours, then beat with a fork, electric mixer or in a food processor, to break up. Return to the freezer for 2 hours.

4 If making by hand, beat the ice cream again, then fold in the clotted cream. Freeze for 2–3 hours. If using an ice cream maker, mix the chilled purée with the whipping cream, add a few drops of green food colouring, if using, and churn until thickened and semi-frozen. Add the clotted cream and continue to churn until thick enough to scoop.

5 To serve, scoop the ice cream into dishes or small plates, decorate with fresh mint sprigs and add a few small meringues to each serving.

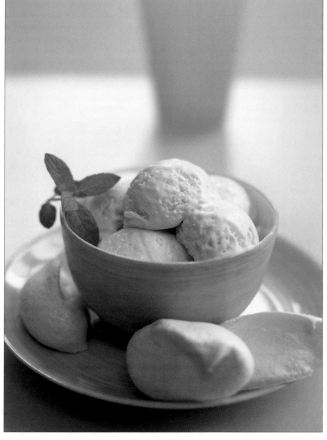

Banana and Toffee Ice Cream

The addition of sweetened condensed milk helps to bring out the natural flavour of the bananas and, surprisingly, the ice cream is not excessively sweet.

INGREDIENTS

Serves 4–6

3 ripe bananas

juice of 1 lemon

370g/12½oz can sweetened condensed
   milk

150ml/¼ pint/⅔ cup whipping cream

150g/5oz toffees

chopped toffees, to decorate

1 Process the bananas to a purée in a food processor or blender, then add the lemon juice and process briefly to mix. Scrape the purée into a plastic tub or similar freezerproof container.

2 Pour in the condensed milk, stirring with a metal spoon, then add the cream. Mix well, cover and freeze for 4 hours or until mushy.

3 Unwrap the toffees and chop them finely, using a sharp knife. If this proves difficult, put them in a double plastic bag and hit them with a rolling pin.

4 Beat the semi-frozen ice cream with a fork or electric mixer to break up the ice crystals, then stir in the toffees. Return the ice cream to the freezer for 3–5 hours or until firm. Scoop on to a plate or into a bowl and decorate with chopped toffees. Serve at once.

COOK'S TIP

To reduce the initial freezing time, start chilling the mixture in a stainless steel roasting pan, transferring to a plastic tub only after adding the toffees. If you are making this ice cream for small children, you may prefer to leave the toffees out or use chopped chocolate instead.

Strawberry Semi-freddo

Serve this quick strawberry and ricotta dessert semi-frozen to enjoy the flavour at its best.

Serves 4–6

250g/9oz/generous 2 cups strawberries

115g/4oz/scant ½ cup strawberry jam

250g/9oz/generous 1 cup ricotta cheese

200g/7oz/scant 1 cup Greek (US strained plain) yogurt

5ml/1 tsp natural vanilla extract

40g/1½oz/3 tbsp caster (superfine) sugar

extra strawberries and mint or lemon balm, to decorate

1 Put the strawberries in a bowl and mash them with a fork until broken into small pieces but not completely puréed. Stir in the strawberry jam. Drain off any whey from the ricotta.

2 Tip the ricotta into a bowl and stir in the Greek yogurt, natural vanilla extract and sugar. Using a dessertspoon, gently fold the mashed strawberries into the ricotta mixture until rippled.

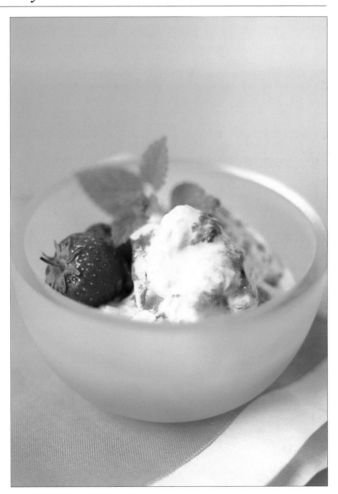

3 Spoon into individual freezerproof dishes and freeze for at least 2 hours until almost solid. Alternatively, freeze until completely solid, then transfer the ice cream to the refrigerator for about 45 minutes to soften before serving. Serve in small bowls with extra strawberries and decorated with mint or lemon balm.

COOK'S TIP

Don't mash the strawberries too much or they'll become too liquid. Freeze in a large freezer container if you don't have suitable small dishes. Transfer to the refrigerator to thaw slightly, then scoop into glasses.

Mango and Passion Fruit Gelato

Fresh and fruity, this tropical ice cream has a delicate perfume. Passion fruit tend to vary in size. If you can locate the large ones, four will be plenty for this dish.

INGREDIENTS

Serves 4

4 large mangoes
grated rind and juice of 1 lime
50g/2oz/¼ cup caster (superfine) sugar
300ml/½ pint/1¼ cups whipping cream
4–6 passion fruit

1 Cut a thick slice from either side of the stone (pit) on each mango. Make criss-cross cuts in the flesh, cutting down as far as the skin.

2 Turn the slices inside out so that the pieces of mango stand proud of the skin, then scoop them into a food processor or blender.

3 Process the mango flesh until smooth, then add the grated lime rind, lime juice and caster sugar and process briefly.

4 If making by hand, whip the cream until it is just thick but will still fall from a spoon. Fold in the puréed mango and lime mixture, then pour into a plastic tub or similar freezerproof container. Freeze for 4 hours until semi-frozen. If using an ice cream maker, churn the fruit mixture for 10–15 minutes, then add the cream and continue to churn until the mixture is thick but still too soft to scoop. Scrape it into a plastic tub.

5 Cut the passion fruit in half and scoop the seeds and pulp into the ice cream mixture, mix well and freeze for 2 hours until firm enough to scoop.

Fresh Strawberry Ice Cream

You can make the ice cream by hand if you freeze it for several hours, whisking it every hour or so, but the texture won't be as good.

INGREDIENTS

Serves 6

300ml/½ pint/1¼ cups creamy milk
1 vanilla pod (bean)
3 large egg yolks
225g/8oz/1½–2 cups strawberries
juice of ½ lemon
75g/3oz/¾ cup icing (confectioners') sugar
300ml/½ pint/1¼ cups double (heavy) cream
sliced strawberries, to serve

3 Meanwhile, purée the strawberries with the lemon juice in a food processor or blender. Press the strawberry purée through a sieve (strainer) into a bowl. Stir in the icing sugar and set aside. In a separate bowl whip the cream until it forms soft peaks.

4 Gently fold the cream into the custard with the strawberry purée. Pour the mixture into an ice cream maker. Churn for 20–30 minutes, or until the mixture holds its shape. Transfer the ice cream to a freezerproof container, cover and freeze until firm. Soften briefly before serving decorated with sliced strawberries.

1 Put the milk and vanilla pod into a pan and slowly bring to the boil. Remove from the heat and leave for 20 minutes. Strain the warm milk into a bowl containing the egg yolks and whisk well.

2 Return the mixture to a clean pan and heat, stirring constantly, until the custard just coats the back of the spoon. Pour into a clean bowl, cover with clear film (plastic wrap) and set aside to cool.

Chocolate Ice Cream

Use good quality chocolate for the best flavour.

INGREDIENTS

Makes about 850ml/1½ pints/3¾ cups

750ml/1¼ pints/3 cups milk

10cm/4in piece of vanilla pod (bean)

4 egg yolks

225g/8oz cooking chocolate, melted

150g/5oz/¾ cup granulated (white) sugar

1 To make the custard, heat the milk with the vanilla pod in a small pan. Remove from the heat as soon as small bubbles start to form. Do not boil.

2 Beat the egg yolks with a wire whisk or electric beater. Gradually incorporate the sugar, and continue beating for about 5 minutes until the mixture is pale yellow. Strain the milk. Slowly add it to the egg mixture drop by drop.

3 Pour the mixture into a double boiler with the melted chocolate. Stir over moderate heat until the water in the pan is boiling, and the custard thickens enough to lightly coat the back of a spoon. Remove from the heat and allow to cool.

4 Freeze in an ice cream maker, or if you do not have an ice cream maker, pour the mixture into a metal or plastic freezer container and freeze until set, about 3 hours. Remove from the container and chop roughly into 7.5cm/3in pieces. Place in the bowl of a food processor and process until smooth. Return to the freezer container, and freeze again until firm. Repeat the freezing-chopping process 2 or 3 times, until a smooth consistency is reached.

Buttermilk Vanilla Ice Cream

*Enriched with just a little double
cream, this unusual ice cream tastes
far more luxurious than it really is.*

INGREDIENTS

Serves 6

250ml/8fl oz/1 cup buttermilk
60ml/4 tbsp double (heavy) cream
1 vanilla pod (bean) or 2.5ml/
   ½ tsp vanilla extract
2 eggs
30ml/2 tbsp clear honey
fresh fruit purée, to serve

1 Place the buttermilk and
cream in a pan with the vanilla
pod, if using, and heat gently over
a low heat until the mixture is
almost boiling. Remove the
vanilla pod.

2 Place the eggs in a bowl over a
pan of hot water and whisk
until they are pale and thick. Add
the heated buttermilk in a thin
stream, while whisking hard.
Continue whisking over the hot
water until the mixture has
thickened slightly.

COOK'S TIP

This basic vanilla ice cream can
be used as a base for other
flavours: stir in puréed fruit,
citrus ring or coffee.

3 Whisk in the honey and vanilla
extract, if using. Spoon the
mixture into a freezerproof
container and freeze until firm.

4 Spoon the firm ice cream
on to a sheet of baking
parchment. Roll it up in the paper
to form a cylinder and freeze again
until firm. Serve the ice cream on
plates in slices.

Frozen Strawberry Mousse Cake

Children love this pretty dessert – it tastes just like an ice cream.

INGREDIENTS

Serves 4–6

425g/15oz can strawberries in syrup
15ml/1 tbsp/1 sachet powdered gelatine
6 trifle sponge cakes
45ml/3 tbsp strawberry jam
200ml/7fl oz/⅞ cup crème fraîche
200ml/7fl oz/⅞ cup whipped cream,
    to decorate

1 Strain the syrup from the strawberries into a large heatproof bowl. Sprinkle over the gelatine and stir well. Stand the bowl in a pan of hot water and stir until the gelatine has dissolved.

2 Leave to cool, then chill for just under 1 hour, until beginning to set. Meanwhile, cut the sponge cakes in half lengthways and spread the cut surfaces with the strawberry jam.

3 Carefully whisk the crème fraîche into the strawberry jelly, then whisk in the canned strawberries. Line a deep, 20cm/8in loose-based cake tin (pan) with baking parchment.

4 Pour half the strawberry mousse mixture into the tin, arrange the sponge cakes over the surface, and then spoon over the remaining mousse mixture, pushing down any sponge cakes which rise up.

5 Freeze for 1–2 hours until firm. Remove the cake from the tin and carefully peel away the lining paper. Transfer to a serving plate. Decorate the mousse with whirls of whipped cream and a few strawberry leaves and a fresh strawberry, if you have them.

Hazelnut Ice Cream

This popular flavour goes very well served with scoops of chocolate and vanilla ice creams.

INGREDIENTS

Serves 4–6

75g/3oz/½ cup hazelnuts
75g/3oz/6 tbsp granulated (white) sugar
475ml/16fl oz/2 cups milk
10cm/4in piece of vanilla pod (bean)
4 egg yolks

1 Spread the hazelnuts on a baking sheet and place under a grill (broiler) for about 5 minutes, shaking frequently to turn the nuts over. Remove from the heat and allow to cool slightly. Place the nuts on a clean dish towel, and rub them with a cloth to remove their dark outer skin. Chop very finely or grind in a food processor with 30ml/2 tbsp of the sugar.

2 Make the custard. Heat the milk with the vanilla pod in a small pan. Remove from the heat as soon as small bubbles start to form on the surface.

3 Beat the egg yolks with a wire whisk or an electric beater. Gradually add the remaining sugar and continue beating until the mixture turns a pale yellow. Discard the vanilla pod and, stirring constantly, very gradually add the milk, pouring it through a sieve (strainer).

4 Pour the mixture into a double boiler, or into a bowl placed over a pan of simmering water. Add the chopped nuts. Stir over a moderate heat until the water in the pan is boiling, and the custard thickens enough to lightly coat the back of a spoon. Remove from the heat and allow to cool.

5 Freeze in an ice cream maker, or transfer the mixture to a freezerproof container and freeze for 5–6 hours. During the freezing time beat twice with a fork, electric whisk or in a food processor until a smooth consistency has been reached. Serve in scoops.

Coffee Ice Cream with Caramelized Pecans

Coffee and sweetened nuts make a mouthwatering combination.

INGREDIENTS

Serves 4–6

For the ice cream

300ml/10fl oz/1¼ cups milk

1 tbsp demerara (raw) sugar

25g/1oz/6 tbsp finely ground coffee or
    15ml/1 tbsp instant coffee granules

1 egg plus 2 yolks

300ml/10fl oz/1¼ cups double
    (heavy) cream

15ml/1 tbsp caster (superfine) sugar

For the pecans

115g/4oz/1 cup pecan halves

50g/2oz/4 tbsp soft dark brown sugar

1 Heat the milk and demerara sugar in a small pan to boiling point. Remove from the heat and sprinkle on the coffee. Leave to stand for 2 minutes, then stir, cover and allow to cool.

2 In a heatproof bowl, beat the egg and extra yolks until the mixture is thick and pale.

COOK'S TIP
〜
You can give good-quality bought ice cream a fillip with the same nutty garnish.

---

3 Strain the coffee mixture into a clean pan, heat to boiling point, then pour on to the eggs in a steady stream, beating hard.

4 Set the bowl over a pan of gently simmering water and stir until it thickens. Cool, then chill in the refrigerator.

5 Whip the cream with the caster sugar. Fold it into the coffee custard and freeze in a covered container. Beat twice at hourly intervals, then leave to freeze firm.

6 To caramelize the nuts, preheat the oven to 180°C/350°F/Gas 4. Spread the nuts on a baking sheet in a single layer. Put them into the oven for 10–15 minutes to toast until they release their fragrance.

7 On the top of the stove, dissolve the brown sugar in 30ml/2 tbsp water in a heavy pan, shaking it about over a low heat until the sugar dissolves completely and the syrup clears.

8 When the syrup begins to bubble, tip in the toasted pecans and cook for a minute or two over a medium heat until the syrup coats and clings to the nuts.

9 Spread the nuts on a lightly oiled baking sheet, separating them with the tip of a knife, and leave to cool. Store when cold in an airtight tin (pan) if they are not to be eaten on the same day.

10 Transfer the ice cream from the freezer to the refrigerator 30 minutes before scooping it into portions and serving with caramelized pecans.

Brown Bread Ice Cream

Delicious on its own and irresistible served with this blackcurrant coulis, brown bread ice cream is a classic that has never lost its popularity.

Serves 6

50g/2oz/½ cup roasted and chopped
   hazelnuts, ground
75g/3oz/1¼ cups wholemeal (whole-
   wheat) breadcrumbs
60ml/4 tbsp soft brown sugar
3 egg whites
115g/4oz/½ cup caster (superfine) sugar
300ml/½ pint/1¼ cups double
   (heavy) cream
few drops of vanilla extract

For the sauce

225g/8oz/2 cups blackcurrants
75g/3oz/6 tbsp caster (superfine) sugar
15ml/1 tbsp creme de cassis
fresh mint to decorate

1 Combine the hazelnuts and breadcrumbs on a baking sheet, then sprinkle over the raw sugar. Place under a medium grill (broiler) and toast, stirring, until the mixture is crisp and evenly browned. Leave to cool.

2 Whisk the egg whites in a bowl until stiff, then gradually whisk in the caster sugar until thick and glossy. Whip the cream until it forms soft peaks and fold into the meringue with the breadcrumb mixture and vanilla extract.

3 Spoon the mixture into a 1.2 litre/2 pint/5 cup loaf tin (pan). Smooth the top level, then cover and freeze for several hours or until firm.

4 Meanwhile, make the sauce. Strip the blackcurrants from their stalks using a fork and put them in a small bowl with the sugar. Toss gently to mix and leave for 30 minutes.

5 Purée the blackcurrants in a blender or food processor, then press through a nylon sieve (strainer) until smooth. Add the crème de cassis and chill well.

6 To serve, turn out the ice cream on to a plate and cut into slices. Arrange each slice on a serving plate, spoon over a little sauce and decorate with fresh mint sprigs.

Indian Ice Cream (Kulfi)

Kulfi-wallahs (ice cream vendors) have always made kulfi, and continue to this day, without using modern freezers. You will need to start making kulfi the day before.

Serves 4–6

3 x 400ml/14fl oz cans evaporated milk

3 egg whites, whisked until peaks form

350g/12oz/3 cups icing
   (confectioners') sugar

5ml/1 tsp cardamom powder

15ml/1 tbsp rose water

175g/6oz/1½ cups pistachio nuts, chopped

75g/3oz/generous ½ cup sultanas
   (golden raisins)

75g/3oz/¾ cup flaked (sliced) almonds

25g/1oz/2 tbsp glacé (candied)
   cherries, halved

1 Remove the labels from the cans of evaporated milk and lay the cans down in a pan with a tight-fitting cover. Fill the pan with water to reach three-quarters up the cans. Bring to the boil, cover and simmer for 20 minutes. When cool, remove and chill the cans in the refrigerator for 24 hours.

2 Open the cans and empty the milk into a large, chilled bowl. Whisk until it doubles in quantity, then fold in the whisked egg whites and icing sugar.

3 Gently fold in the remaining ingredients, seal the bowl with clear film (plastic wrap) and leave in the freezer for 1 hour.

4 Remove the ice cream from the freezer and mix well with a fork. Transfer to a freezer container and return to the freezer for a final setting. Remove from the freezer 10 minutes before serving in scoops.

Turkish Delight Ice Cream

Not strictly a traditional Middle Eastern recipe, but a delicious way of using Turkish Delight. Scatter with rose petals, if you have them.

Serves 6

4 egg yolks

115g/4oz/½ cup caster (superfine) sugar

300ml/½ pint/1¼ cups milk

300ml/½ pint/1¼ cups double (heavy) cream

15ml/1 tbsp rose water

175g/6oz rose-flavoured Turkish
   Delight, chopped

1 Beat the egg yolks and sugar together until pale and thick. In a pan, bring the milk to the boil. Add to the yolks and sugar, stirring, then return to the pan.

2 Continue stirring over a low heat until the custard is thick enough to coat the back of a spoon. Do not boil, or it will curdle. Leave to cool, then stir in the cream and rose water.

3 Put the Turkish Delight in a pan with 30–45ml/2–3tbsp water. Heat gently, until almost melted, but with just a few small lumps. Remove from the heat and stir into the cool custard mixture.

4 Leave the mixture to cool completely, then pour into a shallow freezer container. Freeze for 3 hours until just frozen all over. Transfer the mixture into a mixing bowl.

5 Using a whisk, beat the mixture until smooth, return to the freezer container and freeze for 2 hours more. Repeat the beating process, then return to the freezer for about 3 hours, or until firm. Remove the ice cream from the freezer 20–25 minutes before serving. Serve with thin almond biscuits (cookies) or meringues.

Pineapple Ice Cream

Tropically flavoured, this ice cream can be made at any time of the year, but it is particularly good when made with fresh pineapple.

INGREDIENTS

Serves 8–10

8 eggs, separated

115g/4oz/½ cup caster (superfine) sugar

2.5ml/½ tsp vanilla extract

600ml/1 pint/2½ cups whipping cream

60ml/4 tbsp icing (confectioners') sugar

425g/15oz can pineapple chunks

75g/3oz/¼ cup pistachio nuts, chopped

wafers, to serve

1 Place the egg yolks in a bowl, add the caster sugar and vanilla extract and beat until thick and pale yellow.

2 In a separate bowl, whip the cream and icing sugar to soft peaks. Add to the egg yolk mixture.

3 Whisk the egg whites in a separate large bowl until they are firm and hold stiff peaks. Gently fold the egg whites into the cream mixture and blend well.

COOK'S TIP
〜

Use a small fresh pineapple when available. Remove the rough skin and core, then chop into chunks.

---

4 Cut the pineapple into very small pieces, add the pistachio nuts and stir into the cream mixture, mixing well with a spoon.

5 Pour the mixture into an ice cream container and place in the freezer for a few hours until it is set and firm, stirring it once or twice during the freezing time.

6 Cut into thick slices and serve in a pretty glass dish decorated with wafers.

Coconut Ice Cream

An easy-to-make ice cream that is quite heavenly and will be loved by all for its fresh tropical taste.

INGREDIENTS

Serves 8

400g/14oz can evaporated milk

400g/14oz can sweetened condensed milk

400g/14oz can coconut milk

freshly grated nutmeg

5ml/1 tsp almond extract

lemon balm sprigs, lime slices and
   shredded coconut, to decorate

1 Mix together the evaporated, condensed and coconut milks in a freezerproof bowl and stir in the nutmeg and almond extract.

2 Put in the freezer and chill for an hour or two until the mixture is semi-frozen.

3 Remove from the freezer and whisk the mixture with a hand or electric whisk until it is fluffy and almost doubled in volume.

4 Pour into a freezer container, then cover and freeze until firm. Before serving, allow the ice cream to soften slightly at room temperature. Decorate with a sprig of lemon balm, lime slices and shredded coconut.

Cinnamon and Coffee Swirl Ice Cream

Light ice cream subtly spiced with cinnamon and rippled with a sweet coffee syrup.

INGREDIENTS

Serves 6

300ml/½ pint/1¼ cups single (light) cream
1 cinnamon stick
4 egg yolks
150g/5oz/¾ cup caster (superfine) sugar
300ml/½ pint/1¼ cups double
   (heavy) cream
For the coffee syrup
45ml/3 tbsp ground coffee
45ml/3 tbsp near-boiling water
90g/3½oz/½ cup caster (superfine) sugar
50ml/2fl oz/¼ cup water

1 Slowly bring to the boil the cream and cinnamon stick. Turn off the heat, cover and infuse for 30 minutes. Bring back to the boil and remove the cinnamon.

2 Whisk the yolks and sugar until light. Pour the hot cream over the egg mixture, whisking. Return to the pan and stir over low heat for 1–2 minutes, until it thickens. Allow the mixture to cool.

3 Whip the double cream until peaks form and fold into the custard. Pour into a container and freeze for 3 hours.

4 Meanwhile, put the coffee in a bowl and pour the hot water over. Leave to infuse for 4 minutes, then strain through a sieve (strainer). Discard the coffee grounds.

5 Gently heat the sugar and cold water in a pan until completely dissolved. Bring to the boil and gently simmer for 5 minutes. Cool, then stir in the coffee.

6 Turn the ice cream into a chilled bowl and briefly whisk to break down the ice crystals.

7 Spoon a third back into the container and drizzle over some coffee syrup. Repeat until it is all used.

8 Drag a skewer through the mixture a few times to achieve a marbled effect. Freeze for 4 hours, or until solid. Allow to soften slightly before serving.

Mint Ice Cream

This ice cream is best served slightly softened at room temperature, so take it out of the freezer 20 minutes before you want to serve it. For a special occasion, this looks spectacular served in an ice bowl.

INGREDIENTS

Serves 8

8 egg yolks

75g/3oz/6 tbsp caster (superfine) sugar

600ml/1 pint/2½ cups single (light) cream

1 vanilla pod (bean)

60ml/4 tbsp chopped fresh mint

2 Pour the cream into a separate pan and add the vanilla pod. On a medium heat gently bring the cream just to the boil.

5 Gently heat the mixture until the custard thickens enough to coat the back of a wooden spoon. Leave to cool.

1 Place the egg yolks and sugar in a bowl and beat, using a hand-held electric beater or a balloon whisk, until it is pale and slightly thick. Transfer the mixture to a pan.

3 Remove the vanilla pod and pour the hot cream on to the egg mixture, whisking briskly.

4 Continue whisking to ensure the eggs are thoroughly mixed into the cream.

6 Stir in the mint and place in an ice cream maker to churn and freeze (about 3–4 hours). If you don't have an ice cream maker, freeze the ice cream until mushy and then whisk it well again, to break down the ice crystals. Freeze for another 3 hours until it is softly frozen and whisk again. Finally, freeze the ice cream until hard, preferably overnight.

COOK'S TIP

To make an ice bowl, place a few ice cubes in the bottom of a freezerproof bowl, adding a few sprigs of the herb for decoration. Place a smaller bowl inside, to give a gap of 1cm/½in, level and secure with adhesive tape. Fill the gap with cooled boiled water and freeze until solid. To unmould, pour a little hot water into the inner bowl, then dip briefly in hot water to release the ice bowl.

VARIATION

For an equally refreshing alternative use lemon balm, borage or rose geranium instead of mint. Gather enough sprigs of the chosen herb to make 60ml/4 tbsp of chopped herb and use in the recipe in exactly the same way.

Rocky Road Ice Cream

For chills and thrills, there's nothing to beat this classic sweet ice cream. A perennial favourite, packed with flavour and contrasting textures.

INGREDIENTS

Serves 6

115g/4oz plain (semisweet) chocolate
   broken into squares
150ml/¼ pint/⅔ cup milk
300ml/½ pint/1¼ cups double (heavy)
   cream
115g/4oz/½ cup marshmallows, chopped
50g/2oz/¼ cup glacé (candied) cherries,
   chopped
50g/2oz/1 cup crumbled shortbread
   biscuits (cookies)
30ml/2 tbsp chopped walnuts

1 Melt the chocolate in the milk in a pan over a gentle heat, stirring from time to time. Leave to cool.

2 Whip the cream in a bowl until it just holds it shape. Beat in the chocolate mixture.

3 Tip the chocolate cream mixture into an ice cream maker and churn until thick and almost frozen. Alternatively, pour into a container suitable for use in the freezer, freeze until ice crystals form around the edges, then whisk until completely smooth.

4 Stir the marshmallows, cherries, crushed biscuits and nuts into the iced mixture, then return to the freezer and freeze until firm.

5 Allow the ice cream to soften at room temperature for 15–20 minutes before serving in scoops.

COOK'S TIP

For a quick version, simply stir the flavourings into bought soft-scoop chocolate ice cream and freeze until firm.

Brandied Fruit and Rice Ice Cream

Based on a favourite Victorian rice ice cream, this rich dessert combines spicy rice pudding with a creamy egg custard flecked with brandy-soaked fruits. The mixture is then frozen until it is just firm enough to serve in scoops.

INGREDIENTS

Serves 4–6

50g/2oz/¹/₄ cup ready-to-eat pitted prunes

50g/2oz/¹/₄ cup ready-to-eat dried apricots

50g/2oz/¹/₄ cup glacé (candied) cherries

30ml/2 tbsp brandy

150ml/¹/₄ pint/²/₃ cup single (light) cream

For the rice mixture

40g/1¹/₂oz/generous ¹/₄ cup pudding rice

450ml/³/₄ pint/scant 2 cups full cream (whole) milk

1 cinnamon stick, halved, plus extra cinnamon sticks, to decorate

4 cloves

For the custard

4 egg yolks

75g/3oz/6 tbsp caster (superfine) sugar

5ml/1 tsp cornflour (cornstarch)

300ml/¹/₂ pint/1¹/₄ cups full cream (whole) milk

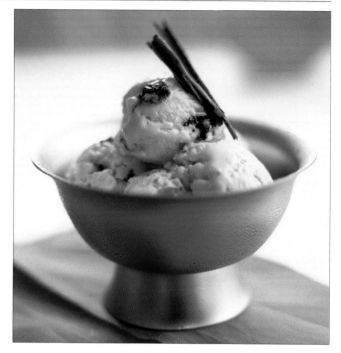

1 Chop the prunes, apricots and glacé cherries finely and put them in a bowl. Pour over the brandy. Cover and leave to soak for 3 hours or overnight if possible.

2 Put the rice, milk and whole spices in a pan. Bring to the boil, then simmer gently for 30 minutes, stirring occasionally, until most of the milk has been absorbed. Lift out the spices and leave the rice to cool.

3 Whisk the egg yolks, sugar and cornflower in a bowl until thick and creamy. Heat the milk in a heavy pan, then gradually pour it on the yolks, whisking constantly. Pour back into the pan and cook, stirring until the custard thickens. Leave to cool, then chill.

4 Mix the chilled custard, rice and single cream together. Pour into a plastic container or similar freezerproof container and freeze for 4–5 hours, until mushy. Beat the ice cream lightly with a fork to break up the ice crystals.

5 Fold in the fruits, then freeze for 2–3 hours until firm enough to scoop.

6 Scoop the ice cream into individual dishes and decorate with cinnamon sticks.

Praline Ice Cream in Baskets

Praline, a delicious crunchy caramel and nut mixture, is a very popular flavouring in France – it can be made with almonds or hazelnuts or a mixture of the two, if you prefer.

INGREDIENTS

Serves 6–8

55g/2oz/½ cup blanched almonds
    or hazelnuts
175g/6oz/⅞ cup caster (superfine) sugar
60ml/4 tbsp water
250ml/8fl oz/1 cup double (heavy) cream
6 egg yolks
500ml/16fl oz/2 cups milk
For the baskets
70g/2½oz/½ cup whole blanched almonds,
    lightly toasted
100g/3½oz/½ cup caster (superfine) sugar
40g/1½oz/3 tbsp unsalted butter,
    softened
2 egg whites
2.5ml/½ tsp almond extract
35g/1¼oz/¼ cup plain (all-purpose)
    flour, sifted

1 Lightly brush a baking sheet with oil. Put the nuts in a pan with 75g/3oz/⅓ cup of the sugar and the water. Bring to the boil over a high heat, swirling the pan to dissolve the sugar, then boil, without stirring, for 4–5 minutes until the syrup and nuts begin to pop. Immediately pour on to the baking sheet (do not touch the hot caramel). Set aside to cool completely then break into pieces.

2 Finely grind the praline in a food processor, using the metal blade. Or, put in a strong polythene bag and crush with a rolling pin.

3 Pour the cream into a cold bowl and set aside. In another bowl whisk the egg yolks and remaining sugar until thick and creamy. Meanwhile, bring the milk just to a simmer over a medium heat, then whisk into the eggs and return the mixture to the pan.

4 With a wooden spoon, stir over a low heat for 3–4 minutes until the sauce thickens and coats the back of the spoon, then strain the custard into the bowl of cream. Cool, then chill until cold. Stir in the praline and freeze in an ice cream maker, or in the freezer, beating once or twice until smooth.

5 Preheat the oven to 200°C/ 400°F/Gas 6. Butter two baking sheets. To make the baskets, put the almonds and 30ml/2 tbsp of the sugar in a food processor and finely grind with the metal blade. Beat the butter until creamy.

6 Add the remaining sugar to the butter and beat until light and fluffy, then gradually beat in the egg whites and the almond extract. Sift the flour over the butter mixture, fold in, then fold in the ground almond mixture.

7 Drop tablespoons of mixture about 20cm/8in apart on to the prepared baking sheets. With the back of a wet spoon, spread into paper-thin rounds 10cm/4in across.

8 Bake the baskets, for 4–5 minutes until the edges are golden and the centres are still pale. Transfer to a wire rack and, working quickly, loosen the edge of a hot basket and carefully transfer to an upturned drinking glass or ramekin, pressing gently over the base to form a fluted basket shape. If the baskets become too crisp to shape, soften them in the oven for 15–30 seconds. Repeat with the remaining baskets. Set aside to cool completely before transferring to a wire rack.

9 To serve, leave the ice cream to soften at room temperature for 5–10 minutes. Place the baskets on dessert plates and fill with scoops of the ice cream.

Black Forest Sundae

Here is a truly indulgent variation on the classic Black Forest gâteau, but this one is spectacularly served in a sundae glass.

INGREDIENTS

Serves 4

400g/14oz can pitted black cherries
    in syrup
15ml/1 tbsp cornflour (cornstarch)
45ml/3 tbsp kirsch
15ml/1 tbsp icing (confectioners') sugar
150ml/¼ pint/ ⅔ cup whipping cream
600ml/1 pint/2½ cups chocolate
    ice cream
115g/4oz ready-made chocolate cake
8 fresh cherries, to decorate
vanilla ice cream, to serve

2 Over a medium heat, bring the syrup in the pan to the boil. Add the cornflour and syrup mixture, stirring until it is well blended, and then simmer briefly to thicken, stirring continuously.

5 Place a spoonful of cherries in the bottom of four sundae glasses. Add a layer of ice cream, then chocolate cake, whipped cream and more cherries, continue until the glasses are full.

1 Strain all but 30ml/2tbsp of the cherry syrup into a pan. Measure the cornflour into a small bowl with the remaining syrup and mix together until smooth and creamy.

3 Add the cherries, stir in the kirsch and then spread on to a baking sheet to cool.

6 To finish the sundaes add a piece of chocolate cake, two scoops of ice cream and another spoonful of cream. Place in the freezer for 5–10 minutes, to firm the ice cream, and serve decorated with fresh cherries.

4 Sift the icing sugar over the cream, fold in and then whip until the mixture is thick and holds its shape.

COOK'S TIP

Bottled black cherries often have a better flavour than canned, especially if the pits are left in. You don't need to remove the pits – but do remember to tell your guests.

Ice Cream Strawberry Shortcake

This pudding is an American classic, and couldn't be easier to make. Fresh juicy strawberries, store-bought flan cases and rich vanilla ice cream are all you need to create an irresistible feast of a dessert.

INGREDIENTS

Serves 4

3x15cm/6in sponge flan cases or
   shortbreads
1.2 litres/2 pints/5 cups vanilla or
   strawberry ice cream
675g/1½lb hulled fresh strawberries
icing (confectioners') sugar, for dusting

1 If using store-bought flan cases, trim the raised edges level with the base, using a serrated knife or bread knife.

2 Start with the flan case, or shortbread, and place one-third of the ice cream and the strawberries on top. Spread them evenly to make a level base. Add another layer of flan case or short-bread and another third of the ice cream and the strawberries. Then the final layer of flan or shortbread.

3 Arrange the remaining ice cream on top and finish with the strawberries. Chill in the freezer before serving dusted with icing sugar.

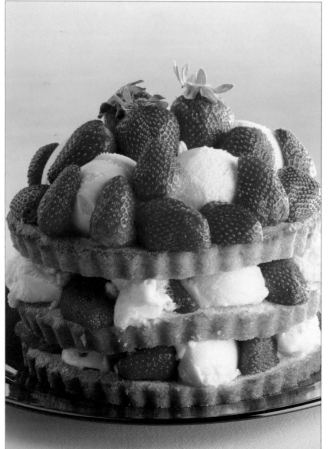

COOK'S TIP
~

Don't worry if the shortbread falls apart when you cut into it. Messy cakes are best. Ice Cream Strawberry Shortbread can be assembled up to 1 hour in advance and kept in the freezer without spoiling the fruit.

Chocolate Mint Ice Cream Pie

This colourful dessert uses ready-made ice cream and it looks and tastes really professional.

INGREDIENTS

Serves 8

75g/3oz plain (semisweet) chocolate chips
40g/1½oz butter or margarine
50g/2oz crisped rice cereal
1 litre/1¾pt mint-chocolate-chip ice cream
75g/3oz plain (semisweet) chocolate

1 In a heatproof bowl set over a pan of barely simmering water, melt the chocolate chips and the butter or margarine.

2 Remove the bowl from the heat and gradually stir in the cereal. Let it cool for 5 minutes.

3 Line a 23cm/9in pie tin (pan) with foil and place a round of baking parchment over the foil in the bottom of the tin. Press the chocolate and cereal mixture over the bottom and around the sides of the lined tin, forming a rim. Chill until set hard.

4 Carefully remove the cereal base from the tin and peel off the foil and baking parchment. Return the base to the pie tin.

5 Remove the ice cream from the freezer and allow to soften for 10 minutes.

6 Spread the ice cream evenly in the crust then freeze for about 1 hour until firm.

7 For the decoration, use the heat of your hands to soften the chocolate slightly. Draw the blade of a swivel-headed vegetable peeler along the smooth surface of the chocolate to shave off short, wide curls. Chill the curls until needed.

8 Just before serving, scatter the chocolate curls over the ice cream to cover the surface.

Pistachio and Nougat Torte

Pistachio nuts, nougat, honey and rose water make a perfect blend of flavours in this quick and easy iced torte.

INGREDIENTS

Serves 6–8

75g/3oz/¾ cup pistachio nuts

150g/5oz nougat

300ml/½ pint/1¼ cups whipping cream

90ml/6 tbsp clear honey

30ml/2tbsp rose water

250g/9oz/generous 1 cup fromage frais

8 trifle sponges

icing (confectioners') sugar, for dusting

fresh raspberries, poached apricots or
    cherries, to serve (optional)

1 Soak the pistachio nuts in boiling water for 2 minutes. Drain them thoroughly, then rub them between pieces of kitchen paper to remove the skins. Peel off any skins that remain, then chop the pistachio nuts roughly.

2 Using a small sharp knife or scissors, cut the nougat into small pieces.

3 Pour the cream into a bowl, add the honey and rose water and whip until it is just beginning to hold its shape. Stir in the fromage frais, chopped pistachio nuts and nougat.

4 Slice the trifle sponges horizontally into three very thin layers.

5 Line a 15–17cm/6–6½in square loose-based cake tin (pan) with baking parchment or clear film (plastic wrap). Arrange a layer of sponge on the bottom of the tin, trimming the pieces to fit.

6 Pack the pistachio and nougat filling into the tin and level the surface. Cover with the remaining sponges, then cover with clear film and freeze overnight.

7 To serve, invert the torte on to a serving plate and dust with icing sugar. Serve with fresh raspberries, poached apricots or cherries, if you like.

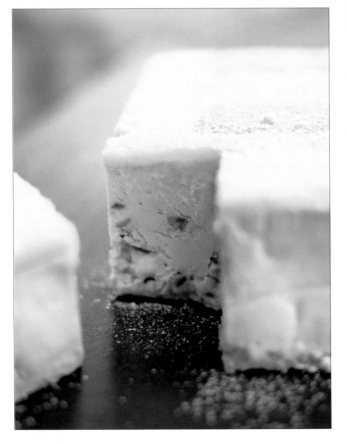

Coffee and Chocolate Bombe

This impressive dessert is known in Italy as zuccotto, *meaning pumpkin. A wide-based bowl gives the most authentic shape, but it will taste delicious whatever shape it is.*

INGREDIENTS

Serves 6-8

175ml/6fl oz/³⁄₄ cup sweet Marsala

15-18 savoiardi (Italian sponge fingers)

75g/3oz amaretti

about 475ml/ 16fl oz/2 cups coffee ice
    cream, softened

about 475ml/ 16fl oz/2 cups vanilla ice
    cream, softened

50g/2oz plain (semisweet) or dark
    (bittersweet) chocolate, grated

chocolate curls and sifted cocoa powder or
    icing (confectioners') sugar, to decorate

1 Line a 1 litre/1³⁄₄ pint/4 cup heatproof bowl with a large piece of damp muslin (cheese-cloth). Pour the Marsala into a shallow dish and dip a sponge finger, turning it quickly to saturate it. Place against the side of the bowl, sugared-side out. Repeat with the remaining sponge fingers, to line the bowl.

2 Fill the base and any gaps around the side with any trimmings of sponge fingers cut to fit. Chill for about 30 minutes.

3 Put the amaretti biscuits in a large bowl and crush them with a large rolling pin. Add the coffee ice cream and any remaining Marsala and beat until mixed. Spoon the mixture into the sponge-finger-lined bowl.

4 Press the ice cream against the sponge to form an even layer with a hollow. Freeze for 2 hours.

5 Put the vanilla ice cream and grated chocolate in a bowl and beat together until evenly mixed. Spoon into the hollow in the centre of the mould. Smooth the top, then cover with the overhanging muslin. Place in the freezer overnight.

6 To serve, run a palette knife between the muslin and the bowl, then unfold the top of the muslin. Place a chilled serving plate on top of the bombe, then invert them so that the bombe is upside down on the plate. Carefully peel off the muslin. Decorate the bombe with the chocolate curls, then sift cocoa powder or icing sugar over. Serve at once.

Maple Coffee and Pistachio Bombes

Real maple syrup tastes infinitely better than the synthetic varieties and is well worth searching for.

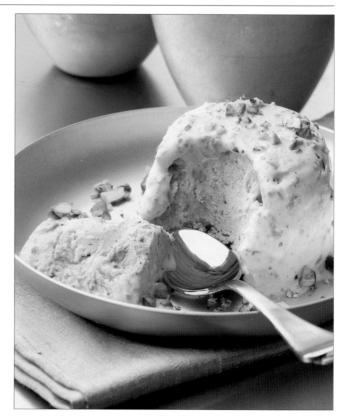

INGREDIENTS

Serves 6

For the pistachio ice cream

50g/2oz/¼ cup caster (superfine) sugar

50ml/2fl oz/¼ cup water

175g/6oz can evaporated milk, chilled

50g/2oz/½ cup shelled and skinned
   pistachio nuts, finely chopped

drop of green food colouring
   (optional)

200ml/7fl oz/scant 1 cup
   whipping cream

For the maple coffee centres

30ml/2 tbsp ground coffee

150ml/¼ pint/⅔ cup single (light) cream

50ml/2fl oz/¼ cup maple syrup

2 egg yolks

5ml/1 tsp cornflour (cornstarch)

150ml/¼ pint/⅔ cup
   whipping cream

1 Put six 175ml/6fl oz/¾ cup mini heatproof bowl or dariole moulds into the freezer to chill. Put the sugar and water in a heavy pan and heat gently until dissolved. Bring to the boil and simmer for 3 minutes. Cool.

2 Stir in the evaporated milk, nuts and colouring, if using. Lightly whip the cream to soft peaks and blend into the mixture.

3 Pour into a freezerproof container and freeze for at least 2 hours. Whisk the ice cream until smooth, then freeze for a further 2 hours or until frozen, but not completely solid.

4 Put the ground coffee in a jug (pitcher). Heat the single cream to near-boiling, pour over the coffee and infuse for 4 minutes. Whisk the maple syrup, egg yolks and cornflour together. Strain the hot coffee cream over the egg mixture, whisking continuously. Return to the pan and cook gently for 1–2 minutes, until the custard thickens. Leave to cool, stirring occasionally.

5 Meanwhile, line the moulds right up to the rim with an even thickness of the ice cream. Freeze until the ice cream is firm.

6 Beat the cream to soft peaks, and fold into the custard. Spoon into the middle of the moulds. Cover and freeze for 2 hours. Serve immediately.

Iced Coffee and Nut Meringue

*This impressive frozen dessert may
seem difficult, but is actually very
easy to prepare.*

INGREDIENTS

Serves 8–10

100g/3½oz/scant 1 cup hazelnuts, toasted

275g/ 10oz/1⅓ cups caster (superfine)
    sugar

5 egg whites

pinch of cream of tartar

1 litre/1¾ pints/4 cups coffee ice cream

For the chocolate cream

500ml/17fl oz/2 cups whipping cream

30ml/2 tbsp coffee liqueur

275g/10oz plain (semisweet) chocolate,
    melted and cooled

white chocolate curls and fresh
    raspberries, to decorate

3 Leave the ice cream to soften
for 15–20 minutes and then
beat until smooth. Spread half the
ice cream over one meringue layer,
and continue layering ice cream
and meringue, finishing with the
last meringue layer on top. Press
down gently, then wrap and freeze
for at least 4 hours until firm.

4 To make the chocolate cream,
beat the whipping cream until
soft peaks form. Quickly fold in
the liqueur and melted chocolate.
Unwrap the frozen meringue and
spread the chocolate cream over
the top and sides, return to the
freezer, rewrapping when firm. To
serve, soften slightly before slicing.

1 Preheat the oven to 180°C/
350°F/Gas 4. Line three baking
sheets with baking parchment.
Using a plate as a guide, mark a
20cm/8in circle on each and
turn the paper over. Process the
hazelnuts in a food processor until
roughly chopped. Add a third of
the sugar and process again until
finely ground.

2 Whisk the egg whites until
frothy, add the cream of tartar
and whisk until they form soft
peaks. Spoon the mixture on to the
paper and spread within the
marked circles. Bake for 1 hour
until firm and dry. Leave to cool in
a turned off oven. Peel off the paper.

Iced Praline Torte

Make this elaborate torte several days ahead, decorate it and return it to the freezer until you are nearly ready to serve it. Allow the torte to stand at room temperature for an hour before serving, or leave it in the refrigerator overnight to soften.

INGREDIENTS

Serves 8

115g/4oz/1 cup almonds or hazelnuts
115g/4oz/8 tbsp caster (superfine) sugar
115g/4oz/⅔ cup raisins
90ml/6 tbsp rum or brandy
115g/4oz dark (bittersweet) chocolate, broken into squares
30ml/2 tbsp milk
450ml/¾ pint/1⅞ cups double (heavy) cream
30ml/2 tbsp strong black coffee
16 sponge finger biscuits (cookies)

To finish

150ml/¼ pint/⅔ cup double (heavy) cream
50g/2oz/½ cup flaked (sliced) almonds, toasted
15g/½oz dark (bittersweet) chocolate, melted

1 To make the praline, have ready an oiled cake tin (pan) or baking sheet. Put the nuts into a heavy pan with the sugar and heat gently until the sugar melts. Swirl the pan to coat the nuts in the hot sugar. Cook slowly until the nuts brown and the sugar caramelizes. Transfer the nuts quickly to the tin or sheet and leave them to cool completely. Break them up and grind them to a fine powder in a blender or food processor.

2 Soak the raisins in 45ml/3 tbsp of the rum or brandy for an hour (or better still overnight), so they soften and absorb the rum. Melt the chocolate with the milk in a bowl over a pan of hot, but not boiling water. Remove and allow to cool. Lightly grease a 1.2 litre/ 2 pint/5 cup loaf tin (pan) and line it with baking parchment.

3 Whisk the cream in a bowl until it holds soft peaks. Whisk in the cold chocolate. Then fold in the praline and the soaked raisins, with any liquid.

4 Mix the coffee and remaining rum or brandy in a shallow dish. Dip in the sponge fingers and arrange half in a layer over the base of the prepared loaf tin.

5 Cover with the chocolate mixture and add another layer of soaked sponge-fingers. Leave in the freezer overnight.

6 Whip the double cream for the topping. Dip the tin briefly into warm water to loosen it and turn the torte out on to a serving plate. Cover with the whipped cream, sprinkle the top with toasted flaked almonds and drizzle the melted chocolate over the top. Return the torte to the freezer until it is needed.

COOK'S TIP
~
Make the praline in advance and store it in an airtight jar until needed.

Chocolate Fudge Sundaes

They look impressive, taste fantastic and only take minutes to make.

INGREDIENTS

Serves 4

4 scoops each vanilla and coffee ice cream

2 small ripe bananas, sliced

whipped cream

toasted flaked (sliced) almonds

For the sauce

50g/2oz/¼ cup soft light brown sugar

120ml/4fl oz/½ cup golden (light corn) syrup

45ml/3 tbsp strong black coffee

5ml/1 tsp ground cinnamon

150g/5oz plain (semisweet) chocolate, chopped

85ml/3fl oz/⅓ cup whipping cream

45ml/3 tbsp coffee liqueur (optional)

1 To make the sauce, place the sugar, syrup, coffee and cinnamon in a heavy pan. Bring to the boil, then boil for about 5 minutes, stirring the mixture constantly.

2 Turn off the heat and stir in the chocolate. When melted and smooth, stir in the cream and liqueur, if using. Leave the sauce to cool slightly. If made ahead, reheat the sauce gently until just warm.

3 Fill four glasses with one scoop of vanilla and another of coffee ice cream.

4 Scatter the sliced bananas over the ice cream. Pour the warm fudge sauce over the bananas, then top each sundae with a generous swirl of whipped cream. Sprinkle toasted almonds over the cream and serve at once.

VARIATION

Ring the changes by choosing other flavours of ice cream such as strawberry, toffee or chocolate. In the summer, substitute raspberries or strawberries for the bananas, and scatter chopped roasted hazelnuts on top in place of the flaked almonds.

Frosted Raspberry and Coffee Terrine

A white chocolate and raspberry layer and contrasting smooth coffee layer, which is jewelled with whole raspberries, makes this attractive dessert doubly delicious.

INGREDIENTS

Serves 6–8

30ml/2 tbsp flavoured ground coffee
250ml/8fl oz/1 cup milk
4 eggs, separated
50g/2oz/¼ cup caster (superfine) sugar
30ml/2 tbsp cornflour (cornstarch)
150ml/¼ pint/⅔ cup double (heavy) cream
150g/5oz white chocolate, roughly chopped
115g/4oz/⅔ cup raspberries
shavings of white chocolate and cocoa
   powder, to decorate

1 Line a 1.5 litre/2½ pint/6¼ cup loaf tin (pan) with clear film (plastic wrap) and chill. Put the ground coffee in a jug (pitcher). Heat 100ml/3½ fl oz/scant ½ cup of the milk to near boiling point and pour over the coffee.

2 Blend the egg yolks, sugar and cornflour in a pan and whisk in the remaining milk and cream. Bring to the boil, stirring, until the mixture has thickened.

3 Divide the mixture between two bowls and add the white chocolate to one, stirring until melted. Strain the coffee through a sieve (strainer) into the other bowl and mix. Cool, stirring occasionally.

4 Whisk two egg whites until stiff and fold into the coffee custard. Spoon into the tin and freeze for 30 minutes. Whisk the remaining whites and fold into the the chocolate mixture with the fruit.

5 Spoon into the tin and level. Freeze for 4 hours. Turn out on to a flat serving plate and peel off the film. Cover with chocolate shavings and dust with cocoa powder before serving.

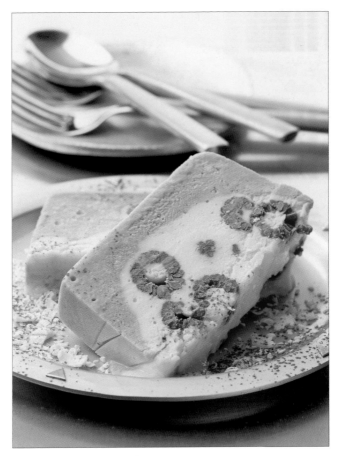

Café Glace

A perfect finish to a summer meal, this delicious dessert is not only very quick and easy to prepare in advance, it needs only minutes to finish and serve. This must be the ultimate no-fuss dessert that looks as good as it tastes.

INGREDIENTS

Serves 4–6

600ml/1 pint/2½ cups water

30-45ml/2-3 tbsp instant dried coffee

15ml/1 tbsp sugar

600ml/1 pint/2½ cups milk

ice cubes

vanilla ice cream

4-6 chocolate flakes

8-12 crisp ice cream biscuits (cookies),
    to serve

1 Bring 120ml/4fl oz/½ cup of the water to the boil, then transfer to a small bowl and stir in the coffee. Add the sugar and stir to dissolve. Chill for 2 hours. Mix together the milk and remaining water in a large jug (pitcher). Add the chilled coffee and stir well.

2 Pour the coffee mixture into long glasses until they are three quarters full. Add ice cubes and the ice cream to the top of each glass and decorate with the chocolate flakes. To serve, place the long glasses on plates with the ice cream biscuits to the side.

COOK'S TIP

You'll need to provide straws and long spoons for eating this dessert. Adjust the amount of coffee and sugar to suit your own taste.

Iced Mint and Chocolate Cooler

Many chocolate drinks are warm and comforting, but this one is really refreshing and ideal for a hot summer's day.

Serves 4

60ml/4 tbsp drinking chocolate
400ml/14fl oz/1⅔ cups chilled milk
150ml/¼ pint/⅔ cup natural (plain) yogurt
2.5ml/½ tsp peppermint extract
4 scoops chocolate ice cream
mint leaves and chocolate shapes,
    to decorate

1 Place the drinking chocolate in a small pan and stir in 120ml/4fl oz/½ cup of the milk. Heat gently, stirring continuously, until almost boiling, then remove from the heat and leave to cool.

COOK'S TIP

Use cocoa powder instead of drinking chocolate if you prefer, but add sugar to taste.

---

2 Pour the cool chocolate milk into a large bowl or jug (pitcher) and whisk in the remaining milk, the yogurt and peppermint extract.

3 Pour the mixture into tall glasses and top each one with a scoop of ice cream. Decorate with mint leaves and chocolate shapes and serve immediately.

Blushing Pina Colada

This is good with or without the rum. Don't be tempted to put roughly crushed ice into the blender; it will not be smooth and will ruin the blades. Make sure you crush it well first.

INGREDIENTS

Serves 2

1 banana, peeled and sliced
1 thick slice pineapple, peeled
3 measures/70ml/4½ tbsp
   pineapple juice
1 scoop strawberry ice cream or sorbet
1 measure/22.5ml/1½ tbsp
   coconut milk
30ml/2 tbsp grenadine
wedges of pineapple and steamed
   maraschino cherries, to decorate

1 Roughly chop the banana. Cut two small wedges from the pineapple for decoration and reserve. Cut up the remainder of the pineapple and place in the blender with the chopped banana. Place two large cocktail glasses in the refrigerator to chill.

VARIATION

For classic pina colada use vanilla ice cream and 1 measure white rum. For a passionate encounter, blend 2 scoops passion fruit sorbet and 15ml/1 tbsp coconut milk with a measure each of pineapple and apricot juice.

2 Add the pineapple juice to the blender and process until the mixture is a smooth paste.

3 Add the strawberry ice cream or sorbet, and the coconut milk plus a small scoop of finely crushed ice, and process until very smooth.

4 Take the chilled cocktail glasses and pour in the mixture, taking care not to splash the sides of the glass.

5 Pour the grenadine syrup slowly on top of the pina colada; it will filter through the drink in a dappled effect.

6 Decorate each glass with a wedge of pineapple and a stemmed cherry and serve immediately with drinking straws.

COOK'S TIP

To crush the ice, place ice cubes into a clean kitchen cloth or a heavy duty plastic bag. Wrap up the cloth or seal the plastic bag, making sure that the ice cubes are quite secure and cannot come out. Place on a firm surface and crush with a wooden rolling pin until the cubes are in tiny pieces.

LOW-FAT DESSERTS

All too often, desserts are the
downfall of anyone trying to
follow a low-fat diet. After a
sensible appetizer and a main
course of fish or chicken and fresh
vegetables, there's an almost
irresistible temptation to award
yourself a large portion of
pudding. The good news is that
you can. You don't have to give up
lovely, luscious desserts – provided
that you stick to the recipes in this
section of the book. Here you will
find low-fat versions of old
favourites such as Bread Pudding,
Fruit Crumble and Angel Cake,
together with new and exotic ideas
such as Papaya Baked with Ginger
and Tropical Fruit Pancakes.

◆ ◆ ◆

Facts About Fats

We all know we need to cut down on the amount of fat we eat – it would be difficult to live in the developed world and be unaware of that fact – but before making changes in our diet, it may be helpful to find out a bit more about the fats that we eat: some types are believed to be less harmful than others.

Fats are essential for the proper functioning of the body. However, we need the right kind of fat and the right amount. The average Western diet contains far too much of the "wrong" type of fat – saturated fat – which leads to obesity, heart problems and strokes. The daily recommended maximum amount of calories that should come from fat is between 30% and 35%. Unfortunately, too many Westerners obtain well over 40% of their calories from fat, often in the form of sweet treats and desserts and pastries.

Fats in our food are made up of different types of fatty acids and glycerol. Fats may be saturated or unsaturated, with unsaturated fat further categorized as mono-unsaturated or polyunsaturated.

Saturated fats

To appreciate the difference between saturated and unsaturated fatty acids, it is necessary to understand a little about their molecular structure. Put very simply, fatty acids are made up of chains of carbon atoms. A common analogy is to a string of beads. Unlike beads, however, which are linked only to each other, the carbon atoms are also able to link up – or bond – with one or more other atoms.

In a saturated fat, all these potential linkages have been made: the carbon atoms are linked to each other and each is further linked to two hydrogen atoms. No further linkages are possible, and the fat is therefore said to be saturated.

Saturated fat is mainly found in foods of animal origin: meat and dairy products such as butter, which is solid at room temperature. However, there are also some saturated fats of vegetable origin, notably coconut oil and also palm oil which is the main vegetable oil used in hard margarines.

Unsaturated fats

Unsaturated fatty acids differ from saturated fatty acids in their structure – not all of the linkages or bonds are complete. Some of the carbon atoms are linked to only one hydrogen atom instead of the usual two, and some of the carbon atoms may be joined to each other by a double bond. Depending on how many double bonds there are, the fatty acid is described as mono-unsaturated (one double bond) or polyunsaturated (many double bonds). The different molecular structures need not concern us here – suffice it to say that unsaturated fats are generally more healthy than saturated fats.

Mono-unsaturated fats

These are found in foods such as olive oil, rapeseed oil, some nuts, oily fish and avocados. Mono-unsaturated fats are believed to be neutral, neither raising or lowering blood cholesterol levels. This, plus the lower saturated fat intake as well as the higher fruit and vegetable intake, which are high in antioxidants, could explain the low incidence of heart disease in the Mediterranean.

Left: A bottle of sunflower oil (left) contains mostly polyunsaturated fats (68%), while olive oil is made of up mainly mono-unsaturated fats (70%).

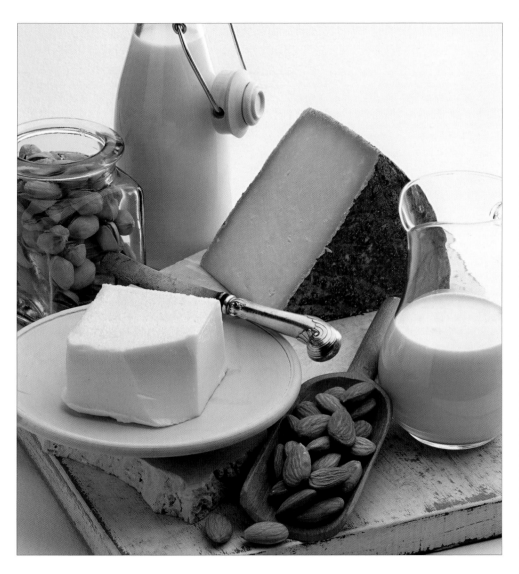

Above: Many common foods contain some fats. Cheese, butter, milk, cream and nuts – all of which are frequently used in desserts – should be strictly limited, unless fat free or very low fat.

Polyunsaturated fats

Polyunsaturated fat has two types. The first (omega 6) is found in vegetable and seed oils, such as sunflower or almond oil, and the second (omega 3) comes from oily fish, green leaves and some seed oils, including rapeseed or canola oil.

Polyunsaturated fats are liquid at room temperature. When vegetable oils are used in soft margarine, they have to be hardened artificially. During this process, the composition of some of the unsaturated fatty acids changes. In the body, these altered or "trans" fatty acids are treated like saturated fats, so, although an oil such as sunflower oil may be high in polyunsaturated fatty acids which lowers cholesterol levels, the same is not necessarily true of a margarine made from that oil.

Although unsaturated fats are healthier then saturated ones, most experts agree that what matters more is reducing our total intake of fat.

A Guide to Low-fat Dessert Ingredients

Watching your fat intake doesn't mean you have to forgo creamy puddings. A wide range of low-fat and virtually fat-free products are on sale in supermarkets, some of them backed by alluring advertising. Clever packaging can sometimes persuade the impulse buyer to make an unwise choice, however, so always check the statistical data printed on the label.

Low-fat spreads have become very popular. These have a high water content, so, while they are perfectly acceptable for spreading on bread and teabreads, they are not necessarily suitable for cooking. When baking puddings or making cakes, look for a spread with a fat content of around 40%. If substituting a reduced-fat spread for butter in a conventional recipe, be prepared to experiment a little, as the results will not necessarily be the same.

Try to avoid using saturated fats such as butter and hard margarine. Oils that are high in polyunsaturates, such as sunflower, corn or safflower, are the healthier option. Cakes and baked puddings made with oil are often excellent. If you must use margarine, choose a brand that is low in saturates and high in polyunsaturates.

Skimmed milk works well in batters and bakes, although you may get a better result using semi-skimmed (low-fat). Yogurt and fromage frais make excellent alternatives to cream, and when combined with honey, liqueur or other flavourings, they make delicious fillings or toppings for cheesecakes and fruit desserts. Many delectable desserts are based on soft cheeses. Cream cheese used to be the preferred option, but low-fat alternatives work just as well and are often easier to mix. If you're not familiar with it already, experiment with Quark, a virtually fat-free cheese that is very versatile.

Oils and low-fat spreads
Corn oil: A polyunsaturated oil, this has a slight flavour, so it is not as good as sunflower oil for baking. Fried foods should be avoided completely if you are trying to limit your fat intake, but if you must fry this is a good choice if used sparingly, as it can reach a high temperature without smoking.
Sunflower oil spread: High in polyunsaturates, this light, delicately flavoured oil is a good choice for puddings, as is safflower oil. Both can be used in cakes and bakes and are particularly good in muffins.
Sunflower light spread: Like reduced-fat butter, this contains about 38% fat, plus emulsified milk solids and water. The flavour is mild.
Olive oil reduced-fat spread: With a fat content of around 63%, this spread is richer than many low-fat spreads, but it has an excellent flavour. It can be used for cooking.

Left: A selection of cooking oils and low-fat spreads. Always check the packaging when buying low-fat spreads – if you are going to use them for cooking, they must have a fat content of about 40%.

Low-fat spread (rich buttermilk blend): This product is made with a high proportion of buttermilk, which is naturally low in fat. Low-fat spreads with a fat content of around 40% can be used for cooking: check the label.

Very low-fat spread: This contains about 20–30% fat and has a high water content; it is not suitable for cooking.

Low-fat milks

Buttermilk: This is the liquid that remains after cream has been churned into butter. Buttermilk produced in this way has a light flavour, similar to skimmed milk. Commercial buttermilk is made by adding a bacterial culture to skimmed milk. This gives it a slightly sharper taste than traditional buttermilk. It is very low in fat (0.5%).

Powdered skimmed milk: This is a useful, low-fat standby. You can make up as little or as much as you need. Always follow the instructions on the packet. Of itself, the powder has quite a high fat content, so if you use too much, the drink will not be the low-fat alternative you wanted.

Semi-skimmed milk: With a fat content of only 1.6%, this milk doesn't taste as rich as full cream (whole) milk. It is favoured by many people for everyday use for precisely this reason. Semi-skimmed milk can be used in all recipes calling for full cream milk.

Skimmed milk: This milk has had virtually all the fat removed, leaving 0.1%. It is ideal for those wishing to reduce their intake of fats.

Low-fat cream substitutes

Crème Fraîche: Look out for half-fat versions of this thick sour cream, where the normal fat content of 40% is reduced to 15%. Crème

Above: Almost all dairy products come in low-fat or reduced-fat versions.

fraîche has a mild, lemony taste and is ideal as a dessert topping.

Greek (US strained plain) yogurt: This thick, creamy yogurt is made from whole milk with a fat content of 9.1%. A low-fat version is also available.

Low-fat natural (plain) yogurt: With a fat content of only about 1%, low-fat natural yogurt is a gift to the dessert cook. Use it instead of cream in whips, as a topping or as an accompaniment. Drizzle a little honey on top if you like.

Low-fat cheeses

Cottage cheese: This low-fat cheese is also available in a half-fat form. Cottage cheese can be used instead of cream cheese in cheesecakes – press it through a sieve to remove the lumps.

Curd cheese: This low-fat soft cheese is generally made from skimmed or

semi-skimmed milk. A simple version can be made at home, using low-fat natural yogurt. Use curd cheese instead of cream cheese.

Edam: Hard cheeses are not widely used in desserts, except in some baked cheesecakes. If a recipe does call for grated hard cheese, however, this is a good choice as it is lower in fat than standards like Cheddar or Cheshire. If you prefer the taste of Cheddar, choose a half-fat version, where the fat will be reduced to 15%.

Fromage frais: This is a fresh, soft cheese with a very mild flavour. It is available in two grades: virtually fat-free (0.2% fat), and a more creamy variety (7.1% fat). Fromage frais is too soft to use on its own as a cheesecake filling, but it can be mixed with curd cheese.

Quark: Perfect for many different types of desserts and puddings, this soft white cheese is virtually fat-free. It is made from fermented skimmed milk.

Fat and Calorie Counts per 100g

The chart below lists both full-fat and low or reduced-fat typical dessert ingredients, so that you can see the savings at a glance if you choose the healthier option.

Ingredient	Fat (g)	Energy	Ingredient	Fat (g)	Energy
Oils and Spreads			Curd cheese 11.7		173 Kcals/723 kJ
Butter 81.7		737 Kcals/3031 kJ	Edam 25		333 Kcals/1382 kJ
Corn oil 99.9		899 Kcals/3696 kJ	Fromage frais (plain) 7.1		113 Kcals/469 kJ
Low-fat spread 40.5		390 Kcals/1605 kJ	Half-fat cheddar 15		261 Kcals/1091 kJ
Margarine 81.6		739 Kcals/3039 kJ	Quark 1.4		86 Kcals/360 kJ
Olive oil 99.9		899 Kcals/3696 kJ	Reduced-fat cottage cheese 1.4		78 Kcals/331 kJ
Olive oil reduced-fat spread 63		571 Kcals/2389 kJ	Very low-fat fromage frais 0.2		58 Kcals/247 kJ
Saffflower oil 99.9		899 Kcals/3696 kJ			
Sunflower oil 99.9		899 Kcals/3696 kJ	*Eggs*		
Sunflower light spread 38		357 Kcals/1494 kJ	about 2 (medium) 10.9		147 Kcals/615 kJ
Very low-fat spread 27		259 Kcals/1084 kJ	Egg white trace		36 Kcals/153 kJ
			Egg yolk 30.5		339 Kcals/1402 kJ
Milk					
Buttermilk 0.5		37 Kcals/157 kJ	*Baking Products and Preserves*		
Semi-skimmed (low-fat) milk 1.6		46 Kcals/195 kJ	Chocolate (milk) 30.3		520 Kcals/2214 kJ
Skimmed milk 0.1		33 Kcals/140 kJ	Chocolate, plain (semisweet) 29.2		510 Kcals/2157 kJ
Skimmed milk powder 0.6		348 Kcals/1482 kJ	Cocoa powder 21.7		359 Kcals/1496 kJ
Full cream (whole) milk 3.9		66 Kcals/275 kJ	Fatless sponge cake 6.1		294 Kcals/1230 kJ
			Honey 0		288 Kcals/1229 kJ
Cream/Cream Substitutes			Sugar (white) 0		394 Kcals/1648 kJ
Crème fraîche 40		380 Kcals/1582 kJ			
Double (heavy) cream 48		449 Kcals/1849 kJ	*Fruit and Nuts*		
Greek (US strained plain) yogurt 9.1		115 Kcals/477 kJ	Almonds 55.8		612 Kcals/2534 kJ
Half-fat crème fraîche 15		166 Kcals/692 kJ	Apples (eating) 0.1		47 Kcals/199 kJ
Low-fat plain (natural) yogurt 0.8		56 Kcals/236 kJ	Bananas 0.3		95 Kcals/403 kJ
Reduced-fat Greek yogurt 5.0		80 Kcals/335 kJ	Brazil nuts 68.2		682 Kcals/2813 kJ
Single (light) cream 19.1		198 Kcals/817 kJ	Dried mixed fruit 0.4		268 Kcals/1114 kJ
Whipping cream 39.3		373 Kcals/1539 kJ	Hazelnuts 63.5		650 Kcals/2685 kJ
			Oranges 0.1		37 Kcals/158 kJ
Cheeses			Peaches 0.1		33 Kcals/142 kJ
Cheddar 34.4		412 Kcals/1708 kJ	Peanut butter (smooth) 53.7		623 Kcals/2581 kJ
Cottage cheese (plain) 3.9		98 Kcals/413 kJ	Pears 0.1		40 Kcals/169 kJ
Cream cheese 47.7		439 Kcals/1807 kJ	Pine nuts 68.6		688 Kcals/2840 kJ

Information from *The Composition of Foods* (5th edition 1991) is reproduced with the permission of the Controller of Her Majesty's Stationery Office.

Making Desserts the Fat-free Way

To many people, dessert means lashings of cream, butter and chocolate. Nowadays, however, it is perfectly possible for a host to hoodwink guests into thinking they are having a luscious, creamy sweet, when all the while, the constituents are fat-free or low in fat.

Many ingredients are available in full-fat and reduced-fat or very low-fat forms. In every supermarket you will find a huge array of low-fat products, such as milk, cream, yogurt, hard and soft cheeses and fromage frais, reduced-fat sweet or chocolate biscuits (cookies); low-fat, half-fat or very low-fat spreads; as well as reduced-fat ready-made desserts. Some ingredients work better than others in cooking, but often a simple substitution will spell success. In a crumb crust, for instance, reduced-fat biscuits work just as well as digestives (graham crackers).

Some of the most delicious desserts are based upon fruit. Serve fresh or dried fruit in a salad or compôte, and there's no need to introduce fats.

If you are making a baked or steamed pudding, or pan-frying fruit such as bananas or pineapple rings, you can get away with using the merest slick of polyunsaturated oil, especially if you use a non-stick pan. Alternatively, use spray oil: a one-second spray of sunflower oil (about 1ml) has 4.6Kcals/18.8kJ and just over half the fat of

Right: This sumptuous pineapple and strawberry mallow meringue looks and tastes delicious even though it is very low in fat.

conventional cooking oil. Spray oil is particularly useful for lightly coating frying pans when making pancakes.

When seeking inspiration for the dessert course for that special dinner party, remember that there are plenty of ingredients that naturally contain very little fat. Rice, flour, rolled oats, bread and cornflakes can all be used to make puddings and toppings, and there's no fat in wine, sherry, sugar or honey, although you may wish to restrict these for other reasons! Meringues are among the most popular puddings – topped with fresh fruit and yogurt or fromage frais, they are irresistible to eat and look great.

Spices and extracts add plenty of extra flavour and colour to desserts, while decorations like rose petals, mint leaves or curls of pared citrus rind improve the appearance and stimulate the appetite.

Low-fat spreads in cooking
Some low-fat spreads can safely be substituted for butter or margarine in baked puddings, but others are only suitable for spreading. The limiting factor is the amount of water in the product. Very low-fat spreads achieve levels of fat of around 20% by virtue of their high water content and cannot be melted successfully. Spreads with a fat content of around 40% are suitable for spreading and for some

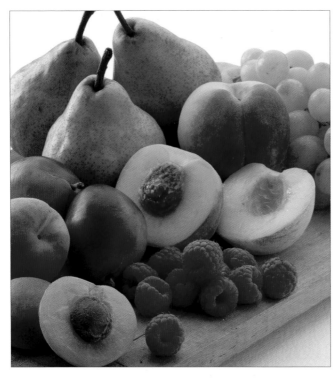

Left: Fresh fruit can be used to make simply superb sweet dishes, and there's no need at all to add any fat.

cooking methods. The information on the label will indicate its suitability. When using low-fat spreads for cooking, the fat may behave slightly differently to full-fat products such as butter or margarine. Be prepared to experiment a little – the results may surprise you. Some recipes actually work better with low-fat ingredients. For example, choux pastry made with half- or low-fat spread is often slightly crisper and lighter in texture than traditional choux pastry. A cheesecake biscuit base made with melted half- or low-fat spread combined with crumbs from reduced-fat biscuits (cookies) may be slightly softer in texture and less crisp than one made using melted butter, but it will still be very good.

Quick Tips for Fat-Free Cooking

• Use heavy or non-stick pans – that way you won't need as much fat for cooking.

• When baking low-fat or reduced-fat cakes, it is advisable to use good quality cookware that doesn't need greasing before use, or line the pan (tin) with non-stick paper and only grease very lightly before filling.

• Look out for non-stick coated fabric sheeting. This reusable material will not stick and is amazingly versatile. It can be cut to size and used to line cake tins, baking sheets or frying pans. Heat resistant to 290°C/550°F and microwave safe, it will last for up to 5 years.

• Bake fruit in a loosely sealed parcel of baking parchment, moistening it with wine, fruit juice or liqueur instead of butter before sealing the parcel.

• When grilling (broiling) fruit, the naturally high moisture content means that it is often unnecessary to add fat. If the fruit looks a bit dry, brush lightly and sparingly with a polyunsaturated oil such as sunflower or corn oil.

• Fruit cooked in the microwave seldom needs additional fat; add spices for extra colour and flavour.

• Poach fresh or dried fruit in natural juice or syrup – there's no need to add any fat.

• Become an expert at cooking with filo pastry. Of itself, filo is extremely low in fat, and if you brush the sheets sparingly with melted low-fat spread, it can be used to make delicious puddings that will not significantly damage a low-fat diet and will replace other high-fat pastries.

• Avoid cooking with chocolate, which is high in fat. If you can't bear to abandon your favourite flavour, use reduced-fat cocoa powder instead.

• Get to know the full range of low- or reduced-fat products, including yogurt, crème fraîche and fromage frais. Low-fat yogurt can be used for making "creamy" sauces, but needs to be treated with a little more care as it can curdle when heated. Stabilize it by stirring in a little cornflour (cornstarch), mixed to a paste with water or skimmed milk.

• Use skimmed milk rather than full cream (whole) milk in rice pudding, semolina pudding and batters.

Above: Many delicious desserts can be made in moments if you have a well-stocked store cupboard.

When heating low-fat spreads, never let them get too hot. Always use a heavy pan over a low heat to avoid the product burning, spitting or spoiling, and stir all the time. Half-fat or low-fat spreads cannot be used for shallow- or deep-frying, traditional pastry making, rich fruit cakes, shortbread and preserves such as lemon curd.

Baked goods, such as cakes, pies and pastries, made using reduced- or low-fat spreads will not keep as well as cakes and teabreads made using butter; this is due to the lower fat content.

Fruit purées
One way of reducing the fat content of a recipe is to replace all or part of the fat with a fruit purée. This is particularly successful with breads, probably because the amount of fat is usually relatively small, and it also works well with some biscuits and bars, such as brownies.

To make a dried fruit purée for this purpose, roughly chop 115g/4oz/²/₃ cup ready-to-eat dried fruit and put it in a blender or food processor. Add 75ml/5 tbsp water and blend to a fairly smooth purée. Scrape into a bowl, cover and keep in the refrigerator for up to 3 days. When baking, simply substitute the same weight of this dried fruit purée for all or just some of the fat in the recipe. You may need to experiment a little to find the proportions that work best. If preferred, you can purée a single variety of dried fruit, such as prunes, apricots, peaches or apples, or substitute mashed fresh fruit, such as ripe bananas or lightly cooked apples. If you choose to purée fresh fruit, omit the water.

Useful Techniques

Cooked or prepared in the right way, delicious desserts like meringues, fruit-filled pancakes and jellies are actually very low in fat. Follow the simple techniques on these pages for certain success.

WHISKING EGG WHITES

1 Place the egg whites in a completely clean, grease-free bowl. If even a speck of egg yolk is present, you will not be able to beat the whites successfully. Use one half of the shell to remove any traces of yolk.

2 Use a balloon whisk in a wide bowl for the greatest volume (egg whites can increase their volume by about eight times), but an electric hand whisk will also do an efficient job. Purists swear that eggs whisked in a copper bowl give the greatest volume.

3 Whisk the whites until they are firm enough to hold either soft or stiff peaks when you lift the whisk – see individual recipes. For stiffly whisked whites, you should be able to hold the bowl upside down without their sliding out, but this is a risky test!

MAKING PANCAKES

1 Apply a light, even coat of spray oil to a 20cm/8in pancake pan, then heat it gently. Pour in about 45ml/3 tbsp of the batter, then quickly tilt the pan so that the batter spreads to cover the bottom thinly and evenly.

2 Cook the pancake for 30–45 seconds, until it has set. Carefully lift the edge with a palette knife; the base of the pancake should have browned lightly. Shake the pan to loosen the pancake, then turn it over with the palette knife or flip it with a quick twist of your wrist.

3 Cook the other side of the pancake for about 30 seconds, then slide the pancake out on to a plate. Make more pancakes in the same way, then spread them with your chosen filling before rolling them or folding them neatly into triangles.

DISSOLVING GELATINE

1 Powdered gelatine is very easy to use. For every 15ml/1 tbsp of gelatine in the recipe, place 45ml/3 tbsp of very hot water in a small bowl.

2 Holding the bowl steady, sprinkle the powdered gelatine lightly and evenly over the hot liquid. Always add the gelatine to the liquid; never the other way round.

3 Stir until the gelatine has dissolved completely and the liquid is clear, with no visible crystals. You may need to stand the bowl in a pan of hot water.

UNMOULDING A JELLY

1 Have ready a serving plate that has been rinsed with cold water. Shake it but leave it damp – this will make it easier to centre the jelly. Run the tip of a knife around the moulded mixture, to loosen it.

2 Dip the mould briefly into a bowl of hot water. One or two seconds is usually enough – if you leave it for too long, the mixture will start to melt around the edges. If the jelly is stuck, dip again. Several short dips are better than one long one.

3 Quickly invert the plate over the mould. Holding mould and plate together, turn both over. Shake firmly to dislodge the jelly; as soon as you feel it drop, lift off the mould. If it does not lift off, give it another shake.

QUICK TIPS FOR GELATINE

Some recipes require gelatine to be dissolved in a cold liquid, such as apple or orange juice. In this case, pour the liquid into a small heat-proof bowl and sprinkle the gelatine on top. Leave until the liquid has absorbed the gelatine and looks spongy, then place the bowl over very hot water until the gelatine has dissolved completely. You could either use a *bain marie* or simply a pan full of boiling water.

Techniques for Tasty Toppings

Although whipped cream is taboo on a low-fat diet, there are some excellent alternatives. Whipped "cream" can be made from skimmed milk powder or yogurt, with very good results. Neither will hold the shape indefinitely, however, so use them as soon as possible after making. Strained yogurt and curd cheese are simple to make at home, and tend to be lower in fat than commercial varieties. Serve strained yogurt with puddings instead of cream, sweetening it with a little honey, if liked. Curd cheese can be used instead of sour cream, cream cheese or butter. Apricot glaze is very useful for brushing over a large variety of fresh fruit toppings. It gives the fruit a lovely shiny appearance.

LOW-FAT WHIPPED CREAM

INGREDIENTS

Makes 150ml/$\frac{1}{4}$ pint/$\frac{2}{3}$ cup
2.5ml/$\frac{1}{2}$ tsp powdered gelatine
75ml/5 tbsp water
50g/2oz/$\frac{1}{4}$ cup skimmed milk powder
15ml/1 tbsp caster (superfine) sugar
15ml/1 tbsp lemon juice

1 Sprinkle the powdered gelatine over 15ml/1 tbsp cold water in a small bowl and leave to "sponge" for 5 minutes. Place the bowl over a pan of hot water and stir until dissolved. Leave to cool.

2 Whisk the milk powder, sugar, lemon juice and remaining water until frothy. Add the dissolved gelatine and whisk. Chill for 30 minutes.

3 Using an electric hand whisk, whisk the chilled mixture again until it holds its shape and is very thick and frothy. Serve within 30 minutes of making.

YOGURT PIPING CREAM

INGREDIENTS

Makes 450ml/$\frac{3}{4}$ pint/scant 2 cups
10ml/2 tsp powdered gelatine
45ml/3 tbsp water
300ml/$\frac{1}{2}$ pint/1$\frac{1}{4}$ cups strained yogurt
15ml/1 tbsp fructose
2.5ml/$\frac{1}{2}$ tsp vanilla extract
1 egg white

1 Sprinkle the gelatine over the water in a small bowl and leave to "sponge" for 5 minutes. Place the bowl over a pan of hot water and stir until dissolved. Leave to cool.

2 Mix together the yogurt, fructose and vanilla extract. Stir in the gelatine. Chill in the refrigerator for 30 minutes, or until just beginning to set around the edges.

3 Whisk the egg white until stiff, then carefully fold it into the yogurt mixture. Spoon into a piping (pastry) bag fitted with a nozzle and use immediately.

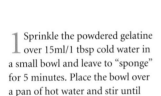

STRAINED YOGURT AND SIMPLE CURD CHEESE

INGREDIENTS

Makes 300ml/½ pint/1¼ cups strained yogurt or 115g/4oz/½ cup curd cheese
600ml/1 pint/2½ cups low-fat yogurt

1 For strained yogurt, line a nylon or stainless steel sieve (strainer) with a double layer of muslin (cheesecloth). Put it over a bowl and carefully pour in the low-fat yogurt.

2 Leave to drain in the refrigerator for 3 hours, by which time it will have separated into thick strained yogurt and watery whey. Discard the whey.

3 For curd cheese, leave to drain in the refrigerator for 8 hours or overnight. Spoon the curd cheese into a serving bowl, cover and keep chilled.

APRICOT GLAZE

1 Place a few spoonfuls of apricot jam in a small pan and add a squeeze of lemon juice. Heat the jam, stirring until it has melted and is runny.

2 Set a wire sieve over a heat-proof bowl. Pour the jam into the sieve, then stir it with a wooden spoon to help it go through the mesh.

3 Return the strained jam to the pan. Keep the glaze warm until needed, then brush it generously over the fresh fruit until evenly coated.

Decorating with Citrus Rind Shreds

Shredded citrus rind makes a very effective decoration for a low-fat dessert. Thinly pare the rind from an orange, lemon or lime, using a swivel vegetable peeler. Take care not to remove any of the white pith, which has a bitter flavour. Cut the strips of

pared rind into very fine shreds with a sharp knife. Boil the shreds for a couple of minutes in water or sugar syrup to soften them.

Right: Shredded citrus rind adds extra colour and appeal to this simple jelly.

HOT LOW-FAT PUDDINGS & DESSERTS

❖ ✦ ❖

Spiced Pear and Blueberry Parcels

This combination makes a delicious dessert for a summer's evening and can be cooked on a barbecue or in the oven.

INGREDIENTS

Serves 4

4 firm, ripe pears
30ml/2 tbsp lemon juice
15ml/1 tbsp low-fat spread, melted
150g/5oz/1¼ cups blueberries
60ml/4 tbsp light muscovado
 (brown) sugar
ground black pepper

NUTRITIONAL NOTES

Per portion:

Energy	146Kcals/614kJ
Fat, total	1.8g
Saturated fat	0.37g
Cholesterol	0.2mg
Fibre	4g

1 Prepare the barbecue or preheat the oven to 200ºC/400ºF/Gas 6. Peel the pears thinly. Cut in half lengthways. Scoop out the core from each half. Brush the pears with lemon juice, to stop them browning. Cut four squares of double-thickness foil, each large enough to wrap a pear.

2 Brush the foil squares with melted spread. Place two pear halves on each, cut side upwards. Gather the foil around them, to hold them level.

3 Mix the blueberries and sugar together and spoon them on top of the pears. Sprinkle with black pepper. Close the foil and barbecue for 20–25 minutes or bake in a hot oven.

Fruit and Spice Bread Pudding

2 Mix together the sultanas, apricots, sugar and spice and sprinkle half the fruit mixture over the bread in the dish.

3 Top with the remaining bread triangles and then the fruit.

4 Beat the eggs, milk and lemon rind together and pour over the bread. Set aside for about 30 minutes, to allow the bread to absorb some of the liquid. Bake for 45–60 minutes, until lightly set and golden brown. Serve hot or cold.

An easy-to-make fruity dessert with a hint of spice, this is delicious served either hot or cold.

INGREDIENTS

Serves 4

6 slices wholemeal (whole-wheat) bread
50g/2oz apricot or strawberry jam
low-fat spread, for greasing
50g/2oz/1/3 cup sultanas (golden raisins)
50g/2oz/1/4 cup ready-to-eat dried
   apricots, chopped
50g/2oz/1/3 cup soft light brown sugar
5ml/1 tsp ground mixed (apple pie) spice
2 eggs
600ml/1 pint/2 1/2 cups skimmed milk
finely grated rind of 1 lemon

1 Preheat the oven to 160°C/ 325°F/Gas 3. Remove and discard the crusts from the bread. Spread the bread slices with jam and cut into small triangles. Place half the bread triangles in a lightly greased ovenproof dish.

NUTRITIONAL NOTES

Per portion:

Energy	305Kcals/1293kJ
Fat, total	4.51g
Saturated fat	1.27g
Cholesterol	99.3mg
Fibre	3.75g

Fruity Bread Pudding

2 Remove the pan from the heat and stir in the bread cubes, spice and banana. Spoon the mixture into a shallow 1.2 litre/ 2 pint/5 cup ovenproof dish and pour over the milk.

3 Sprinkle with demerara sugar and bake for 25–30 minutes, until firm and golden brown. Serve hot or cold, with natural yogurt if you like.

A delicious family favourite from grandmother's kitchen, with a lighter, healthier touch for today.

INGREDIENTS

Serves 4

75g/3oz/1/2 cup mixed dried fruit
150ml/1/4 pint/2/3 cup unsweetened
    apple juice
115g/4oz/3–4 slices day-old brown or
    white bread, cubed
5ml/1 tsp mixed (apple pie) spice
1 large banana, sliced
150ml/1/4 pint/2/3 cup skimmed milk
15ml/1 tbsp demerara (raw) sugar
low-fat natural (plain) yogurt, to serve
    (optional)

1 Preheat the oven to 200ºC/ 400ºF/Gas 6. In a small pan, bring the dried fruit and apple juice to the boil.

Baked Apples with Red Wine

Special-occasion baked apples include a delicious filling of sultanas soaked in spiced red wine.

Serves 6

65g/2¹/2 oz/scant ¹/2 cup sultanas
   (golden raisins)
350ml/12fl oz/1¹/2 cups red wine
pinch of grated nutmeg
pinch of ground cinnamon
50g/2oz/¹/4 cup granulated (white) sugar
pinch of grated lemon rind
35ml/7 tsp low-fat spread
6 baking apples of even size

1 Put the sultanas in a small bowl and pour over the wine. Stir in the grated nutmeg, ground cinnamon, sugar and lemon rind. Cover and leave to stand for approximately 1 hour.

2 Preheat the oven to 190ºC/ 375ºF/Gas 5. Use a little of the low-fat spread to grease a baking dish. Core the apples, without cutting right through to the bottom.

3 Divide the sultana mixture among the apples. Spoon in a little extra spiced wine. Arrange the apples in the prepared baking dish.

4 Pour the remaining wine around the apples. Top the filling in each apple with 5ml/1 tsp of the low-fat remaining spread. Bake for 40–50 minutes, or until the apples are soft but not mushy. Serve hot or at room temperature.

NUTRITIONAL NOTES

Per portion:

Energy	187Kcals/784kJ
Fat, total	2.7g
Saturated fat	0.61g
Cholesterol	0.4mg
Fibre	2.6g

Baked Apples with Apricot Nut Filling

Omit the low-fat spread if you want to reduce the fat content further.

Serves 6

75g/3oz/^{1}/$_2$ cup chopped dried apricots
20g/^{3}/$_4$ oz/3 tbsp chopped walnuts
5ml/1 tsp grated lemon rind
1.5ml/^{1}/$_4$ tsp ground cinnamon
115g/4oz/^{2}/$_3$ cup soft light brown sugar
30ml/2 tbsp low-fat spread
6 Bramley or other cooking apples

3 Stand the apples in a baking dish just large enough to hold them comfortably side by side.

4 Melt the remaining spread and brush it over the apples. Bake for 40–45 minutes until tender. Serve hot.

1 Preheat the oven to 190ºC/ 375ºF/Gas 5. In a bowl, combine the apricots, walnuts, lemon rind and cinnamon. Add the sugar and rub in two-thirds of the low-fat spread until combined.

2 Core the apples, without cutting all the way through to the base. Peel the top third of each apple. With a small knife, widen the top of each cavity by about 4cm/1½in for the filling. Spoon the filling into the apples.

NUTRITIONAL NOTES
Per portion:

Energy	263Kcals/1095kJ
Fat, total	4.9g
Saturated fat	0.89g
Cholesterol	0.3mg
Fibre	4.3g

Baked Apples in Honey and Lemon

A classic combination of flavours in a traditional family pudding.

INGREDIENTS

Serves 4

4 Bramley or other cooking apples
15ml/1 tbsp clear honey
grated rind and juice of 1 lemon
15ml/1 tbsp low-fat spread
skimmed milk custard, to serve (optional)

NUTRITIONAL NOTES

Per portion:

Energy	78Kcals/326kJ
Fat, total	1.7g
Saturated fat	0.37g
Cholesterol	0.2mg
Fibre	2.4g

1 Preheat the oven to 180ºC/ 350ºF/Gas 4. Remove the cores from the apples, taking care not to go right through the bottoms of the apples.

2 With a cannelle knife or a narrow bladed, sharp knife, cut lines through the apple skin at intervals. Stand the apples in an ovenproof dish.

3 Mix together the honey, lemon rind, juice and low-fat spread.

4 Spoon the mixture into the apples and cover the dish with foil or a lid. Bake for 40–45 minutes, or until the apples are tender. Serve with skimmed milk custard, if you wish.

Date, Chocolate and Walnut Pudding

2 Separate the whole egg and place the yolk in a heatproof bowl. Add vanilla extract and sugar. Place over a pan of hot water and whisk to thicken.

3 Sift the flour and cocoa into the mixture and fold in. Stir in the milk. Whisk the egg whites and fold in.

Proper puddings are not totally taboo when you're reducing your fat intake – this one is just within the rules!

1 Preheat the oven to 180°C/ 350°F/Gas 4. Grease a 1.2 litre/ 2 pint/5 cup heatproof bowl and place a small circle of baking parchment in the base. Spoon in the walnuts and dates.

4 Spoon the mixture into the lined bowl and bake for 40–45 minutes, until the pudding has risen well and is firm to the touch. Run a knife around the pudding then turn it out and serve hot.

INGREDIENTS

Serves 4

low-fat spread, for greasing

15g/1/2 oz/1 tbsp chopped walnuts

25g/1oz/2 tbsp chopped dates

1 egg plus 1 egg white

5ml/1 tsp pure vanilla extract

30ml/2 tbsp golden caster (superfine) sugar

20g/3/4 oz/3 tbsp wholemeal (whole-wheat) flour

15ml/1 tbsp cocoa powder

30ml/2 tbsp skimmed milk

NUTRITIONAL NOTES

Per portion:

Energy	126Kcals/530kJ
Fat, total	4.9g
Saturated fat	1.15g
Cholesterol	48.3mg
Fibre	1.3g

Sultana and Couscous Puddings

Most couscous is the pre-cooked variety, which hardly needs cooking, but check the pack instructions first.

INGREDIENTS

Serves 4

50g/2oz/1/3 cup sultanas (golden raisins)

475ml/16fl oz/2 cups unsweetened
    apple juice

90g/31/2 oz/scant 1 cup couscous

2.5ml/1/2 tsp mixed (apple pie) spice

skimmed milk custard, to serve (optional)

NUTRITIONAL NOTES

Per portion:

Energy	132Kcals/557kJ
Fat, total	0.4g
Saturated fat	0.09g
Cholesterol	0mg
Fibre	0.3g

1 Lightly grease four 250ml/ 8fl oz/1 cup heatproof bowls. Place the sultanas and apple juice in a pan.

2 Bring the apple juice to the boil, then lower the heat and simmer the mixture gently for 2–3 minutes, to plump up the fruit. Place about half the fruit in the bottom of the bowls.

3 Add the couscous and mixed spice to the pan and bring the liquid back to the boil, stirring. Cover and leave over a low heat for 8–10 minutes, or until all the liquid has been absorbed.

4 Spoon the couscous into the bowls, spread it level, then cover the bowls tightly with foil. Place the bowls in a steamer over boiling water, cover and steam for about 30 minutes. Run a knife around the edges, turn the puddings out carefully and serve hot, with skimmed milk custard, if you like.

COOK'S TIP
~
These puddings can also be cooked in the microwave. Use microwaveproof bowls or teacups, cover, and cook on High for 8–10 minutes.

Blackberry Batter Pudding

Batter puddings are easy to make – this one has a juicy compôte under a crunchy batter blanket.

INGREDIENTS

Serves 8

800g/1³/4 lb/7 cups blackberries

250g/9oz/generous 1 cup granulated
  (white) sugar

45ml/3 tbsp plain (all-purpose) flour

grated rind of 1 lemon

1.5ml/¹/4 tsp grated nutmeg

For the topping

225g/8oz/2 cups plain (all-purpose) flour

225g/8oz/1 cup granulated (white) sugar

15ml/1 tbsp baking powder

pinch of salt

250ml/8fl oz/1 cup skimmed milk

75g/3oz/6 tbsp low-fat spread, melted

1 Preheat the oven to 180ºC/350ºF/Gas 4. In a large mixing bowl, combine the blackberries with 225g/8oz/1 cup of the sugar. Add the flour and lemon rind. Using a large spoon, stir gently to blend. Transfer to a 2 litre/3¹/2 pint/8 cup baking dish.

2 Make the topping. Sift the flour, sugar, baking powder and salt into a large bowl. Set aside. In a jug, combine the milk and melted low-fat spread.

3 Gradually stir the milk mixture into the dry ingredients and stir until the batter is just smooth.

4 Spoon the batter over the berries. Mix the remaining sugar with the nutmeg, then sprinkle the mixture over the pudding. Bake for about 50 minutes, until the topping is set. Serve hot.

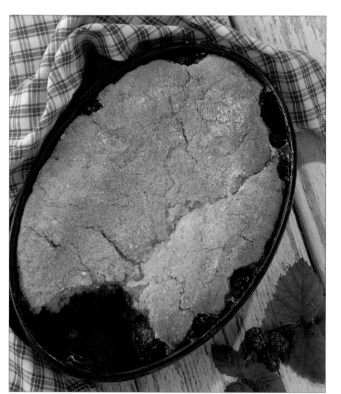

NUTRITIONAL NOTES

Per portion:

Energy	427Kcals/1812kJ
Fat, total	4.5g
Saturated fat	1g
Cholesterol	1.2mg
Fibre	4.1g

Peach Cobbler

All the flavour of the traditional and popular pudding, with less fat than in a conventional cobbler.

INGREDIENTS

Serves 6

1.5kg/3–3¹/₂lb/5 cups peaches, peeled
   and sliced
40g/1¹/₂oz/3 tbsp sugar
30ml/2 tbsp peach brandy
15ml/1 tbsp fresh lemon juice
15ml/1 tbsp cornflour (cornstarch)

For the topping

115g/4oz/1 cup plain (all-purpose) flour
7.5ml/1¹/₂ tsp baking powder
1.5ml/¹/₄ tsp salt
20g/³/₄oz/¹/₄ cup ground almonds
65g/2¹/₂oz sugar
30ml/2 tbsp low-fat spread
75ml/5 tbsp skimmed milk
1.5ml/¹/₄ tsp almond extract
ice cream, to serve (optional)

1 Preheat the oven to 220ºC/
425ºF/Gas 7. In a bowl, toss the peaches with the sugar, peach brandy, lemon juice and cornflour. Spoon the peach mixture into a 2 litre/3¹/₂ pint/8 cup baking dish.

2 Using a fine sieve (strainer), sift the flour, baking powder and salt into a mixing bowl. Add the ground almonds and 50g/2oz of the sugar. With 2 knives, cut in the spread until the mixture resembles coarse crumbs.

3 Add the milk and almond extract. Stir until the mixture is combined.

4 Drop the almond mixture on to the peaches and sprinkle with the sugar.

5 Bake for 30–35 minutes until piping hot. The cobbler topping should be lightly browned. Serve hot, with ice cream, if you like.

NUTRITIONAL NOTES	
Per portion:	
Energy	393Kcals/1661kJ
Fat, total	4.4g
Saturated fat	0.68g
Cholesterol	0.6mg
Fibre	4g

Apple Brown Betty

A traditional favourite, this tasty dessert is good served with low-fat yogurt or fromage frais.

Serves 6

50g/2oz/1 cup fresh white breadcrumbs
low-fat spread, for greasing
175g/6oz/1 cup light brown sugar
2.5ml/¹/2 tsp ground cinnamon
1.5ml/¹/4 tsp ground cloves
1.5ml/¹/4 tsp grated nutmeg
900g/2lb eating apples
juice of 1 lemon
30ml/2 tbsp low-fat spread
20g/³/4oz/3 tbsp finely chopped walnuts

1 Preheat the grill (broiler). Spread the breadcrumbs on a baking sheet and toast under the grill until golden, stirring so that they colour evenly. Set aside.

2 Preheat the oven to 190°C/ 375°F/Gas 5. Grease a 2 litre/ 3¹/2 pint/8 cup baking dish. Mix the sugar with the cinnamon, cloves and nutmeg in a mixing bowl.

3 Peel, core and slice the apples. Place in a bowl. Toss the slices with the lemon juice to prevent them from turning brown.

4 Sprinkle about 45ml/3 tbsp of the breadcrumbs over the bottom of the prepared dish. Cover with one-third of the apples and sprinkle one-third of the sugar-spice mixture on top.

5 Add another layer of bread-crumbs and dot with one-quarter of the spread. Repeat the layers two more times, ending with a layer of breadcrumbs. Sprinkle with the nuts, and dot with the remaining spread.

6 Bake for 35–40 minutes, until the apples are tender and the top is golden brown. Serve warm.

NUTRITIONAL NOTES	
Per portion:	
Energy	257Kcals/1073kJ
Fat, total	4.7g
Saturated fat	0.73g
Cholesterol	0.3mg
Fibre	2.9g

Blueberry Buckle

This fruity dessert is an American speciality and can be served with low-fat Greek yogurt, if you like.

INGREDIENTS

Serves 8

low-fat spread, for greasing
225g/8oz/2 cups plain (all-purpose) flour
10ml/2 tsp baking powder
2.5ml/1/2 tsp salt
30ml/2 tbsp low-fat spread
175g/6oz/3/4 cup granulated (white) sugar
1 egg
2.5ml/1/2 tsp pure vanilla extract
175ml/6fl oz/3/4 cup skimmed milk
450g/1lb/4 cups fresh blueberries
low-fat Greek (US strained plain) yogurt,
    to serve (optional)

For the topping

115g/4oz/2/3 cup soft light brown sugar
50g/2oz/1/2 cup plain (all-purpose) flour
2.5ml/1/2 tsp salt
2.5ml/1/2 tsp ground allspice
45ml/3 tbsp low-fat spread
10ml/2 tsp skimmed milk
5ml/1 tsp pure vanilla extract

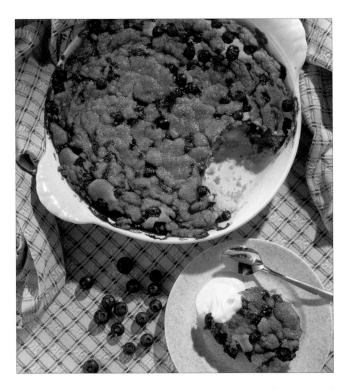

1 Preheat the oven to 190ºC/ 375ºF/Gas 5. Grease a 23cm/ 9in round gratin dish or shallow baking dish. Sift the flour, baking powder and salt into a bowl. Set aside.

2 Cream the spread and sugar. Beat in the egg and vanilla. Add the flour mix and milk alternately, beginning and ending with flour.

3 Pour the mixture into the prepared dish and sprinkle over the blueberries.

4 Make the topping. Mix the brown sugar, flour, salt and allspice in a bowl. Rub in the spread until the mixture resembles coarse crumbs.

NUTRITIONAL NOTES	
Per portion:	
Energy	338Kcals/1432kJ
Fat, total	4.9g
Saturated fat	1.14g
Cholesterol	25.1mg
Fibre	2.1g

5 Mix the milk and vanilla extract together. Drizzle over the flour mixture and mix with a fork. Sprinkle the topping over the blueberries. Bake for 45 minutes, or until an inserted skewer comes out clean. Serve warm, with low-fat Greek yogurt, if you like.

Apple and Walnut Crumble

Another American classic, combining delicious apples with crunchy walnuts, for a simple, but tasty, dessert.

INGREDIENTS

Serves 6

low-fat spread, for greasing
900g/2lb eating apples, peeled and sliced
grated rind of $1/2$ lemon
15ml/1 tbsp fresh lemon juice
115g/4oz/$1/2$ cup light brown sugar
75g/3oz/$3/4$ cup plain (all-purpose) flour
1.5ml/$1/4$ tsp salt
1.5ml/$1/4$ tsp grated nutmeg
2.5ml/$1/2$ tsp ground cardamom
2.5ml/$1/2$ tsp ground cinnamon
30ml/2 tbsp low-fat spread
20g/$3/4$oz/3 tbsp walnut pieces, chopped

1 Preheat the oven to 180ºC/ 350ºF/Gas 4. Grease a 23cm/ 9in shallow baking dish. Toss the apples with the lemon rind and juice. Arrange them evenly in the bottom of the dish.

2 In a mixing bowl, combine the brown sugar, flour, salt, nutmeg, cardamom and cinnamon. Rub in the spread until the mixture resembles coarse crumbs. Mix in the walnuts.

3 Sprinkle the crumble mixture evenly over the apples. Cover with foil and bake for 30 minutes.

4 Remove the foil and continue baking for about 30 minutes more, until the apples are tender and the crumble topping is crisp. Serve warm.

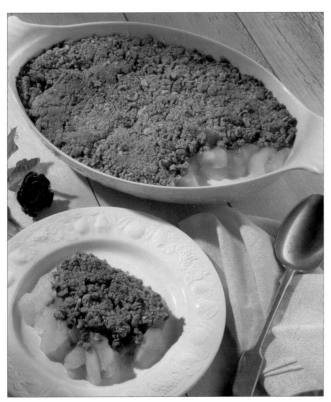

NUTRITIONAL NOTES

Per portion:

Energy	240Kcals/1003kJ
Fat, total	4.7g
Saturated fat	0.76g
Cholesterol	0.3mg
Fibre	3.1g

Strawberry and Apple Crumble

A high-fibre, low-fat version of apple crumble. Fresh or frozen raspberries can be used instead of strawberries.

INGREDIENTS

Serves 4

450g/1lb cooking apples

150g/5oz/1¼ cups strawberries, hulled

30ml/2 tbsp caster (superfine) sugar

2.5ml/½ tsp ground cinnamon

30ml/2 tbsp orange juice

low-fat custard or yogurt, to serve (optional)

For the crumble

45ml/3 tbsp plain (all-purpose) wholemeal (whole-wheat) flour

50g/2oz/⅔ cup rolled oats

30ml/2 tbsp low-fat spread

1 Preheat the oven to 180ºC/ 350ºF/Gas 4. Peel, core and cut the apples into approximately 5mm/¼in-size slices. Halve the strawberries.

2 Toss together the apples, strawberries, sugar, cinnamon and orange juice. Tip the mixture into a 1.2 litre/2 pint/5 cup ovenproof dish.

3 Make the crumble. Combine the flour and oats in a bowl and mix in the low-fat spread with a fork.

4 Sprinkle the crumble evenly over the fruit. Bake for 40–45 minutes, until golden brown and bubbling. Serve warm, with low-fat custard or yogurt, if you like.

NUTRITIONAL NOTES

Per portion:

Energy	173Kcals/729kJ
Fat, total	3.9g
Saturated fat	0.85g
Cholesterol	0.4mg
Fibre	3.5g

Blackberry Charlotte

This delicious classic pudding is the perfect reward for an afternoon's blackberry picking.

INGREDIENTS

Serves 4

30ml/2 tbsp low-fat spread
175g/6oz/3 cups fresh white breadcrumbs
50g/2oz/¼ cup soft light brown sugar
60ml/4 tbsp golden (light corn) syrup
finely grated rind and juice of 2 lemons
450g/1lb cooking apples
450g/1lb/4 cups blackberries

NUTRITIONAL NOTES

Per portion:

Energy	346Kcals/1462kJ
Fat, total	4.2g
Saturated fat	0.74g
Cholesterol	0.5mg
Fibre	6.3g

1 Preheat the oven to 180ºC/ 350ºF/Gas 4. Melt the spread in a pan with the breadcrumbs. Sauté for 5–7 minutes, until the crumbs are golden and fairly crisp. Leave to cool slightly.

2 Heat the sugar, syrup, lemon rind and juice gently in a small pan. Add the crumbs and mix well.

3 With a sharp knife, cut the apples into quarters, peel them and remove the cores. Slice the wedges thinly.

4 Arrange a thin layer of blackberries in a baking dish. Top with a thin layer of crumbs, then a thin layer of apple, topping the fruit with another thin layer of crumbs. Repeat the process with another layer of blackberries, followed by another layer of crumbs.

5 Continue until you have used up all the ingredients, finishing with a layer of crumbs.

6 Bake for 30 minutes, until the crumbs are golden and the fruit is soft.

Peach Pudding

On chilly days, try this delicious hot fruit pudding with its tantalizing, feather-light sponge topping.

INGREDIENTS

Serves 4

400g/14oz can peach slices in natural juice
50g/2oz/¼ cup low-fat spread
40g/1½oz/¼ cup soft light brown sugar
1 egg, beaten
65g/2½oz/½ cup plain (all-purpose) wholemeal (whole-wheat) flour
50g/2oz/½ cup plain (all-purpose) flour
5ml/1 tsp baking powder
2.5ml/½ tsp ground cinnamon
60ml/4 tbsp skimmed milk
2.5ml/½ tsp vanilla extract
10ml/2 tsp icing (confectioners') sugar, for dusting
low-fat, ready-to-serve custard, to serve

NUTRITIONAL NOTES
Per portion:

Energy	255Kcals/1071kJ
Fat, total	6.78g
Saturated fat	1.57g
Cholesterol	0.5mg
Fibre	2.65g

1 Preheat the oven to 180°C/350°F/Gas 4. Drain the peaches and put into a 1 litre/1¾ pint/4 cup pie dish with 30ml/2 tbsp of the juice.

2 Put all the remaining ingredients, except the icing sugar and custard, into a mixing bowl. Beat for 3–4 minutes, until thoroughly combined.

3 Spoon the sponge mixture over the peaches and level the top. Cook in the oven for 35–40 minutes, until springy to the touch. Lightly dust the top with icing sugar before serving hot with the custard.

Chunky Apple Bake

This filling, economical family pudding is a good way of using up bread that is a day or so old.

INGREDIENTS

Serves 4

450g/1lb cooking apples
75g/3oz wholemeal (whole-wheat) bread,
    about 3 slices, without crusts
115g/4oz/1/2 cup low-fat cottage cheese
45ml/3 tbsp light muscovado (brown) sugar
200ml/7fl oz/scant 1 cup skimmed milk
5ml/1 tsp demerara (raw) sugar

1 Preheat the oven to 220ºC/
425ºF/Gas 7. Peel the apples,
cut them in quarters and remove
the cores.

VARIATION

You could experiment with other
types of bread such as oat, rye or
white. Pears could be used instead
of apples.

NUTRITIONAL NOTES

Per portion:

Energy	158Kcals/669kJ
Fat, total	1g
Saturated fat	0.38g
Cholesterol	2.4mg
Fibre	2.3g

2 Using a sharp knife, roughly
chop the apples into even-size
pieces, about 1cm/1/2in in width
and depth.

3 Cut the bread into 1cm/1/2in
cubes. Do not use the crusts
as these will be too thick for
the mixture.

4 Put the apples in a bowl and
add the bread cubes, cottage
cheese and muscovado sugar. Toss
lightly and mix thoroughly.

5 Stir in the skimmed milk and
then tip the mixture into a
wide ovenproof dish. Sprinkle
demerara sugar over the top of
the mixture.

6 Bake for 30–35 minutes, or
until the apple bake is golden
brown and bubbling. Serve hot.

COOK'S TIP

You may need to adjust the
amount of milk used, depending
on the dryness of the bread; the
more stale the bread, the more
milk it will absorb. The texture
should be very moist but not
falling apart.

Apple Couscous Pudding

This unusual mixture makes a delicious family pudding with a rich fruity flavour, but virtually no fat.

INGREDIENTS

Serves 4

600ml/1 pint/2¹/2 cups unsweetened
   apple juice
115g/4oz/²/3 cup couscous
40g/1¹/2oz/¹/4 cup sultanas (golden raisins)
2.5ml/¹/2 tsp mixed spice
2 large cooking apples
30ml/2 tbsp demerara (raw) sugar
low-fat natural (plain) yogurt, to serve

NUTRITIONAL NOTES
Per portion:

Energy	194Kcals/815kJ
Fat, total	0.58g
Saturated fat	0.09g
Cholesterol	0mg
Fibre	0.75g

1 Preheat the oven to 200ºC/ 400ºF/Gas 6. Bring to boil the apple juice, couscous, sultanas and spice in a pan, stirring. Lower heat, cover and simmer.

2 Spoon half the couscous mix into a 1.2 litre/2 pint/5 cup ovenproof dish. Peel, core and slice the apples and arrange half the slices on top, then add the remaining couscous.

3 Arrange the remaining apple slices over the top and sprinkle with demerara sugar. Bake for 25–30 minutes or until golden brown. Serve while still hot, with low-fat yogurt.

COOK'S TIP

Couscous is a pre-cooked wheat that is widely available.

Baked Fruit Compote

This marvellous medley of dried fruit looks good, tastes even better and is quick and easy to make.

INGREDIENTS

Serves 6

115g/4oz/²/3 cup ready-to-eat dried figs
115g/4oz/¹/2 cup ready-to-eat dried apricots
50g/2oz/¹/2 cup ready-to-eat dried
    apple rings
50g/2oz/¹/4 cup ready-to-eat prunes
50g/2oz/¹/2 cup ready-to-eat dried pears
50g/2oz/¹/2 cup ready-to-eat dried peaches
300ml/¹/2 pint/1¹/4 cups unsweetened
    apple juice
300ml/¹/2 pint/1¹/4 cups unsweetened
    orange juice
6 cloves
1 cinnamon stick
a few toasted flaked (sliced) almonds,
    to decorate

2 Mix together the unsweetened apple and orange juices and pour evenly over the fruit, thoroughly coating all the dried fruit with the apple and orange juices. Add the cloves and cinnamon stick and stir gently to mix.

3 Bake for about 30 minutes until the fruit mixture is hot, stirring once or twice during cooking. Set aside and soak for 20 minutes, then discard the cloves and cinnamon stick.

4 Spoon into serving bowls and serve warm or cold, decorated with toasted flaked almonds.

COOK'S TIP

Pineapple and orange or grape and apple juice can be used instead.

1 Preheat the oven to 180ºC/350ºF/Gas 4. Place the figs, apricots, apple rings, prunes, pears and peaches in a shallow ovenproof dish and stir to mix.

NUTRITIONAL NOTES
Per portion:

Energy	174Kcals/744kJ
Fat, total	0.8g
Saturated fat	0.05g
Cholesterol	0mg
Fibre	5.16g

Kumquat Compote

2 Pare the orange rind and add to the pan. Peel and grate the ginger and add to the pan. Crush the cardamom pods and add the seeds to the mixture, with the cloves.

3 Reduce the heat, cover, and simmer gently for 30 minutes, until the fruit is tender, stirring occasionally.

Warm, spicy and full of sun-ripened ingredients, this is the perfect winter dessert to remind you of summer days.

4 Add the squeezed orange juice to the compote. Sweeten with the honey, sprinkle with the almonds and serve warm.

INGREDIENTS

Serves 4

200g/7oz/2 cups kumquats

200g/7oz/scant 1 cup dried apricots

30ml/2 tbsp sultanas (golden raisins)

400ml/14fl oz/1²/3 cups water

1 orange

2.5cm/1in piece of fresh root ginger

4 cardamom pods

4 cloves

30ml/2 tbsp clear honey

15ml/1 tbsp flaked (sliced) almonds,
   toasted

1 Wash the kumquats, and, if they are large, cut them in half. Place them in a pan with the apricots, sultanas and water. Bring to the boil.

NUTRITIONAL NOTES
Per portion:

Energy	198Kcals/833kJ
Fat, total	2.9g
Saturated fat	0.25g
Cholesterol	0mg
Fibre	6.9g

Russian Blackcurrant Pudding

This Russian pudding is traditionally made from the thickened juice of stewed red or blackcurrants.

INGREDIENTS

Serves 4

225g/8oz/2 cups red or blackcurrants or
    a mixture of both
225g/8oz/2 cups raspberries
150ml/¼ pint/⅔ cup water
50g/2oz/¼ cup caster (superfine) sugar
25ml/1½ tbsp arrowroot
15ml/1 tbsp crème de mûre
low-fat yogurt, to serve (optional)

1 Place the currants and raspberries, water and sugar in a pan. Cover the pan and cook over a low heat for 12–15 minutes, until the fruit is soft.

2 Blend the arrowroot to a paste with a little water in a small bowl and stir into the hot fruit mixture. Bring the fruit mixture back to the boil, stirring all the time until thickened and smooth.

3 Remove the pan from the heat and leave the fruit compote to cool slightly, then gently stir in the crème de mûre.

4 Pour the compote into four glass serving bowls and leave until cold, then chill until required. Serve solo or with low-fat yogurt.

NUTRITIONAL NOTES

Per portion:

Energy	105Kcals/443kJ
Fat, total	0.2g
Saturated fat	0g
Cholesterol	0mg
Fibre	3.3g

COOK'S TIP
Crème de mûre is a blackberry liqueur available from large supermarkets – you could use crème de cassis instead, if you prefer.

Cornflake-topped Peach Bake

With a few store cupboard ingredients, this golden, crisp-crusted pudding can be rustled up in next to no time.

INGREDIENTS

Serves 4

400g/14oz can peach slices in juice
30ml/2 tbsp sultanas (golden raisins)
1 cinnamon stick
strip of pared orange rind
30ml/2 tbsp low-fat spread
50g/2oz/1¹/2 cups cornflakes
10ml/2 tsp sesame seeds

1 Preheat the oven to 200ºC/ 400ºF/Gas 6. Drain the peaches, reserving the juice in a pan. Arrange the peaches in a shallow ovenproof dish.

2 Bring to the boil the sultanas, cinnamon, orange rind and juice. Lower the heat and simmer, to reduce the liquid by half. Remove the rind and cinnamon and spoon over the peaches.

3 Melt the low-fat spread in a small pan, stir in the cornflakes and sesame seeds.

4 Spread the cornflake mixture over the fruit. Bake for 15–20 minutes, or until the topping is crisp and golden. Serve hot.

NUTRITIONAL NOTES

Per portion:

Energy	150Kcals/633kJ
Fat, total	4.6g
Saturated fat	1g
Cholesterol	0.5mg
Fibre	1.3g

Rhubarb Spiral Cobbler

3 Roll out the dough on a floured surface to a 25cm/10in square. Mix the orange rind, demerara sugar and ginger, then sprinkle this over the dough.

4 Roll up quite tightly, then cut into about 10 slices using a sharp knife. Arrange the slices over the rhubarb.

5 Bake for 20–25 minutes, or until the spirals are well risen and golden brown. Serve warm.

The tangy taste of rhubarb combines perfectly with the ginger spice in this unusual cobbler.

INGREDIENTS

Serves 4

675g/1½lb rhubarb, sliced
45ml/3 tbsp unsweetened orange juice
75g/3oz/6 tbsp caster (superfine) sugar
200g/7oz/1¾ cups self-raising (self-rising) flour
about 250ml/8fl oz/1 cup low-fat natural (plain) yogurt
grated rind of 1 orange
30ml/2 tbsp demerara (raw) sugar
5ml/1 tsp ground ginger

1 Preheat the oven to 200°C/400°F/Gas 6. Mix the rhubarb, orange juice and 50g/2oz/4 tbsp of the caster sugar in a pan. Cover and cook over a low heat for 10 minutes or until tender. Tip into an ovenproof dish.

2 To make the topping, mix the flour and remaining caster sugar in a bowl, then stir in enough of the yogurt to bind to a soft dough.

NUTRITIONAL NOTES

Per portion:

Energy	320Kcals/1343kJ
Fat, total	1.2g
Saturated fat	0.34g
Cholesterol	2mg
Fibre	3.92g

COOK'S TIP

In the summer you could substitute halved plums, sliced nectarines or peaches for the rhubarb, if you prefer.

Plum, Apple and Banana Scone Pie

This is one of those simple, satisfying puddings that everyone enjoys. Serve hot or cold with low-fat natural yogurt.

INGREDIENTS

Serves 4

450g/1lb plums
1 cooking apple
1 large banana
150ml/¼ pint/⅔ cup water
115g/4oz/1 cup wholemeal (whole-wheat) flour, or half wholemeal and half plain (all-purpose) flour
10ml/2 tsp baking powder
25g/1oz/3 tbsp raisins
about 60ml/4 tbsp sour milk or low-fat natural (plain) yogurt
low-fat natural (plain) yogurt, to serve (optional)

1 Preheat the oven to 180°C/ 350°F/Gas 4. Cut the plums in half and ease out the stones (pits). Peel, core and chop the apple, then slice the banana.

NUTRITIONAL NOTES

Per portion:

Energy	195Kcals/831kJ
Fat, total	1g
Saturated fat	0.2g
Cholesterol	0.6mg
Fibre	5.2g

2 Mix the fruit in a pan. Pour in the water. Bring to simmering point and cook gently for 15 minutes or until the fruit is completely soft.

3 Spoon the fruit mixture into a pie dish. Level the surface.

4 Mix the flour, baking powder and raisins in a bowl. Add the sour milk or low-fat natural yogurt and mix to a very soft dough.

5 Transfer the scone dough to a lightly floured surface and divide it into 6–8 portions, then pat them into flattish scones.

6 Cover the plum and apple mixture with the scones. Bake the pie for 40 minutes until the scone topping is cooked through. Serve the pie hot with natural yogurt, or leave it until cold.

COOK'S TIP

To prevent the banana discoloring before cooking, dip each slice in fresh lemon juice.

Griddle Cakes with Mulled Plums

These light little pancakes, with their rich, spicy plum sauce, can easily be cooked on the barbecue.

Serves 6

500g/1¼lb red plums
90ml/6 tbsp light muscovado
   (brown) sugar
1 cinnamon stick
2 whole cloves
1 piece star anise
90ml/6 tbsp unsweetened apple juice
low-fat Greek (US strained plain) yogurt
   or fromage frais, to serve (optional)
For the griddle cakes
50g/2oz/½ cup plain (all-purpose) flour
10ml/2 tsp baking powder
pinch of salt
50g/2oz/½ cup fine cornmeal
30ml/2 tbsp light muscovado
   (brown) sugar
1 egg, beaten
300ml/½ pint/1¼ cups skimmed milk
15ml/1 tbsp corn oil

1 Halve, stone (pit) and quarter the plums. Place in a pan, with the sugar, spices and apple juice.

2 Place on a hot barbecue or stove and bring to the boil. Lower heat, cover and simmer gently for 8–10 minutes, stirring, until the plums are soft. Remove the spices and keep warm.

3 For the griddle cakes, sift the flour, baking powder and salt into a large bowl and stir in the cornmeal and sugar.

4 Make a well in the centre and add the egg; gradually beat in the milk. Beat with a wooden spoon to a smooth batter. Beat in 5ml/1 tsp of the oil.

5 Heat a griddle or a heavy frying-pan on a hot barbecue or stove. When it is very hot, brush with oil and then drop tablespoons of batter on to it. Cook the griddle cakes for about a minute, until bubbles appear on the surface and the underside is golden.

6 Turn the cakes over and cook the other side for a further minute, or until golden. Bake the other cakes. Serve hot with the mulled plums. Add a spoonful of low-fat Greek yogurt or fromage frais, if you like.

COOK'S TIP

Use spray oil on the griddle if you prefer, and cut the fat content still further.

NUTRITIONAL NOTES
Per portion:

Energy	159Kcals/669kJ
Fat, total	3.3g
Saturated fat	0.58g
Cholesterol	33.1mg
Fibre	1.7g

Barbecued Bananas with Spicy Vanilla Spread

Baked bananas are easy because they bake in their own skins.

INGREDIENTS

Serves 4

4 bananas
6 green cardamom pods
1 vanilla pod (bean)
finely grated rind of 1 small orange
30ml/2 tbsp brandy
60ml/4 tbsp light muscovado (brown) sugar
45ml/3 tbsp low-fat spread

COOK'S TIP

If making this for children, use orange juice instead of the brandy or, if the fat content is no object, drizzle the cooked bananas with melted chocolate.

---

2 Meanwhile, split the cardamom pods, remove the seeds and crush them lightly with a pestle and mortar.

3 Split the vanilla pod lengthways and scrape out the tiny seeds. Mix with the cardamom, orange rind, sugar brandy and spread, to make a paste.

4 Slit the skin of each banana, open out slightly and spoon in a little of the paste. Serve immediately.

1 Place the bananas, in their skins, on the hot barbecue and leave for 6–8 minutes, turning occasionally, until they are turning brownish-black.

NUTRITIONAL NOTES

Per portion:

Energy	215Kcals/900kJ
Fat, total	4.9g
Saturated fat	1.22g
Cholesterol	0.7mg
Fibre	1.1g

Hot Spiced Bananas

Baking bananas in a rum and fruit syrup makes for a dessert with negligible fat and maximum flavour.

INGREDIENTS

Serves 6

low-fat spread, for greasing

6 ripe bananas

200g/7oz/generous 1 cup light brown sugar

250ml/8fl oz/1 cup unsweetened
   pineapple juice

120ml/4fl oz/1/2 cup dark rum

2 cinnamon sticks

12 whole cloves

NUTRITIONAL NOTES
Per portion:

Energy	290Kcals/1215kJ
Fat, total	0.3g
Saturated fat	0.11g
Cholesterol	0mg
Fibre	1.1g

1 Preheat the oven to 180ºC/
350ºF/Gas 4. Grease a 23cm/
9in shallow baking dish.

2 Peel the bananas and cut them
diagonally into 2.5cm/1in
pieces. Arrange the banana pieces,
to spread evenly over the bottom
of the prepared baking dish.

3 Mix the sugar and pineapple
juice in a pan. Heat gently
until the sugar has dissolved,
stirring. Add the rum, cinnamon
and cloves. Bring to the boil, then
remove from the heat.

4 Pour the hot pineapple and
spice mixture over the bananas
in the baking dish. Bake in the
oven for 25–30 minutes until the
bananas are tender. Serve while
still hot.

Rum and Raisin Bananas

*Choose almost-ripe bananas with
evenly coloured skins, either all
yellow or just green at the tips.*

INGREDIENTS

Serves 4

40g/1½oz/¼ cup seedless raisins

75ml/5 tbsp dark rum

15ml/1 tbsp low-fat spread

60ml/4 tbsp soft light brown sugar

4 ripe bananas, peeled and
   halved lengthways

1.5ml/¼ tsp grated nutmeg

1.5ml/¼ tsp ground cinnamon

15ml/1 tbsp slivered almonds, toasted

low-fat fromage frais or low-fat vanilla
   ice cream, to serve (optional)

1 Put the raisins in a bowl and
pour over the rum. Leave
them to soak for about 30 minutes
until plump.

2 Melt the spread in a frying pan,
add the sugar and stir until it
has completely dissolved. Add the
bananas and cook for a few minutes
until tender, turning occasionally.

3 Sprinkle the spices over the
bananas, then pour over the
rum and raisins. Carefully set
alight using a long-handled match;
stir gently to mix.

4 Scatter over the slivered
almonds and serve immediately
with low-fat fromage frais or low-
fat vanilla ice cream, if you like.

COOK'S TIP

For an accompaniment that
won't add too much fat, make
your own frozen yogurt by
churning extra low-fat yogurt in
an ice-cream maker.

NUTRITIONAL NOTES

Per portion:

Energy	263Kcals/1110kJ
Fat, total	4.1g
Saturated fat	0.51g
Cholesterol	0.2mg
Fibre	1.6g

Caribbean Bananas

Tender baked bananas in a rich and spicy sauce – a dessert for those with a sweet tooth!

INGREDIENTS

Serves 4

30ml/2 tbsp low-fat spread

8 firm ripe bananas

juice of 1 lime

75g/3oz/¹/2 cup soft dark brown sugar

5ml/1 tsp ground allspice

2.5ml/¹/2 tsp ground ginger

seeds from 6 cardamoms crushed

30ml/2 tbsp rum

pared lime rind, to decorate

low-fat crème fraîche, to serve (optional)

1 Preheat the oven to 200°C/ 400°F/Gas 6. Use a little of the spread to grease a shallow baking dish large enough to hold the bananas snugly in a single layer.

2 Peel the bananas and cut them in half lengthways. Arrange the bananas in the dish and pour over the lime juice.

3 Mix the sugar, allspice, ginger and crushed cardamom seeds in a bowl. Scatter the mixture over the bananas. Dot with the remaining low-fat spread. Bake, basting once, for 15 minutes, or until the bananas are soft.

4 Remove the dish from the oven. Warm the rum in a small pan or metal soup ladle, pour it over the bananas and set it alight.

5 As soon as the flames die down, decorate the dessert with the pared lime rind. Serve while still hot and add a dollop of low-fat crème fraîche to each portion, if you like.

VARIATION

For a version that will appeal more to children, use orange juice instead of lime and leave out the rum.

NUTRITIONAL NOTES
Per portion:

Energy	310Kcals/1306kJ
Fat, total	3.2g
Saturated fat	0.87g
Cholesterol	0.4mg
Fibre	2.2g

Barbecued Pineapple Boats with Rum Glaze

Pineapple is full of flavour when barbecued; this spiced rum glaze turns it into a special dessert.

Serves 4

1 medium pineapple, about 600g/1lb 6oz

30ml/2 tbsp dark muscovado
   (molasses) sugar

5ml/1 tsp ground ginger

45ml/3 tbsp low-fat spread, melted

30ml/2 tbsp dark rum

COOK'S TIP
~

For an easier version, cut off the
skin and then slice the whole
pineapple into thick slices and
cook as shown.

---

1 With a large, sharp knife, cut
the pineapple lengthways into
quarters. Cut out and discard the
hard centre core from each quarter.
Take care when handling the rough
outer skin.

2 Cut between the flesh and
skin, to release the flesh, but
not cut the skin. Slice the flesh
across, into chunks.

3 Push a bamboo skewer
lengthways through each
quarter and into the stalk, to hold
the chunks in place.

4 Mix together the sugar, ginger,
melted spread and rum and
brush over the pineapple. Cook the
quarters on a hot barbecue for
3–4 minutes; pour the remaining
glaze over the top and serve.

NUTRITIONAL NOTES
Per portion:

Energy	155Kcals/646kJ
Fat, total	4.9g
Saturated fat	1.14g
Cholesterol	0.7mg
Fibre	1.8g

Nectarines with Amaretto

Amaretto, the sweet almond-flavoured liqueur from Italy, adds a touch of luxury to these low-fat nectarines.

INGREDIENTS

Serves 4

6 ripe nectarines

30ml/2 tbsp clear honey

60ml/4 tbsp Amaretto

half-fat crème fraîche, to serve (optional)

NUTRITIONAL NOTES	
Per portion:	
Energy	150Kcals/627kJ
Fat, total	0.2g
Saturated fat	0g
Cholesterol	0mg
Fibre	2.7g

1 Cut the nectarines in half by running a small sharp knife down the side of each fruit from top to bottom, cutting right through to the stone (pit). Gently ease the nectarine apart and remove the stone. Handle the fruit carefully as nectarines bruise easily.

2 Place the nectarines cut side up in an ovenproof dish and drizzle 2.5ml/½ tsp honey and 5ml/1 tsp Amaretto over each half. Preheat the grill (broiler) until very hot and then grill (broil) the fruit until slightly charred. Serve with a little half-fat crème fraîche, if you like.

Nectarines with Marzipan and Yogurt

A luscious dessert that few can resist; a wonderful combination of flavours.

INGREDIENTS

Serves 4

4 firm, ripe nectarines or peaches
75g/3oz marzipan
75ml/5 tbsp low-fat Greek (US strained
   plain) yogurt
3 amaretti, crushed

1 Cut the nectarines or peaches in half, removing the stones (pits).

2 Cut the marzipan into eight pieces and press one piece into the stone cavity of each nectarine half.

COOK'S TIP

If the stone (pit) does not pull out easily when you halve the fruit, use a small, sharp knife to cut around it.

3 Preheat the grill (broiler), unless you are cooking on the barbecue. Spoon the low-fat Greek yogurt on top. Sprinkle the crushed amaretti over the yogurt.

4 Place the fruits on a hot barbecue or under a hot grill. Cook for 3–5 minutes, until the yogurt starts to melt.

NUTRITIONAL NOTES

Per portion:

Energy	176Kcals/737kJ
Fat, total	4.3g
Saturated fat	0.98g
Cholesterol	3.2mg
Fibre	2.3g

Spiced Nectarines with Fromage Frais

This easy dessert is good at any time of year – use canned peach halves if fresh nectarines are not available.

INGREDIENTS

Serves 4

4 ripe nectarines or peaches
15ml/1 tbsp light muscovado (brown)
    sugar
115g/4oz/^{1}/2 cup low-fat fromage frais
2.5ml/^{1}/2 tsp ground star anise or
    mixed (apple pie) spice

NUTRITIONAL NOTES	
Per portion:	
Energy	108Kcals/450kJ
Fat, total	3.3g
Saturated fat	2g
Cholesterol	14.4mg
Fibre	1.5g

2 Arrange the fruit, cut-side upwards, in a wide flameproof dish or on a baking sheet.

3 Stir the sugar into the fromage frais. Using a teaspoon, spoon the mixture into the hollow of each half.

1 With a sharp knife cut the nectarines or peaches in half and remove the stones (pits).

4 Sprinkle the fruit with the ground star anise or mixed spice. Place under a moderately hot grill (broiler) for 6–8 minutes, or until the fruit is hot and bubbling. Serve warm.

Barbecued Orange Parcels

This is one of the most delicious ways of rounding off a barbecue party. Serve on their own, or with low-fat fromage frais.

INGREDIENTS

Serves 4

30ml/2 tbsp low-fat spread, plus extra, melted, for brushing

4 oranges

30ml/2 tbsp maple syrup

30ml/2 tbsp Cointreau or Grand Marnier liqueur

low-fat fromage frais, to serve (optional)

1 Cut four double-thickness squares of foil, large enough to wrap the oranges. Melt about 10ml/2 tsp of the low-fat spread and brush it over the centre of each piece of foil.

NUTRITIONAL NOTES

Per portion:

Energy	127Kcals/532kJ
Fat, total	3.2g
Saturated fat	0.74g
Cholesterol	0.5mg
Fibre	2.7g

2 Remove some shreds of orange rind, for the decoration. Blanch and dry them and set aside. Peel the oranges, removing the white pith and peel and catching the juice in a bowl.

3 Slice the oranges crossways into thick slices. Reassemble, and place each orange on a square of foil.

4 Create a cup shape by tucking the foil up high around the oranges. This will keep them in shape, but leave the foil open at the top.

5 Mix together the reserved orange juice, maple syrup and liqueur and spoon the mixture over the oranges.

6 Add a dab of low-fat spread to each parcel and fold over the foil, to seal in the juices. Place the parcels on a hot barbecue for 10–12 minutes, until hot. Serve topped with shreds of orange rind and fromage frais, if you like.

COOK'S TIP

To make the orange shreds for the decoration, slice off several pieces of orange rind, taking care to avoid the bitter white pith, then cut them into thin matchsticks. Add to a small pan of boiling water, for 1 minute, then drain and dry on kitchen paper.

Apples and Raspberries in Rose Syrup

Inspiration for this dessert stems from the fact that the apple and the raspberry belong to the rose family.

INGREDIENTS

Serves 4

5ml/1 tsp rose pouchong tea

900ml/1½ pints/3¾ cups boiling water

5ml/1 tsp rose water (optional)

50g/2oz/¼ cup granulated (white) sugar

5ml/1 tsp lemon juice

5 dessert apples

175g/6oz/1½ cups fresh raspberries

1 Warm a large tea pot. Add the rose pouchong tea, then pour on the boiling water, together with the rose water, if using. Allow to stand and infuse for 4 minutes.

2 Measure the sugar and lemon juice into a stainless steel pan. Strain in the tea and stir to dissolve the sugar.

3 Peel and core the apples, then cut into quarters.

4 Poach the apples in the syrup for about 5 minutes.

5 Transfer the apples and syrup to a large metal baking sheet and leave to cool to room temperature.

6 Pour the cooled apples and syrup into a bowl, add the raspberries and mix to combine. Spoon into individual dishes or bowls and serve while still warm.

NUTRITIONAL NOTES

Per portion:

Energy	125Kcals/526kJ
Fat, total	0.4g
Saturated fat	0g
Cholesterol	0mg
Fibre	3.6g

Papaya Baked with Ginger

Ginger enhances the flavour of papaya in this recipe, which takes no more than ten minutes to prepare. Don't overcook the papaya or it will become watery.

INGREDIENTS

Serves 4

2 ripe papayas

2 pieces stem ginger in syrup, drained, plus 15ml/1 tbsp syrup from the jar

8 dessert biscuits (cookies), coarsely crushed

45ml/3 tbsp raisins

shredded, finely pared rind and juice of 1 lime

15ml/1 tbsp light muscovado (brown) sugar

60ml/4 tbsp low-fat Greek (US strained plain) yogurt, plus extra to serve (optional)

15ml/1 tbsp finely chopped unsalted pistachio nuts

1 Preheat the oven to 200ºC/ 400ºF/Gas 6. Cut the papayas in half and scoop out their seeds. Place the halves in a baking dish and set aside. Cut the stem ginger into fine matchsticks.

2 Make the filling. Combine the crushed biscuits, stem ginger matchsticks and raisins in a bowl. Make sure they are all mixed well together.

3 Stir in the lime rind and juice, then add the sugar and the yogurt. Mix well.

4 Fill the papaya halves and drizzle with the ginger syrup. Sprinkle with the pistachio nuts.

5 Bake for about 25 minutes or until tender. Serve hot, with extra low-fat Greek yogurt, if you like.

NUTRITIONAL NOTES

Per portion:

Energy	218Kcals/922kJ
Fat, total	4.2g
Saturated fat	1.23g
Cholesterol	6mg
Fibre	3.8g

Baked Peaches with Raspberry Sauce

Pretty as a picture – that's the effect when you serve these tasty stuffed peaches to delighted dinner party guests.

INGREDIENTS

Serves 6

30ml/2 tbsp low-fat spread
50g/2oz/1/4 cup granulated (white) sugar
1 egg, beaten
20g/3/4oz/1/4 cup ground almonds
6 ripe peaches
glossy leaves and plain or frosted
    raspberries, to decorate
For the sauce
225g/8oz/2 cups raspberries
15ml/1 tbsp icing (confectioners') sugar

NUTRITIONAL NOTES
Per portion:

Energy	137Kcals/576kJ
Fat, total	4.7g
Saturated fat	0.81g
Cholesterol	32.3mg
Fibre	2.8g

1 Preheat the oven to 180ºC/ 350ºF/Gas 4. Beat the low-fat spread and sugar together, then beat in the egg and the ground almonds.

2 Cut the peaches in half and remove the stones (pits). With a spoon, scrape out some of the flesh from each peach half, slightly enlarging the hollow left by the stone. Save the excess peach for the sauce.

3 Stand the peach halves on a baking sheet, supporting them with crumpled foil to keep them steady. Fill each peach hollow with the almond mixture. Bake for 30 minutes, or until the almond filling is puffed and golden and the peaches are very tender.

4 Meanwhile, process the raspberries, icing sugar and the reserved peach flesh in a food processor or blender, until smooth. Press through a sieve (strainer) over a bowl to remove fibres and seeds.

5 Let the peaches cool slightly. Spoon the sauce on each plate and arrange two peach halves on top. Decorate with the leaves and raspberries and serve immediately.

COOK'S TIP

For a special occasion, stir about 15ml/1 tbsp framboise or peach brandy into the raspberry sauce.

Stuffed Peaches with Almond Liqueur

Together amaretti have an intense
almond flavour, and make a natural
partner for peaches.

INGREDIENTS

Serves 4

4 ripe but firm peaches

50g/2oz/¹/₂ cup amaretti

30ml/2 tbsp low-fat spread

30ml/2 tbsp caster (superfine) sugar

1 egg yolk

60ml/4 tbsp almond liqueur

low-fat spread, for greasing

250ml/8fl oz/1 cup dry white wine

8 tiny sprigs of fresh basil, to decorate

low-fat ice cream, to serve (optional)

1 Preheat the oven to 180ºC/
350ºF/Gas 4. Cut the peaches in
half and remove the stones (pits).
Scrape out some of the flesh from
each peach half, slightly enlarging
the hollow, chop and set aside.

2 Put the amaretti in a bowl and
crush them finely with the end
of a rolling pin.

3 Cream the low-fat spread and
sugar together in a separate
bowl until smooth. Stir in the
reserved chopped peach flesh, the
egg yolk and half the liqueur with
the amaretti crumbs. Lightly grease
a baking dish that is just large
enough to hold the peach halves in
a single layer.

NUTRITIONAL NOTES

Per portion:

Energy	232Kcals/971kJ
Fat, total	5g
Saturated fat	1.37g
Cholesterol	54.7mg
Fibre	1.9g

4 Stand the peaches in the dish
and spoon the stuffing into
them. Mix the remaining liqueur
with the wine, pour over the
peaches and bake for 25 minutes
or until the peaches feel tender.
Decorate with basil and serve
immediately, with low-fat ice
cream, if you like.

Coconut Dumplings with Apricot Sauce

These delicate little dumplings are simple to make. The sharp flavour of the sauce offsets them perfectly.

Serves 4

75g/3oz/6 tbsp low-fat cottage cheese
1 egg white
15ml/1 tbsp low-fat spread
15ml/1 tbsp light muscovado
   (brown) sugar
30ml/2 tbsp self-raising (self-rising)
   wholemeal (whole-wheat) flour
finely grated rind of 1/2 lemon
15ml/1 tbsp desiccated (dry unsweetened
   shredded) coconut, toasted
For the sauce
225g/8oz can apricot halves in
   natural juice
15ml/1 tbsp lemon juice

1 Half-fill a steamer with boiling water and put it on to boil. If you do not own a steamer, place a heatproof plate or shallow dish over a pan of boiling water.

2 Beat together the cottage cheese, egg white and low-fat spread until they are evenly mixed.

3 Stir in the sugar, flour, lemon rind and coconut, mixing everything evenly to a fairly firm dough.

4 Place 8–12 spoonfuls of the mixture in the steamer or on the plate, leaving a small space between them.

5 Cover the steamer or pan tightly with a lid or a plate and steam for about 10 minutes, until the dumplings have risen and are firm to the touch.

6 Meanwhile make the sauce. Purée the can of apricots and stir in the lemon juice. Pour into a small pan and heat until boiling, then serve with the dumplings. Sprinkle with extra coconut to serve, if you like and can afford the extra fat.

NUTRITIONAL NOTES
Per portion:

Energy	112Kcals/470kJ
Fat, total	4.3g
Saturated fat	2.56g
Cholesterol	1.2mg
Fibre	1.7g

COOK'S TIP

The mixture should be quite stiff; if it is not stiff enough to hold its shape, stir in a little more flour.

Pineapple Flambé

Flambéing means adding alcohol and then burning it off so that the flavour is not too overpowering.

Serves 4

1 large, ripe pineapple, about 600g/1lb 6oz

30ml/2 tbsp low-fat spread

40g/1^{1}/2oz/^{1}/4 cup soft light brown sugar

60ml/4 tbsp fresh orange juice

30ml/2 tbsp brandy or vodka

15g/^{1}/2oz/1 tbsp slivered almonds, toasted

1 Cut away the top and base of the pineapple. Then cut down the sides, removing all the dark "eyes".

2 Cut the pineapple into thin slices. Using an apple corer, remove the hard, central core from each slice.

VARIATION

Try this with nectarines, peaches or cherries. Omit the almonds if you want to reduce the fat content.

3 Melt the spread in a frying pan, with the sugar. Add the orange juice. Stir until hot, then add as many pineapple slices as the pan will hold. Cook for 1–2 minutes, turning once. Remove each slice as it browns.

4 Return all the pineapple slices to the pan, heat briefly, then pour over the brandy or vodka and light with a long-handled match. Let the flames die down, then sprinkle with the almonds. Serve immediately.

NUTRITIONAL NOTES

Per portion:

Energy	171Kcals/711kJ
Fat, total	5g
Saturated fat	0.62g
Cholesterol	0.4mg
Fibre	2.1g

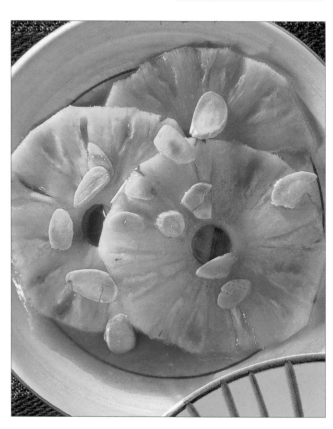

Warm Pears in Cider

*Serve these pears with low-fat Greek
yogurt or fromage frais if you must,
but they are very good on their own.*

INGREDIENTS

Serves 4

1 lemon

50g/2oz/¼ cup caster (superfine) sugar

a little grated nutmeg

250ml/8fl oz/1 cup sweet cider

4 firm, ripe pears

low-fat Greek (US strained plain) yogurt
   or fromage frais, to serve (optional)

NUTRITIONAL NOTES

Per portion:

Energy	11Kcals/46kJ
Fat, total	0g
Saturated fat	0g
Cholesterol	0mg
Fibre	3.3g

1 Using a vegetable peeler
remove the rind from the
lemon in thin strips, leaving any
white pith behind.

2 Squeeze the juice from the
lemon and pour it into a
pan. Add the lemon rind, sugar,
grated nutmeg and cider and heat
gently until the sugar has
completely dissolved.

3 Peel the pears, leaving the
stalks on if possible, and place
in the pan of cider. Poach for
10–15 minutes until almost tender,
turning them frequently.

4 Transfer the pears to individual
serving dishes using a slotted
spoon. Simmer the liquid over a
high heat until it reduces slightly
and becomes syrupy. Pour the
warm syrup over the pears.
Serve immediately.

COOK'S TIP

To make sure that the pears are
firm enough for this dish, buy
them slightly under-ripe and
then wait a day or more.

Fanned Poached Pears in Port Syrup

The perfect choice for autumn dining, this easy, simple dessert has a beautiful rich colour and fantastic flavour.

INGREDIENTS

Serves 4

2 ripe, firm pears

pared rind of 1 lemon

175ml/6fl oz/³/4 cup ruby port

50g/2oz/¹/4 cup caster (superfine) sugar

1 cinnamon stick

60ml/4 tbsp cold water

half-fat crème fraîche, to serve (optional)

To decorate

15ml/1 tbsp sliced hazelnuts, toasted

fresh mint, pear or rose leaves

1 Peel the pears, cut them in half and remove the cores. Place the lemon rind, port, sugar, cinnamon stick and water in a shallow pan. Bring to the boil over a low heat. Add the pears, cover and poach for 5 minutes. Let the pears cool in the syrup.

2 When the pears are cold, transfer them to a bowl with a slotted spoon. Return the syrup to the heat. Boil rapidly until it has reduced to form a syrup. Remove the cinnamon stick and lemon rind and leave the syrup to cool.

3 To serve, place each pear half on a board, cut side down. Keeping it intact at the stalk end, slice lengthways. Carefully lift it off, using a palette knife, and place on a dessert plate. Press gently to fan out the pears. Spoon over the port syrup, top with a few hazelnuts and decorate with fresh mint, pear or rose leaves. Serve with half-fat crème fraîche, if you like.

NUTRITIONAL NOTES

Per portion:

Energy	173Kcals/725kJ
Fat	2.5g
Saturated fat	0.17g
Cholesterol	0mg
Fibre	1.9g

Mulled Pears with Ginger and Brandy

The flavours improve with keeping, so you can mull the pears several days before you want to serve them.

INGREDIENTS

Serves 8

600ml/1 pint/2¹/2 cups red wine

225g/8oz/1 cup caster (superfine) sugar

1 cinnamon stick

6 cloves

finely grated rind of 1 orange

10ml/2 tsp grated fresh root ginger

8 even-sized firm pears, with stalks

15ml/1 tbsp brandy

25g/1oz/¹/4 cup almonds or hazelnuts, toasted, to decorate

low-fat whipped cream, to serve (optional)

1 Put all the ingredients except the pears, brandy and nuts into a large pan and heat slowly until the sugar has dissolved. Simmer for 5 minutes.

2 Peel the pears, leaving the stalks on. Arrange them upright in the pan. Cover and simmer until tender, for 45–50 minutes.

3 Gently remove the pears from the syrup with a slotted spoon, being very careful not to dislodge the stalks. Put the cooked pears in a serving bowl or individual bowls, if you prefer.

NUTRITIONAL NOTES
Per portion:

Energy	246Kcals/1038kJ
Fat, total	1.9g
Saturated fat	0.13g
Cholesterol	0mg
Fibre	3.5g

4 Boil the syrup until it thickens and reduces. Cool slightly, add the brandy and strain over the pears. Decorate with toasted nuts. Serve with whipped cream, if you like.

Poached Pears in Maple-yogurt Sauce

Poach the pears in advance, and have the cooled syrup ready to spoon on to the plates just before you serve.

INGREDIENTS

Serves 6

6 firm dessert pears
15ml/1 tbsp lemon juice
250ml/8fl oz/1 cup sweet white wine
   or cider
thinly pared rind of 1 lemon
1 cinnamon stick
30ml/2 tbsp maple syrup
2.5ml/½ tsp arrowroot
150ml/¼ pint/⅔ cup low-fat Greek
   (US strained plain) yogurt

1 Peel the pears thinly, leaving them whole and with the stalks. Brush them with lemon juice, to prevent them from browning. Use a vegetable peeler or small knife to scoop out the core from the base of each pear.

2 Place them in a wide, heavy pan and add the wine or cider, with cold water to almost cover the pears.

3 Add the lemon rind and cinnamon stick and bring to the boil. Reduce the heat, cover and simmer gently for 30–40 minutes, or until tender. Turn the pears so that they cook evenly. Lift out carefully, draining them well.

4 Boil the liquid uncovered to reduce to about 120ml/ 4fl oz/½ cup. Strain into a jug (pitcher) and add the maple syrup. Blend a little of the liquid with the arrowroot, then return the mixture to the jug; mix well. Return to the pan and cook, stirring, until thick and clear. Cool.

COOK'S TIP

The cooking time will vary, depending upon the type and ripeness of the pears. They should be ripe, but firm; soft pears will not keep their shape.

5 Slice each pear about three-quarters of the way through, leaving the slices attached at the stem end. Fan each pear out on a serving plate.

6 Stir 30ml/2 tbsp of the cooled syrup into the yogurt and spoon it around the pears. Drizzle with the remaining syrup and serve immediately.

NUTRITIONAL NOTES

Per portion:

Energy	136Kcals/573kJ
Fat, total	1.4g
Saturated fat	0.79g
Cholesterol	1.8mg
Fibre	3.3g

Blushing Pears

Pears poached in rosé wine and sweet spices absorb all the subtle flavours and turn a soft pink colour.

INGREDIENTS

Serves 6

6 firm eating pears
300ml/$\frac{1}{2}$ pint/$1\frac{1}{4}$ cups rosé wine
150ml/$\frac{1}{4}$ pint/$\frac{2}{3}$ cup cranberry juice
  or clear apple juice
strip of thinly pared orange rind
4 whole cloves
1 cinnamon stick
1 bay leaf
75ml/5tbsp caster (superfine) sugar
small bay leaves, to decorate

1 Thinly peel the pears with a sharp knife or vegetable peeler, leaving the stalks attached.

2 Pour the wine and cranberry or apple juice into a large heavy pan. Add the orange rind, cloves, cinnamon stick, bay leaf and sugar.

3 Heat gently, stirring all the time until the sugar has dissolved. Add the pears and stand them upright in the pan. Pour in enough cold water to barely cover them. Cover and cook very gently for 20–30 minutes, or until just tender, turning and basting occasionally to ensure even cooking.

4 Using a slotted spoon, gently lift the pears out of the syrup and transfer to a serving dish.

5 Bring the syrup to the boil and boil rapidly for 10–15 minutes, or until it has reduced by half.

6 Strain the syrup and pour over the pears. Serve hot, decorated with bay leaves.

NUTRITIONAL NOTES
Per portion:

Energy	148Kcals/620kJ
Fat, total	0.16g
Saturated fat	0g
Cholesterol	0mg
Fibre	1.9g

COOK'S TIP

Check the pears by piercing with a skewer or sharp knife towards the end of the poaching time and carefully lift out any that have cooked more quickly than others.

Chargrilled Apples on Cinnamon Toasts

This yummy treat makes a fabulous finale to a summer barbecue.

INGREDIENTS

Serves 4

4 sweet dessert apples

juice of ½ lemon

4 individual brioche

15ml/1 tbsp low-fat spread, melted

30ml/2 tbsp golden caster (superfine) sugar

5ml/1 tsp ground cinnamon

low-fat Greek (US strained plain) yogurt,
    to serve (optional)

1 Core the apples and cut them horizontally in three or four thick slices. Sprinkle with the lemon juice.

VARIATION

Other fruit in season could be used for this recipe. Try pears, peaches or pineapple for variety. Nutmeg or mixed (apple pie) spice could also replace the cinnamon.

NUTRITIONAL NOTES	
Per portion:	
Energy	241Kcals/1016kJ
Fat, total	4.9g
Saturated fat	1.63g
Cholesterol	0.2mg
Fibre	3.0g

2 Cut the brioche into thick slices. Brush sparingly with melted low-fat spread on both sides using a pastry brush.

3 Mix together the sugar and ground cinnamon. Preheat the grill (broiler) if not using a barbecue.

4 Place the apple and brioche slices on the hot barbecue or under the grill and cook them for 3–4 minutes, turning once, until they are beginning to turn golden brown.

5 Sprinkle half the cinnamon sugar over the apple slices and toasts and cook for 1 minute more, until they are a rich golden brown.

6 To serve, arrange the apple slices over the toasts and sprinkle them with the remaining cinnamon sugar. Serve hot, with low-fat Greek yogurt, if you like.

COOK'S TIP

To keep the quantity of fat within acceptable levels, make this simple, scrumptious dessert with brioche, but for a rare splurge, use muffins or similar sweet bread.

Banana, Maple and Lime Pancakes

Pancakes are a sweet treat. They can be made in advance and stored in the freezer for convenience.

INGREDIENTS

Serves 4

115g/4oz/1 cup plain (all-purpose) flour

1 egg white

250ml/8fl oz/1 cup skimmed milk

60ml/4 tbsp cold water

spray oil, for frying

shreds of lime rind, to decorate

For the filling

4 bananas, sliced

45ml/3 tbsp maple syrup or golden
   (light corn) syrup

30ml/2 tbsp fresh lime juice

1 Make the pancake batter by beating together the flour, egg white, milk and water in a bowl until smooth and bubbly. Cover and chill until needed.

2 Apply a light coat of spray oil to a non-stick frying pan. Heat the pan, then pour a little batter, swirling it around the pan to coat evenly.

3 Cook the pancake until golden, then toss and cook the other side. Slide on to a plate, cover with foil and keep hot while cooking all the pancakes.

4 Make the filling. Mix the bananas, syrup and lime juice in a pan and simmer gently for 1 minute. Spoon into the pancakes and fold into quarters. Decorate with lime rind.

NUTRITIONAL NOTES

Per portion:

Energy	282Kcals/1185kJ
Fat, total	2.79g
Saturated fat	0.47g
Cholesterol	1.25mg
Fibre	2.12g

COOK'S TIP

Pancakes freeze well. To store for later use, interleave them with non-stick baking parchment, wrap and freeze for up to 3 months.

Chinese Chestnut Pancakes

Thin pancakes, spread with chestnut purée and fried in a little oil, make a deliciously different dessert.

INGREDIENTS

Serves 4

90g/3oz canned sweetened chestnut purée
15ml/1 tbsp vegetable oil, for frying
caster (superfine) sugar, to serve
For the pancakes
150g/5oz/1¼ cups plain (all-purpose)
   flour, plus extra for dusting
about 105ml/7 tbsp boiling water
2.5ml/½ tsp vegetable oil

1 Make the pancakes. Sift the flour and then pour in the boiling water, stirring as you pour. Mix in the oil and knead the mixture into a dough. Cover with a damp dish towel and leave to stand for 30 minutes.

2 Knead the dough until smooth, then roll it out into a long sausage, cut into eight pieces and roll each into a ball. Flatten then roll it to a 15cm/6in pancake.

3 Heat an ungreased frying pan until hot, then reduce the heat to low and place the pancakes, one at a time, in the pan. Turn them when small brown spots appear on the underside. Keep under a damp cloth until all are cooked.

4 Spread about 15ml/1 tbsp of the chestnut purée over each pancake, then roll it up.

5 Heat the oil in a non-stick wok or frying pan. Add the rolls in batches and fry them briefly until golden brown, turning once.

6 Cut each pancake roll into three or four pieces and sprinkle with caster sugar. Serve immediately.

NUTRITIONAL NOTES
Per portion:

Energy	192Kcals/809kJ
Fat, total	3.8g
Saturated fat	0.47g
Cholesterol	0mg
Fibre	1.8g

Tropical Fruit Pancakes

Fresh fruit, coated with a citrus and honey sauce, makes the perfect pancake filling for this light dessert.

Serves 4

115g/4oz/1 cup self-raising (self-rising) flour
pinch of grated nutmeg
15ml/1 tbsp caster (casterfine) sugar
1 egg
300ml/¹/2 pint/1¹/4 cups skimmed milk
15ml/1 tbsp melted low-fat spread
15ml/1 tbsp desiccated (dry unsweetened shredded) coconut (optional)
light sunflower spray oil for frying
icing (confectioners') sugar, for dusting
low-fat Greek (US strained plain) yogurt, to serve (optional)

For the filling

225g/8oz ripe, firm mango
2 bananas
2 kiwi fruit
1 large orange
15ml/1 tbsp lemon juice
30ml/2 tbsp unsweetened orange juice
15ml/1 tbsp clear honey

1 Sift the flour, nutmeg and caster sugar into a large bowl. In a separate bowl, beat the egg lightly, then beat in most of the milk. Add to the flour mixture and beat to make a thick, smooth batter. Add the remaining milk, melted spread and coconut, if using, and continue beating until the batter is smooth and of a fairly thin, dropping consistency.

2 Spray a large non-stick frying pan with a very thin coating of oil. Heat, then pour in a little batter to cover the base. Fry until golden brown, then toss or turn with a spatula.

3 Repeat Step 2 with the remaining mixture to make about eight pancakes. Dice the mango, chop the bananas and slice the kiwi fruit. Peel the orange and cut into segments.

4 Place the fruit in a bowl. Mix the lemon and orange juices and honey, then pour over the fruit.

5 Spoon a little fruit down the centre of a pancake and fold over each side. Repeat with the remaining pancakes. Dust with icing sugar and serve solo or with low-fat Greek yogurt.

NUTRITIONAL NOTES
Per portion:

Energy	303Kcals/1280kJ
Fat, total	4.7g
Saturated fat	0.98g
Cholesterol	49.9mg
Fibre	4.2g

Blueberry Pancakes

3 Heat a few drops of oil in a pancake pan or heavy frying pan until just hazy. Pour on about 30ml/2 tbsp of the batter and swirl it around until it makes a neat pancake.

4 Cook for 2–3 minutes. When almost set on top, sprinkle over 15–30ml/1–2 tbsp of the blueberries. As soon as the base is loose and golden brown, turn the pancake over.

5 Cook on the second side for only about 1 minute, until golden and crisp. Slide the pancake on to a plate and keep warm while you make 17 more pancakes in the same way. Serve drizzled with maple syrup, if you like, and offer lemon wedges for squeezing.

These American-style pancakes became popular as a breakfast option, but are equally good as a dessert.

INGREDIENTS

Serves 6

115g/4oz/1 cup self-raising (self-rising) flour
pinch of salt
40g/1 1/2 oz/3 tbsp caster (superfine) sugar
2 eggs
120ml/4fl oz/1/2 cup skimmed milk
15ml/1 tbsp vegetable oil
115g/4oz fresh or frozen blueberries
maple syrup and lemon wedges, to serve

1 Sift the flour and salt into a bowl. Add the sugar. In a separate bowl, beat the eggs thoroughly. Make a well in the flour and stir in the eggs.

2 Gradually blend in a little of the milk to make a smooth batter. Whisk in the rest of the milk for 1–2 minutes. Rest for 20–30 minutes.

COOK'S TIP

Instead of blueberries you could use fresh or thawed and drained frozen blackberries or raspberries.

NUTRITIONAL NOTES	
Per portion:	
Energy	146Kcals/618kJ
Fat, total	3.9g
Saturated fat	0.76g
Cholesterol	64.6mg
Fibre	0.9g

Apple and Blackcurrant Pancakes

These pancakes are made with a wholemeal batter and are filled with a delicious fruit mixture.

INGREDIENTS

Serves 4

115g/4oz/1 cup wholemeal (whole-wheat)
    flour
300ml/1/2 pint/11/4 cups skimmed milk
1 egg, beaten
15ml/1 tbsp sunflower oil
spray oil, for greasing
half-fat crème fraîche, to serve (optional)
toasted nuts or sesame seeds,
    for sprinkling (optional)
For the filling
450g/1lb cooking apples
225g/8oz/2 cups blackcurrants
30–45ml/2–3 tbsp water
30ml/2 tbsp demerara (raw) sugar

1 Make the pancake batter. Place the flour in a mixing bowl and make a well in the centre.

2 Add a little of the milk with the egg and the oil. Whisk the flour into the liquid, then gradually whisk in the rest of the milk, keeping the batter smooth. Cover the batter and put it in the refrigerator while you prepare the filling.

3 Quarter, peel and core the apples. Slice them into a pan and add the blackcurrants and water. Cook over a gentle heat for 10–15 minutes until the fruit is soft. Stir in enough demerara sugar to sweeten.

4 Apply a light, even coat of spray oil to a pancake pan. Heat the pan, pour in about 30ml/ 2 tbsp batter, swirl it around and cook for about 1 minute. Flip the pancake over with a palette knife and cook the other side. Keep the pancake hot while cooking the remaining pancakes (unless cooking to order).

5 Fill the pancakes with the apple and blackcurrant mixture and fold or roll them up. Serve with a dollop of crème fraîche, if using, and sprinkle with nuts or sesame seeds, if you like.

NUTRITIONAL NOTES
Per portion:

Energy	120Kcals/505kJ
Fat, total	3g
Saturated fat	0.5g
Cholesterol	25mg
Fibre	0g

Cherry Pancakes

These pancakes are virtually fat-free, and lower in calories and higher in fibre than traditional ones.

INGREDIENTS

Serves 4

50g/2oz/1/2 cup plain (all-purpose) flour
50g/2oz/1/2 cup wholemeal (whole-wheat) flour
pinch of salt
1 egg white
150ml/1/4 pint/2/3 cup skimmed milk
150ml/1/4 pint/2/3 cup water
spray oil for frying
For the filling
425g/15oz can black cherries in syrup
7.5ml/1 1/2 tsp arrowroot

2 Apply a light coat of spray oil to a non-stick frying pan. Heat the pan, then pour a little batter, swirling the pan to cover the base evenly.

3 Cook until the pancake is set and golden, then turn to cook the other side. Slide on to kitchen paper and cook the remaining 8 pancakes.

4 Drain the cherries, reserving the syrup. Mix about 30ml/2 tbsp of the syrup with the arrowroot in a pan. Stir in the rest of the syrup. Heat gently, stirring, until the mixture boils, thickens and clears. Add the cherries and stir until heated. Spoon the cherries into the pancakes and fold them in quarters. Serve immediately.

1 Sift the flours and salt into a bowl, adding any bran left in the sieve (strainer) to the bowl at the end. Make a well in the centre of the flour and add the egg white, then the milk and water. Beat with a wooden spoon, gradually incorporating the flour mixture, then whisk the batter hard until it is smooth and bubbly.

NUTRITIONAL NOTES
Per portion:

Energy	190Kcals/800kJ
Fat, total	1.7g
Saturated fat	0.23g
Cholesterol	0.8mg
Fibre	2.2g

Summer Berry Crêpes

The delicate flavour of these fluffy crêpes contrasts beautifully with tangy summer berry fruits.

Serves 4

115g/4oz/1 cup self-raising (self-rising) flour
1 large egg
300ml/1/2 pint/11/4 cups skimmed milk
a few drops of pure vanilla extract
spray oil, for greasing
icing (confectioners') sugar, for dusting
For the fruit
15ml/1 tbsp low-fat spread
50g/2oz/1/4 cup caster (superfine) sugar
juice of 2 oranges
thinly pared rind of 1/2 orange
350g/12oz/3 cups mixed summer berries, such as sliced strawberries, yellow raspberries, blueberries and redcurrants
45ml/3 tbsp Grand Marnier or other orange-flavoured liqueur

1 Preheat the oven to 150ºC/ 300ºF/Gas 2. To make the crêpes, sift the flour into a large bowl and make a well in the centre. Break in the egg and gradually whisk in the milk to make a smooth batter. Stir in the vanilla extract. Set the batter aside in a cool place for up to half an hour.

2 Apply a light, even coat of spray oil to an 18cm/7in non-stick frying pan. Whisk the batter, then pour a little of it into the hot pan, swirling to cover the base evenly. Cook until the mixture comes away from the sides and the crêpe is golden underneath.

3 Flip the crêpe over with a large palette knife and cook the other side briefly until golden. Slide the crêpe on to a heatproof plate. Make seven more crêpes in the same way. Cover the crêpes with foil or another plate and keep them hot in a warm oven.

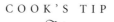

COOK'S TIP

For safety, when igniting a mixture for flambéing, use a long taper or long wooden match and stand back.

4 Melt the spread in a heavy frying pan, stir in the sugar and cook gently. Add the orange juice and rind and cook until syrupy. Then add the fruits and warm through (reserve some for decoration), add the liqueur and set it alight. Shake the pan until the flame dies down.

5 Fold the pancakes into quarters and arrange two on each plate. Spoon over the fruit mixture and dust with icing sugar. Serve the remaining fruit separately.

NUTRITIONAL NOTES

Per portion:

Energy	285Kcals/1203kJ
Fat, total	5g
Saturated fat	1.06g
Cholesterol	59.5mg
Fibre	3.5g

Blueberry and Orange Crêpe Baskets

Impress your guests with these fruit-filled crêpes. When blueberries are out of season, try raspberries.

INGREDIENTS

Serves 6

150g/5oz/1¼ cups plain (all-purpose)
    flour
pinch of salt
2 egg whites
200ml/7fl oz/scant 1 cup skimmed milk
150ml/¼ pint/⅔ cup orange juice
spray oil, for greasing
For the filling
4 medium-size oranges
225g/8oz/2 cups blueberries

NUTRITIONAL NOTES

Per portion:

Energy	165Kcals/697kJ
Fat, total	1.4g
Saturated fat	0.16g
Cholesterol	0.7mg
Fibre	3.2g

1 Preheat the oven to 200ºC/
400ºF/Gas 6. Sift the flour and
salt into a bowl. Make a well in the
centre and add the egg whites,
milk and orange juice. Beat the
liquid, gradually incorporating the
surrounding flour mixture, then
whisk the batter until it is smooth
and bubbly.

2 Apply a light, even coat of
spray oil to a heavy or non-
stick pancake pan and heat it. Pour
in just enough batter to cover the
base of the pan, swirling it to cover
the pan evenly.

3 Cook until the pancake has
set and is golden underneath
and then turn it to cook on the
other side. Slide the pancake on
to a sheet of kitchen paper. Cook
the remaining batter, to make
six pancakes.

4 Invert six small ovenproof
bowls or moulds on a baking
sheet and drape a pancake over
each. Bake them in the oven for
about 10 minutes, until they are
crisp and set into shape. Carefully
lift the "baskets" off the moulds
and set aside.

5 Pare a thin piece of orange
rind from one orange and cut
it in fine strips. Blanch the strips in
boiling water for 30 seconds, rinse
them in cold water and drain well.
Cut all the peel and white pith

6 Cut the oranges into segments,
working over a bowl to catch
the juice. Add the segments and
juice to the blueberries in a pan
and warm through gently. Spoon
the fruit into the baskets and
scatter the shreds of rind over
the top.

COOK'S TIP

Don't fill the pancake baskets
until you are ready to serve
them, because they will absorb
the fruit juice and begin
to soften.

Ginger and Honey Syrup

Particularly good for winter puddings, this virtually fat-free sauce can be served hot or cold with fruit salad.

INGREDIENTS

Serves 4

1 lemon

4 green cardamom pods

1 cinnamon stick

150ml/¼ pint/⅔ cup clear honey

3 pieces stem ginger, plus

   30ml/2 tbsp syrup from the jar

60ml/4 tbsp water

3 Place the lemon rind, cardamoms, cinnamon stick, honey, ginger syrup and water lower in a pan Boil then simmer for 2 minutes.

4 Chop the ginger and stir it into the sauce with the lemon juice. Pour over a winter fruit salad or try it with a baked fruit compote. Chill to serve.

1 Thinly pare two strips of rind from the lemon with a vegetable peeler.

2 Lightly crush the cardamom pods with the back of a heavy knife. Cut the lemon in half. Reserve half for another recipe and squeeze the juice from the remaining half. Set the juice aside.

NUTRITIONAL NOTES
Per portion:

Energy	145Kcals/611kJ
Fat, total	0.1g
Saturated fat	0g
Cholesterol	0mg
Fibre	0g

Lemon and Lime Sauce

This tangy sauce goes well with pancakes or fruit tarts, or as an accompaniment to an orange or mandarin cheesecake.

INGREDIENTS

Serves 4

1 lemon

2 limes

50g/2oz/¹/4 cup caster (superfine) sugar

25ml/1¹/2 tbsp arrowroot

300ml/¹/2 pint/1¹/4 cups water

freshly made pancakes, to serve

fresh lemon balm or mint leaves, to decorate

NUTRITIONAL NOTES

Per portion:

Energy	75Kcals/317kJ
Fat, total	0.1g
Saturated fat	0g
Cholesterol	0mg
Fibre	0g

1 Using a citrus zester, pare the rinds thinly from the lemon and limes. Squeeze the juice from the fruit.

VARIATION

This sauce can also be made with orange and lemon rind if you prefer.

2 Place all the rind in a pan, cover with water and bring to the boil. Drain through a sieve (strainer) and set it aside.

3 Mix a little sugar and the arrowroot with enough water to give a smooth paste. Add to the remaining water, heat, and stir until the sauce boils and thickens.

4 Stir in the remaining sugar, the citrus juice and the reserved rind. Serve hot with freshly made pancakes. Decorate with lemon balm or mint.

COLD LOW-FAT PUDDINGS & DESSERTS

❖ ◆ ❖

Rich Blackcurrant Coulis

There can be few more impressive desserts than this – port wine jelly with swirled cream hearts.

Serves 8

6 sheets of leaf gelatine
475ml/16fl oz/2 cups water
225g/8oz/2 cups blackcurrants
225g/8oz/1 cup caster (superfine) sugar
150ml/¼ pint/⅔ cup ruby port
30ml/2 tbsp crème de cassis
120ml/4fl oz/½ cup single (light) cream,
   to decorate

1 In a small bowl, soak the gelatine in 75ml/5 tbsp of the water until soft.

2 Place the blackcurrants, sugar and 300ml/½ pint/1¼ cups of the remaining water in a large pan. Bring to the boil, lower the heat and simmer for 20 minutes.

3 Strain through a sieve (strainer) and reserve the cooking liquid in a large jug (pitcher). Put the blackcurrants in a bowl and pour over 60ml/4 tbsp of the reserved cooking liquid.

4 Squeeze the water out of the gelatine and place in a pan with the port, cassis and remaining water. Heat gently to dissolve the gelatine. Stir the gelatine mixture into the jug of blackcurrant liquid.

5 Run 6–8 jelly moulds under cold water, drain and place in a roasting pan. Fill with the port mixture. Chill for at least 6 hours until set. Tip the bowl of blackcurrants into a food processor, purée until smooth, then pass through a fine sieve.

6 Run a fine knife around each jelly. Dip each mould in hot water for 5–10 seconds, then turn the jelly out on to your hand. Place on a plate and spoon the coulis around the jelly.

7 To decorate, drop a little cream at intervals on to the coulis. Draw a cocktail stick (toothpick) through the cream dots, dragging each into a heart shape.

NUTRITIONAL NOTES	
Per portion:	
Energy	276Kcals/1163kJ
Fat, total	3.8g
Saturated fat	2.4g
Cholesterol	11mg
Fibre	2.7g

Raspberry Muesli Layer

As well as being a delicious dessert, this can also be served for breakfast.

Serves 4

225g/8oz/2 cups fresh or frozen and thawed raspberries

250ml/8fl oz/1 cup low-fat natural (plain) yogurt

75g/3oz/¹/2 cup Swiss-style muesli (granola)

3 Sprinkle a layer of Swiss-style muesli over the yogurt.

4 Continue the layers until all the ingredients have been used. Top each dessert with a whole raspberry.

1 Reserve four raspberries to decorate, then spoon a few raspberries into four glass dishes.

2 Top the raspberries in each glass with yogurt.

NUTRITIONAL NOTES
Per portion:

Energy	114Kcals/481kJ
Fat, total	1.7g
Saturated fat	0.48g
Cholesterol	2.3mg
Fibre	2.6g

Strawberries in Spiced Grape Jelly

The cinnamon combines with the sun-ripened strawberries to make a dessert for a summer dinner party.

Serves 4

475ml/16fl oz/2 cups red grape juice

1 cinnamon stick

1 small orange

15ml/1 tbsp powdered gelatine

225g/8oz/2 cups strawberries, chopped, plus extra to decorate

1 Pour the grape juice into a pan and add the cinnamon stick. Pare the rind from the orange. Add most of it to the pan but shred some pieces and set them aside for the decoration. Place the pan over a very low heat for 10 minutes, then remove the flavourings.

2 Squeeze the juice from the orange into a bowl and sprinkle over the powdered gelatine. When the mixture is spongy, stir into the grape juice until it has completely dissolved. Allow the jelly to cool in the bowl until just beginning to set.

3 Stir in the strawberries and quickly tip into a 1 litre/1¾ pint/4 cup mould or serving dish. Chill until set.

4 Dip the mould quickly into hot water and invert on to a serving plate. Decorate with strawberries and shreds of orange rind.

NUTRITIONAL NOTES

Per portion:

Energy	85Kcals/355kJ
Fat, total	0.2g
Saturated fat	0g
Cholesterol	0mg
Fibre	1.04g

Chilled Oranges in Syrup

This popular classic is light and
refreshing. A perfect dish to serve
after a heavy main course.

INGREDIENTS

Serves 4

4 oranges

600ml/1 pint/2^1/2 cups water

350g/12oz/1^1/2 cups granulated (white)
   sugar

30ml/2 tbsp lemon juice

30ml/2 tbsp orange flower water or
   rose water

40g/1^1/2oz/^{1}/3 cup unsalted pistachio nuts,
   shelled and chopped

NUTRITIONAL NOTES

Per portion:

Energy	467Kcals/1980kJ
Fat, total	4.9g
Saturated fat	0.59g
Cholesterol	0mg
Fibre	3.1g

2 Cut the peel into strips and
boil in fresh water several
times to remove the bitterness.
Drain on kitchen paper.

3 Place the water, sugar and
lemon juice in a pan. Bring to
the boil, add the pared rind and
simmer until the syrup thickens.
Add the orange flower or rose
water, stir and then cool.

1 Peel the oranges with a
vegetable peeler, avoiding
the pith.

COOK'S TIP

Almonds could be substituted
for the pistachio nuts, if you like,
but don't be tempted to increase
the quantity or you'll raise the
level of fat.

4 Remove any pith and slice the
oranges. Arrange in a serving
dish, pour over the syrup and
chill for 1–2 hours. Serve with
pistachio nuts.

Grapes in Grape-yogurt Jelly

This light, refreshing combination makes a great special-occasion dessert, but takes very little time to make.

INGREDIENTS

Serves 4

200g/7oz/1³/4 cups white seedless grapes

450ml/³/4 pint/scant 2 cups unsweetened white grape juice

15ml/1 tbsp powdered gelatine

120ml/4fl oz/¹/2 cup low-fat natural (plain) yogurt

1 Set aside four tiny bunches of grapes for decoration. Pull the rest off their stalks and cut them in half.

2 Divide the grapes among four stemmed glasses and tilt the glasses on one side, propping them firmly in a bowl of ice.

3 Heat the grape juice in a pan until almost boiling. Remove it from the heat and sprinkle the gelatine over the surface, stirring until it dissolves.

4 Pour half the grape juice over the grapes and leave to set.

5 Cool the remaining grape juice until on the verge of setting, then stir in the low-fat natural yogurt.

6 Stand the set glasses upright and pour in the yogurt mixture. Chill to set, then decorate the rim of each glass with grapes, and serve.

NUTRITIONAL NOTES

Per portion:

Energy	113Kcals/480kJ
Fat, total	0.4g
Saturated fat	0.16g
Cholesterol	1.3mg
Fibre	0g

COOK'S TIP

For an easier version, stand the glasses upright rather than at an angle – then they can be put in the refrigerator to set rather than packed with ice in a container.

Fresh Citrus Jelly

Fresh fruit jellies really are worth the effort – they're packed with fresh flavour, natural colour and vitamins.

Serves 4

3 medium oranges

1 lemon

1 lime

300ml/½ pint/1¼ cups water

75g/3oz/6 tbsp golden caster (superfine) sugar

15ml/1 tbsp powdered gelatine

extra slices of citrus fruit, to decorate

1 With a sharp knife, cut all the peel and white pith from one orange and carefully remove the segments. Arrange in the base of a 900ml/1½ pint/3¾ cup mould. Chill.

2 Remove some shreds of citrus rind and reserve them for decoration. Grate the remaining rind from the lemon and lime and one orange. Place in a pan, with the water and sugar.

3 Heat gently, without boiling, until the sugar has dissolved. Take off the heat. Squeeze the juice from all the rest of the fruit and stir into the pan.

4 Strain the hot liquid into a measuring jug (cup) to remove the rind. You should have about 600ml/1 pint/2½ cups of liquid; if necessary, make up the amount with hot water. Sprinkle the gelatine over the liquid and stir until it has dissolved.

COOK'S TIP

To speed up the setting of the fruit segments in jelly, stand the dish in a bowl of ice. Or, if you're short of time, simply stir the segments into the liquid jelly, pour into a serving dish and set it all together.

5 Pour a little of the jelly over the orange segments and chill until set. Leave the remaining jelly at room temperature to cool, but not set.

6 Pour the remaining cooled jelly into the dish and chill until set. To serve, turn out the jelly and decorate it with the reserved citrus rind shreds and extra slices of citrus fruit.

NUTRITIONAL NOTES
Per portion:

Energy	137Kcals/580kJ
Fat, total	0.2g
Saturated fat	0g
Cholesterol	0mg
Fibre	2.1g

Orange-blossom Jelly

The natural flavour of fresh orange juice has a cleansing quality.

INGREDIENTS

Serves 4

65g/2¹/2oz/¹/3 cup caster (superfine) sugar
150ml/¹/4 pint/²/3 cup water
25g/1oz powdered gelatine
600ml/1 pint/2¹/2 cups fresh orange juice
30ml/2 tbsp orange flower water

NUTRITIONAL NOTES

Per portion:

Energy	135Kcals/573kJ
Fat, total	0g
Saturated fat	0g
Cholesterol	0mg
Fibre	0.2g

1 Place the caster sugar and water in a small pan and heat gently to dissolve the sugar. Pour into a heatproof bowl and leave to cool.

2 Sprinkle the gelatine over the surface of the syrup. Leave to stand until it has absorbed all the liquid.

3 Gently melt the gelatine over a pan of simmering water until it becomes clear and transparent. Leave to cool. When the gelatine is cold, mix it with the orange juice and orange flower water.

4 Wet a jelly mould and pour in the jelly. Chill in the refrigerator for at least 2 hours, or until set. Turn out to serve.

Ground Rice Pudding

This light ground rice pudding is the perfect end to a spicy meal.

Serves 4–6

50g/2oz/1/2 cup coarsely ground rice
25g/1oz/2 tbsp ground almonds
4 green cardamom pods, crushed
900ml/1 1/2 pints/3 3/4 cups semi-skimmed
    (low-fat) milk
75g/3oz/6 tbsp caster (superfine) sugar
15ml/1 tbsp rose water
15ml/1 tbsp crushed pistachio nuts,
    to decorate (optional)

1 Place the ground rice and almonds in a pan with the green cardamom pods. Add 600ml/1 pint/2 1/2 cups milk and bring to the boil over a medium heat, stirring occasionally.

2 Add the remaining milk and cook over a medium heat for about ten minutes or until the rice mixture thickens to the consistency of a creamy chicken soup.

3 Stir in the sugar and rose water and continue to cook for a further 2 minutes. Serve garnished with pistachio nuts, if wished.

NUTRITIONAL NOTES

Per portion:

Energy	201Kcals/844kJ
Fat, total	8.78g
Saturated fat	2.57g
Cholesterol	14.70mg
Fibre	0g

Clementine Jelly

This jelly has a clear fruity taste and can be made extra special by adding a little white rum or Cointreau.

INGREDIENTS

Serves 4

12 clementines

clear unsweetened white grape juice
 (see method for amount)

15ml/1 tbsp powdered gelatine

30ml/2 tbsp caster (superfine) sugar

60ml/4 tbsp half-fat crème fraîche,
 for topping

VARIATION

Use ruby grapefruit instead of clementines, if you prefer. Squeeze the juice from half the grapefruit and segment the rest.

1 Squeeze the juice from eight of the clementines and pour it into a jug (pitcher). Make up to 600ml/1 pint/2½ cups with the grape juice, then strain the juice mixture through a fine sieve (strainer).

2 Pour half the juice mixture into a pan. Sprinkle the gelatine on top, leave for 5 minutes, then heat gently until the gelatine has dissolved. Stir in the sugar and remaining juice; set aside.

3 Pare the rind very thinly from the remaining fruit and set it aside. Using a sharp knife, cut between the membrane and fruit to separate the citrus segments. Discard the membrane and pith.

4 Place half the segments in four dessert glasses and cover with some of the liquid fruit jelly. Place in the refrigerator to set.

5 Arrange the remaining segments on top. Pour over the remaining jelly and chill until set. Cut the clementine rind into shreds. Serve the jellies topped with a spoonful of crème fraîche scattered with clementine shreds.

NUTRITIONAL NOTES

Per portion:

Energy	142Kcals/600kJ
Fat, total	2.5g
Saturated fat	1.4g
Cholesterol	15.8mg
Fibre	1.5g

Mexican Lemony Rice Pudding

Rice pudding is popular the world over. This Mexican version is light and attractive.

INGREDIENTS

Serves 4

75g/3oz/¹/2 cup raisins

90g/3¹/2oz/¹/2 cup short grain rice

2.5cm/1in strip of pared lime or
    lemon rind

250ml/8fl oz/1 cup water

475ml/16fl oz/2 cups skimmed milk

225g/8oz/1 cup granulated (white) sugar

1.5ml/¹/4 tsp salt

2.5cm/1in cinnamon stick

1 egg yolk, well beaten

15ml/1 tbsp low-fat spread

10ml/2 tsp toasted flaked (sliced) almonds
    to decorate

orange segments to serve

3 Discard the cinnamon stick. Drain the raisins well. Add the raisins, egg yolk and low-fat spread, stirring constantly until the spread has been absorbed, the raisins evenly distributed and the pudding is rich and creamy.

4 Cook the pudding for a few minutes longer. Tip the rice into a serving dish and allow to cool. Decorate with the toasted flaked almonds and add a few orange segments to each serving.

NUTRITIONAL NOTES
Per portion:

Energy	450Kcals/1903kJ
Fat, total	4.9g
Saturated fat	0.88g
Cholesterol	53mg
Fibre	1.4g

1 Put the raisins into a small bowl. Cover with warm water and set aside to soak. Put the rice into a pan together with the pared lime or lemon rind and water. Bring slowly to the boil, then lower the heat. Cover the pan and simmer gently for about 20 minutes or until all the water has been absorbed.

2 Remove the rind from the rice and discard it. Add the milk, sugar, salt and cinnamon stick. Cook, stirring, over a very low heat until the milk has been absorbed. Do not cover the pan.

Fragrant Rice with Dates

Moroccan rice puddings are sprinkled with either nuts and honey or wrapped in pastry. This is a low-fat version.

INGREDIENTS

Serves 4

75g/3oz/½ cup short grain rice

about 900ml/1½ pints/3¾ cups
  skimmed milk

30ml/2 tbsp ground rice

50g/2oz/¼ cup caster (superfine) sugar

15g/½oz/2 tbsp ground almonds

5ml/1 tsp vanilla extract

2.5ml/½ tsp almond extract

a little orange flower water (optional)

30ml/2 tbsp chopped dates

30ml/2 tbsp unsalted, pistachio nuts,
  finely chopped

1 Place the rice in a pan with 750ml/1¼ pints/3 cups of the milk and gradually heat until simmering. Cook, uncovered, over a very low heat for 30–40 minutes, until the rice is completely tender, stirring frequently.

2 Blend the ground rice with the remaining milk and add to the pan, stirring. Slowly bring back to the boil and cook for 1 minute.

3 Stir in the sugar, ground almonds, vanilla and almond extracts and orange flower water, if using. Cook until the pudding is thick and creamy.

4 Pour into serving bowls and sprinkle with the chopped dates and pistachiosto decorate. Allow to cool before serving.

NUTRITIONAL NOTES
Per portion:

Energy	270Kcals/1135kJ
Fat, total	4.8g
Saturated fat	0.55g
Cholesterol	4.5mg
Fibre	0.4g

Rice Pudding with Mixed Berry Sauce

*A compote of red berries contrasts
beautifully with creamy rice
pudding for a richly flavoured
cool dessert.*

INGREDIENTS

Serves 6

low-fat spread, for greasing

400g/14oz/2 cups short grain rice

325ml/11fl oz/scant 1¹/2 cups
skimmed milk

pinch salt

115g/4oz/²/3 cup soft light brown sugar

5ml/1 tsp pure vanilla extract

2 eggs, beaten

grated rind of 1 lemon

5ml/1 tsp lemon juice

30ml/2 tbsp low-fat spread

strawberry leaves, to decorate

For the sauce

225g/8oz/2 cups strawberries, hulled
and quartered

225g/8oz/2 cups raspberries

115g/4oz/¹/2 cup granulated (white) sugar

grated rind of 1 lemon

1 Preheat the oven to 160°C/
325°F/Gas 3. Grease a deep
2 litre/3¹/2 pint/8 cup baking dish.
Add the rice to boiling water and
boil for 5 minutes. Drain. Transfer
the rice to the prepared baking dish.

2 Combine the milk, salt, brown
sugar, vanilla, eggs, lemon
rind and juice. Pour over the rice
and stir.

3 Dot the surface of the rice
mixture with the spread. Bake
for 50 minutes until the rice is
cooked and creamy.

4 Meanwhile, mix the berries
and sugar in a pan. Stir over
low heat until the sugar has
dissolved and the fruit is becoming
soft and pulpy.

5 Transfer to a bowl and stir in
the lemon rind. Cool, then
chill the sauce until required.

6 Remove the rice pudding
from the oven. Leave to cool.
Serve with the berry sauce.
Then decorate with fresh
strawberry leaves.

NUTRITIONAL NOTES
Per portion:

Energy	474Kcals/1991kJ
Fat, total	4.9g
Saturated fat	0.95g
Cholesterol	65.5mg
Fibre	1.4g

Fresh Fruit with Caramel Rice

This creamy rice pudding with a crisp caramel crust sounds wickedly indulgent, but is relatively low in fat.

INGREDIENTS

Serves 4

50g/2oz/generous ¼ cup short grain rice

low-fat spread, for greasing

75ml/5 tbsp demerara (raw) sugar

pinch of salt

400g/14oz can light evaporated milk made
  up to 600ml/1 pint/2½ cups with water

2 crisp eating apples

1 small fresh pineapple

10ml/2 tsp lemon juice

1 Preheat the oven to 150°C/ 300°F/Gas 2. Wash the rice under cold water. Drain well and put into a lightly greased soufflé dish.

2 Add 30ml/2 tbsp of the sugar to the dish, with the salt. Pour on the diluted evaporated milk and stir gently. Bake for 2 hours, then leave to cool for 30 minutes.

3 Meanwhile, peel, core and cut the apples and pineapple into thin slices, then cut the pineapple into chunks. Toss the fruit in lemon juice, coating thoroughly, and set aside.

4 Preheat the grill (broiler) and sprinkle the remaining sugar over the rice. Grill (broil) for 5 minutes to caramelize the sugar. Leave to stand for 5 minutes to harden the caramel. Serve with the fresh fruit.

NUTRITIONAL NOTES

Per portion:

Energy	309Kcals/1293kJ
Fat, total	4.6g
Saturated fat	2.51g
Cholesterol	34mg
Fibre	2.8g

Rice Fruit Sundae

*Cook a rice pudding on top of the
stove instead of in the oven for a
light creamy texture.*

INGREDIENTS

Serves 4

50g/2oz/1/3 cup short grain rice
600ml/1 pint/2 1/2 cups skimmed milk
5ml/1 tsp pure vanilla extract
2.5ml/1/2 tsp ground cinnamon
25g/1oz/2 tbsp granulated (white) sugar
200g/7oz/1 3/4 cups strawberries,
    raspberries or blueberries, to serve

1 Put the rice, milk, vanilla
extract, cinnamon and sugar
into a medium-sized pan. Bring to
the boil, stirring constantly, and
then turn down the heat so that
the mixture barely simmers.

2 Cook the rice for 30–40
minutes, stirring occasionally,
until the grains are soft. Tip into a
bowl and allow the rice to cool,
stirring occasionally. Chill the rice
in the refrigerator.

NUTRITIONAL NOTES

Per portion:

Energy	169Kcals/711kJ
Fat, total	3.3g
Saturated fat	0.1g
Cholesterol	3mg
Fibre	0.9g

3 Just before serving, stir the rice
and spoon into four sundae
dishes. Top with the prepared fruit.

VARIATION

Instead of simple short grain rice
try using a Thai fragrant or
jasmine rice for a delicious natural
flavour. For a firmer texture, an
Italian arborio rice makes a good
pudding too. You could also use
other toppings, such as toasted,
chopped hazelnuts or toasted
coconut flakes. Another fruit
combination could be mango,
pineapple and banana for a fresh
tropical taste.

Summer Pudding

Summer pudding is an annual treat, and need not be high in fat if you avoid serving it with cream.

INGREDIENTS

Serves 6

1 loaf of white crusty bread,
   1–2 days old, sliced
675g/1½lb/6 cups fresh redcurrants
75g/3oz/6 tbsp granulated (white) sugar
60ml/4 tbsp water
450g/1lb/4 cups mixed berries, plus extra
   to decorate
sprig of mint, to decorate
juice of ½ lemon

NUTRITIONAL NOTES

Per portion:

Energy	272Kcals/1152kJ
Fat, total	1.6g
Saturated fat	0g
Cholesterol	0mg
Fibre	7.6g

1 Trim the crusts from the bread slices and cut a round to fit in the bottom of a 1.5 litre/2½ pint/6 cup heatproof bowl. Line the bowl with bread slices, overlapping them slightly. Reserve enough to cover the top of the bowl. Mix the redcurrants with 50g/2oz/¼ cup of the sugar and the water in a pan. Heat gently, lightly crushing the berries. When the sugar has dissolved, remove from the heat.

2 Tip the redcurrant mixture into a food processor and process until smooth. Press through a fine sieve (strainer) set over a bowl. Discard the pressed fruit pulp left in the sieve.

3 Put the mixed berries in a bowl with the remaining sugar and the lemon juice. Stir well.

4 One at a time, remove the cut bread pieces from the bowl and dip them in the redcurrant purée. Replace to line the bowl evenly.

5 Spoon the berries into the lined bowl, pressing them down evenly. Top with the reserved cut bread slices, which have been dipped in the redcurrant purée.

6 Cover the bowl with clear film (plastic wrap). Set a small plate, just big enough to fit inside the rim of the bowl, on top of the pudding. Weigh it down with cans of food. Chill in the refrigerator for 8–24 hours.

7 To turn out, remove the weights, plate and clear film. Run a knife between the bowl and the pudding to loosen it. Invert on to a serving plate. Decorate with a sprig of mint and a few berries. Serve in wedges.

Autumn Pudding

Here is an autumn version of the traditional summer pudding.

INGREDIENTS

Serves 6

450g/1lb eating apples

450g/1lb plums, halved and stoned (pitted)

225g/8oz/2 cups blackberries

60ml/4 tbsp apple juice

sugar or honey, to sweeten (optional)

8 slices of wholemeal (whole-wheat) bread,
    crusts removed

mint sprig and blackberry, to decorate

half-fat crème fraîche, to serve (optional)

3 Spoon the fruit into the bowl with enough juice to moisten.

4 Set aside any remaining juice. Cover the fruit completely with bread. Fit a plate on the top, resting just below the rim and stand the bowl in a larger bowl to catch any juice. Weight the plate and chill overnight.

5 Turn the pudding out on a plate and pour the reserved juice over any areas that have not absorbed the juice. Decorate with the mint sprig and blackberry. Serve with half-fat crème fraîche, if you like.

1 Quarter the apples, remove the cores and peel, and slice them into a pan. Add the plums, blackberries and apple juice. Cover and cook gently for 10–15 minutes until tender. Sweeten, if necessary, with a little sugar or honey.

2 Line the bottom and sides of a 1.2 litre/2 pint/5 cup heatproof bowl with slices of bread, cut to fit. Press together tightly.

NUTRITIONAL NOTES
Per portion:

Energy	141Kcals/595kJ
Fat, total	1.1g
Saturated fat	0.17g
Cholesterol	0mg
Fibre	5.4g

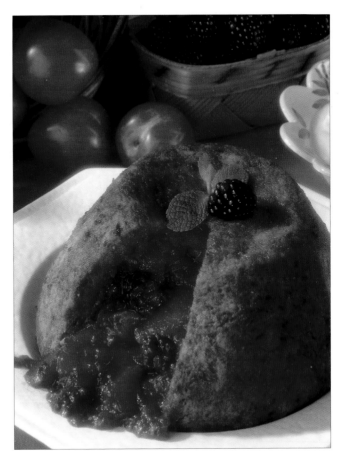

Two-tone Yogurt Ring with Tropical Fruit

A light and colourful dessert with a truly tropical flavour, combining mango, kiwi fruit, lime juice and physalis together.

Serves 6

175ml/6fl oz/³⁄4 cup tropical fruit juice
15ml/1 tbsp powdered gelatine
3 egg whites
150ml/¹⁄4 pint/²⁄3 cup low-fat natural (plain) yogurt
finely grated rind of 1 lime
For the filling
1 mango
2 kiwi fruit
10–12 physalis, plus extra to decorate
juice of 1 lime

1 Pour the tropical fruit juice into a small pan and sprinkle the powdered gelatine over the surface. Heat gently until the gelatine has completely dissolved.

NUTRITIONAL NOTES
Per portion:

Energy	87Kcals/364kJ
Fat, total	0.5g
Saturated fat	0.13g
Cholesterol	1mg
Fibre	2.3g

2 Whisk the egg whites in a grease-free bowl until they hold peaks. Continue whisking hard, gradually adding the yogurt and lime rind.

3 Continue whisking hard and pour in the hot gelatine mixture in a steady stream, until evenly mixed.

4 Quickly pour the mixture into a 1.5 litre/2¹⁄2 pint/6¹⁄4 cup ring mould. Chill the mould in the refrigerator until set. The mixture will separate into two layers.

5 Halve, stone (pit), peel and dice the mango. Peel and slice the kiwi fruit. Remove the husks from the physalis and cut them in half. Toss all the fruits in a bowl and stir in the lime juice.

6 Run a knife around the edge of the ring to loosen the mixture. Dip the mould quickly into hot water, then turn it out on to a serving plate. Spoon all the prepared fruit into the centre of the ring, decorate with the reserved physalis and serve immediately.

VARIATION

Any mixture of fruit works in this recipe, depending on the season. Try using apple juice in the ring mixture and fill it with luscious, red summer fruits.

Fruited Rice Ring

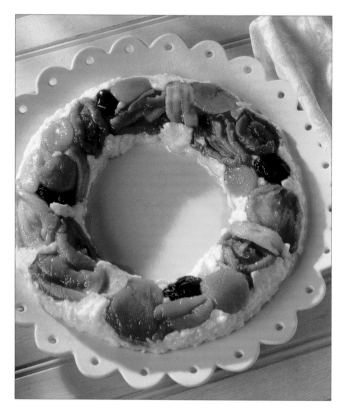

This looks beautiful turned out of a
ring mould, but you can stir the
fruit into the rice and serve in
individual dishes.

Serves 4

65g/2¹/2oz/5 tbsp short grain rice
900ml/1¹/2 pints/3³/4 cups semi-skimmed
    (low-fat) milk
1 cinnamon stick
175g/6oz/1¹/2 cups dried fruit salad
350ml/12fl oz/1¹/2 cups orange juice
45ml/3 tbsp caster (superfine) sugar
finely grated rind of 1 small orange
low-fat oil, for greasing

1 Mix the rice, milk and
cinnamon stick in a large pan
and bring to the boil. Lower the
heat, cover and simmer, stirring
occasionally, for about 1¹/2 hours,
until no free liquid remains.

2 Meanwhile, mix the dried fruit
salad and orange juice in a
pan and bring to the boil. Cover,
then simmer very gently for about
1 hour, until tender and no free
liquid remains.

3 Remove the cinnamon stick
from the rice and stir in the
sugar and orange rind, mixing
thoroughly.

4 Tip the fruit into the base of a
lightly oiled 1.5 litre/2¹/2 pint/
6¹/4 cup ring mould. Spoon the
rice over, smoothing down firmly.
Chill in the refrigerator.

5 Run a knife around the edge of
the mould and turn out the
rice carefully on to a serving plate.

NUTRITIONAL NOTES

Per portion:

Energy	343Kcals/1440kJ
Fat, total	4.4g
Saturated fat	2.26g
Cholesterol	15.75mg
Fibre	1.07g

Dried Fruit Fool

This light, fluffy dessert can be made with a single dried fruit – try dried peaches, prunes, apples or apricots.

INGREDIENTS

Serves 4

300g/11oz/1 1/4 cups ready-to-eat
    dried fruit such as apricots, peaches,
    prunes or apples
300ml/1/2 pint/1 1/4 cups fresh orange juice
250ml/8fl oz/1 cup low-fat fromage frais
2 egg whites
fresh mint sprigs, to decorate

NUTRITIONAL NOTES

Per portion:

Energy	180Kcals/757kJ
Fat, total	0.63g
Saturated fat	0.06g
Cholesterol	0.5mg
Fibre	4.8g

1 Put the dried fruit in a pan, add the orange juice and heat gently until boiling. Lower the heat, cover and simmer gently for 3 minutes.

2 Cool slightly. Tip into a food processor or blender and process until smooth. Stir in the fromage frais.

3 Whisk the egg whites in a grease-free bowl until stiff enough to hold soft peaks, then slowly fold into the fruit mixture until it is all combined.

4 Spoon into four stemmed glasses or one large serving dish. Chill for at least 1 hour. Decorate with the mint sprigs just before serving.

COOK'S TIP

To make a speedier fool leave out the egg whites and simply swirl together the fruit mixture and fromage frais.

Passion Fruit and Apple Foam

Passion fruit have an exotic flavour that lifts this simple apple dessert. You could use two finely chopped kiwi fruit instead.

Serves 4

450g/1lb cooking apples

90ml/6 tbsp unsweetened apple juice

3 passion fruit

3 egg whites

1 red-skinned eating apple, to decorate

5ml/1 tsp lemon juice

1 Peel, core and roughly chop the cooking apples. Put them in a pan with the apple juice.

2 Bring the liquid to the boil, then lower the heat and cover the pan. Cook gently, stirring occasionally, until the apple is very tender.

3 Remove from the heat and beat the apple mixture with a wooden spoon until it forms a fairly smooth purée (or purée the apple in a food processor if you prefer).

4 Cut the passion fruit in half and scoop out the flesh. Stir into the apple purée to mix thoroughly.

5 Place the egg whites in a grease-free bowl and whisk until they form soft peaks. Fold them into the apple mixture. Spoon the apple foam into four serving dishes. Leave to cool.

6 Thinly slice the red-skinned apple and brush the slices with lemon juice to prevent them from browning. Arrange the slices on top of the apple foam and serve cold.

COOK'S TIP

It is important to use a good cooking apple for this recipe, because the fluffy texture of a cooking apple breaks down easily to a purée. You can use dessert apples, but will probably have to purée them in a food processor.

NUTRITIONAL NOTES

Per portion:

Energy	80Kcals/338kJ
Fat, total	0.2g
Saturated fat	0g
Cholesterol	0mg
Fibre	2.9g

Raspberry and Mint Bavarois

A sophisticated dessert that can be made a day in advance to impress guests at a special dinner party.

INGREDIENTS

Serves 6

450g/1lb/4 cups fresh or thawed
    frozen raspberries
30ml/2 tbsp icing (confectioners') sugar
30ml/2 tbsp lemon juice
15ml/1 tbsp finely chopped fresh mint
30ml/2 tbsp powdered gelatine
75ml/5 tbsp boiling water
300ml/1/2 pint/1 1/4 cups low-fat custard
250ml/8fl oz/1 cup low-fat Greek
    (US strained plain) yogurt
fresh mint sprigs, to decorate

1 Reserve a few raspberries for decoration. Place the remaining raspberries in a food processor. Add the icing sugar and lemon juice and process to a smooth purée.

NUTRITIONAL NOTES

Per portion:

Energy	131Kcals/554kJ
Fat, total	2.4g
Saturated fat	1.36g
Cholesterol	4.1mg
Fibre	1.9g

2 Press the purée through a sieve (strainer) to remove the seeds. Pour into a measuring jug (cup) and stir in the mint.

3 Sprinkle 5ml/1 tsp of the gelatine over 30ml/2 tbsp of the boiling water, stirring until it has dissolved. Stir into 150ml/ 1/4 pint/2/3 cup of fruit purée.

4 Pour this jelly into a 1 litre/1 3/4 pint/4 cup mould, and chill in until just setting. Tip the mould to swirl the setting jelly around the sides, and chill until set completely.

5 Mix the custard and low-fat Greek yogurt in a bowl and stir in the remaining fruit purée. Dissolve the rest of the gelatine in the remaining boiling water and stir it in quickly.

6 Pour the raspberry custard into the mould and chill it until it has set completely. To serve, dip the mould quickly into a bowl of hot water and then turn it out on a serving plate. Decorate with the reserved raspberries and the mint sprigs.

COOK'S TIP

You can make this dessert using frozen raspberries, which have a good colour and flavour. Allow them to thaw at room temperature, and use any juice in the jelly.

Raspberry and Cranberry Jelly

INGREDIENTS

Serves 6–8

140g/4¾oz packet raspberry jelly
150ml/¼ pint/⅔ cup boiling water
250ml/8fl oz/1 cup raspberry and
    cranberry juice
115g/4oz/1 cup fresh strawberries
115g/4oz/⅔ cup raspberries
    (fresh or frozen)
1 large red-skinned apple,
    cored and chopped

NUTRITIONAL NOTES

Per portion:

Energy	276Kcals/1163kJ
Fat, total	3.8g
Saturated fat	2.4g
Cholesterol	11mg
Fibre	2.7g

1 Break up the jelly into a heat-proof measuring jug (cup) and pour over the boiling water. Stir until dissolved. Pour in the raspberry and cranberry juice and leave until the jelly is starting to set.

2 Halve or quarter the strawberries, depending on their size. If using frozen raspberries, leave them in the freezer until you put the jelly to set. Prepare the apple last.

3 Have ready a pretty 1.2 litre/2 pint/5 cup mould, rinsed out with cold water. When the jelly is beginning to thicken, stir in the fruits. Spoon into the mould and chill until set.

4 Turn out the jelly on to a serving plate and serve with custard, fromage frais or frozen yogurt ice.

Blackberry and Apple Romanoff

INGREDIENTS

Serves 6–8

350g/12oz (3–4) sharp eating apples,
    peeled, cored and chopped
45ml/3 tbsp caster (superfine) sugar
250ml/8fl oz/1 cup half-fat double
    (heavy) cream
5ml/1 tsp grated lemon rind
90ml/6 tbsp Greek (US strained
    plain) yogurt
50g/2oz (4–6) crisp meringues,
    roughly crumbled
225g/8oz/2 cups blackberries
    (fresh or frozen)
whipped reduced-fat cream, a few
    blackberries and mint leaves,
    to decorate

1 Line a 1–1.2 litre/1¾–2 pint/4–5 cup freezerproof heatproof bowl with clear film (plastic wrap).

2 Toss the apples into a pan with 30ml/2 tbsp sugar and cook for 2–3 minutes, or until softening. Mash with a fork and leave to cool.

3 Whip the cream and fold in the lemon rind, yogurt, the remaining sugar, the apples and meringues.

4 Gently stir in the blackberries, then tip the mixture into the lined freezerproof heatproof bowl and freeze for 1–3 hours.

5 Turn out on to a plate and remove the clear film. Decorate with whirls of cream, blackberries and mint.

NUTRITIONAL NOTES

Per portion:

Energy	148Kcals/621kJ
Fat, total	7.0g
Saturated fat	4.3g
Cholesterol	17mg
Fibre	1.7g

Clementines in Cinnamon Caramel

The combination of sweet, yet sharp clementines and caramel sauce with a hint of spice is divine.

Serves 4

8–12 clementines, about 450–500g/
   1–1¹/₄lb
225g/8oz/1 cup granulated (white) sugar
300ml/¹/₂ pint/1¹/₄ cups warm water
2 cinnamon sticks
30ml/2 tbsp orange-flavoured liqueur
25g/1oz/¹/₄ cup shelled, unsalted
   pistachio nuts

1 Using a vegetable peeler pare the rind from two clementines and cut it into fine strips. Set aside.

2 Peel the clementines, removing all the pith but keeping each fruit intact. Put the fruits in a heatproof serving bowl.

3 Gently heat the sugar in a pan until it dissolves and turns a rich golden brown. Immediately turn off the heat.

4 Protecting your hand with a dish towel, carefully pour in the warm water (the mixture will bubble and splutter). Bring slowly to the boil, stirring, until the caramel has completely dissolved.

5 Add the shredded peel and cinnamon sticks to the pan, then simmer for 5 minutes. Stir in the orange liqueur.

6 Cool the syrup for 10 minutes, then pour it from the pan over the clementines. Cover the bowl, cool, then chill for several hours or overnight.

7 Blanch the unsalted pistachio nuts in boiling water. Drain, cool and remove outer skins. Decorate the clementines by scattering the nuts over the top. Serve immediately.

NUTRITIONAL NOTES

Per portion:

Energy	328Kcals/1392kJ
Fat, total	3.5g
Saturated fat	0.42g
Cholesterol	0mg
Fibre	1.4g

Yogurt with Apricots and Pistachio Nuts

Drain the yogurt overnight to make it thick and add honeyed apricots and nuts for an exotic dessert.

INGREDIENTS

Serves 4

250ml/8fl oz/1 cup low-fat Greek (US strained plain) yogurt

250ml/8fl oz/1 cup low-fat natural (plain) yogurt

175g/6oz/3/4 cup ready-to-eat dried apricots, snipped

15ml/1 tbsp clear honey

10ml/2 tsp roughly chopped unsalted pistachio nuts, plus extra for sprinkling

ground cinnamon, for sprinkling

1 Mix the yogurts and place in a sieve (strainer) over a bowl. Drain overnight in the refrigerator.

2 Discard the yogurt whey. In a pan cover the apricots with water, simmer to soften. Drain, cool, then tip into a bowl and add the honey.

3 Add the yogurt to the apricot mixture, then add the nuts. Spoon into sundae dishes, sprinkle over a little cinnamon and nuts and chill.

NUTRITIONAL NOTES
Per portion:

Energy	164Kcals/689kJ
Fat, total	4.5g
Saturated fat	2g
Cholesterol	5.5mg
Fibre	2.8g

Raspberries and Fruit Purée

Three fruit purées, swirled together, make a kaleidoscopic garnish for a nest of raspberries.

Serves 4–6

200g/7oz/1 cup raspberries
120ml/4fl oz/¹/2 cup red wine
icing (confectioners') sugar, for dusting
For the decoration
1 large mango, peeled and chopped
400g/14oz kiwi fruit, peeled and chopped
200g/7oz/1 cup raspberries
icing (confectioners') sugar, to taste

1 Place the raspberries in a bowl with the red wine and allow to macerate for about 2 hours.

2 Purée separately in a food processor, the mango, kiwi fruit, and the remaining raspberries, adding water if necessary. Press each purée through a sieve (strainer) into a bowl. Sweeten the purées with sifted icing sugar.

3 Spoon each purée on to a serving plate, separating the kiwi and mango with the raspberry purée as if creating a four-wedged pie. Gently tap the plate on the work surface to settle the purées against each other.

4 Using a skewer, draw a spiral outwards from the centre of the plate to the rim. Drain the macerated raspberries, dust them heavily with icing sugar and pile them in the centre of the purées.

NUTRITIONAL NOTES	
Per portion:	
Energy	154Kcals/648kJ
Fat, total	0.9g
Saturated fat	0g
Cholesterol	0mg
Fibre	6.7g

Caramel with Fresh Fruit

A creamy caramel dessert is a wonderful way to end a meal. It is light and delicious, and this recipe is very simple.

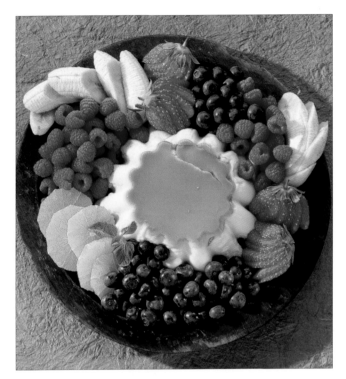

Serves 6

For the caramel

25g/1oz/2 tbsp sugar

30ml/2 tbsp water

For the custard

6 medium eggs

4 drops vanilla extract

90g/3^1/2oz/^{1}/2 cup caster (superfine) sugar

750ml/1^1/4 pints/3 cups semi-skimmed
   (low-fat) milk

fresh fruit for serving

1 To make the caramel, place the sugar and water in a heatproof dish and place in a microwave. Cook for 4 minutes on high or until the sugar has caramelized. Alternatively, melt in a pan until pale gold in colour. Pour on to a 1.2 litre/2 pint/5 cup soufflé dish. Leave to cool.

2 Preheat the oven to 180°C/ 350°F/Gas 4. To make the custard, break the eggs into a medium mixing bowl and whisk until frothy.

3 Stir in the vanilla extract and gradually add the sugar, then the milk, whisking continuously.

4 Pour the custard over the top of the caramel.

5 Cook in the preheated oven for 35–40 minutes. Remove from the oven and leave to cool.

6 Loosen the custard from the side of the dish with a knife. Place a serving dish on top of the soufflé dish and invert, giving a gentle shake.

7 Arrange any fruit of your choice around the caramel and serve.

NUTRITIONAL NOTES

Per portion:

Energy	229Kcals/964kJ
Fat, total	7.40g
Saturated fat	2.77g
Cholesterol	201.25mg
Fibre	0g

Figs with Ricotta Cream

This simple recipe makes the most of the natural sweetness of ripe figs.

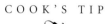

INGREDIENTS

Serves 4

4 ripe, fresh figs

115g/4oz/½ cup ricotta cheese

45ml/3 tbsp half-fat crème fraîche

15ml/1 tbsp clear honey

2.5ml/½ tsp pure vanilla extract

freshly grated nutmeg, to decorate

COOK'S TIP

The honey can be omitted and replaced with a little artificial sweetener.

---

1 Using a small sharp knife, trim the stalks from the figs. Make four cuts through each fig from the stalk-end, cutting them almost through but being careful to leave them joined at the base.

2 Place the figs on serving plates and open them out.

3 In a bowl, mix together the ricotta cheese, crème fraîche, honey and vanilla extract.

4 Spoon a little ricotta cream mixture on to each plate and sprinkle with grated nutmeg to serve.

NUTRITIONAL NOTES

Per portion:

Energy	97Kcals/405kJ
Fat, total	5.0g
Saturated fat	3.04g
Cholesterol	26.2mg
Fibre	0.8g

Apple Foam with Blackberries

This lovely light dish is perfect if you fancy a dessert, but don't want anything too rich or too filling.

Serves 4

225g/8oz/2 cups blackberries
150ml/¼ pint/⅔ cup unsweetened
    apple juice
5ml/1 tsp powdered gelatine
15ml/1 tbsp clear honey
2 egg whites

1 Place the blackberries in a pan with 60ml/4 tbsp of the apple juice and heat gently until the fruit is soft. Remove from the heat, cool, then chill.

2 Sprinkle the gelatine over the remaining apple juice in a small pan and stir over low heat until dissolved. Stir in the honey.

3 Whisk the egg whites until they hold stiff peaks. Continue whisking hard and pour in the hot gelatine mixture gradually, until well mixed.

4 Quickly spoon the foam into rough mounds on individual plates. Chill. Serve with the blackberries and juice spooned around the foam.

NUTRITIONAL NOTES	
Per portion:	
Energy	49Kcals/206kJ
Fat, total	0.2g
Saturated fat	0g
Cholesterol	0mg
Fibre	1.7g

Sensational Strawberries

Strawberries release their finest flavour when moistened.

INGREDIENTS

Serves 4

350g/12oz/2 cups raspberries, fresh
   or frozen
45ml/3 tbsp caster (superfine) sugar
1 passion fruit
675g/1¹/2lb/6 cups small strawberries
dessert biscuits (cookies), to serve (optional)

1 Mix the raspberries and sugar in a pan and heat gently until they release their juices. Simmer for 5 minutes. Leave to cool.

2 Cut the passion fruit in half and scoop out the seeds and juice into a small bowl.

3 Tip the raspberry mixture into a food processor, add the passion fruit and blend to a smooth purée.

4 Press the purée through a fine nylon sieve (strainer) placed over a bowl, to remove the seeds.

5 Fold the strawberries into the sauce, then spoon into four stemmed glasses. Serve with the dessert biscuits, if you like, but these will increase the total fat content of the dessert.

NUTRITIONAL NOTES	
Per portion:	
Energy	115Kcals/484kJ
Fat, total	0.5g
Saturated fat	0g
Cholesterol	0mg
Fibre	4.2g

Crunchy Fruit Layer

This simple, almost instant, dessert contrasts smooth and crunchy textures. Other fruits can equally well be used.

INGREDIENTS

Serves 2

1 peach or nectarine
115g/4oz/1 cup muesli (granola)
150g/5oz/2/3 cup low-fat plain (natural) yogurt
15ml/1 tbsp jam
15ml/1 tbsp fruit juice

1 Remove the stone (pit) from the peach or nectarine and cut the fruit into bite-size pieces with a sharp knife.

2 Divide the fruit evenly between two tall glasses, reserving a few pieces for decoration.

3 Sprinkle the muesli over the fruit in an even layer, then top with the low-fat yogurt.

4 Stir the jam and the fruit juice together in a cup, then drizzle the mixture over the yogurt. Decorate with the reserved peach or nectarine pieces and serve immediately.

NUTRITIONAL NOTES

Per portion:

Energy	227Kcals/950kJ
Fat, total	2.7g
Saturated fat	0.98g
Cholesterol	3.0mg
Fibre	3.6g

Soft Fruit Pavlova

There is rather a lot of sugar in meringue, but for special occasions this is the queen of desserts.

INGREDIENTS

Serves 4

4 egg whites

pinch salt

175g/6oz/³/4 cup caster (superfine) sugar

30ml/2 tbsp redcurrant jelly

15ml/1 tbsp rose water

300ml/¹/2 pint/1¹/4 cups low-fat Greek
   (US strained plain) yogurt

450g/1lb/4 cups mixed soft fruits, such as
   blackberries, blueberries, redcurrants,
   raspberries or loganberries

10ml/2 tsp sifted icing (confectioners')
   sugar

1 Preheat the oven to 140ºC/
275ºF/Gas 1. Oil a baking
sheet. Whisk the egg whites with a
pinch of salt in a spotlessly clean
bowl, until they are white and stiff.
Slowly add the caster sugar and
keep whisking until the mixture
forms stiff, glossy peaks.

NUTRITIONAL NOTES

Per portion:

Energy	302Kcals/1280kJ
Fat, total	3.9g
Saturated fat	2.37g
Cholesterol	5.3mg
Fibre	3.1g

2 Spoon the meringue into a
25cm/10in round on the
baking sheet, making a slight
indentation in the centre to give it
a swirled rim. Bake for 1–1¹/2
hours until the meringue is firm.
Keep checking as the meringue can
easily overcook and brown. Transfer
the meringue to a serving plate.

3 Melt the redcurrant jelly in a
small heatproof bowl resting
over hot water. Cool slightly, then
spread the jelly in the centre of the
meringue. Gently mix the rose
water with the low-fat Greek
yogurt and spoon into the centre
of the meringue. Pile the fruits on
top and dust with icing sugar.

Passion Fruit Creams

3 Bake for 25–30 minutes or until set, then leave to cool before chilling. Run a knife round the rim of the ramekins to help loosen the creams.

4 Run a knife round the insides of the creams, then invert them on to serving plates, tapping the base firmly. Carefully peel off the baking parchment and chill. Just before serving, spoon on a little passion fruit flesh and add mint leaves to serve.

VARIATIONS

You can also serve these creams hot, straight from their dishes, with an extra passion fruit half on the side. To make a crème caramel-style dessert, coat each ramekin with caramel instead of the baking parchment lining.

These delicately perfumed creams are very light and the passion fruit gives them a fresh, citrusy flavour.

INGREDIENTS

Serves 5–6

butter, for greasing
600ml/1 pint/2¹/2 cups double (heavy)
    cream, or a mixture of single (light) and
    double cream
a few drops of vanilla extract
6 passion fruits
30–45ml/2–3 tbsp caster (superfine) sugar
5 eggs
30ml/2 tbsp lemon curd
mint leaves, to serve

2 Bring the cream and vanilla to boiling point. Strain the flesh of four passion fruits and beat together with the sugar, eggs and lemon curd. Whisk in the hot cream. Ladle into the ramekins and half fill the roasting pan with boiling water.

1 Preheat the oven to 180ºC/ 350ºF/Gas 4. Lightly butter 6 ramekins and place a circle of baking parchment in the bases. Place them in a roasting pan.

NUTRITIONAL NOTES

Per portion:

Energy	585Kcals/2414kJ
Fat, total	58.4g
Saturated fat	34.7g
Cholesterol	296mg
Fibre	0.5g

Low-fat Pastries, Cakes & Pies

✦ ✦ ✦

Spiced Mango Filo Fingers

Mangoes have a wonderful texture and look great next to these crunchy filo fingers.

INGREDIENTS

Serves 8

4 mangoes

6 filo pastry sheets

90g/3½oz/7 tbsp butter, melted

45g/3 tbsp soft light brown sugar

20ml/4 tsp ground cinnamon

icing (confectioners') sugar, for dusting

1 Preheat the oven to 200°C/ 400°F/Gas 6. Set one mango aside for the decoration. Peel the remaining mangoes and slice the flesh. Cut the flesh across into 3mm/⅛in thick slices.

2 Keeping the rest of the filo covered with a damp cloth, lay one sheet on a baking sheet and brush with melted butter. Mix the brown sugar and cinnamon and sprinkle one-fifth of the mixture over the filo. Lay a sheet on top and repeat for the other 5 sheets, ending with a filo sheet.

3 Brush the top filo sheet with butter, trim off the excess pastry and lay the sliced mango in neat rows across the layered filo, to cover it completely. Brush with reserved butter and bake for 30 minutes. Allow to cool on the baking sheet, then cut into fingers.

4 Slice the flesh from either side of the stone of the reserved mango. Cut each piece in half lengthways. Make four long cuts, almost to the end, in each quarter. Dust with icing sugar. Put on a plate and carefully fan out the slices. Serve with the mango fingers.

NUTRITIONAL NOTES

Per portion:

Energy	207Kcals/861kJ
Fat, total	5.0g
Saturated fat	2.75g
Cholesterol	11.5mg
Fibre	3.6g

Filo Rhubarb Chiffon Pie

Filo pastry is low in fat and is easy to bake. Keep a pack in the freezer, ready to make impressive puddings like this one.

INGREDIENTS

Serves 3

500g/1¼ lb pink rhubarb
5ml/1 tsp mixed (apple pie) spice
finely grated rind and juice of 1 orange
15ml/1 tbsp granulated (white) sugar
15ml/1 tbsp low-fat spread
3 sheets filo pastry, thawed if frozen

VARIATION

Other fruit such as apples, pears, peaches, cherries or gooseberries can be used in this pie – try it with whatever is in season.

1 Preheat the oven to 200°C/400°F/Gas 6. Trim the leaves and ends from the rhubarb and chop them in 2.5cm/1in pieces. Place them in a medium-sized mixing bowl.

2 Add the mixed spice, orange rind and juice and sugar; toss well to coat evenly. Tip the rhubarb into a 1 litre/1¾ pint/4 cup pie dish.

3 Melt the spread and brush over the filo sheets. Crumple loosely and arrange over the filling.

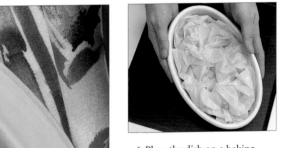

4 Place the dish on a baking sheet and bake the pie for 20 minutes, until golden brown. Reduce the heat to 180°C/350°F/Gas 4 and bake for 10–15 minutes more until the rhubarb is tender. Serve warm.

NUTRITIONAL NOTES

Per portion:

Energy	118Kcals/494kJ
Fat, total	3g
Saturated fat	0.65g
Cholesterol	0.3mg
Fibre	2.4g

Apricot and Pear Filo Roulade

This is a very quick way of making a strudel, it tastes delicious all the same!

Serves 6

115g/4oz/¹/₂ cup ready-to-eat dried
   apricots, chopped

30ml/2 tbsp apricot conserve

5ml/1 tsp lemon juice

50g/2oz/¹/₃ cup soft light brown sugar

2 pears, peeled, cored and chopped

30ml/2 tbsp flaked (sliced) almonds

30ml/2 tbsp low-fat spread, melted

8 sheets filo pastry, thawed if frozen

5ml/1 tsp icing (confectioners') sugar,
   for dusting

1 Put the apricots, apricot conserve, lemon juice, brown sugar and pears into a pan and heat for 5–7 minutes.

2 Remove from the heat and cool. Mix in the flaked almonds. Preheat the oven to 200°C/400°F/Gas 6. Melt the low-fat spread completely.

3 Lightly grease a baking sheet. Layer the pastry on the baking sheet, brushing each layer with the melted low-fat spread.

4 Spoon the filling down the filo, keeping it to one side of the centre and within 2.5cm/1in of each end. Lift the other side of the pastry up by sliding a palette knife underneath.

5 Fold this pastry over the filling, tucking the edge under. Seal the ends neatly and brush all over with spread again. Bake for 15–20 minutes, until golden. Dust with icing sugar and serve hot, cut into diamonds.

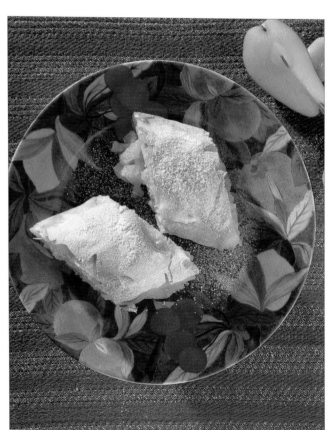

NUTRITIONAL NOTES	
Per portion:	
Energy	190Kcals/794kJ
Fat, total	4.1g
Saturated fat	0.54g
Cholesterol	0.1mg
Fibre	2.6g

Apricot Parcels

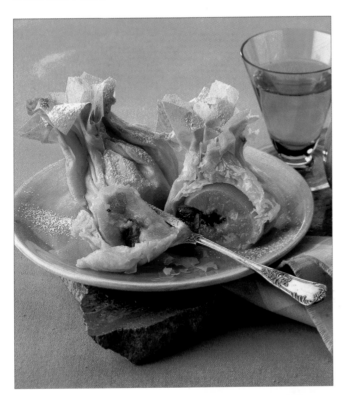

NUTRITIONAL NOTES	
Per portion:	
Energy	234Kcals/982kJ
Fat, total	4.4g
Saturated fat	1.1g
Cholesterol	3.7mg
Fibre	1.5g

These filo parcels are a good way to use up mincemeat and marzipan that have been in your cupboard since Christmas!

INGREDIENTS

Serves 8

350g/12oz filo pastry, thawed if frozen
30ml/2 tbsp low-fat spread, melted
8 apricots, halved and stoned (pitted)
60ml/4 tbsp luxury mincemeat
12 ratafia biscuits (almond macaroons),
  crushed
30ml/2 tbsp grated marzipan
icing (confectioners') sugar, for dusting

1 Preheat the oven to 200°C/
400°F/Gas 6. Cut the filo into
thirty-two 18cm/7in squares. Brush
4 of the squares with melted spread
and stack them, giving each layer a
quarter turn forming a star shape.
Repeat to make 8.

2 Place an apricot half, hollow
up, in the centre of each pastry
star. Mix together the mincemeat,
crushed biscuits and marzipan and
spoon a little of the mixture into
the hollow in each apricot.

3 Top with another apricot half,
then bring the corners of each
pastry together and squeeze to
make a gathered purse.

4 Place the purses on a baking
sheet and brush each with a
little melted spread. Bake for
15–20 minutes or until the pastry
is golden and crisp. Lightly dust
with icing sugar to serve.

COOK'S TIP

If you have run out of
mincemeat, use mixed vine
fruits instead.

Filo Fruit Scrunchies

Quick and easy to make, these pastries are ideal to serve at teatime.

INGREDIENTS

Serves 6

5 apricots or plums

4 sheets filo pastry, thawed if frozen

20ml/4 tsp low-fat spread, melted

50g/2oz/1/3 cup demerara (raw) sugar

30ml/2 tbsp flaked (sliced) almonds

icing (confectioners') sugar, for dusting

1 Preheat the oven to 190ºC/ 375ºF/Gas 5. Halve the apricots or plums, remove the stones (pits) and slice the fruit. Cut the filo pastry into twelve 18cm/7in squares. Pile the squares on top of each other and cover with a damp cloth to prevent them drying out.

2 Remove one square of filo and brush it with melted spread. Lay a second filo square on top, then, using your fingers, mould into folds.

3 Quickly make five more scrunchies in the same way so that the pastry does not dry out. Arrange a few slices of fruit in the folds of each scrunchie, then sprinkle generously with the demerara sugar and almonds.

4 Place the scrunchies on a baking sheet. Bake for 8–10 minutes until golden brown, then loosen the scrunchies from the baking sheet with a palette knife and transfer to a wire rack. Dust with icing sugar and serve immediately.

NUTRITIONAL NOTES
Per portion:

Energy	132Kcals/555kJ
Fat, total	4.19g
Saturated fat	0.63g
Cholesterol	0mg
Fibre	0.67g

Plum Filo Pockets

*Cheese-filled plums provide a
wonderful mix of sweet and savoury.*

INGREDIENTS

Serves 4

115g/4oz/$^{1}/2$ cup low-fat soft cheese

15ml/1 tbsp light muscovado (brown)
sugar

2.5ml/$^{1}/2$ tsp ground cloves

8 large, firm plums, halved and stoned
(pitted)

8 sheets filo pastry, thawed if frozen

sunflower oil, for brushing

icing (confectioners') sugar, for dusting

1 Preheat the oven to 220ºC/
425ºF/Gas 7. Mix together the
low-fat soft cheese, muscovado
sugar and ground cloves to make a
firm paste.

2 Sandwich the plum halves
together with a spoonful of
the cheese mixture. Stack the
filo pastry sheets and cut into
16 pieces, each 23cm/9in square.
Brush each piece with oil and place
them diagonally over each other.

3 Place a plum on each filo
pastry square, lift up the sides
and pinch the corners together.
Place on a baking sheet. Bake for
15–18 minutes, until golden, then
dust with icing sugar.

NUTRITIONAL NOTES

Per portion:

Energy	188Kcals/790kJ
Fat, total	1.87g
Saturated fat	0.27g
Cholesterol	0.29mg
Fibre	2.55g

Tropical Fruit Filo Clusters

These fruity filo clusters are ideal for a family treat or a dinner party.

INGREDIENTS

Serves 8

1 banana, sliced

1 small mango, peeled, stoned (pitted) and diced

lemon juice, for sprinkling

1 small cooking apple, coarsely grated

6 fresh or dried dates, stoned (pitted) and chopped

50g/2oz/1/3 cup ready-to-eat dried pineapple, chopped

50g/2oz/1/3 cup sultanas (golden raisins)

50g/2oz/1/3 cup soft light brown sugar

5ml/1 tsp mixed (apple pie) spice

8 sheets filo pastry, thawed if frozen

30ml/2 tbsp sunflower oil

icing (confectioners') sugar, for dusting

NUTRITIONAL NOTES

Per portion:

Energy	197Kcals/833kJ
Fat, total	3.58g
Saturated fat	0.44g
Cholesterol	0mg
Fibre	2.31g

1 Preheat the oven to 200ºC/ 400ºF/Gas 6. Line a baking sheet with baking parchment. In a medium-sized mixing bowl, toss the banana slices and diced mango in lemon juice to prevent discoloration.

2 Add the apple, dates, pineapple, sultanas, sugar and spice to the bowl and mix well.

3 To make each fruit cluster, cut each sheet of filo pastry in half crossways to make two squares or rectangles (16 pieces in total). Lightly brush two pieces of pastry with oil and place one on top of the other at a 45º angle to form a star shape.

COOK'S TIP

To prevent filo pastry drying out and crumbling, cover with a damp cloth before brushing with the oil.

4 Spoon some fruit filling into the centre, gather the pastry up over the filling and secure with string. Place the cluster on the prepared baking sheet and lightly brush all over with oil.

5 Repeat with the remaining pastry squares and filling to make a total of 8 fruit clusters. Bake for 25–30 minutes, until golden brown and crisp.

6 Carefully snip and remove the string from each cluster and serve hot or cold, dusted with icing sugar.

Redcurrant Filo Baskets

Filo pastry is low in fat and needs only a fine brushing of oil before use; a light oil such as sunflower is best.

INGREDIENTS

Serves 6

3 sheets filo pastry, thawed if frozen

15ml/1 tbsp sunflower oil

175g/6oz/1½ cups redcurrants

250ml/8fl oz/1 cup low-fat Greek (US strained plain) yogurt

5ml/1 tsp icing (confectioners') sugar

1 Preheat the oven to 200ºC/ 400ºF/Gas 6. Cut the sheets of filo pastry into eighteen 10cm/ 4in squares.

2 Brush each filo square very thinly with oil, then arrange three squares in each of six small patty tins (pans), placing each one at a different angle so that they form star-shaped baskets. Bake for 6–8 minutes, until crisp and golden. Lift the baskets out carefully and leave them to cool on a wire rack.

3 Set aside a few sprigs of redcurrants on their stems for decoration and string the rest. Stir the redcurrants into the low-fat Greek yogurt.

4 Spoon the yogurt into the filo baskets. Decorate with the reserved sprigs of redcurrants and sprinkle them with the icing sugar to serve.

NUTRITIONAL NOTES
Per portion:

Energy	80Kcals/335kJ
Fat, total	3.8g
Saturated fat	1.35g
Cholesterol	2.3mg
Fibre	1g

Filo Fruit Baskets

*Crisp filo teamed with fruit in a
strawberry yogurt cream makes a
fine finish for a summer meal.*

INGREDIENTS

Serves 6

4 large or 8 small sheets of filo pastry,
    thawed if frozen
25g/1oz/5 tsp low-fat spread, melted
250ml/8fl oz/1 cup low-fat Greek
    (US strained plain) yogurt
60ml/4 tbsp whole-fruit strawberry jam
15ml/1 tbsp Curaçao or other orange liqueur
115g/4oz/1 cup seedless red grapes, halved
115g/4oz/1 cup seedless green grapes, halved
175g/6oz/1 cup fresh pineapple cubes
225g/8oz/2 cups raspberries
30ml/2 tbsp icing (confectioners') sugar
6 small sprigs of fresh mint, for decorating

1 Preheat the oven to 180ºC/
350ºF/Gas 4. Grease 6 cups of a
bun tin (muffin pan).

2 Stack the filo sheets and
cut into twenty-four
12cm/4½in squares.

NUTRITIONAL NOTES
Per portion:

Energy	207Kcals/867kJ
Fat, total	4.6g
Saturated fat	1.84g
Cholesterol	3.2mg
Fibre	1.4g

3 Lay 4 squares of pastry in each
of the 6 bun tins, rotating to
make star-shapes. Press the filo
firmly down.

4 Brush the pastry baskets
lightly with melted low-fat
spread. Bake for 5–7 minutes, until
the pastry is crisp and golden.
Cool on a wire rack.

5 In a bowl, mix the yogurt
with the strawberry jam and
orange liqueur.

6 Just before serving, spoon a
little of the cream mixture into
each pastry basket. Top with the
fresh fruit. Sprinkle with icing
sugar and decorate each basket
with a small sprig of mint.

Filo-topped Apple Pie

With its scrunchy filo topping and only a small amount of low-fat spread, this makes a healthy dessert.

INGREDIENTS

Serves 6

900g/2lb cooking apples
75g/3oz/6 tbsp caster (superfine) sugar
grated rind of 1 lemon
15ml/1 tbsp lemon juice
75g/3oz/$1/2$ cup sultanas (golden raisins)
2.5ml/$1/2$ tsp ground cinnamon
4 large sheets filo pastry, thawed if frozen
30ml/2 tbsp low-fat spread, melted
icing (confectioners') sugar, for dusting

1 Peel, core and dice the apples. Place them in a pan with the sugar and lemon rind. Drizzle the lemon juice over. Bring to the boil, stir well, then cook for 5 minutes or until the apples soften.

2 Stir in the sultanas and cinnamon. Spoon the fruit mixture into a 1.2 litre/2 pint/ 5 cup pie dish and level the top. Leave to cool.

NUTRITIONAL NOTES

Per portion:

Energy	199Kcals/837kJ
Fat, total	2.5g
Saturated fat	0.56g
Cholesterol	0.3mg
Fibre	1.9g

3 Preheat the oven to 180ºC/ 350ºF/Gas 4. Place a pie funnel in the centre of the fruit. Brush each sheet of filo with melted spread. Scrunch up loosely and place on the fruit to cover.

4 Bake for 20–30 minutes until the filo is golden. Dust the pie with icing sugar before serving.

VARIATION

To make filo crackers, cut the greased filo into 20cm/8in wide strips. Spoon a little of the filling along one end of each strip, leaving the sides clear. Roll up and twist the ends to make a cracker. Brush with more melted low-fat spread, bake for 20 minutes.

Pineapple and Strawberry Meringue

This is a gooey meringue that has a wonderful marshmallow texture.

INGREDIENTS

Serves 6

5 egg whites, at room temperature

pinch of salt

5ml/1 tsp cornflour (cornstarch)

15ml/1 tbsp distilled malt vinegar

few drops of vanilla extract

275g/10oz/1¼ cups caster (superfine)
   sugar

250ml/8fl oz/1 cup low-fat Greek (US
   strained plain) yogurt

175g/6oz fresh pineapple, cut into chunks

175g/6oz/1⅓ cups fresh strawberries,
   halved

strawberry leaves, to decorate (optional)

1 Preheat the oven to 160°C/
325°F/Gas 3. Line a baking
sheet with baking parchment.

2 Whisk the egg whites in a large
grease-free bowl until they
hold stiff peaks. Add the salt,
cornflour, vinegar and vanilla
extract; whisk again until stiff.

NUTRITIONAL NOTES

Per portion:

Energy	247Kcals/1050kJ
Fat, total	2.2g
Saturated fat	1.31g
Cholesterol	2.9mg
Fibre	0.7g

3 Gently whisk in half the sugar,
then carefully fold in the rest.
Spoon the meringue on to the
baking sheet and swirl into a
20cm/8in round with the back of a
large spoon.

4 Bake for 20 minutes, then
reduce the temperature to
150°C/300°F/Gas 2 and bake for
40 minutes more.

5 While still warm, transfer the
meringue to a serving plate,
then leave to cool. To serve, top
with Greek yogurt, pineapple
chunks and halved strawberries.
Decorate with strawberry leaves, if
you have them.

COOK'S TIP

You can also cook this in a
deep, 20cm/8in loose-bottomed
cake tin (pan) that is greased
and lined.

Nectarine and Hazelnut Meringues

Sweet nectarines and yogurt paired with crisp hazelnut meringues make a really superb sweet.

INGREDIENTS

Serves 5

3 egg whites

175g/6oz/³/4 cup caster (superfine) sugar

50g/2oz/¹/2 cup chopped hazelnuts, toasted

300ml/¹/2 pint/1¹/4 cups low-fat Greek (US strained plain) yogurt

15ml/1 tbsp sweet dessert wine

2 nectarines, stoned (pitted) and sliced

fresh mint sprigs, to decorate

VARIATIONS

Use apricots instead of nectarines if you prefer, or you could try this with a raspberry topping.

1 Preheat the oven to 140°C/ 275°F/Gas 1. Line two large baking sheets with baking parchment. Whisk the egg whites in a grease-free bowl until they form stiff peaks. Gradually whisk in the caster sugar a spoonful at a time until the mixture forms a stiff, glossy meringue.

2 Fold in two thirds of the hazelnuts, then spoon five large ovals on to each baking sheet. Scatter the remaining hazelnuts over five of the meringue ovals. Flatten the remaining five ovals.

3 Bake the meringues for 1–1¹/4 hours until dry, carefully lift them off the baking parchment and cool completely.

4 Mix the Greek yogurt lightly with the dessert wine. Spoon some of this mixture on to each of the plain meringues. Arrange a few nectarine slices on each. Put each meringue on a dessert plate with a hazelnut-topped meringue. Decorate each portion with mint sprigs and serve the meringues immediately.

NUTRITIONAL NOTES

Per portion:

Energy	293Kcals/1236kJ
Fat, total	4.9g
Saturated fat	2.34g
Cholesterol	4.2mg
Fibre	1.4g

Blackberry Brown Sugar Meringue

A brown sugar meringue looks very effective, when contrasted with a dark topping.

INGREDIENTS

Serves 6

175g/6oz/1 cup soft light brown sugar

3 egg whites

5ml/1 tsp distilled malt vinegar

2.5ml/¹/2 tsp vanilla extract

For the topping

30ml/2 tbsp crème de cassis

350g/12oz/3 cups blackberries

15ml/1 tbsp icing (confectioners') sugar, sifted

300ml/¹/2 pint/1¹/4 cups low-fat Greek (US strained plain) yogurt

small blackberry leaves, to decorate

1 Preheat the oven to 160°C/ 325°F/Gas 3. Draw a 20cm/ 8in circle on a sheet of baking parchment, turn over and place on a baking sheet.

2 Spread out the brown sugar on a second baking sheet and dry in the oven for 8–10 minutes. Strain to remove lumps.

3 Whisk the egg whites in a clean grease-free bowl until stiff. Add half the dried brown sugar, 15ml/1 tbsp at a time, whisking well after each addition. Add the vinegar and vanilla extract, then fold in the remaining sugar.

4 Spoon the meringue on to the circle, leaving a central hollow. Bake for 45 minutes, turn off the oven but leave the meringue in the oven with the door slightly open, until cold.

5 In a bowl, sprinkle crème de cassis over the blackberries. Leave to macerate for 30 minutes.

6 When the meringue is cold, peel off the baking parchment, carefully, and transfer the meringue to a serving plate. Stir the icing sugar into the low-fat Greek yogurt and spoon into the centre.

7 Top with the blackberries and decorate with small blackberry leaves. Serve immediately.

NUTRITIONAL NOTES

Per portion:

Energy	199Kcals/833kJ
Fat, total	2.6g
Saturated fat	1.58g
Cholesterol	3.5mg
Fibre	1.8g

Floating Islands in Hot Plum Sauce

The plum sauce for this pudding can be made in advance, and reheated just before you cook the meringues.

INGREDIENTS

Serves 4

450g/1lb red plums
300ml/½ pint/1¼ cups unsweetened
    apple juice
2 egg whites
30ml/2 tbsp concentrated apple juice
freshly grated nutmeg

1 Halve the plums and discard the stones (pits). Place them in a wide pan with the unsweetened apple juice.

2 Bring to the boil, lower the heat, cover and simmer gently for 15–20 minutes or until the plums are tender.

3 Meanwhile, place the egg whites in a grease-free bowl and whisk them until they hold soft peaks.

4 Gradually whisk in the concentrated apple juice, whisking continuously until the meringue holds fairly firm peaks.

NUTRITIONAL NOTES

Per portion:

Energy	77Kcals/324kJ
Fat, total	0.3g
Saturated fat	0g
Cholesterol	0mg
Fibre	1.7g

5 Using a tablespoon, scoop the meringue mixture into the gently simmering plum sauce. You may need to cook the "islands" in two batches.

6 Cover and allow to simmer gently for 2–3 minutes, until the meringues are just set. Serve straight away, sprinkled with a little freshly grated nutmeg.

COOK'S TIP
Concentrated apple juice is a useful sweetener, or use a little honey.

VARIATION

Add an extra dimension to this dessert by using a fruit liqueur such as Calvados, apricot brandy or Grand Marnier instead of the concentrated apple juice.

Raspberry Vacherin

Meringue rounds filled with orange-flavoured fromage frais and raspberries make a perfect dinner-party dessert.

INGREDIENTS

Serves 6
3 egg whites
175g/6oz/3/4 cup caster (superfine) sugar
5ml/1 tsp chopped almonds
icing (confectioners') sugar, for dusting
raspberry leaves, to decorate (optional)
For the filling
175g/6oz/3/4 cup low-fat soft cheese
15ml/1 tbsp clear honey
15ml/1 tbsp Cointreau or other orange-flavoured liqueur
120ml/4fl oz/1/2 cup low-fat fromage frais
225g/8oz/2 cups raspberries

1 Preheat the oven to 140°C/ 275°F/Gas 1. Draw a 20cm/8in circle on each of two pieces of baking parchment. Turn the paper over so the marking is on the underside and use it to line two heavy baking sheets.

NUTRITIONAL NOTES
Per portion:

Energy	248Kcals/1041kJ
Fat, total	2.22g
Saturated fat	0.82g
Cholesterol	4mg
Fibre	1.06g

2 Whisk the egg whites in a grease-free bowl until very stiff, then gradually whisk in the caster sugar to make a stiff meringue mixture.

3 Spoon the mixture on to the circles on the prepared baking sheets, spreading the meringue evenly to the edges. Sprinkle one meringue round with the chopped almonds.

4 Bake for 1 1/2–2 hours, then lift the meringues off the baking sheets, peel away the paper and cool on a wire rack.

5 To make the filling, cream the soft cheese with the honey and liqueur in a bowl. Fold in the fromage frais and raspberries, reserving three of the best for decoration.

6 Place the plain meringue round on a board, carefully spread with the filling and top with the nut-covered round. Dust with icing sugar, transfer to a serving plate and decorate with the reserved raspberries, and a sprig of raspberry leaves, if you like.

COOK'S TIP

When making the meringue, whisk the egg whites until they are so stiff that you can turn the bowl upside-down without them falling out.

Baked Blackberry Cheesecake

This light, low-fat cheesecake is best made with wild blackberries, but cultivated ones will do.

INGREDIENTS

Serves 5

low-fat spread, for greasing
175g/6oz/3/4 cup low-fat cottage cheese
150ml/1/4 pint/2/3 cup low-fat natural
  (plain) yogurt
15ml/1 tbsp wholemeal (whole-wheat)
  flour
25g/1oz/2 tbsp golden caster (superfine)
  sugar
1 egg
1 egg white
finely grated rind and juice of 1/2 lemon
200g/7oz/13/4 cups fresh or thawed
  frozen blackberries

1 Preheat the oven to 180ºC/
350ºF/Gas 4. Lightly grease and base-line an 18cm/7in sandwich cake tin (pan).

COOK'S TIP

If fresh blackberries are not in season, you can use canned blackberries. Choose those canned in natural juice and drain the fruit well before adding it to the cheesecake mixture.

2 Place the cottage cheese in a food processor and process until smooth. Alternatively, rub it through a sieve (strainer), to obtain a smooth mixture.

3 Stir in the yogurt, flour, sugar, egg and egg white. Add the lemon rind, juice and blackberries, reserving a few for decoration.

4 Tip the mixture into the prepared tin and bake it for 30–35 minutes, or until it is just set. Turn off the oven and leave for a further 30 minutes.

5 Run a knife around the edge of the cheesecake, and then turn it out. Remove the lining paper, and place the cheesecake on a warm serving plate.

6 Decorate the cheesecake with the reserved blackberries, and serve it while still warm.

NUTRITIONAL NOTES

Per portion:

Energy	95Kcals/402kJ
Fat, total	1.9g
Saturated fat	0.77g
Cholesterol	41.5mg
Fibre	1.4g

Tofu Berry Cheesecake

Strictly speaking, this isn't a cheese-cake at all, as it is based on tofu – but who would guess?

INGREDIENTS

Serves 6

For the base

30ml/2 tbsp low-fat spread

30ml/2 tbsp unsweetened apple juice

115g/4oz/2¹/2 cups bran flakes or other high-fibre cereal

For the filling

275g/10oz/1¹/2 cups silken tofu

250ml/8fl oz/1 cup low-fat natural (plain) yogurt

60ml/4 tbsp apple juice

15ml/1 tbsp powdered gelatine

For the topping

175g/6oz/1¹/2 cups mixed summer soft fruit, such as strawberries, raspberries, redcurrants and blackberries

30ml/2 tbsp redcurrant jelly

30ml/2 tbsp hot water

1 For the base, place the low-fat spread and apple juice in a pan and heat them gently until the spread has melted. Crush the cereal and stir it into the pan, mixing well. Tip into a 23cm/9in round flan tin (pie pan) and press down firmly. Leave to set.

2 Make the filling. Place the tofu and yogurt in a food processor and process until smooth. Pour the apple juice into a cup and sprinkle the gelatine on top. Leave until spongy, then place over hot water until melted. Stir quickly into the tofu mixture.

3 Spread the tofu mixture over the chilled base. Chill until set. Remove the flan tin, place the cheesecake on a serving plate. Arrange the fruits on top.

4 Melt the redcurrant jelly with the hot water. Let it cool, then spoon over the fruit to serve.

NUTRITIONAL NOTES

Per portion:

Energy	163Kcals/688kJ
Fat, total	4.4g
Saturated fat	0.93g
Cholesterol	1.6mg
Fibre	3.2g

Angel Cake

3 Gently fold in the flour mixture with a large metal spoon. Spoon into an ungreased 25cm/10in angel cake tin (pan), smooth the surface and bake for about 45–50 minutes, until the cake springs back when pressed.

Serve this light-as-air cake with low-fat fromage frais – it makes a perfect dessert or tea-time treat.

1 Preheat the oven to 180ºC/ 350ºF/Gas 4. Sift both flours on to a sheet of baking parchment.

4 Sprinkle a sheet of baking parchment with caster sugar and set an egg cup in the centre. Invert the cake tin over the paper, balancing it on the egg cup. When cold, the cake will drop out of the tin. Transfer to a plate, dust with icing sugar, or decorate and serve.

INGREDIENTS

Serves 10

40g/1¹/2oz/¹/3 cup cornflour (cornstarch)
40g/1¹/2oz/¹/3 cup plain (all-purpose) flour
8 egg whites
225g/8oz/1 cup caster (superfine) sugar, plus extra for sprinkling
5ml/1 tsp pure vanilla extract
icing (confectioners') sugar, for dusting

2 Whisk the egg whites in a large grease-free bowl until very stiff, then gradually add the sugar and vanilla extract, whisking until the mixture is thick and glossy.

NUTRITIONAL NOTES

Per portion:

Energy	139Kcals/582kJ
Fat, total	0.08g
Saturated fat	0.01g
Cholesterol	0mg
Fibre	0.13g

COOK'S TIP

Make a lemony icing by mixing 175g/6oz/1¹/2 cups icing sugar with 15–30ml/1–2 tbsp lemon juice. Drizzle over the cake and decorate with physalis.

Chocolate and Orange Angel Cake

This light-as-air sponge with its fluffy icing is virtually fat-free, yet it tastes heavenly and looks great too.

INGREDIENTS

Serves 10

25g/1oz/¼ cup plain (all-purpose) flour
15g/½oz/2 tbsp fat-reduced cocoa powder
30ml/2 tbsp cornflour (cornstarch)
pinch of salt
5 egg whites
2.5ml/½ tsp cream of tartar
115g/4oz/½ cup caster (superfine) sugar
pared rind of 1 orange, blanched,
   to decorate
For the icing
200g/7oz/scant 1 cup caster (superfine)
   sugar
75ml/5 tbsp water
1 egg white

2 Add the caster sugar to the egg whites a spoonful at a time, whisking for a few minutes each time. Sift a third of the flour and cocoa mixture over the meringue and gently fold in with a palette knife. Repeat the procedure, sifting and folding in the flour and cocoa mixture twice more. times.

5 Whisk the egg white in a grease-free bowl until soft peaks occur. Add the syrup in a thin stream, whisking all the time. Continue to whisk until very thick and fluffy.

1 Preheat the oven to 180°C/ 350°F/Gas 4. Sift the flour, cocoa powder, cornflour and salt together three times. Beat the egg whites in a large grease-free bowl until foamy. Add the cream of tartar, then whisk to soft peaks.

3 Spoon the mixture into a 20cm/8in ring mould and level the top. Bake for 35 minutes or until springy when lightly pressed. Turn upside-down on a wire rack and leave to cool in the tin.

4 Make the icing. Put the sugar in a pan with the water. Stir over a low heat until dissolved. Boil until the syrup reaches a temperature of 120°C/250°F on a sugar thermometer, or when a drop of the syrup makes a soft ball when dropped into a cup of cold water. Remove from the heat.

6 Turn out the cake on to a serving plate. Spread the icing over the top and sides of the cooled cake. Sprinkle the orange rind over the top of the cake and serve.

COOK'S TIP
~

Do not over-beat the egg whites. They should form soft peaks, to allow for expansion.

NUTRITIONAL NOTES

Per portion:

Energy	153Kcals/644kJ
Fat, total	0.27g
Saturated fat	0.13g
Cholesterol	0mg
Fibre	0.25g

Cinnamon Apple Gâteau

Make this lovely cinnamon-spiced cake for an autumn celebration when apples are at their best.

INGREDIENTS

Serves 8

3 eggs

115g/4oz/$^1\!/_2$ cup caster (superfine) sugar

75g/3oz/$^3\!/_4$ cup plain (all-purpose) flour

5ml/1 tsp ground cinnamon

For the filling and topping

4 large eating apples

60ml/4 tbsp clear honey

15ml/1 tbsp water

75g/3oz/$^1\!/_2$ cup sultanas (golden raisins)

2.5ml/$^1\!/_2$ tsp ground cinnamon

350g/12oz/1$^1\!/_2$ cups low-fat soft cheese

60ml/4 tbsp low-fat fromage frais

10ml/2 tsp lemon juice

45ml/3 tbsp smooth apricot jam, warmed

fresh mint sprigs, to decorate

1 Preheat the oven to 190ºC/ 375ºF/Gas 5. Grease and line a 23cm/9in sandwich cake tin (pan). Place the eggs and caster sugar in a bowl and whisk until thick and mousse-like (when the whisk is lifted, a trail should remain on the surface of the mixture for at least 15 seconds).

2 Sift the flour and cinnamon over the egg mixture and carefully fold in. Pour into the prepared tin and bake for 25–30 minutes or until the cake springs back when lightly pressed. Slide a palette knife between the cake and the tin to loosen the edge, then turn the cake on to a wire rack to cool.

3 To make the filling, peel, core and slice three of the apples and put them in a pan. Add 30ml/2 tbsp of the honey and the water. Cover and cook over a gentle heat for about 10 minutes until the apples have softened. Add the sultanas and cinnamon, stir well, replace the lid and leave to cool.

4 Put the soft cheese in a bowl with the remaining honey, the fromage frais and half the lemon juice. Beat until the mixture is smooth.

5 Halve the cake horizontally, place the bottom half on a board and drizzle over any liquid from the apple mixture. Spread with two-thirds of the cheese mixture, then top with the apple filling. Fit on the top of the cake.

6 Swirl the remaining cheese mixture over the top of the sponge. Core and slice the remaining apple, sprinkle with the remaining lemon juice and use to decorate the cake edge. Brush the apple with apricot jam and decorate with mint sprigs.

NUTRITIONAL NOTES	
Per portion:	
Energy	244Kcals/1023kJ
Fat, total	4.05g
Saturated fat	1.71g
Cholesterol	77.95mg
Fibre	1.5g

Peach Swiss Roll

A feather-light sponge with a filling of peach jam – delicious at tea time or as a dinner-party dessert.

INGREDIENTS

Serves 6–8

low-fat spread, for greasing

3 eggs

115g/4oz/¹/2 cup caster (superfine) sugar

75g/3oz/³/4 cup plain (all-purpose)
   flour, sifted

15ml/1 tbsp boiling water

90ml/6 tbsp peach jam

icing (confectioners') sugar, for dusting

NUTRITIONAL NOTES
Per portion:

Energy	178Kcals/746kJ
Fat, total	2.45g
Saturated fat	0.67g
Cholesterol	82.5mg
Fibre	0.33g

1 Preheat the oven to 200ºC/
400ºF/Gas 6. Grease a 30 ×
20cm/12 × 8in Swiss roll tin (jelly
roll pan) and line with baking
parchment. Combine the eggs and
sugar in a bowl. Whisk until thick
and mousse-like (when the whisk
is lifted, a trail should remain on
the surface of the mixture for at
least 15 seconds).

2 Carefully fold in the flour with
a large metal spoon, then add
the boiling water in the same way.

3 Spoon into the prepared tin,
spread evenly to the edges and
bake for about 10–12 minutes
until the cake springs back when
lightly pressed.

4 Spread a sheet of baking
parchment on a flat surface,
sprinkle it with caster sugar, then
invert the cake on top. Peel off the
lining paper.

5 Neatly trim the edges of the
cake. Make a neat cut two-
thirds of the way through the cake,
about 1cm/¹/2in from the short
edge nearest you.

6 Spread the cake with the
peach jam and roll up quickly
from the partially cut end. Hold
in position for a minute, making
sure the join is underneath. Cool
on a wire rack. Decorate with
glacé icing (see Cook's Tip) or
simply dust with icing sugar
before serving.

COOK'S TIP

Decorate the Swiss roll with
glacé icing. Put 115g/4oz glacé
icing in a piping (pastry) bag
fitted with a small writing nozzle
and pipe lines over the top
of the Swiss roll.

Apricot and Orange Roulade

This elegant dessert is very low in fat, so serving it with yogurt or fromage frais would not be disastrous.

INGREDIENTS

Serves 6

low-fat spread, for greasing

4 egg whites

115g/4oz/$\frac{1}{2}$ cup golden caster (superfine) sugar

50g/2oz/$\frac{1}{2}$ cup plain (all-purpose) flour

finely grated rind of 1 small orange

45ml/3 tbsp orange juice

For the filling

115g/4oz/$\frac{1}{2}$ cup ready-to-eat dried apricots, roughly chopped

150ml/$\frac{1}{4}$ pint/$\frac{2}{3}$ cup orange juice

To decorate

10ml/2 tsp icing (confectioners') sugar

shreds of pared orange rind, to decorate

1 Preheat the oven to 200ºC/ 400ºF/Gas 6. Grease a 23 × 33cm/9 × 13in Swiss roll tin (jelly roll pan) and line it with baking parchment. Grease the parchment.

COOK'S TIP
~

Make and bake the sponge mixture a day in advance and keep it cool, rolled in the paper. Fill with the fruit purée 2–3 hours before serving. The sponge can also be stored frozen.

2 Place the egg whites in a large grease-free bowl and whisk them they hold soft peaks. Gradually add the sugar, whisking hard each time.

3 Fold in the flour, orange rind and juice. Spoon the mixture into the prepared tin and spread it evenly.

4 Bake for 15-18 minutes, or until the sponge is firm and pale gold in colour. Turn out on to baking parchment, and roll it up loosely from one short side. Leave to cool.

5 Make the filling. Place the apricots in a pan, with the orange juice. Cover the pan and leave to simmer until most of the liqud has been absorbed. Purée the apricots in a food processor.

6 Unroll the roulade and spread with the apricot mixture. Roll up, arrange strips of paper diagonally across the roll, sprinkle lightly with lines of icing sugar, remove the paper and scatter with shreds of pared orange rind. Serve in slices.

NUTRITIONAL NOTES
Per portion:

Energy	154Kcals/652kJ
Fat, total	0.3g
Saturated fat	0.01g
Cholesterol	0mg
Fibre	1.5g

Lemon Chiffon Cake

Lemon mousse provides a tangy filling for this light lemon sponge, which is simple to prepare.

INGREDIENTS

Serves 8

low-fat spread, for greasing
2 eggs
75g/3oz/6 tbsp caster (superfine) sugar
grated rind of 1 lemon
50g/2oz/½ cup plain (all-purpose) flour, sifted
thinly pared lemon rind, cut in shreds
For the filling
2 eggs, separated
75g/3oz/6 tbsp caster (superfine) sugar
grated rind and juice of 1 lemon
30ml/2 tbsp water
15ml/1 tbsp powdered gelatine
120ml/4fl oz/½ cup low-fat fromage frais
For the icing
115g/4oz/1 cup icing (confectioners') sugar, sifted
15ml/1 tbsp lemon juice

2 Bake for 20–25 minutes until the cake springs back when lightly pressed in the centre. Turn on to a wire rack to cool. Once cold, split the cake in half horizontally and return the lower half to the clean cake tin. Set aside.

3 Make the filling. Put the egg yolks, sugar, lemon rind and juice in a bowl. Beat with a hand-held electric whisk until thick, pale and creamy.

5 Pour the lemon mousse over the sponge in the cake tin, spreading it to the edges. Set the second layer of sponge on top and chill until set.

6 Slide a palette knife between the tin and the cake to loosen it, then transfer to a serving plate. Make the icing by adding enough lemon juice to the icing sugar to make a mixture thick enough to coat the back of a wooden spoon. Pour over the cake and decorate with the lemon rind.

1 Preheat the oven to 180°C/ 350°F/Gas 4. Grease and line a 20cm/8in loose-bottomed cake tin (pan). Whisk the eggs, sugar and lemon rind until thick and mousse-like. Gently fold in the flour, then turn the mixture into the prepared tin.

4 Pour the water into a small heatproof bowel and sprinkle the gelatine on top. Leave until spongy, then place over simmering water and stir until dissolved. Cool slightly, then whisk into the yolk mixture. Fold in the fromage frais. When the mixture begins to set, quickly whisk the egg whites to soft peaks. Fold a spoonful into the mousse mixture to lighten it, then fold in the rest.

NUTRITIONAL NOTES	
Per portion:	
Energy	202Kcals/849kJ
Fat, total	2.81g
Saturated fat	0.79g
Cholesterol	96.41mg
Fibre	0.2g

Tia Maria Gâteau

A feather-light coffee sponge with a creamy liqueur-flavoured filling and a hint of ginger.

INGREDIENTS

Serves 8

low-fat spread, for greasing

75g/3oz/¾ cup plain (all-purpose) flour

30ml/2 tbsp instant coffee powder

3 eggs

115g/4oz/½ cup caster (superfine) sugar

coffee beans, to decorate

For the filling

175g/6oz/¾ cup low-fat soft cheese

15ml/1 tbsp clear honey

15ml/1 tbsp Tia Maria

50g/2oz/¼ cup stem ginger,
   roughly chopped

For the icing

225g/8oz/2 cups icing (confectioners')
   sugar, sifted

10ml/2 tsp coffee extract

15ml/1 tbsp water

5ml/1 tsp cocoa powder, preferably
   fat-reduced

1 Preheat the oven to 190ºC/ 375ºF/Gas 5. Grease and line a 20cm/8in deep round cake tin (pan). Sift the flour and coffee powder together on to a sheet of baking parchment.

2 Whisk the eggs and sugar in a bowl until thick (when the whisk is lifted, a trail should remain on the mixture's surface for 10–15 seconds).

3 Gently fold in the flour mixture with a metal spoon, being careful not to knock out any air. Turn the mixture into the prepared tin. Bake for 30–35 minutes or until it springs back when lightly pressed. Turn on to a wire rack and leave to cool completely.

4 Make the filling. Mix the soft cheese with the honey in a bowl. Beat until smooth, then stir in the Tia Maria and the chopped stem ginger.

5 Split the cake in half and sandwich them with the Tia Maria filling.

6 Make the icing. Mix the icing sugar and coffee extract with enough of the water to make an icing that will coat the back of a wooden spoon. Spread three-quarters of the icing over the cake. Stir the cocoa into the remaining icing until smooth. Spoon into a piping (pastry) bag fitted with a writing nozzle and pipe the mocha icing over the coffee icing. Decorate with coffee beans.

NUTRITIONAL NOTES

Per portion:

Energy	226Kcals/951kJ
Fat, total	3.14g
Saturated fat	1.17g
Cholesterol	75.03mg
Fibre	0.64g

LOW-FAT CUSTARDS, SOUFFLÉS & WHIPS

◆ ◆ ◆

Bread and Sultana Custard

An old favourite gets the low-fat treatment and proves how successful this can be.

INGREDIENTS

Serves 4

15ml/1 tbsp low-fat spread
3 thin slices of bread, crusts removed
475ml/16fl oz/2 cups skimmed milk
2.5ml/1/2 tsp mixed (apple pie) spice
45ml/3 tbsp demerara (raw) sugar
2 eggs, whisked
75g/3oz/1/2 cup sultanas (golden raisins)
freshly grated nutmeg
a little icing (confectioners') sugar,
    for dusting

1 Preheat the oven to 180ºC/
350ºF/Gas 4. Lightly grease an ovenproof dish. Spread the bread with low-fat spread and cut into small pieces.

2 Place the bread in several layers in the prepared dish.

3 Whisk the skimmed milk, mixed spice, demerara sugar and eggs in a large mixing bowl. Pour the mixture over the bread, to cover. Sprinkle over the sultanas and stand for 30 minutes.

4 Grate a little nutmeg over the top and bake for 30–40 minutes until the custard is just set and golden. Serve sprinkled with icing sugar.

NUTRITIONAL NOTES
Per portion:

Energy	246Kcals/1037kJ
Fat, total	5g
Saturated fat	1.37g
Cholesterol	99.2mg
Fibre	0.7g

Poppy seed Custard with Red Fruit

Poppy seeds add a nutty flavour to this custard without increasing the amount of fat too much.

INGREDIENTS

Serves 6

low-fat spread, for greasing
600ml/1 pint/2¹/2 cups skimmed milk
2 eggs
15ml/1 tbsp caster (superfine) sugar
15ml/1 tbsp poppy seeds
115g/4oz/1 cup each of strawberries,
 raspberries and blackberries
15ml/1 tbsp soft light brown sugar
60ml/4 tbsp red grape juice

3 Pour the custard into the soufflé dish and bake in the preheated oven for 50–60 minutes, until the custard is just set and golden on top.

4 While the custard is baking, mix the fruit with the soft brown sugar and fruit juice. Chill until ready to serve with the warm baked custard.

NUTRITIONAL NOTES

Per portion:

Energy	109Kcals/460kJ
Fat, total	3.1g
Saturated fat	0.69g
Cholesterol	66.2mg
Fibre	1.3g

1 Preheat the oven to 150°C/ 300°F/Gas 2. Grease a soufflé dish very lightly with low-fat spread. Heat the milk until just below boiling point, but do not boil. Beat the eggs in a bowl with the caster sugar and poppy seeds until creamy.

2 Whisk the milk into the egg mixture until well mixed. Stand the prepared soufflé dish in a shallow roasting pan, then pour in hot water from the kettle to come halfway up the sides of the dish.

VARIATION

If you don't like poppy seeds, sprinkle the surface with grated nutmeg or ground cinnamon.

Orange Yogurt Brûlées

*Luxurious treats, much lower in fat
than classic brûlées, which are made
with cream, eggs and lots of sugar.*

INGREDIENTS

Serves 4

2 oranges

150ml/¼ pint/⅔ cup low-fat Greek
  (US strained plain) yogurt

60ml/4 tbsp half-fat crème fraîche

45ml/3 tbsp golden caster (superfine)
  sugar

30ml/2 tbsp light muscovado
  (brown) sugar

1 With a sharp knife, cut away all
the peel and white pith from
the oranges and segment the fruit,
removing all the membrane.

2 Place the fruit in the bottom of
four individual flameproof
dishes. Mix together the yogurt
and crème fraîche and spoon over
the oranges.

3 Mix together the two sugars
and sprinkle them evenly over
the tops of the dishes.

4 Place the dishes under a
preheated, very hot grill
(broiler) for 3–4 minutes or until
the sugar melts and turns to a rich
golden brown. Serve warm or cold.

NUTRITIONAL NOTES
Per portion:

Energy	154Kcals/648kJ
Fat, total	3.8g
Saturated fat	2.35g
Cholesterol	15.8mg
Fibre	1.4g

Tofu Berry Brûlée

Brûlée is usually out-of-bounds on a low-fat diet, but this version is perfectly acceptable as it uses tofu.

INGREDIENTS

Serves 4

300g/11oz packet silken tofu

45ml/3 tbsp icing (confectioners') sugar

225g/8oz/2 cups red berry fruits,
    such as raspberries, strawberries
    and redcurrants

about 75ml/5 tbsp demerara (raw) sugar

NUTRITIONAL NOTES

Per portion:

Energy	180Kcals/760kJ
Fat, total	3.01g
Saturated fat	0.41g
Cholesterol	0mg
Fibre	1.31g

1 Mix the tofu and icing sugar in a food processor or blender and process until smooth.

COOK'S TIP

Choose silken tofu as it gives a smoother texture than firm tofu in this type of dish. Firm tofu is better for cooking in chunks.

2 Stir in the fruits, then spoon into a 900ml/1½ pint/3¾ cup flameproof dish. Flatten the top.

3 Sprinkle the top with demerara sugar to cover evenly. Place under a very hot grill (broiler) until the sugar melts and caramelizes. Chill before serving.

Passion Fruit Brûlée

Fruit brûlées are usually made with double cream, but Greek yogurt works just as well.

INGREDIENTS

Serves 4

4 passion fruit

300ml/¹/₂ pint/1¹/₄ cups low-fat Greek
   (US strained plain) yogurt

75g/3oz/¹/₂ cup soft light brown sugar

15ml/1 tbsp water

COOK'S TIP

Watch the caramel closely. It is
ready when it darkens to a rich
golden brown. At this stage it
will be very hot, so protect your
hand and pour it with great care.

1 Cut the passion fruit in half,
using a very sharp knife. Use a
teaspoon to scoop out all the pulp
and seeds and divide among four
ovenproof ramekins.

2 Spoon equal amounts of
the yogurt on the fruit and
smooth the surface level. Chill for
at least 2 hours.

3 Put the sugar in a small pan
with the water and heat gently,
stirring, until the sugar has melted
and caramelized. Pour over the
yogurt; the caramel will harden
within 1 minute. Keep the brûlées
in a cool place until ready to serve.

NUTRITIONAL NOTES
Per portion:

Energy	139Kcals/590kJ
Fat, total	3.8g
Saturated fat	2.37g
Cholesterol	5.3mg
Fibre	0.5g

Mango and Ginger Clouds

The sweet, perfumed flavour of ripe mango combines beautifully with ginger.

Serves 6

3 ripe mangoes

3 pieces stem ginger, plus 45ml/3 tbsp
    syrup from the jar

75g/3oz/1/2 cup silken tofu

3 egg whites

6 unsalted pistachio nuts, chopped

1 Cut the mango flesh off the stone (pit), remove the peel and chop.

2 Put the mango flesh in a food processor and add the ginger, syrup and tofu. Process until smooth. Spoon into a bowl.

NOTE

Raw or lightly cooked egg whites should be avoided by young children and women during pregnancy.

3 Whisk the egg whites in a grease-free bowl to form soft peaks. Fold them lightly into the mango mixture.

4 Spoon the mixture into wide dishes or glasses and chill before serving, sprinkled with the pistachio nuts.

NUTRITIONAL NOTES

Per portion:

Energy	141Kcals/592kJ
Fat, total	1.9g
Saturated fat	0.21g
Cholesterol	0mg
Fibre	3.9g

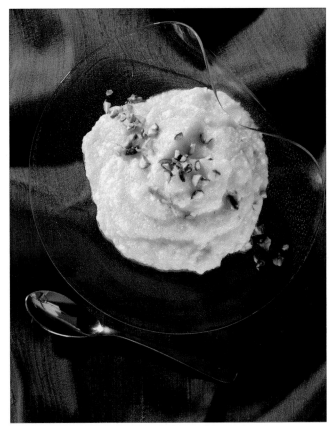

Raspberry Passion Fruit Swirls

2 Place alternate spoonfuls of the raspberry pulp and the fromage frais mixture into stemmed glasses or serving dishes.

3 Stir lightly to create a swirled effect. Decorate each dessert with a whole raspberry and a sprig of fresh mint. Serve chilled.

If passion fruit is not available, this simple dessert can be made with raspberries alone.

INGREDIENTS

Serves 4

300g/11oz/2¹/₂ cups raspberries

2 passion fruit

400ml/14fl oz/1²/₃ cups low-fat
   fromage frais

30ml/2 tbsp caster (superfine) sugar

raspberries and fresh mint sprigs,
   to decorate

COOK'S TIP

Over-ripe, slightly soft fruit can be used in this recipe. Use frozen raspberries when fresh are not available, but thaw them first.

1 Using a fork, mash the raspberries in a small bowl until the juice runs. Place the fromage frais and sugar in a separate bowl. Halve the passion fruit and scoop out the seeds. Add to the fromage frais and mix well.

NUTRITIONAL NOTES

Per portion:

Energy	110Kcals/462kJ
Fat, total	0.47g
Saturated fat	0.13g
Cholesterol	1mg
Fibre	2.12g

Chocolate Vanilla Timbales

You really can allow yourself the occasional chocolate treat, especially if it's a dessert as light as this one.

INGREDIENTS

Serves 6

350ml/12fl oz/1½ cups skimmed milk

30ml/2 tbsp cocoa powder, plus extra, for sprinkling

2 eggs, separated

5ml/1 tsp pure vanilla extract

45ml/3 tbsp caster (superfine) sugar

15ml/1 tbsp powdered gelatine

45ml/3 tbsp hot water

For the sauce

120ml/4fl oz/½ cup low-fat Greek (US strained plain) yogurt

2.5ml/½ tsp pure vanilla extract

1 Mix the milk and cocoa in a pan; stir over a moderate heat until the milk boils. Beat the egg yolks, vanilla and sugar in a bowl, until smooth. Pour in the chocolate milk, beating well.

2 Return the mixture to the pan and stir constantly over a gentle heat, without boiling, until it thickens slightly and is smooth. Dissolve the gelatine in the hot water and then quickly stir it into the milk mixture. Let it cool until on the point of setting.

3 Whisk the egg whites in a grease-free bowl until they hold soft peaks. Fold them quickly into the chocolate milk mixture, then divide among six individual moulds. Chill until set.

4 To serve the timbales, run a knife around the edge of each mould, dip the moulds quickly into hot water and turn out on to serving plates. For the sauce, stir the yogurt and vanilla extract together, then spoon on to the plates. Sprinkle the sauce with cocoa powder just before serving.

NUTRITIONAL NOTES

Per portion:

Energy	118Kcals/497kJ
Fat, total	4.1g
Saturated fat	1.89g
Cholesterol	66.7mg
Fibre	0.7g

Peach and Ginger Paskha

This low-fat version of the Russian Easter favourite is made with peaches and stem ginger.

INGREDIENTS

Serves 4

350g/12oz/1½ cups low-fat cottage cheese

2 ripe peaches or nectarines

90g/3½oz/scant ½ cup low-fat natural (plain) yogurt

2 pieces stem ginger in syrup, drained and chopped, plus 30ml/2 tbsp syrup from the jar

2.5ml/½ tsp pure vanilla extract

To decorate

1 peach or nectarine, peeled and sliced

10ml/2 tsp slivered almonds, toasted

1 Drain the cottage cheese and rub it through a sieve (strainer) into a bowl. Stone (pit) and roughly chop the fruit.

2 In a bowl, mix together the peaches or nectarines, the low-fat cottage cheese, yogurt, stem ginger, syrup and vanilla extract.

3 Line a new, clean flower pot or a sieve with a piece of clean, fine cloth such as muslin (cheesecloth).

4 Tip in the cheese mixture, wrap over the cloth and weight down. Leave over a bowl in a cool place to drain overnight. Unwrap the cloth and invert the paskha on to a plate. Decorate with fruit slices and almonds.

NUTRITIONAL NOTES
Per portion:

Energy	147Kcals/621kJ
Fat, total	2.9g
Saturated fat	0.89g
Cholesterol	5.3mg
Fibre	1.1g

COOK'S TIP

For individual paskhas, line four to six ramekins with the clean cloth and divide the mixture among them.

Strawberry Rose-petal Paskha

This lighter version of a traditional Russian dessert is ideal for dinner parties – make it a day or two in advance.

INGREDIENTS

Serves 4

350g/12oz/1¹/2 cups low-fat cottage cheese
175ml/6fl oz/³/4 cup low-fat natural
   (plain) yogurt
30ml/2 tbsp clear honey
2.5ml/¹/2 tsp rose water
275g/10oz/2¹/2 cups strawberries
handful of scented pink rose petals,
   to decorate

VARIATION

Use small porcelain heart-shaped moulds with draining holes for a pretty alternative.

1 Drain any liquid from the cottage cheese. Tip the cheese into a sieve (strainer). Using a wooden spoon to rub it through the sieve into a bowl. Stir the yogurt, honey and rose water into the cheese.

2 Roughly chop about half the strawberries and fold them into the cheese mixture.

3 Line a new, clean flowerpot or a sieve with fine muslin (cheesecloth) and tip the cheese mixture in. Drain over a bowl for several hours, or overnight.

4 Invert the flowerpot or sieve on to a serving plate, turn out the paskha and lift off the muslin. Cut the remaining strawberries in half and arrange them around the paskha. Scatter the rose petals over. Serve the paskha chilled.

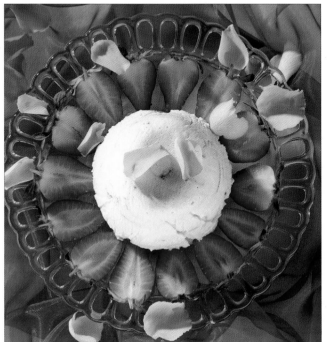

NUTRITIONAL NOTES

Per portion:

Energy	133Kcals/561kJ
Fat, total	1.6g
Saturated fat	1g
Cholesterol	6.1mg
Fibre	0.8g

Lemon Hearts with Strawberry Sauce

These elegant little hearts are perfect for a romantic celebration, such as a Valentine's Day dinner.

INGREDIENTS

Serves 6

175g/6oz/³/4 cup low-fat cottage cheese
150ml/¹/4 pint/²/3 cup half-fat
  crème fraîche
15ml/1 tbsp granulated (white) sugar
finely grated rind of ¹/2 lemon
30ml/2 tbsp lemon juice
10ml/2 tsp powdered gelatine
2 egg whites
low-fat spread, for greasing
For the sauce
225g/8oz/2 cups fresh or frozen and
  thawed strawberries, plus extra
  to decorate
15ml/1 tbsp lemon juice

1 Press the cottage cheese through a sieve (strainer) into a bowl. Beat in the crème fraîche, sugar and lemon rind.

COOK'S TIP
~

Don't worry if you haven't got heart-shaped (coeur à la crème) moulds. Simply use individual fluted moulds – or even ordinary teacups.

---

2 Pour the lemon juice into a small heatproof bowl and sprinkle the gelatine over the surface. When it has sponged, place the bowl over a pan of hot water and stir until dissolved.

3 Quickly stir the gelatine into the cheese mixture, mixing it in evenly.

4 Beat the egg whites in a grease-free bowl until they form soft peaks. Quickly fold them into the cheese mixture with metal spoon.

5 Spoon the mixture into six lightly greased, individual heart-shaped moulds, and chill the moulds until set.

6 Make the sauce. Mix the strawberries and lemon juice in a food processor or blender and process until smooth. Pour the sauce on to serving plates and invert the lemon hearts on top of the sauce. Decorate with slices of strawberry.

NUTRITIONAL NOTES
Per portion:

Energy	94Kcals/397kJ
Fat, total	4.2g
Saturated fat	2.60g
Cholesterol	27.7mg
Fibre	0.4g

Souffléed Rice Pudding

The fluffy egg whites in this rice pudding make the portions more substantial, without adding extra fat.

INGREDIENTS

Serves 4

65g/2¹/2 oz/¹/3 cup short-grain rice
45ml/3 tbsp clear honey
750ml/1¹/4 pints/3 cups semi-skimmed (low-fat) milk
1 vanilla pod (bean) or 2.5ml/¹/2 tsp vanilla extract
2 egg whites
5ml/1 tsp freshly grated nutmeg

1 Place the rice, honey and milk in a heavy or non-stick pan and bring the milk to the boil. Add the vanilla pod, if using.

2 Lower the heat, cover and simmer over the lowest possible heat for approximately 1–1¹/4 hours, stirring occasionally to prevent sticking, until most of the liquid has been absorbed.

3 Remove the vanilla pod, or, if using vanilla extract, add this to the rice mixture now. Set the pan aside, so that the mixture cools slightly. Preheat the oven to 220ºC/425ºF/Gas 7.

4 Place the egg whites in a grease-free bowl and whisk until they hold soft peaks when the whisk is lifted.

5 Using a metal spoon or spatula, fold the egg whites evenly into the rice mixture, then tip it into a 1 litre/1³/4 pint/4 cup ovenproof dish.

6 Sprinkle with grated nutmeg and bake for 15–20 minutes, until the pudding has risen well and is golden brown. Serve hot.

NUTRITIONAL NOTES

Per portion:

Energy	186Kcals/782kJ
Fat, total	3.7g
Saturated fat	1.88g
Cholesterol	13.1mg
Fibre	0g

COOK'S TIP

If you like, use skimmed milk instead of semi-skimmed, but take care when it is simmering as, with so little fat, it tends to boil over very easily.

Cinnamon and Apricot Soufflés

Don't expect this to be difficult simply because it's a soufflé – it really couldn't be easier.

INGREDIENTS

Serves 4

low-fat spread, for greasing

plain (all-purpose) flour, for dusting

3 eggs

115g/4oz/1/2 cup apricot fruit spread

finely grated rind of 1/2 lemon

5ml/1 tsp ground cinnamon, plus extra
   to decorate

NUTRITIONAL NOTES
Per portion:

Energy	134Kcals/560kJ
Fat, total	4.1g
Saturated fat	1.15g
Cholesterol	144.4mg
Fibre	0g

1 Preheat the oven to 190ºC/
375ºF/Gas 5. Lightly grease
four individual soufflé dishes and
dust them lightly with flour.

VARIATION

Other fruit spreads would be
delicious in this soufflé. Try peach
or blueberry for a change.

2 Separate the eggs and place the
yolks in a bowl with the fruit
spread, lemon rind and cinnamon.

3 Whisk hard until the mixture
is thick and pale in colour.

4 Place the egg whites in a
grease-free bowl and whisk
them until they form soft peaks
when the whisk is lifted from
the bowl.

5 Using a metal spoon, gradually
fold the egg whites evenly into
the yolk mixture.

6 Divide the soufflé mixture
among the prepared dishes
and bake for 10–15 minutes, until
well-risen and golden brown. Serve
at once, dusted with a little extra
ground cinnamon.

COOK'S TIP

Puréed fresh or well-drained
canned fruit can be used instead
of the apricot spread, but make
sure that the mixture is not
too wet or the soufflés will
not rise properly.

Apple Soufflé Puddings

Stewed fruit, such as plums, rhubarb or gooseberries sweetened with honey or sugar, would also make a good base for this soufflé.

INGREDIENTS

Serves 4

4 crisp eating apples
a little lemon juice
300ml/1/2 pint/11/4 cups milk
40g/11/2oz/3 tbsp butter
40g/11/2oz/1/3 cup plain (all-purpose)
    flour
25g/1oz/2 tbsp caster (superfine) sugar
2.5ml/1/2 tsp vanilla extract
2 eggs, separated

1 Preheat the oven to 200°C/ 400°F/Gas 6. Butter an ovenproof dish 20–23cm/8–9in in diameter and 5cm/2in deep. Peel, core and slice the apples. Put them in the dish and sprinkle with lemon juice.

2 Put the milk, butter and flour in a pan. Stirring continuously with a whisk, cook over medium heat until the sauce thickens and comes to the boil.

3 Let it bubble gently for 1–2 minutes, stirring well to make sure it does not stick and burn on the bottom of the pan.

4 Pour into a bowl, add the sugar and vanilla extract, and then stir in the egg yolks.

5 In a separate bowl, whisk the egg whites until stiff peaks form. With a metal spoon fold the egg whites into the custard.

6 Pour the custard mixture over the apples in the dish. Put into the hot oven and cook for about 40 minutes until puffed up, deep golden brown and firm to the touch. Serve straight out of the oven, before the soufflé topping begins to fall.

NUTRITIONAL NOTES
Per portion:

Energy	240Kcals/1006kJ
Fat, total	12.5g
Saturated fat	6.8g
Cholesterol	121mg
Fibre	1.9g

Hot Blackberry and Apple Soufflés

It's always worth freezing a bag of blackberries to have on hand for treats such as this delicious soufflé.

INGREDIENTS

Serves 6

low-fat spread, for greasing

150g/5oz/2/3 cup caster (superfine) sugar, plus extra for dusting

350g/12oz/3 cups blackberries

1 large cooking apple, peeled, cored and finely diced

grated rind and juice of 1 orange

3 egg whites

icing (confectioners') sugar, for dusting

COOK'S TIP
~

Running a table knife around the edge of the soufflés before baking helps them to rise evenly.

---

1 Preheat the oven to 200°C/ 400°F/Gas 6 and heat a baking sheet. Grease six 150ml/1/4 pint/ 2/3 cup soufflé dishes and dust with caster sugar.

2 In a pan, cook the blackberries, diced apple, orange rind and juice for 10 minutes. Press through a sieve (strainer) into a bowl. Stir in 50g/2oz/1/4 cup of the caster sugar. Set aside to cool.

3 Put a spoonful of the fruit purée into each prepared dish and smooth the surface. Set the dishes aside.

4 Whisk the egg whites in a large grease-free bowl until they form stiff peaks. Very gradually whisk in the remaining caster sugar to make a stiff, glossy meringue mixture.

5 Fold in the remaining fruit purée and spoon the flavoured meringue into the prepared dishes. Level the tops with a palette knife, and run a table knife around the edge of each dish.

6 Place the dishes on the hot baking sheet and bake for 10–15 minutes until the soufflés have risen well and are lightly browned. Dust the tops with icing sugar and serve at once.

NUTRITIONAL NOTES	
Per portion:	
Energy	138Kcals/584kJ
Fat, total	0.3g
Saturated fat	0.5g
Cholesterol	0mg
Fibre	2.7g

Souffléed Orange Semolina

If you have a bad opinion of semolina, treat yourself to a taste of this version.

Serves 4

50g/2oz/¼ cup semolina

600ml/1 pint/2½ cups semi-skimmed (low-fat) milk

30ml/2 tbsp muscovado (molasses) sugar

1 large orange

1 egg white

NUTRITIONAL NOTES
Per portion:

Energy	158Kcals/665kJ
Fat, total	2.67g
Saturated fat	1.54g
Cholesterol	10.5mg
Fibre	0.86g

1 Preheat the oven to 200ºC/ 400ºF/Gas 6. Put the semolina in a non-stick pan and add the milk and sugar. Stir over a moderate heat until thickened and smooth. Remove from the heat.

COOK'S TIP
〜

When using the rind of citrus fruit, scrub the fruit thoroughly before use, or buy unwaxed fruit.

---

2 Scrub the orange rind and pare a few long shreds of rind, save for decoration. Finely grate the remaining rind. Cut all the peel and white pith from the orange and separate the flesh into equal segments. Stir the segments into the semolina, with the orange rind.

3 Whisk the egg white in a grease-free bowl until stiff, then fold lightly and evenly into the mixture. Spoon into a 1 litre/ 1¾ pint/4 cup ovenproof dish and bake for 15–20 minutes, until risen and golden brown. Scatter the orange shreds and serve.

Quick Apricot Blender Whip

One of the quickest desserts you could make – and also one of the prettiest with its swirl of apricot.

INGREDIENTS

Serves 4

400g/14oz can apricot halves in juice
15ml/1 tbsp Grand Marnier or brandy
175ml/6fl oz/3/4 cup low-fat Greek
 (US strained plain) yogurt
15ml/1 tbsp flaked (sliced) almonds

3 Alternately spoon fruit purée and yogurt into four tall glasses or glass dishes, swirling them together slightly to give a marbled effect.

4 Lightly toast the almonds until they are golden. Let them cool slightly and then sprinkle them on top of each whip. Serve at once.

1 Drain the juice from the apricots and place the fruit and liqueur in a blender or food processor.

2 Process the apricots until the mixture is smooth.

NUTRITIONAL NOTES
Per portion:

Energy	88Kcals/369kJ
Fat, total	4.4g
Saturated fat	1.38g
Cholesterol	3.1mg
Fibre	0.9g

Prune and Orange Pots

A simple, store-cupboard dessert, made in minutes. It can be served straight away, but it is best chilled.

Serves 4

225g/8oz/1¹/2 cups ready-to-eat
    dried prunes
150ml/¹/4 pint/²/3 cup orange juice
250ml/8fl oz/1 cup low-fat natural
    (plain) yogurt
shreds of thinly pared orange rind,
    to decorate

2 Bring the juice to the boil, stirring. Lower the heat, cover and simmer for 5 minutes, until the prunes are tender and the liquid is reduced by half.

3 Remove from the heat, allow to cool slightly, then beat well with a wooden spoon, until the fruit breaks down to a rough purée.

5 Spoon the mixture into stemmed glasses or individual serving dishes, smoothing the tops.

6 Top each pot with a few shreds of thinly pared orange rind, to decorate. Chill before serving.

1 Remove the pits (if any), then roughly chop the prunes. Place them in a pan with the orange juice.

COOK'S TIP

This dessert can also be made with other ready-to-eat dried fruit, such as apricots or peaches. If using dried apricots, try the unsulphured variety for a rich colour and flavour. For a special occasion, add a dash of brandy or Cointreau with the yogurt.

4 Transfer the mixture to a bowl. Stir in the yogurt, swirling the yogurt and fruit purée together lightly, to give an attractive marbled effect.

NUTRITIONAL NOTES
Per portion:

Energy	125Kcals/529kJ
Fat, total	0.7g
Saturated fat	0.28g
Cholesterol	2.3mg
Fibre	3.2g

Gooseberry Cheese Cooler

Gooseberries are one of the less common summer fruits, so they're well worth snapping up.

INGREDIENTS

Serves 4

450g/1lb/4 cups fresh or frozen
   gooseberries
1 small orange
15ml/1 tbsp clear honey
250g/9oz/1 cup low-fat cottage cheese

NUTRITIONAL NOTES

Per portion:

Energy	93Kcals/392kJ
Fat, total	1.4g
Saturated fat	0.56g
Cholesterol	3.1mg
Fibre	3.4g

1 Top and tail the gooseberries and place them in a medium-sized pan. Finely grate the rind from the orange and squeeze out all of the juice; then add the orange rind and juice to the pan. Cover the pan and cook gently, stirring occasionally, until the fruit is completely tender.

2 Remove from the heat and stir in the honey. Purée the gooseberries with the cooking liquid in a food processor until almost smooth. Cool.

3 Press the cottage cheese through a sieve (strainer), or process it in a food processor, until smooth. Stir half the gooseberry purée into the cheese.

4 Spoon the cheese mixture into four serving dishes or glasses. Top each with a spoonful of the gooseberry purée. Serve chilled.

Grape Cheese Whips

A deliciously cool dessert of low-fat cheese and honey, topped with sugar-frosted grapes as decoration.

INGREDIENTS

Serves 4

150g/5oz/1¼ cups black or green seedless grapes, plus tiny bunches
2 egg whites
15ml/1 tbsp caster (superfine) sugar
finely grated rind and juice of ½ lemon
225g/8oz/1 cup low-fat soft cheese
45ml/3 tbsp clear honey
30ml/2 tbsp brandy (optional)

NUTRITIONAL NOTES
Per portion:

Energy	135Kcals/563kJ
Fat, total	3g
Saturated fat	1.2g
Cholesterol	0.56mg
Fibre	0g

1 Brush the tiny bunches of grapes lightly with egg white and sprinkle with sugar to coat. Leave to dry.

2 In a bowl, mix together the lemon rind and juice, cheese, honey and brandy if using. Chop the remaining grapes and stir them into the mixture.

3 Whisk the egg whites in a grease-free bowl until stiff enough to hold soft peaks. Fold the whites into the grape mixture, then spoon into four serving glasses.

4 Top with the sugar-frosted grapes and serve chilled.

Apricot Delight

A fluffy mousse base with a layer of fruit jelly on top makes this dessert doubly delicious.

Serves 8

2 × 400g/14oz cans apricots in natural juice

60ml/4 tbsp fructose

15ml/1 tbsp lemon juice

25ml/1½ tbsp powdered gelatine

425g/15oz low fat ready-to-serve custard

150ml/¼ pint/⅔ cup low-fat natural (plain) yogurt, strained

To decorate

1 quantity yogurt piping cream

1 apricot, sliced

1 sprig of fresh apple mint

1 Line the base of a 1.2 litre/ 2 pint/5 cup heart-shaped or round cake tin (pan) with baking parchment.

COOK'S TIP

〰

Don't use a loose-bottomed cake tin (pan) for this recipe as the mixture may seep through before it sets.

---

2 Drain the apricots, reserving the juice. Put the drained apricots in a food processor or blender. Add the fructose and 60ml/4 tbsp of the apricot juice. Blend to a smooth purée.

3 Measure 30ml/2 tbsp of the apricot juice into a small bowl, add lemon juice, then sprinkle over 10ml/2 tsp of the gelatine. Leave for 5 minutes.

4 Stir the gelatine into half the apricot purée and pour into the tin. Chill in the refrigerator for 1½ hours.

---

5 Sprinkle the remaining 15ml/ 1 tbsp gelatine over 60ml/ 4 tbsp of the apricot juice. Soak and dissolve as before. Mix the remaining purée with the custard, yogurt and gelatine. Pour on to the layer of set fruit purée and chill in the refrigerator for 3 hours.

6 Dip the cake tin into hot water for a few seconds and unmould the mousse on to a serving plate. Decorate with yogurt piping cream, the sliced apricot and a sprig of fresh apple mint.

LOW-FAT FRUIT SALADS

❖

Strawberries with Cointreau

Strawberries at the height of their season are the best summer pleasure.

Serves 4

1 unwaxed orange

40g/1¹/₂oz/3 tbsp granulated (white) sugar

75ml/5 tbsp water

450g/1lb/3¹/₂ cups strawberries, hulled

45ml/3 tbsp Cointreau or other orange-
   flavoured liqueur

250ml/8fl oz/1 cup low-fat Greek
   (US strained plain) yogurt

1 With a vegetable peeler, remove wide strips of rind from the orange, taking care to avoid the pith. Then cut into very thin julienne strips.

2 Mix the sugar and water in a small pan. Heat gently, swirling the pan occasionally until the sugar has dissolved. Bring to the boil, add the julienne strips, then simmer for 10 minutes.

3 Remove the pan from the heat and leave the syrup to cool. Reserve four strawberries for decoration and cut the rest lengthways in halves or quarters. Put them in a bowl. Stir the Cointreau or chosen liqueur into the syrup and pour it over the fruit. Add the orange rind. Set aside for at least 30 minutes or for up to 2 hours.

NUTRITIONAL NOTES

Per portion:

Energy	155Kcals/653kJ
Fat, total	3.2g
Saturated fat	1.97g
Cholesterol	4.4mg
Fibre	1.2g

4 Whip the yogurt, then sweeten to taste with a little of the strawberry syrup.

5 To serve, spoon the chopped strawberries into glass serving dishes and top with dollops of the sweetened Greek yogurt. Decorate with strawberries.

Fresh Figs with Honey and Wine

Fresh figs are naturally sweet, and taste wonderful in a honeyed wine syrup. Any variety can be used in this recipe.

INGREDIENTS

Serves 6

450ml/³⁄4 pint/scant 2 cups dry
    white wine
75g/3oz/¹⁄3 cup clear honey
50g/2oz/¹⁄4 cup caster (superfine) sugar
1 small orange
8 whole cloves
450g/1lb fresh figs
1 cinnamon stick
bay leaves, to decorate

For the sauce

300ml/¹⁄2 pint/1¹⁄4 cups low-fat Greek
    (US strained plain) yogurt
5ml/1 tsp pure vanilla extract
5ml/1 tsp caster (superfine) sugar

1 Put the wine, honey and sugar in a heavy pan and heat gently until the sugar dissolves.

2 Stud the orange with the cloves and add to the syrup with the figs and cinnamon. Cover and simmer until the figs are soft then leave to cool.

3 Flavour the low-fat Greek yogurt with the vanilla extract and sugar. Spoon it into a serving dish. Transfer the fruit to another serving dish. With a sharp knife cut one or two of the figs in half, if you like, to show off their pretty centres. Decorate with the bay leaves and serve with the yogurt.

NUTRITIONAL NOTES

Per portion:

Energy	201Kcals/845kJ
Fat, total	2.7g
Saturated fat	1.58g
Cholesterol	3.5mg
Fibre	1.5g

Persian Melon Cups

This typical Persian dessert uses fresh fruits flavoured with rose water and a hint of aromatic mint.

INGREDIENTS

Serves 4

2 small melons

225g/8oz/2 cups strawberries, sliced

3 peaches, peeled and cut into small cubes

1 bunch of seedless grapes, about 225g/8oz

30ml/2 tbsp caster (superfine) sugar

15ml/1 tbsp rose water

15ml/1 tbsp lemon juice

crushed ice

4 sprigs of mint, to decorate

COOK'S TIP

If you don't have a melon baller, scoop out the melon flesh using a large spoon.

---

2 Reserve four strawberries and slice the rest. Place in a bowl with the melon balls, the peaches, grapes, sugar, rose water and lemon juice.

3 Pile the fruit into the melon shells and chill in the refrigerator for 2 hours.

4 To serve, sprinkle with crushed ice and decorate each melon shell with a whole strawberry and a sprig of mint.

1 Carefully cut the melons in half and remove the seeds. Scoop out the flesh with a melon baller, taking care not to damage the skin. Reserve the melon shells for later.

NUTRITIONAL NOTES

Per portion:

Energy	137Kcals/579kJ
Fat, total	0.4g
Saturated fat	0g
Cholesterol	0mg
Fibre	3.2g

Fragrant Mandarins with Pistachio Nuts

Mandarins, tangerines, clementines, mineolas: any of these lovely citrus fruits could be used for this dessert.

INGREDIENTS

Serves 4

10 mandarins

15ml/1 tbsp icing (confectioners') sugar

10ml/2 tbsp orange flower water

15ml/1 tbsp chopped pistachio nuts

3 Mix the reserved mandarin juice, icing sugar and orange flower water and pour it over the fruit. Cover the dish and place in the refrigerator for at least an hour to chill.

4 Blanch the shreds of rind in boiling water for 30 seconds. Drain and cool on kitchen paper, then sprinkle them over the mandarins, with the pistachio nuts, to serve.

1 Pare a little mandarin rind and cut into shreds. Squeeze the juice from two mandarins and set aside.

2 Peel the remaining fruit, removing all the pith and place in a bowl.

NUTRITIONAL NOTES
Per portion:

Energy	91Kcals/382kJ
Fat, total	2.2g
Saturated fat	0.25g
Cholesterol	0mg
Fibre	2g

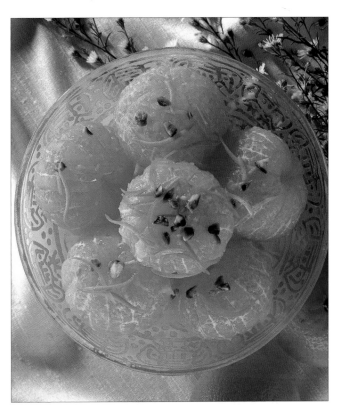

Orange and Date Salad

This Moroccan dessert is simplicity itself, yet it is wonderfully light at the end of a rich meal.

INGREDIENTS

Serves 6

6 oranges

15–30ml/1–2 tbsp orange flower water or rose water (optional)

lemon juice (optional)

115g/4oz/^{2}/$_3$ cup stoned (pitted) dates

40g/1^1/$_2$oz/scant ^{1}/$_2$ cup pistachio nuts

15ml/1 tbsp icing (confectioners') sugar, plus extra for dusting

5ml/1 tsp toasted almonds

3 Chop the dates and pistachio nuts and sprinkle over the salad with the icing sugar. Chill for 1 hour.

4 Just before serving, sprinkle the salad with the toasted almonds and extra icing sugar.

NUTRITIONAL NOTES
Per portion:

Energy	147Kcals/616kJ
Fat, total	4.3g
Saturated fat	0.45g
Cholesterol	0mg
Fibre	3.5g

1 Peel the oranges with a sharp knife, removing all the pith. Cut into segments, catching all the juice in a bowl. Place in a serving dish.

2 Stir in the juice from the bowl, with a little orange flower or rose water, if using, and sharpen with lemon juice, if liked.

COOK'S TIP

Use fresh dates, if you can, although if you can't get hold of them dried dates are delicious in this salad, too.

Fresh Fruit Salad and Almond Curd

2 In a separate pan, dissolve the sugar in the remaining water over the heat. Add the milk and the almond extract. Blend well, but do not boil.

3 Pour the agar-agar, isinglass or gelatine mixture into a large serving bowl. Add the flavoured milk gradually, stirring all the time. When cool, put in the refrigerator for 2–3 hours to set. To serve, cut the curd into small cubes and spoon into a serving dish or into individual bowls. Spoon the fruit salad over the curd and serve.

This is a wonderfully light Chinese dessert usually made from agar-agar or isinglass, though gelatine can be used.

INGREDIENTS

Serves 6

10g/¹/₄oz agar-agar or isinglass
   or 25g/1oz gelatine
about 600ml/1 pint/2¹/₂ cups water
50g/2oz/¹/₄ cup caster (superfine) sugar
300ml/¹/₂ pint/1¹/₄ cups semi-skimmed
   (low-fat) milk
5ml/1 tsp almond extract
fresh fruit salad

1 In a pan, dissolve the agar-agar or isinglass in about half of the water over a gentle heat. This will take at least 10 minutes. If using gelatine, follow the instructions on the sachet.

NUTRITIONAL NOTES

Per portion:

Energy	117Kcals/499kJ
Fat, total	1.2g
Saturated fat	0.75g
Cholesterol	5.3mg
Fibre	0g

Fresh Pineapple with Coconut

This refreshing dessert can also be made with vacuum-packed pineapple, and it is very simple to make and light to eat.

INGREDIENTS

Serves 4

1 fresh pineapple, about
    675g/1½ lb, peeled
few slivers of fresh coconut
300ml/½ pint/1¼ cups unsweetened
    pineapple juice
60ml/4 tbsp coconut liqueur
2.5cm/1in piece stem ginger, plus 45ml/
    3 tbsp syrup from the jar

1 Peel and slice the pineapple, arrange in a serving dish and scatter the coconut slivers on top.

2 Place the pineapple juice and coconut liqueur in a pan and heat gently.

3 Thinly slice the stem ginger and add to the pan with the ginger syrup. Bring just to the boil, then simmer gently until the liquid is slightly reduced and the sauce is fairly thick.

4 Pour the sauce over the pineapple and coconut, leave to cool, then chill in the refrigerator before serving.

NUTRITIONAL NOTES
Per portion:

Energy	177Kcals/743kJ
Fat, total	2.2g
Saturated fat	1.55g
Cholesterol	0mg
Fibre	2.2g

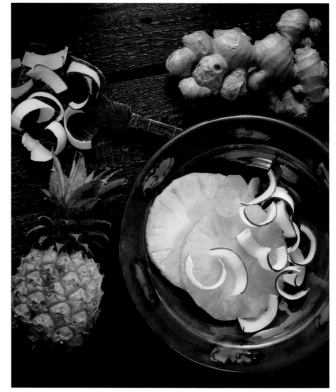

Perfumed Pineapple Salad

Prepare this fruit salad ahead to give the fruit time to absorb the perfumed flavour of the orange flower water.

Serves 4

1 small ripe pineapple
15ml/1 tbsp icing (confectioners') sugar
15ml/1 tbsp orange flower water, or
  more if liked
115g/4oz/²⁄₃ cup fresh dates, stoned
  (pitted) and quartered
225g/8oz/ 2 cups fresh strawberries, sliced
a few fresh mint sprigs, to serve

1 Cut the skin from the pineapple and, using the tip of a vegetable peeler, remove as many brown "eyes" as possible. Quarter the pineapple lengthways, remove the core from each wedge, then slice.

2 Lay the pineapple slices in a shallow glass serving bowl. Sprinkle with icing sugar and drizzle over the orange flower water.

3 Add the dates and strawberries to the pineapple, cover and chill for at least 2 hours, stirring once or twice. Serve, decorated with a few mint sprigs.

COOK'S TIP

Orange flower water is available from Middle Eastern food stores or good delicatessens.

NUTRITIONAL NOTES

Per portion:

Energy	127Kcals/534kJ
Fat, total	0.4g
Saturated fat	0g
Cholesterol	0mg
Fibre	2.9g

Iced Pineapple Crush

The sweet tropical flavours of pineapple and lychees combine well with richly scented strawberries.

INGREDIENTS

Serves 4

2 small pineapples
450g/1lb/4 cups strawberries
400g/14oz can lychees
45ml/3 tbsp kirsch or white rum
30ml/2 tbsp icing (confectioners') sugar

1 Remove the crown from both pineapples by twisting sharply. Reserve the leaves for decoration.

VARIATION

You could use other tropical fruit such as mango, papaya or guava as well as the pineapple.

2 Cut the fruit in half diagonally with a large serrated knife.

3 Cut around the flesh inside the skin with a small serrated knife, keeping the skin intact. Remove the core from the pineapple.

4 Chop the pineapple and combine with the strawberries and lychees, taking care not to damage the fruit.

5 Combine the kirsch or rum with the icing sugar, pour over the fruit and freeze for 45 minutes.

6 Turn the fruit out into the pineapple skins and decorate with the pineapple leaves. Serve chilled.

NUTRITIONAL NOTES

Per portion:

Energy	251Kcals/1058kJ
Fat, total	0.7g
Saturated fat	0g
Cholesterol	0mg
Fibre	5.2g

COOK'S TIP

A ripe pineapple will resist pressure when squeezed and will have a sweet, fragrant smell. In winter, freezing conditions can cause the flesh to blacken.

Pineapple Wedges with Allspice and Lime

2 Loosen the flesh on each wedge by sliding a knife between the flesh and the skin. Cut the flesh into slices, leaving it on the skin.

3 Using a sharp-pointed or canelle knife, remove a few shreds of rind from the lime. Squeeze out the juice.

Fresh pineapple is easy to prepare and always looks festive, so this dish is perfect for easy entertaining.

INGREDIENTS

Serves 4

1 ripe pineapple, about 800g/1¾lb

1 lime

15ml/1 tbsp dark muscovado (molasses) sugar

5ml/1 tsp ground allspice

1 Cut the pineapple lengthways into quarters and remove the hard core from each wedge.

NUTRITIONAL NOTES

Per portion:

Energy	96Kcals/403kJ
Fat, total	0.5g
Saturated fat	0.03g
Cholesterol	0mg
Fibre	2.3g

4 Sprinkle the pineapple with the lime juice and rind, sugar and allspice. Serve immediately, or chill for up to an hour.

Papaya and Mango Medley with Iced Yogurt

Tropical fruit with iced mango yogurt makes a wonderful dessert. Buy very ripe fruit for this dessert.

INGREDIENTS

Serves 4

2 large ripe mangoes, total weight about 675g/1½ lb

300ml/½ pint/1¼ cups low-fat Greek (US strained plain) yogurt

8 dried apricots, halved

150ml/¼ pint/⅔ cup unsweetened orange juice

1 ripe papaya, about 300g/11oz

1 Take one thick slice from one of the mangoes and, while still on the skin, slash the flesh in a criss-cross pattern to make cubes.

3 Meanwhile, put the apricots and orange juice in a pan. Bring to boil, then simmer until the apricots are soft, adding a little water, if needed, so that the apricots remain moist. Remove from the heat and set aside to cool. Peel, stone (pit) and chop the mangoes.

4 Halve the papaya, remove seeds and peel. Dice the flesh and add to the mango. Pour the apricot sauce over.

5 Stir the mango yogurt a few times. Serve the fruit topped with the mango yogurt.

2 Turn the piece of mango inside-out and cut away the cubed flesh from the skin. Place in a bowl, mash to a pulp with a fork, then add the yogurt and mix well. Spoon into a freezer tub and freeze for 1–1½ hours until half frozen.

NUTRITIONAL NOTES
Per portion:

Energy	231Kcals/967kJ
Fat, total	4.3g
Saturated fat	2.44g
Cholesterol	5.3mg
Fibre	7.5g

Pineapple and Passion Fruit Salsa

Serve this fruity salsa solo or as a filling for halved baby cantaloupes.

Serves 6

1 small fresh pineapple

2 passion fruit

150ml/¼ pint/⅔ cup low-fat Greek (US strained plain) yogurt

30ml/2 tbsp light muscovado (brown) sugar

meringues, to serve (optional)

1 Cut off the top and bottom of the pineapple so that it will stand firmly on a chopping board. Using a large sharp knife, slice off the peel.

2 Use a small sharp knife to carefully cut out the eyes from around the pineapple.

VARIATION

Use low-fat fromage frais instead of the yogurt, if you like.

3 Slice the pineapple and use a small pastry (cookie) cutter to stamp out the tough core. Finely chop the flesh.

4 Cut the passion fruit in half, remove the seeds and scoop out the pulp into a bowl.

NUTRITIONAL NOTES

Per portion:

Energy	82Kcals/342kJ
Fat, total	1.5g
Saturated fat	0.79g
Cholesterol	1.8mg
Fibre	1.3g

5 Stir in the chopped pineapple and yogurt. Cover and chill.

6 Stir in the muscovado sugar just before serving the salsa. Serve with meringues, if you like.

Grapefruit Salad with Campari and Orange

The bittersweet flavour of Campari combines especially well with citrus fruit for this sophisticated dessert.

INGREDIENTS

Serves 4

150ml/¹/4 pint/²/3 cup water
45ml/3 tbsp caster (superfine) sugar
60ml/4 tbsp Campari
30ml/2 tbsp lemon juice
4 grapefruit
5 oranges
4 sprigs fresh mint

COOK'S TIP

When buying citrus fruit, choose brightly coloured varieties that feel heavy for their size.

---

1 Bring the water to the boil in a small pan, add the sugar and simmer until dissolved. Cool in a metal tray, then add the Campari and lemon juice. Chill until ready to serve.

2 Peel the grapefruit and oranges. Working over a bowl, to catch the juice, cut the fruit into segments. Add them to the bowl, stir in the Campari syrup and chill again.

3 Spoon the salad into four dishes and finish with a sprig of fresh mint.

NUTRITIONAL NOTES
Per portion:

Energy	182Kcals/764kJ
Fat, total	0.4g
Saturated fat	0g
Cholesterol	0mg
Fibre	5.3g

Muscat Grape Frappé

2 Remove the seeds from the grapes with a pair of tweezers. If you have time, peel the grapes.

3 Scrape the frozen wine with a tablespoon to make a fine ice. Combine the grapes with the ice and spoon into four glasses.

The flavour and perfume of the Muscat grape is rarely more enticing than when captured in this icy-cool salad.

INGREDIENTS

Serves 4

1/2 bottle Muscat wine, Beaumes de Venise, Frontignan or Rivesaltes

150ml/1/4 pint/2/3 cup water

450g/1lb/4 cups Muscat grapes

1 Pour the wine into a stainless-steel or non-stick baking sheet, add the water and freeze for 3 hours or until solid.

COOK'S TIP

To make this frappé alcohol-free, substitute 300ml/1/2 pint/ 1 1/4 cups apple or grape juice for the wine.

NUTRITIONAL NOTES

Per portion:

Energy	155Kcals/651kJ
Fat, total	0g
Saturated fat	0g
Cholesterol	0mg
Fibre	1g

Cool Green Fruit Salad

A sophisticated, simple fruit salad, which would look wonderful served on a bed of crushed ice.

INGREDIENTS

Serves 6

3 Ogen or Galia melons

115g/4oz/1 cup green seedless grapes

2 kiwi fruit

1 star fruit, plus extra slices to garnish

1 green-skinned apple

1 lime

175ml/6fl oz/¾ cup unsweetened
    sparkling grape juice

3 Thinly pare the rind from the lime and cut it in fine strips. Blanch in boiling water for 30 seconds, and then drain them and rinse them in cold water. Squeeze the juice from the lime and pour it over the fruit. Toss lightly.

4 Spoon the prepared fruit into the reserved melon shells; then chill the shells until required. To serve, spoon the sparkling grape juice over the fruit and scatter with lime rind. Decorate with slices of star fruit.

1 Halve the melons and scoop out the seeds. Keeping the shells intact, scoop out the flesh and cut into bite-size cubes. Reserve the melon shells.

2 Cut any large grapes in half. Peel and chop the kiwi fruit. Slice the star fruit and set aside a few slices for decoration. Core and slice the apple and place in a bowl, with the other fruit.

NUTRITIONAL NOTES

Per portion:

Energy	91Kcals/382kJ
Fat, total	0.4g
Saturated fat	0.00g
Cholesterol	0.0mg
Fibre	1.6g

Blackberry Salad with Rose Granita

The blackberry is a member of the rose family and combines especially well with rose water.

INGREDIENTS

Serves 4

600ml/1 pint/2½ cups water
150g/5oz/⅔ cup caster (superfine) sugar
petals from 1 fresh red rose, finely chopped
5ml/1 tsp rose water
10ml/2 tsp lemon juice
450g/1lb/4 cups blackberries
icing (confectioners') sugar, for dusting
For the meringue
2 egg whites
115g/4oz/½ cup caster (superfine) sugar

1 Bring 150ml/¼ pint/⅔ cup of the water to the boil in a stainless-steel or enamel pan. Add the sugar and chopped rose petals, then lower the heat and simmer for 5 minutes. Strain the syrup into a deep metal tray, add the remaining water, the rose water and lemon juice; leave to cool. Freeze the mixture for approximately 3 hours or until solid.

2 Preheat the oven to 140°C/ 275°F/Gas 1. Line a baking sheet with six layers of newspaper and cover with baking parchment.

3 Make the meringue. Whisk the egg whites in a grease-free bowl until they form soft peaks. Whisk in the caster sugar, a little at a time, then continue to whisk until the meringue forms stiff peaks when the whisk is lifted out of the bowl.

4 Spoon the meringue into a piping (pastry) bag fitted with a 1cm/½in plain nozzle. Pipe the meringue in lengths on the lined baking sheet. Dry in the bottom of the oven for 1½–2 hours.

5 Break the meringue into 5cm/ 2in lengths and place three or four lengths on each of four large plates. Pile the blackberries next to the meringue. With a tablespoon, scrape the granita finely. Shape into ovals and place over the meringue. Dust with icing sugar and serve immediately.

COOK'S TIP
〜

Serve the dessert as soon as possible after piling the granita on the meringue, or the meringue will soon go soggy.

NUTRITIONAL NOTES
Per portion:

Energy	310Kcals/1318kJ
Fat, total	0.2g
Saturated fat	0g
Cholesterol	0mg
Fibre	3.5g

VARIATION

Other soft fruits such as blueberries, raspberries or loganberries would work equally well with this dessert.

Blueberry and Orange Salad Meringues

What could be prettier than this simple salad of delicate blueberries, oranges and meringues flavoured with lavender?

INGREDIENTS

Serves 4

6 oranges

350g/12oz/3 cups blueberries

8 sprigs fresh lavender

For the meringue

2 egg whites

115g/4oz/$\frac{1}{2}$ cup caster (superfine) sugar

5ml/1 tsp fresh lavender flowers

1 Preheat the oven to 140°/ 275°F/Gas 1. Line a baking sheet with six layers of newspaper and cover with baking parchment. Whisk the egg whites in a large grease-free bowl until they hold soft peaks. Add the sugar a little at a time, whisking thoroughly after each addition. Fold in the lavender flowers.

2 Spoon the meringue into a piping (pastry) bag fitted with a 5mm/$\frac{1}{4}$in plain nozzle. Pipe small buttons of meringue on to the prepared baking sheet. Dry the meringue near the bottom of the oven for 1$\frac{1}{2}$–2 hours.

3 To segment the oranges, remove the peel from the top, bottom and sides with a serrated knife. Loosen the segments by cutting with a paring knife between the flesh and the membranes, holding the fruit over a bowl to catch the juice.

4 Arrange the segments on four plates, fanning them out.

5 Combine the blueberries with the lavender meringues and pile in the centre of each plate. Decorate with sprigs of lavender and serve immediately.

VARIATION

You could use blackberries or firm raspberries with fresh rosemary leaves and flowers for this dessert. You would also make 7.5cm/3in circles of meringue instead of small buttons and layer the soft fruit in between circles of meringue.

NUTRITIONAL NOTES
Per portion:

Energy	198Kcals/838kJ
Fat, total	0.3g
Saturated fat	0g
Cholesterol	0mg
Fibre	3.5g

COOK'S TIP

Always use fresh or recently dried lavender, and avoid artificially scented bunches that are sold for dried flower displays.

Mixed Fruit Salad

A really good fruit salad is always refreshing, especially when it comes bathed in fresh orange and lemon juices.

INGREDIENTS

Serves 4

juice of 3 large sweet oranges
juice of 1 lemon
1 banana
1–2 apples
1 ripe pear
2 peaches or nectarines
4–5 apricots or plums
115g/4oz/1 cup black or green grapes
115g/4oz/1 cup strawberries or raspberries
any other fruits in season
sugar, to taste (optional)
30–45ml/2–3 tbsp Kirsch, Maraschino or other liqueur (optional)

COOK'S TIP

For a herb infused flavour add chopped fresh herbs, try pineapple mint, lemon balm or borage flowers.

NUTRITIONAL NOTES
Per portion:

Energy	133Kcals/558kJ
Fat, total	0.4g
Saturated fat	0.03g
Cholesterol	0mg
Fibre	3.8g

1 Place the fresh orange and lemon juices into a large serving bowl.

2 Prepare all the fruits by washing or peeling them as necessary. Cut them into bite-size pieces. Halve the grapes and remove any seeds. Core and slice the apples. Stone (pit) and slice soft fruits and leave small berries whole. As soon as each fruit is prepared, add it to the juices in the bowl.

3 Taste the salad, adding sugar if needed. Liqueur can also be added, if you like. Cover the bowl and put it in the refrigerator for at least 2 hours. Mix well before serving.

Spiced Fruit Platter

The spicy sour flavour of chat masala may seem a little strange at first, but this Indian dessert can become addictive!

INGREDIENTS

Serves 6

1 pineapple
2 papayas
1 small melon
juice of 2 limes
2 pomegranates
chat masala, to taste
sprigs of fresh mint, to decorate

NUTRITIONAL NOTES
Per portion:

Energy	102Kcals/429kJ
Fat, total	0.5g
Saturated fat	0g
Cholesterol	0mg
Fibre	4.8g

1 Peel the pineapple. Remove the core and any remaining "eyes", then cut the flesh lengthways into thin wedges. Peel the papayas, cut them in half, and then into thin wedges. Halve the melon and remove the seeds from the middle. Cut it into thin wedges and remove the skin.

2 Arrange the fruit on six individual plates and sprinkle with the lime juice. Cut the pomegranates in half and scoop out the seeds, discarding any pith. Scatter the seeds over the fruit. Serve, sprinkled with a little chat masala to taste. Scatter over a few sprigs of mint, to decorate.

Ruby Fruit Salad

After a rich main course, this port-flavoured fruit salad is light and refreshing. Use any fruit available.

Serves 8

300ml/¹/2 pint/1¹/4 cups water
115g/4oz/¹/2 cup caster (superfine) sugar
1 cinnamon stick
4 cloves
pared rind of 1 orange
300ml/¹/2 pint/1¹/4 cups port
2 oranges
1 small ripe Ogen, Charentais or
   honeydew melon
4 small bananas
2 dessert apples
225g/8oz/2 cups seedless grapes

1 Put the water, sugar, spices and pared orange rind into a pan and stir over a gentle heat to dissolve the sugar. Then bring to the boil, lower the heat, cover and simmer for 10 minutes. Leave to cool, then add the port.

NUTRITIONAL NOTES
Per portion:

Energy	212Kcals/895kJ
Fat, total	0.2g
Saturated fat	0.04g
Cholesterol	0mg
Fibre	1.9g

2 Strain the liquid into a bowl. With a sharp knife, cut off all the skin and pith from the oranges. Then, holding each orange over the bowl to catch the juice, cut it into segments, and drop them into the syrup. Squeeze the remaining pulp to release any juice.

3 Cut the melon in half, remove the seeds and scoop out the flesh or cut it in small cubes. Add it to the syrup.

4 Peel the bananas and cut them diagonally in 1cm/¹/2in slices. Quarter and core the apples and cut the wedges in small cubes. Leave the skin on, or peel them if it is tough. Halve the grapes if large or leave them whole. Stir all the fruit into the syrup, cover with clear film (plastic wrap) and chill for an hour before serving.

Winter Fruit Salad

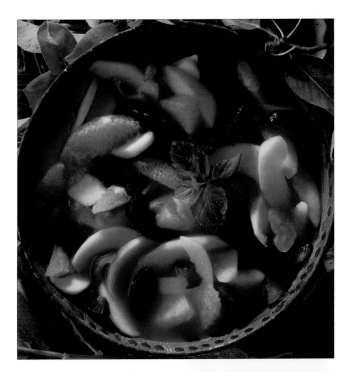

A refreshing and nutritious fruit
salad, this makes an excellent choice
for a winter buffet.

INGREDIENTS

Serves 6

225g/8oz can pineapple cubes in fruit juice
200ml/7fl oz/scant 1 cup fresh orange juice
200ml/7fl oz/scant 1 cup unsweetened
    apple juice
30ml/2 tbsp orange- or apple-flavoured
    liqueur
30ml/2 tbsp clear honey (optional)
2 oranges, peeled
2 green-skinned eating apples
2 pears
4 plums, stoned (pitted) and chopped
12 fresh dates, stoned (pitted)
    and chopped
115g/4oz/1/2 cup ready-to-eat
    dried apricots
fresh mint sprigs, to decorate

2 Segment the oranges, catching
any juice in the bowl, then add
the orange segments and pineapple
to the fruit juice mixture.

3 Core and chop the apples
and pears and add them to
the bowl.

4 Stir in the plums, dates and
apricots. Cover and chill for
several hours. Decorate with fresh
mint sprigs to serve.

1 Drain the pineapple, reserving
the juice in a large serving
bowl. Add the orange juice, apple
juice, liqueur and honey, if using,
and stir.

NUTRITIONAL NOTES	
Per portion:	
Energy	227Kcals/967kJ
Fat, total	0.37g
Saturated fat	0g
Cholesterol	0mg
Fibre	5.34g

Mixed Melon Salad

Several melon varieties are combined with wild or woodland strawberries for a delicious salad.

INGREDIENTS

Serves 4

1 cantaloupe or Charentais melon
1 Galia melon
900g/2lb watermelon
175g/6oz/1½ cups wild strawberries
4 sprigs fresh mint

NUTRITIONAL NOTES
Per portion:

Energy	91Kcals/381kJ
Fat, total	0.7g
Saturated fat	0g
Cholesterol	0mg
Fibre	2.7g

1 Cut the cantaloupe or Charentais melon, Galia melon and watermelon in half.

2 Using a spoon, scoop out the seeds from the cantaloupe or Charentais, and the Galia.

3 With a melon scoop, take out as many balls as you can from all three melons. Mix them together in a large bowl, cover and put the bowl in the refrigerator. Chill for 2–3 hours.

4 Just before serving, add the wild strawberries and mix lightly. Spoon into four stemmed glass dishes.

5 Decorate with sprigs of mint and serve at once.

Fresh Fruit with Mango Sauce

This bright, flavourful sauce is easy to prepare and turns a simple fruit salad into something very special.

Serves 6

1 large ripe mango, peeled, stoned (pitted)
   and chopped
rind of 1 unwaxed orange
juice of 3 oranges
caster (superfine) sugar to taste
2 peaches
2 nectarines
1 small mango, peeled
2 plums
1 pear or 1/2 small melon
juice of 1 lemon
25–50g/1–2oz/2–4 tbsp wild strawberries
25–50g/1–2oz/2–4 tbsp raspberries
25–50g/1–2oz/2–4 tbsp blueberries
small mint sprigs, to decorate

1 In a food processor fitted with a metal blade, process the large mango until smooth. Add the orange rind, juice and sugar to taste and process again until very smooth. Press through a sieve (strainer) into a bowl and chill the sauce.

2 Peel the peaches if liked, then slice and stone (pit) the peaches, nectarines, small mango and plums. Quarter the pear and remove the core and seeds, or, if using, slice the melon thinly and remove the peel.

3 Place the sliced fruits on a large plate, sprinkle with lemon juice and chill, covered with clear film (plastic wrap), for up to 3 hours before serving. (Some fruits may discolour if cut too far ahead of time.)

4 To serve, arrange the sliced fruits on individual serving plates, spoon the berries on top, drizzle with a little of the mango sauce and decorate with the mint sprigs. Serve the remaining sauce separately.

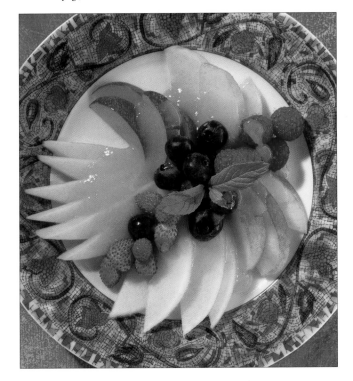

NUTRITIONAL NOTES	
Per portion:	
Energy	229Kcals/997kJ
Fat, total	0.6g
Saturated fat	0g
Cholesterol	0.0mg
Fibre	4.9g

Marzipan Figs with Dates

Sweet Mediterranean figs and dates combine well with dessert apples.

Serves 4

6 large apples
juice of 1/2 lemon
150g/5oz/1 cup fresh dates
25g/1oz white marzipan
5ml/1 tsp orange flower water
60ml/4 tbsp low-fat natural (plain) yogurt
4 green or purple figs
4 almonds, toasted

1 Core the apples. Slice thinly and cut into fine matchsticks. Moisten with lemon juice to prevent them browning.

2 Remove the stones (pits) from the dates and cut the flesh into fine strips, then mix with the apple matchsticks in a bowl.

3 Soften the marzipan with orange flower water and combine with the low-fat yogurt. Mix well.

4 Pile the apples and dates in the centre of four plates. Remove the stem from each of the figs and cut the fruit into quarters without slicing the base. Squeeze the base with the thumb and forefinger to open the fruit.

5 Place a fig in the centre of the salad, spoon in the yogurt filling and decorate each portion with a toasted almond.

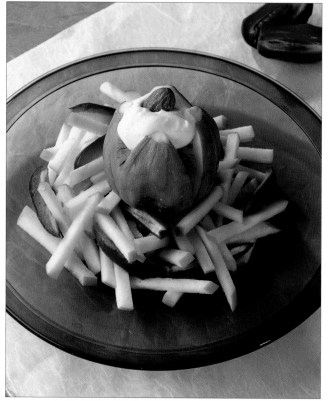

NUTRITIONAL NOTES	
Per portion:	
Energy	210Kcals/884kJ
Fat, total	3.1g
Saturated fat	0.15g
Cholesterol	0.6mg
Fibre	5.4g

Dried Fruit Salad with Summer Berries

This is a wonderful combination of fresh and dried fruit.

INGREDIENTS

Serves 4

115g/4oz/¹/2 cup dried apricots
115g/4oz/¹/2 cup dried peaches
1 fresh pear
1 fresh apple
1 fresh orange
115g/4oz/²/3 cup mixed raspberries
    and blackberries
550ml/18fl oz/2¹/2 cups water
1 cinnamon stick
50g/2oz/¹/4 cup sugar
15ml/1 tbsp honey

1 Soak the apricots and peaches in water for 1–2 hours until plump, then drain and halve or quarter.

2 Peel and core the pear and apple and cut into cubes. Peel the orange with a sharp knife, removing all the pith, and cut into wedges. Place all the fruit in a large pan with the raspberries and blackberries.

3 Add the water, the cinnamon, sugar and honey.

4 Bring to a boil, then cover the pan and simmer very gently for 10–12 minutes, until the fruit is just tender, stirring occasionally.

NUTRITIONAL NOTES

Per portion:

Energy	190Kcals/811kJ
Fat, total	0.4g
Saturated fat	0g
Cholesterol	0.0mg
Fibre	5.1g

Tropical Fruit Salad

Like all nuts, coconut is a significant source of fat, so go easy on the strips used to decorate this delicious salad.

INGREDIENTS

Serves 4–6

1 medium pineapple, about 600g/1lb 5oz
400g/14oz can guava halves in syrup
2 medium bananas, sliced
1 large mango, peeled, stoned (pitted)
   and diced
115g/4oz stem ginger, plus 30ml/2 tbsp of
   the syrup from the jar
60ml/4 tbsp thick coconut milk
10ml/2 tsp granulated (white) sugar
2.5ml/1/2 tsp freshly grated nutmeg
2.5ml/1/2 tsp ground cinnamon
a few fine strips of coconut, to decorate

1 Peel, core and cube the pineapple, and place in a serving bowl. Drain the guavas, reserving the syrup, and chop. Add the guavas to the bowl with half the sliced banana and the mango.

NUTRITIONAL NOTES

Per portion:

Energy	340Kcals/1434kJ
Fat, total	1.8g
Saturated fat	0.83g
Cholesterol	0mg
Fibre	8.1g

2 Chop the stem ginger and add to the fruit mixture.

3 Pour 30ml/2 tbsp of the ginger syrup, and the reserved guava syrup, into a blender or food processor. Add the remaining banana slices with the coconut milk and the sugar. Blend to a smooth purée.

4 Pour the banana and coconut mixture over the tropical fruit. Add a little grated nutmeg and a sprinkling of cinnamon on the top. Serve chilled, decorated with fine strips of coconut.

Melon and Strawberry Salad

This colourful fruit salad can be served either as a dessert or as a refreshing appetizer before a meal.

INGREDIENTS

Serves 4

1 Galia melon
1 honeydew melon
1/2 watermelon
225g/8oz/2 cups fresh strawberries,
　 halved if large
15ml/1 tbsp lemon juice
15ml/1 tbsp clear honey
15ml/1 tbsp water
15ml/1 tbsp chopped fresh mint

2 Mix the lemon juice, honey and water in a jug (pitcher) and stir into the fruit.

3 Sprinkle the chopped mint over the fruit and serve.

NUTRITIONAL NOTES
Per portion:

Energy	139Kcals/584kJ
Fat, total	0.84g
Saturated fat	0g
Cholesterol	0mg
Fibre	2g

1 Prepare the melons by cutting them in half and scraping out the seeds. Use a melon baller to scoop out the flesh into balls or a knife to cut it into cubes. Place these in a fruit bowl and add the fresh strawberries.

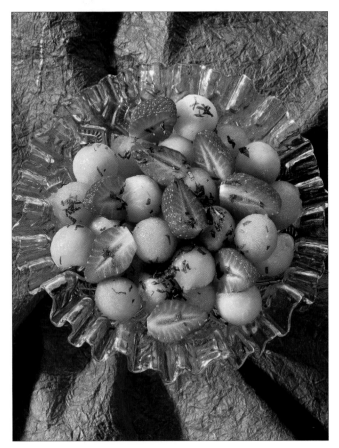

Papaya and Green Grapes with Mint Syrup

This wonderful combination of textures and flavours makes the perfect dessert to follow a spicy main course.

INGREDIENTS

Serves 4

2 large papayas

225g/8oz/2 cups seedless green grapes

juice of 3 limes

2.5cm/1in fresh root ginger, peeled and finely grated

15ml/1 tbsp clear honey

5 fresh mint leaves, cut into thin strips, plus extra whole leaves, to decorate

1 Peel the papaya and cut into small cubes, discarding the seeds. Cut the grapes in half.

2 In a bowl, mix together the lime juice, grated root ginger, clear honey and mint leaf strips.

3 Add the papaya and grapes and toss well. Cover and leave in a cool place to marinate for 1 hour.

4 Serve in a large dish or individual stemmed glasses, garnished with the whole fresh mint leaves.

NUTRITIONAL NOTES
Per portion:

Energy	120Kcals/507kJ
Fat, total	0.2g
Saturated fat	0g
Cholesterol	0mg
Fibre	4.4g

Papaya Skewers with Passion Fruit Coulis

Tropical fruits make a simple, exotic dessert. The passion fruit flesh can be used without puréeing or straining.

Serves 6

3 ripe papayas

10 passion fruit or kiwi fruit

30ml/2 tbsp fresh lime juice

30ml/2 tbsp icing (confectioners') sugar

30ml/2 tbsp white rum

lime slices, to garnish

NUTRITIONAL NOTES
Per portion:

Energy	94Kcals/399kJ
Fat, total	0.3g
Saturated fat	0g
Cholesterol	0mg
Fibre	4.1g

3 Press the fruit pulp through a sieve (strainer) placed over a bowl; discard the seeds. Add the lime juice, icing sugar and rum, then stir the coulis well until the sugar has dissolved.

4 Spoon a little coulis onto plates and place the skewers on top. Scoop the flesh from the remaining passion or kiwi fruit and spoon over. Serve at once, garnished with lime slices.

1 Cut the papayas in half and scoop out the seeds. Peel them and cut the flesh into even-size chunks. Thread the chunks on to six bamboo skewers.

2 Halve eight of the passion fruit or kiwi fruit and scoop out the flesh. Purée the flesh for a few seconds in a blender or food processor.

Three-fruit Compote

Mixing dried fruits with fresh ones makes a good combination, especially with orange flower water.

Serves 6

175g/6oz/1 cup ready-to-eat dried apricots
300ml/1/2 pint/11/4 cups water
1 small ripe pineapple
1 small ripe melon, about 450g/1lb
15ml/1 tbsp orange flower water
mint sprigs, to decorate

NUTRITIONAL NOTES

Per portion:

Energy	86Kcals/360kJ
Fat, total	0.4g
Saturated fat	0g
Cholesterol	0mg
Fibre	3.2g

2 Peel and quarter the pineapple, cut the core from each quarter and discard. Cut the flesh into small chunks.

3 Cut the melon in half and out the seeds. Working over a bowl to catch the juices, scoop balls from the flesh. Tip the juices into the apricots.

4 Put the apricots, with the juices, into a bowl. Stir in the orange flower water. Add the pineapple and melon and mix all the fruits gently.

5 Pour into a serving dish or individual dishes. Decorate with a mint sprig and chill in the refrigerator before serving.

1 Put the apricots into a pan and pour in the water. Bring to the boil, then lower the heat and simmer for 5 minutes. Leave to cool.

VARIATION

A good fruit salad needn't consist of a mixture of fruits. For a delicious red fruit salad, try berry fruits with sliced plums, or for green fruits, try apple, kiwi fruit and green grapes.

Apricot and Banana Compote

3 Spoon the fruit and juices into a large serving dish.

4 Serve immediately, or cover and chill for several hours first. Sprinkle with flaked almonds just before serving.

This compote is delicious with low-fat custard or ice cream. Served for breakfast, it makes a tasty start to the day.

INGREDIENTS

Serves 4

225g/8oz/1 cup ready-to-eat dried apricots
300ml/1/2 pint/1 1/4 cups unsweetened
  orange juice
150ml/1/4 pint/2/3 cup unsweetened
  apple juice
5ml/1 tsp ground ginger
3 medium bananas, sliced
25g/1oz/1/4 cup toasted flaked
  (sliced) almonds

1 Put the apricots in a pan with the fruit juices and ginger and stir. Cover, bring to the boil and then simmer gently for 10 minutes, stirring constantly.

2 Set aside to cool, leaving the lid on. Once the compote is cool, stir in the sliced bananas.

COOK'S TIP

Use other combinations of dried and fresh fruit such as prunes or figs and apples or peaches.

NUTRITIONAL NOTES

Per portion:

Energy	241Kcals/1022kJ
Fat, total	4.18g
Saturated fat	0.37g
Cholesterol	0mg
Fibre	4.91g

Spiced Fruits Jubilee

Based on the classic Cherries Jubilee, this is a great way to use a glut of fruit. The spiced syrup is a bonus.

INGREDIENTS

Serves 6

115g/4oz/¹/₂ cup caster (superfine) sugar

thinly pared rind of 1 lemon

4 whole cloves

1 cinnamon stick

300ml/¹/₂ pint/1¹/₄ cups water

225g/8oz tart red plums, stoned (pitted) and sliced

225g/8oz nectarines, stoned (pitted) and chopped

225g/8oz/2 cups cherries, pitted

5ml/1 tsp arrowroot

75ml/5 tbsp brandy

low-fat vanilla ice cream, to serve (optional)

1 Put the sugar, lemon rind, cloves, cinnamon stick and water in a pan. Bring to the boil, stirring, then simmer for 5 minutes. Lift out the spices with a slotted spoon and discard.

2 Add the fruit, cover the pan and simmer for 5 minutes. Drain the fruit and set it aside; return the syrup to the pan. Boil it, uncovered, for 2 minutes or until thick and syrupy.

3 Put the arrowroot in a small bowl and stir in 30ml/2 tbsp of the brandy. Stir the mixture into the syrup. Continue cooking and stirring, until the sauce thickens. Return the fruit to the pan.

4 If serving with ice cream, place a scoop in each serving bowl and spoon the hot fruit over the top. Warm the remaining brandy in a small pan, then set it alight. For maximum dramatic effect, ladle it over the fruit at the table.

NUTRITIONAL NOTES	
Per portion:	
Energy	151Kcals/639kJ
Fat, total	0.1g
Saturated fat	0g
Cholesterol	0mg
Fibre	1g

Italian Fruit Salad and Ice Cream

Macerated soft fruits are delectable on their own, and also make a wonderful ice cream.

INGREDIENTS

Serves 6

900g/2lb/8 cups mixed soft fruits, such as strawberries, raspberries, loganberries, redcurrants, blueberries, peaches, apricots, plums and melons

juice of 6–8 oranges

juice of 1 lemon

15ml/1 tbsp pear and apple concentrate

60ml/4 tbsp very low-fat fromage frais

30ml/2 tbsp orange-flavoured liqueur

fresh mint sprigs, to decorate

1 Prepare the fruit according to type. Cut it into reasonably small pieces, large enough to hold their shape.

2 Put the fruit pieces in a serving bowl and pour over enough orange juice to cover. Add the lemon juice, stir gently, cover and chill for 2 hours.

3 Set half the macerated fruit aside to serve as it is. Purée the remainder in a blender or food processor.

4 Gently warm the pear and apple concentrate and stir it into the fruit purée. Whip the fromage frais and fold it in, then add the liqueur.

NUTRITIONAL NOTES

Per portion:

Energy	60Kcals/254kJ
Fat, total	0.2g
Saturated fat	0.01g
Cholesterol	0.1mg
Fibre	3.2g

5 Churn in an ice cream maker. Alternatively, place in a container and freeze until ice crystals form around the edge, then beat until smooth. Repeat once or twice, then freeze until firm. Soften slightly before serving decorated with mint. Serve accompanied by the macerated fruit.

LOW-FAT ICES & SORBETS

❖◆❖

Redcurrant and Raspberry Coulis

3 Blend the cornflour with the orange juice, then stir into the fruit purée. Transfer to a pan and bring to the boil, stirring continuously, and cook for 1–2 minutes until smooth and thick. Leave until cold.

4 Spoon the sauce over each plate. Drip the cream from a teaspoon to make small dots evenly around the edge. Draw a cocktail stick (toothpick) through the dots to form heart shapes. Scoop or spoon sorbet into the middle and decorate with flowers.

A sauce to serve with meringues and fruit sorbets. Make it pretty with a fresh flowers and leaves.

INGREDIENTS

Serves 6

225g/8oz/2 cups redcurrants
450g/1lb/4 cups raspberries
50g/2oz/1/2 cup icing (confectioners') sugar
15ml/1 tbsp cornflour (cornstarch)
juice of 1 orange
30ml/2 tbsp low-fat cream
edible flowers, to decorate

1 Strip the redcurrants from their stalks. Place them in a blender with the sugar and raspberries, and blend to a purée.

2 Press the fruit mixture through a fine sieve (strainer) into a bowl and discard the seeds and pulp.

NUTRITIONAL NOTES	
Per portion:	
Energy	81Kcals/340kJ
Fat, total	1.2g
Saturated fat	0.6g
Cholesterol	0mg
Fibre	3.2g

Christmas Cranberry Bombe

This alternative to Christmas pudding is light and low in fat, but still very festive and luxurious.

INGREDIENTS

Serves 6

250ml/8fl oz/1 cup buttermilk

60ml/4 tbsp low-fat crème fraîche

1 vanilla pod (bean)

2 eggs

30ml/2 tbsp clear honey

30ml/2 tbsp chopped angelica

30ml/2 tbsp mixed peel

10ml/2 tsp flaked (sliced) almonds, toasted

For the sorbet

175g/6oz/1½ cups fresh or
    frozen cranberries

150ml/¼ pint/⅔ cup fresh orange juice

finely grated rind of ½ orange

2.5ml/½ tsp mixed (apple pie) spice

50g/2oz/¼ cup golden caster (superfine)
    sugar

1 Heat the buttermilk, crème fraîche and vanilla pod until the mixture is almost boiling. Remove the vanilla pod.

NUTRITIONAL NOTES	
Per portion:	
Energy	153Kcals/644kJ
Fat, total	4.6g
Saturated fat	1.58g
Cholesterol	75.5mg
Fibre	1.5g

2 Place the eggs in a heatproof bowl over a pan of hot water and whisk until they are pale and thick. Pour in the heated buttermilk in a thin stream, whisking hard. Continue whisking over the hot water until the mixture thickens slightly.

3 Whisk in the honey and then cool. Spoon the mixture into a freezer container and freeze until slushy, tip into a bowl and stir in the chopped angelica, mixed peel and almonds.

4 Pack into a 1.2 litre/2 pint/5 cup heatproof bowl and hollow out the centre. Freeze until firm.

5 Meanwhile, make the sorbet centre. Put the cranberries, orange juice, rind and spice in a pan and cook gently until the cranberries are soft. Set some cranberries aside for decorating. Add the sugar to the rest, then purée in a food processor until almost smooth, but still with some texture. Leave to cool.

6 Fill the hollowed-out centre of the bombe with the cranberry mixture, smooth over and freeze until firm. To serve, allow to soften slightly at room temperature, then turn out and serve in medium-sized slices, decorated with the reserved cranberries.

Summer Fruit Salad Ice Cream

What could be more cooling on a hot summer day than fresh fruits, lightly frozen in this irresistible ice?

INGREDIENTS

Serves 6

900g/2lb/6 cups mixed soft summer fruit, such as raspberries, strawberries, blackcurrants or redcurrants
2 eggs
250ml/8fl oz/1 cup low-fat Greek (US strained plain) yogurt
175ml/6fl oz/³/4 cup red grape juice
15ml/1 tbsp powdered gelatine

2 Separate the eggs, whisk the yolks and the yogurt into the fruit purée.

4 Whisk the dissolved gelatine mixture into the fruit purée. Cool, then pour the mixture into a freezerproof container. Freeze until half-frozen and slushy.

1 Reserve half the fruit for the decoration; purée the rest in a food processor, then strain it over a bowl to make a smooth purée.

VARIATION

You could use other combinations of summer fruit such as apricots, peaches and nectarines, with apple or orange juice for a more delicate ice cream.

3 Heat the grape juice until almost boiling, then remove it from the heat. Sprinkle the gelatine over the grape juice and stir to dissolve the gelatine completely.

5 Whisk the egg whites in a grease-free bowl until stiff. Quickly fold them into the half-frozen mixture.

6 Return the ice cream to the freezer and freeze until almost firm. Scoop into individual dishes and decorate with the reserved soft fruits.

NUTRITIONAL NOTES
Per portion:

Energy	116Kcals/489kJ
Fat, total	3.9g
Saturated fat	1.69g
Cholesterol	66.8mg
Fibre	3.6g

COOK'S TIP

Red grape juice has a good flavour and improves the colour of the ice, but if it is not available, use cranberry, apple or orange juice instead.

Frozen Apple and Blackberry Terrine

This pretty, three-layered terrine can be frozen, so you can enjoy it at any time of year.

Serves 6

450g/1lb cooking or eating apples

300ml/¹/2 pint/1¹/4 cups sweet cider

15ml/1 tbsp clear honey

5ml/1 tsp pure vanilla extract

200g/7oz/scant 2 cups fresh or frozen and thawed blackberries

15ml/1 tbsp powdered gelatine

2 egg whites

fresh apple slices and blackberries, to decorate

1 Peel, core and chop the apples and place them in a pan with half the cider. Bring the cider to the boil, then lower the heat, cover the pan and let the apples simmer gently until tender.

2 Tip the apples into a food processor and process to a smooth purée. Stir in the honey and vanilla extract. Add half the blackberries to half the apple purée, and process again until smooth. Strain to remove the pips.

3 Heat the remaining cider until almost boiling, then sprinkle the gelatine over and stir until the gelatine has dissolved completely. Add half the gelatine mixture to the apple purée and half to the blackberry purée.

4 Leave both purées to cool until almost set. Whisk the egg whites until they are stiff. Quickly fold them into the apple purée. Remove half the purée to another bowl. Stir the remaining whole blackberries into half the apple purée, and then tip this into a 1.75 litre/3 pint/7¹/2 cup loaf tin (pan), packing it down firmly.

5 Top with the blackberry purée and spread it evenly. Finally, add a layer of the plain apple purée and smooth it evenly. If necessary, freeze each layer until firm before adding the next.

6 Freeze until firm. When ready to serve, remove from the freezer and allow to stand at room temperature for about 20 minutes to soften. Serve in slices, decorated with fresh apple slices and blackberries.

VARIATION

For a quicker version the mixture can be set without the layering. Purée the apples and blackberries together, stir the dissolved gelatine and whisked egg whites into the mixture, turn the whole thing into the tin (pan) and leave the mixture to set.

NUTRITIONAL NOTES

Per portion:

Energy	83Kcals/346kJ
Fat, total	0.2g
Saturated fat	0g
Cholesterol	0mg
Fibre	2.6g

Ginger and Kiwi Sorbet

Freshly grated root ginger gives a lively, aromatic flavour to sorbets and ices. Here, it is combined with kiwi fruit to make a refreshing sorbet.

INGREDIENTS

Serves 6

150g/2oz fresh root ginger
115g/4oz/^{1}/$_{2}$ cup caster (superfine) sugar
300ml/^{1}/$_{2}$ pint/1^{1}/$_{4}$ cups water
5 kiwi fruit
fresh mint sprigs or chopped kiwi fruit,
   to decorate

1 Peel the ginger and finely grate. Put the sugar and water in a pan and heat gently until the sugar has dissolved. Add the ginger and cook for 1 minute, then leave to cool. Strain into a bowl and chill until very cold.

2 Peel the kiwi fruit and blend until smooth. Add the purée to the chilled syrup and mix well.

3 Pour the mixture into a container and freeze for 3–4 hours, beating twice as it thickens. Return to the freezer until ready to serve.

4 Spoon into glasses, decorate with mint sprigs or chopped kiwi fruit, and serve.

NUTRITIONAL NOTES
Per portion:

Energy	100Kcals/426kJ
Fat, total	0.3g
Saturated fat	0g
Cholesterol	0mg
Fibre	1g

COOK'S TIP

If using an ice cream maker prepare the ingredients as described in steps 1 and 2, then churn the mixture until it thickens. Transfer to a plastic tub or similar freezerproof container and freeze until ready to serve.

Ruby Grapefruit Sorbet

*On a hot day, nothing slips down
more easily than a smooth sorbet.
This one looks as good as it tastes.*

INGREDIENTS

Serves 8

175g/6oz/³/4 cup granulated (white) sugar
120ml/4fl oz/¹/2 cup water
1 litre/1³/4 pints/4 cups strained freshly
    squeezed ruby grapefruit juice
15ml/1 tbsp fresh lemon juice
15ml/1 tbsp icing (confectioners') sugar
mint leaves, to decorate

1 In a small heavy pan, dissolve
the granulated sugar in the
water over a medium heat, without
stirring. When the sugar has
dissolved, boil the syrup for
3–4 minutes. Remove from the
heat and leave to cool.

2 Pour the cooled sugar syrup
into the grapefruit juice. Stir
well. Taste the mixture and adjust
the flavour by adding the lemon
juice or the icing sugar, if necessary,
but do not make it too sweet.

3 Pour the mixture into a metal
or plastic freezer container and
freeze for about 3 hours, or until
softly set.

4 Remove from the container
and chop roughly into
7.5cm/3in pieces. Place in a
food processor and process
until smooth. Return the mixture
to the freezer container and
freeze again until set. Repeat this
freezing and chopping process
2 or 3 times, until a smooth
consistency is obtained.

5 Alternatively, freeze the
sorbet in an ice cream maker,
following the manufacturer's
instructions. Serve, decorated
with mint leaves.

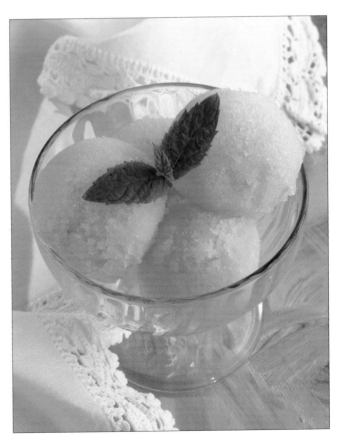

NUTRITIONAL NOTES

Per portion:

Energy	133Kcals/568kJ
Fat, total	0.1g
Saturated fat	0g
Cholesterol	0mg
Fibre	0g

Mango Sorbet with Mango Sauce

After a heavy meal, this Indian speciality makes a refreshing dessert. Remove from the freezer 10 minutes before serving.

INGREDIENTS

Serves 4

900g/2lb/5 cups mango pulp

2.5ml/1/2 tsp lemon juice

grated rind of 1 orange and 1 lemon

4 egg whites

50g/2oz/1/4 cup caster (superfine) sugar

120ml/4fl oz/1/2 cup low-fat Greek
   (US strained plain) yogurt

50g/2oz/1/2 cup icing (confectioners')
   sugar

NUTRITIONAL NOTES

Per portion:

Energy	259Kcals/1090kJ
Fat, total	1.7g
Saturated fat	0.79g
Cholesterol	1.8mg
Fibre	5.9g

1 In a large, chilled bowl that can safely be used in the freezer, mix half of the mango pulp with the lemon juice and the grated citrus rind.

2 Whisk the egg whites in a grease-free bowl to soft peaks and fold into the mango mixture with the caster sugar. Cover, freeze for at least 1 hour.

3 Remove the sorbet from the freezer and beat again. Transfer to an ice cream container, and freeze until solid.

4 Lightly whisk the yogurt with the icing sugar and the remaining pulp. Spoon into a bowl and chill for 24 hours. Scoop individual servings of sorbet and cover with mango sauce.

Lychee and Elderflower Sorbet

The flavour of elderflowers is famous for bringing out the extract of gooseberries, and it complements lychees wonderfully.

INGREDIENTS

Serves 4

175g/6oz/3/4 cup caster (superfine) sugar
400ml/14fl oz/1 2/3 cups water
500g/1 1/4lb fresh lychees, peeled and stoned (pitted)
15ml/1 tbsp undiluted elderflower cordial
dessert biscuits (cookies), to serve

NUTRITIONAL NOTES
Per portion:

Energy	249Kcals/1058kJ
Fat, total	0.1g
Saturated fat	0g
Cholesterol	0mg
Fibre	0.9g

1 Heat the sugar and water until the sugar has dissolved. Then boil for 5 minutes and add the lychees. Lower the heat and simmer for 7 minutes. Remove from the heat and allow to cool.

2 Purée the fruit and syrup. Place a sieve (strainer) over a bowl and press the purée through it with a spoon.

3 Stir the elderflower cordial into the strained purée, then pour the mixture into a freezerproof container. Freeze for approximately 2 hours, until ice crystals start to form around the edges.

4 Remove the sorbet from the freezer and process briefly in a food processor or blender to break up the crystals. Repeat this process twice more, then freeze until firm.

5 Transfer to the refrigerator for 10 minutes to soften slightly before serving in scoops. Crisp dessert biscuits can be served with the sorbet, but aren't really necessary. If you do serve them, remember that they will increase the fat content of the dessert.

Plum and Port Sorbet

*Rather a grown-up sorbet, this one,
but you could use still red grape juice
instead of port if you prefer.*

INGREDIENTS

Serves 6

900g/2lb ripe red plums, halved
   and stoned (pitted)
75g/3oz/6 tbsp caster (superfine) sugar
45ml/3 tbsp water
45ml/3 tbsp ruby port or red wine
biscuits (cookies), to serve (optional)

1 Put the plums in a pan with
the sugar and water. Stir over a
gentle heat until the sugar has
melted, then cover and simmer
gently for about 5 minutes, until
the fruit is soft.

2 Tip into a food processor
and purée until smooth,
then stir in the port or wine.
Cool completely, then tip into a
container that can safely be used in
the freezer and freeze until firm
around the edges.

3 Spoon into the food processor
and process until smooth.
Return to the freezer and freeze
until solid.

4 Soften slightly at room
temperature then serve in
scoops, with biscuits if you like,
but they will add fat content.

NUTRITIONAL NOTES

Per portion:

Energy	166Kcals/699kJ
Fat, total	0.25g
Saturated fat	0g
Cholesterol	0mg
Fibre	3.75g

Raspberry Sorbet with a Soft Fruit Garland

This stunning fresh fruit and herb garnish creates a bold border for the scoops of sorbet.

INGREDIENTS

Serves 8

175g/6oz/³/4 cup caster (superfine) sugar

250ml/8fl oz/1 cup water

450g/1lb fresh or thawed
   frozen raspberries

strained juice of 1 orange

For the decoration

1 bunch mint

selection of soft fruits, including
   strawberries, raspberries, redcurrants
   and blueberries

1 Heat the caster sugar with the water in a pan, until dissolved, stir occasionally. Bring to the boil, then set aside to cool. Purée the raspberries with the orange juice, then strain, to remove any seeds.

2 Mix the syrup with the puréed raspberries and pour into a suitable container for the freezer. Freeze for 2 hours or until ice crystals form around the edges. Whisk until smooth, then return to the freezer for 4 hours.

3 About 30 minutes before serving, transfer the sorbet to the refrigerator to soften slightly. Place a large sprig of mint on the rim of a serving plate, then build up a garland, using more mint sprigs.

4 Leaving on the leaves, cut the strawberries in half. Arrange on the mint with the other fruit. Place the fruits at different angles and link the leaves with strings of redcurrants. Place scoops of sorbet in the centre.

NUTRITIONAL NOTES

Per portion:

Energy	158Kcals/669kJ
Fat, total	0.4g
Saturated fat	0g
Cholesterol	0mg
Fibre	3.4g

Blackcurrant Sorbet

If not serving immediately, cover this blackcurrant sorbet tightly and freeze it again, for up to one week.

INGREDIENTS

Serves 4

100g/3¹/2 oz/scant ¹/2 cup caster
   (superfine) sugar
120ml/4fl oz/¹/2 cup water
450g/1lb/4 cups blackcurrants
juice of ¹/2 lemon
15ml/1 tbsp egg white

1 Mix the sugar and water in a small pan. Heat gently, stirring until the sugar dissolves, then boil the syrup for 2 minutes. Remove the pan from the heat and set aside to cool.

2 Remove the blackcurrants from the stalks by pulling them through the tines of a fork. Wash thoroughly and drain.

3 Using a metal blade, process the blackcurrants and lemon juice until smooth. Or, chop the blackcurrants coarsely, then add the lemon juice. Stir in the sugar syrup.

4 Press the purée through a sieve (strainer) to remove the seeds.

5 Pour the blackcurrant purée into a non-metallic dish that can safely be used in the freezer. Cover the dish with a lid and freeze until the sorbet is nearly firm, but still slushy.

6 Cut the sorbet into pieces and process in a food processor until smooth. With the machine running, add the egg white through the feeder tube and process until well mixed. Tip the sorbet back into the dish and freeze until almost firm. Chop the sorbet again and process until smooth. Serve immediately.

NUTRITIONAL NOTES
Per portion:

Energy	132Kcals/558kJ
Fat, total	0g
Saturated fat	0g
Cholesterol	0mg
Fibre	4.1g

Mango and Lime Sorbet in Lime Shells

This richly flavoured sorbet looks pretty served in the lime shells, but is also good served in scoops.

INGREDIENTS

Serves 4

4 large limes

1 ripe mango

7.5ml/1½ tsp powdered gelatine

2 egg whites

15ml/1 tbsp caster (superfine) sugar

strips of pared lime rind, to decorate

1 Slice the top and bottom off each lime. Squeeze the juice, then scrape out the shell.

2 Halve, stone (pit), peel and chop the mango. Purée in a food processor with 30ml/2 tbsp of the lime juice.

3 Sprinkle the gelatine over 45ml/3 tbsp of the lime juice in a small heatproof bowl. Set aside until spongy, then place over a pan of hot water.

4 Stir the mixture until the gelatine has dissolved. Stir it into the mango mixture. Whisk the egg whites in a grease-free bowl until they hold soft peaks. Whisk in the sugar. Fold the egg white mixture quickly into the mango mixture. Spoon the sorbet into the lime shells. Any leftover sorbet can be frozen in small ramekins.

NUTRITIONAL NOTES

Per portion:

Energy	83Kcals/350kJ
Fat, total	0.4g
Saturated fat	0g
Cholesterol	0mg
Fibre	2.3g

5 Place the filled shells in the freezer until the sorbet is firm. Overwrap the shells in clear film (plastic wrap). Before serving, allow the shells to stand at room temperature for about 10 minutes; decorate them with knotted strips of pared lime rind.

Watermelon Sorbet

A slice of this refreshing sorbet is the perfect way to cool down on a hot day. Ensure the watermelon is perfectly ripe.

Serves 6

1/2 small watermelon, about 1kg/2¼lb
75g/3oz/6 tbsp caster (superfine) sugar
60ml/4 tbsp unsweetened cranberry
   juice or water
30ml/2 tbsp lemon juice
sprigs of fresh mint, to decorate

1 Cut the watermelon into six equal-size wedges. Scoop out the pink flesh, discarding the seeds but reserving the shell.

2 Select a bowl that can safely be used in the freezer. Line it with clear film (plastic wrap). Arrange the melon skins in the bowl to re-form the shell, fitting them together snugly so that there are no gaps. Put in the freezer.

3 Mix the sugar and cranberry juice or water in a pan and stir over a low heat until the sugar dissolves. Bring to the boil, then lower the heat and simmer for 5 minutes. Leave the sugar syrup to cool.

4 Put the melon flesh and lemon juice in a blender and process to a smooth purée. Stir in the sugar syrup and pour into a freezer-proof container. Freeze for 3–3½ hours, or until slushy.

5 Tip the sorbet into a chilled bowl and whisk to break up the ice crystals. Return to the freezer for another 30 minutes, whisk again, then tip into the melon shell and freeze until solid.

6 Carefully remove the sorbet-filled melon shell from the freezer and turn it upside down. Use a sharp knife to separate the segments, then quickly place them on individual plates. Decorate with mint sprigs and serve.

NUTRITIONAL NOTES
Per portion:

Energy	125Kcals/525kJ
Fat, total	0.52g
Saturated fat	0g
Cholesterol	0mg
Fibre	0.26g

COOK'S TIP

Watermelon seeds make a delicious and nutritious snack if toasted in a moderate oven until brown and hulled to remove the outer shell.

Rhubarb and Orange Water-ice

Pink rhubarb, with sweet oranges and honey – the perfect summer ice. Add more honey or sugar if needed, to taste.

INGREDIENTS

Serves 4

350g/12oz pink rhubarb
1 orange
15ml/1 tbsp clear honey
5ml/1 tsp powdered gelatine
orange slices, to decorate

NUTRITIONAL NOTES
Per portion:

Energy	38Kcals/158kJ
Fat, total	0.1g
Saturated fat	0g
Cholesterol	0mg
Fibre	2g

1 Trim the rhubarb and slice into 2.5cm/1in lengths. Place the rhubarb in a non-reactive pan.

2 Finely grate the rind from the orange and squeeze out the juice. Add about half the orange juice and the grated rind to the rhubarb in the pan and simmer until the rhubarb is just tender. Stir in the honey.

3 Heat the remaining orange juice and stir in the gelatine to dissolve. Stir it into the rhubarb. Tip the whole mixture into a rigid container that can safely be used in the freezer; freeze for about 2 hours or until slushy.

4 Remove the mixture from the freezer, tip into a bowl and beat well to break up the ice crystals. Freeze until firm. Soften slightly at room temperature before serving in scoops, decorated with orange slices.

Orange Ice with Strawberries

*Juicy oranges and really ripe
strawberries make a tasty ice that does
not need any additional sweetness.*

INGREDIENTS

Serves 4

6 large juicy oranges
350g/12oz/3 cups ripe strawberries
finely pared strips of orange rind,
  to decorate

NUTRITIONAL NOTES

Per portion:

Energy	124Kcals/518kJ
Fat, total	0.4g
Saturated fat	0g
Cholesterol	0mg
Fibre	5.6g

1 Squeeze the juice from the
oranges and pour into a
shallow freezer-proof bowl.
Freeze until ice crystals form
around the edge of the mixture,
beat thoroughly and freeze again.
Repeat this process at 30-minute
intervals over a 4-hour period.

2 Halve the strawberries and
arrange them on a serving
plate. Scoop the ice into serving
glasses, decorate with strips of
orange rind and serve immediately
with the strawberries.

COOK'S TIP

The ice will keep for up to
3 weeks in the freezer. Sweet
ruby grapefruits or deep red
blood oranges can be used for a
different flavour and colour.

Iced Oranges

These little sorbets served in the fruit shell are easy to eat – just the thing for serving at a barbecue or picnic.

INGREDIENTS

Serves 8
150g/5oz/²⁄₃ cup granulated (white) sugar
juice of 1 lemon
200ml/7fl oz/scant 1 cup water
14 oranges
8 fresh bay leaves, to decorate

1 Put the sugar in a heavy pan. Add half the lemon juice, then pour in 120ml/4fl oz/¹⁄₂ cup of the water. Heat gently, stirring occasionally, until the sugar has dissolved, then bring to the boil, and boil for 2–3 minutes, until the syrup is clear. Leave to cool.

2 Slice the tops off eight of the oranges, to make "hats". Scoop out the flesh from inside each, taking care not to damage the shell, and set it aside. Put the empty orange shells and the "hats" on a baking sheet and place in the freezer until needed.

NUTRITIONAL NOTES

Per portion:

Energy	167Kcals/703kJ
Fat, total	0.3g
Saturated fat	0g
Cholesterol	0mg
Fibre	4.3g

3 Grate the rind of the six remaining oranges and add this to the syrup. Squeeze the juice from the oranges, and from the reserved flesh. There should be 750ml/1¹⁄₄ pints/3 cups. Top up with water, if necessary.

4 Stir the orange juice into the syrup, with the remaining lemon juice and water. Pour the mixture into a shallow container that can safely be used in the freezer. Freeze for 3 hours.

5 Turn the mixture into a bowl, and whisk to break down the ice crystals. Return to the freezer container and freeze for 4 hours more, until firm, but not solid.

6 Pack the mixture into the orange shells, mounding it up, and set the "hats" on top. Freeze until ready to serve. Just before serving, make a hole in the top of each "hat", using a skewer, and push in a bay leaf as decoration.

COOK'S TIP
~
Use crumpled foil to keep the shells upright on the baking sheet.

Fresh Orange Granita

A granita is like a water ice, but coarser and quite grainy in texture.

INGREDIENTS

Serves 6

4 large oranges

1 large lemon

150g/5oz/2/3 cup granulated (white) sugar

475ml/16fl oz/2 cups water

biscuits (cookies), to serve (optional)

pared strips of orange and lemon rind,
    to decorate

1 Thinly pare the orange and lemon rind, avoiding the white pith, and set aside for the decoration. Cut the fruit in half and squeeze the juice into a jug (pitcher). Set aside.

2 Heat the sugar and water in a heavy pan, stir until the sugar dissolves. Bring to the boil, and boil without stirring, until a syrup forms. Remove from the heat, add the orange and lemon rind and shake the pan. Cover and cool.

3 Strain the sugar syrup into a shallow freezer container, add the fruit juice. Stir well then freeze, uncovered, for 4 hours until slushy.

COOK'S TIP

Slice orange and lemon rind into thin strips. Blanch for 2 minutes, refresh in cold water and dry.

4 Remove the half-frozen mixture from the freezer and mix with a fork, return to the freezer and freeze again for 4 hours or until frozen hard.

5 To serve, turn into a bowl and leave to soften for about 10 minutes, break up again and pile into long-stemmed glasses. Decorate with the orange and lemon rind. Serve with biscuits, if you like, but the fat content must be taken into account.

NUTRITIONAL NOTES
Per portion:

Energy	139Kcals/589kJ
Fat, total	0.2g
Saturated fat	0g
Cholesterol	0mg
Fibre	1.6g

Lemon Granita

Nothing is more refreshing for dessert on a hot summer's day than a fresh lemon granita.

INGREDIENTS

Serves 4

475ml/16fl oz/2 cups water
115g/4oz/1/2 cup granulated (white) sugar
2 large lemons

NUTRITIONAL NOTES

Per portion:

Energy	114Kcals/488kJ
Fat, total	0g
Saturated fat	0g
Cholesterol	0mg
Fibre	0g

1 In a large pan, heat the water and sugar together over a low heat until the sugar dissolves. Bring to the boil, stirring occasionally. Remove from the heat and allow to cool.

2 Grate the rind from one lemon, then squeeze the juice from both. Stir the grated rind and juice into the sugar syrup. Place it in a shallow container or freezer tray, and freeze until solid.

3 Plunge the bottom of the frozen container or tray in very hot water for a few seconds. Turn the frozen mixture out, and chop it into large chunks.

4 Place the mixture in a food processor fitted with metal blades, and process until it forms small crystals. Spoon into serving glasses or dishes.

Coffee Granita

A granita is a cross between a frozen drink and a flavoured ice, and can be made at home with the help of a food processor. The consistency should be slushy, not solid.

INGREDIENTS

Serves 4

475ml/16fl oz/2 cups water
115g/4oz/1/2 cup granulated (white) sugar
250ml/8fl oz/1 cup very strong espresso
  coffee, cooled

NUTRITIONAL NOTES

Per portion:

Energy	115Kcals/488kJ
Fat, total	0g
Saturated fat	0g
Cholesterol	0mg
Fibre	0g

1 Heat the water and sugar together gently until the sugar dissolves. Bring to the boil, stirring occasionally. Remove from the heat and allow to cool.

2 Stir the coffee and sugar syrup together. Place it in a container and freeze until solid. Plunge the bottom of the frozen container or tray in very hot water. Turn the mixture out, and chop into chunks.

3 Place the mixture in a food processor and process until it forms small crystals. Spoon into tall glasses and serve.

COOK'S TIP

To store a granita, pour the processed mixture back into a container, cover, and freeze again. Allow to thaw slightly before serving.

Index

A

Allspice and lime with
pineapple wedges, 456
Almond chocolate
meringue, 130
Almond cream and pear
tart, 161
Almond cream with peach
tart, 146–7
Almond curd and fresh fruit
salad, 451
Almonds, caramelized, with
lemon soufflé, 203
Almost instant banana
pudding, 176–7
Amaretti chocolate
peaches, 47
Amaretto soufflé, 191
Amaretto, nectarines
with, 307
Amaretto with stuffed
peaches, 315
American spiced pumpkin
pie, 165
Angel cake, 403
Angel food cake, 114
Apples
Apple and cider water
ice, 218
Apple foam with
blackberries, 375
Apple pie, 156–7
Apple pie, filo-topped, 392
Apple soufflé puddings,
434
Apricot nut filling
baked, 278
Blackberry Romanoff,
368–9
Blackberry terrine, 488–9
Blackcurrant pancakes, 332
Brown Betty, 284
Caramel sauce baked, 28–9
Chargrilled apples on
cinnamon toasts, 326–7
Chunky bake, 290–1
Cinnamon gâteau, 406–7
Couscous pudding, 292
Cranberry lattice pie, 141
Eve's pudding, 30–1
Fritters, 48–9
Honey and lemon
baked, 279
Hot blackberry
soufflés, 435
Lemon risotto with
poached plums, 58

Passion fruit and apple
foam, 364–5
Plum and banana scone
pie, 298–9
Raspberries in rose
syrup, 312
Red wine baked, 277
Soufflé omelette, 195
Strawberry crumble, 287

Strudel, 52–3
Tarte Tatin, 163
Walnut crumble, 286
Apricots
Apricot delight, 442–3
Apricot glaze, 271
Apricot parcels, 385
Apricots in Marsala, 84–5
Baked apples with apricot
nut filling, 278
Banana compote, 479
Cinnamon soufflés, 432–3
Coconut dumplings with
apricot sauce, 316–17
Glazed apricot sponge,
44–5
Orange cream, 68–9
Orange jelly, 64–5
Orange roulade, 410–11
Pear filo roulade, 384
Quick blender whip, 437
Yogurt and pistachio
nuts, 371

Australian hazelnut
pavlova, 127
Autumn pudding, 359

B

Baked apples in honey and
lemon, 279
Baked apples with apricot
nut filling, 278
Baked apples with caramel
sauce, 28–9
Baked apples with red
wine, 277
Baked blackberry
cheesecake, 400–1
Baked fruit compote, 293
Baked peaches with
raspberry sauce, 314
Bakewell tart, 155
Bananas
Almost instant banana
pudding, 176–7
Apricot compote, 479
Banana ginger parkin, 103
Banana orange loaf, 102
Banana and toffee ice
cream, 220
Barbecued with spicy
vanilla spread, 302
Boston banoffee pie, 159
Brazilian coffee, 95
Caribbean, 305

Chocolate chip pudding, 43
Hot spiced bananas, 303
Maple and lime
pancakes, 328
Passion fruit whip, 186
Pineapple mousse, 81
Plum and apple scone pie,
298–9
Rum and raisin, 304
Thai fried bananas, 56–7
Barbecued orange parcels,
310–11
Barbecued pineapple boats
with rum glaze, 306
Bitter chocolate mousse, 94
Black and white pound
cake, 119
Black Forest gâteau, 113
Black Forest sundae, 242–3
Blackberries
Apple foam with, 375
Apple Romanoff, 368–9
Apple terrine, 488–9
Baked cheesecake, 400–1
Batter pudding, 282
Brown sugar meringue, 395
Charlotte, 288
Hot apple soufflés, 435
Lemon soufflé, 194
Salad with rose granita,
462–3
Blackcurrant apple
pancakes, 332
Blackcurrant coulis, 342
Blackcurrant pudding, 295
Blackcurrant sorbet, 496
Blueberry and orange crêpe
baskets, 336–7
Blueberry and orange salad
meringues, 464–5
Blueberry and peach pie,
132–3
Blueberry and spiced pear
parcels, 274
Blueberry buckle, 285
Blueberry pancakes, 331
Blueberry-hazelnut
cheesecake, 108–9
Blushing pears, 324–5
Blushing pina colada, 256–7
Boodles orange fool, 64–5
Boston banoffee pie, 159
Brandied fruit and rice ice
cream, 239
Brandy butter, 20
Brandy ginger mulled
pears, 321

Brazilian coffee bananas, 95
Bread and sultana
     custard, 418
Bread pudding, fruit
     spice, 275
Bread pudding, fruity, 276
Bread pudding with pecan
     nuts, 42
Brown bread ice cream, 230
Buttermilk, 263
Buttermilk vanilla ice
     cream, 225
Butterscotch sauce, 20

C
Cabinet pudding, 30–1
Café glace, 254
Calories: count chart, 264
Cappuccino coffee cups, 187
Caramel rice pudding, 60
Caramel with fresh fruit, 373
Cardamom coffee
     zabaglione, 174
Caribbean bananas, 305
Carrot cake with maple
     butter frosting, 118
Chargrilled apples on
     cinnamon toasts, 326–7
Cheese, 263
     Figs with ricotta cream, 374
     Gooseberry cooler, 440
     Grape cheese whips, 441
     Kiwi ricotta cheese tart, 149
     Spiced nectarines with
          fromage frais, 309
Cheesecake
     Baked blackberry, 400–1
     Blueberry-hazelnut, 108–9
     Chocolate, 106–7
     Classic, 106–7
     Raspberry and white
          chocolate, 124
     Tofu berry, 402
Cherries jubilee, 84–5
Cherry and chocolate
     polenta cake, 115
Cherry compote, 48–9
Cherry pancakes, 333
Cherry pie, 138–9
Cherry syllabub, 70–1
Chestnut and chocolate
     pots, 73
Chestnut pancakes,
     Chinese 329
Chestnut pudding, 93
Chilled coffee praline
     soufflé, 201
Chilled oranges in syrup, 345
Chocolate
     Almond meringue pie, 130
     Amaretti peaches, 47
     Angel cake, 404–5
     Banana pudding, 43

Bitter chocolate mousse, 94
Black and white cake, 119
Black Forest gâteau, 113
Cheesecake, 106–7
Cherry polenta cake, 115
Chestnut pots, 73
Chiffon pie, 144
Coffee and vanilla stripe,
     74–5
Coffee bombe, 247
Crêpes with plums and
     port, 32
Date and walnut
     pudding, 280

Death by chocolate, 121
Devil's food cake, 112
Double chocolate
     snowball, 77
Fruit fondue, 52–3
Fruits of the forest with
     chocolate creams, 208–9
Fudge sauce, 21
Fudge sundaes, 252
Greek mousse tartlets, 162
Hazelnut galettes, 76
Hot chocolate cake, 41
Hot chocolate zabaglione,
     170
Ice cream, 224
Iced mint cooler, 255
Iced pear terrine with
     chocolate sauce, 211
Layer cake, 100
Magic mud pudding, 37
Mandarin trifle, 178–9
Marbled Swiss roll, 125
Mint ice cream pie, 245
Orange Scotch pancakes, 25

Orange soufflé, 34–5
Pear tart, 151
Pears in fudge blankets, 33
Pecan torte, 135
Profiteroles, 160
Raspberry and white
     chocolate cheesecake, 124
Rich berry tart, 154
Risotto, 59
Rocky road ice cream, 238
Sachertorte, 126
Simple chocolate cake, 122
Sorbet with red fruits, 216
Soufflé crêpes, 198

Soufflés, 199
Steamed fruit puddings, 40
Strawberry layer cake, 120
Vanilla timbales, 425
White chocolate mousse
     with dark sauce, 80
White chocolate parfait,
     78–9
Choux pastry, 12
Christmas cranberry
     bombe, 485
Christmas pudding, 38–9
Chunky apple bake, 290–1
Cider and warm pears, 319
Cinnamon and coffee swirl
     ice cream, 235
Cinnamon apple gâteau,
     406–7
Cinnamon apricot soufflés,
     432–3
Cinnamon pastry mince
     pies, 140
Cinnamon toasts, chargrilled
     apples on, 326–7

Citrus rind shreds, 271
Classic cheesecake, 106–7
Classic coffee crème
     caramel, 172
Clementine jelly, 352
Clementines in cinnamon
     caramel, 370
Coconut
     Coconut cream pie, 145
     Coconut ice cream, 234
     Coffee trifle, 182–3
     Cold mango soufflés, 197
     Creole ambrosia, 72
     Dumplings with apricot
          sauce, 316–17
     Fresh pineapple, 452
     Lemon layer cake, 116–17
Coffee
     Brazilian coffee bananas, 95
     Café glace, 254
     Cappuccino cups, 187
     Cardamom zabaglione, 174
     Chocolate bombe, 247
     Cinnamon swirl ice
          cream, 235
     Classic crème caramel, 172
     Coconut trifle, 182–3
     Coeur à la crème, 168
     Coffee granita, 504–5
     Crêpes with peaches and
          cream, 87
     Frosted raspberry
          terrine, 253
     Hot mocha rum
          soufflés, 196
     Ice cream with caramelized
          pecans, 228–9
     Maple and pistachio
          bombes, 248
     Mocha cream pots, 189
     Nut meringue, 249
     Petits pots de cappuccino,
          175
     Praline soufflé, 201
     Tiramisù, 169
     Twice-baked mocha
          soufflé, 202
     Vanilla and chocolate
          stripe, 74–5
Cointreau and strawberries,
     446
Cold mango soufflés with
     toasted coconut, 197
Compote
     Apricot and banana, 479
     Baked fruit, 293
     Cherry, 48–9
     Kumquat , 294
     Russian fruit , 90–1
     Three-fruit, 478
Cool green fruit salad, 461
Corn oil, 262
Cornflake-topped peach

bake, 296
Coulis, 18
  Passion fruit, 477
  Redcurrant and raspberry,
    18, 484
  Rich blackcurrant, 342
Couscous apple pudding, 292
Couscous sultana
  puddings, 281
Cranberry bombe, 485
Cranberry-apple lattice
  pie, 141
Cranberry raspberry jelly,
  368–9
Cream substitute,
  making, 270
Crème anglaise, 19
Crème brûlée, 173
Crème caramel, 171, 172
Crème fraîche, 263
Creole ambrosia, 72
Crêpes Suzette, 54–5
Crunchy fruit layer, 377
Crunchy gooseberry
  crumble, 46
Custard
  Bread and sultana, 418
  Cabinet pudding, 30–1
  Floating islands, 92
  Pineapple and rum, 185
  Plum and custard
    creams, 190
  Poppyseed with red
    fruit, 419
  Vermont baked maple, 188

D
Damson and iced gin
  soufflés, 200
Date and orange salad, 450
Date and walnut cake,
  spiced, 101
Date, chocolate and walnut
  pudding, 280
Dates with fragrant rice, 354
Dates with marzipan figs, 472
Death by chocolate, 121
Devil's food cake with
  orange frosting, 112
Double chocolate
  snowball, 77
Dried fruit fool, 363
Dried fruit salad with
  summer berries, 473

E
Egg whites, whisking, 268
Elderflower and gooseberry
  cream, 67
Elderflower lychee sorbet, 493
Eve's pudding, 30–1

F
Fanned poached pears in
  port syrup, 320
Fats, 260–1
  count chart, 264
Fig and honey pudding, 90–1
Figs with dates, 472
Figs with honey and
  wine, 447
Figs with ricotta cream, 374
Filo fruit baskets, 391
Filo fruit scrunchies, 386
Filo plum pockets, 387
Filo redcurrant baskets, 390

Filo rhubarb chiffon pie, 383
Filo roulade, apricot and
  pear, 384
Filo spiced mango fingers, 382
Filo tropical fruit clusters,
  388–9
Filo-topped apple pie, 392
Floating islands, 92
Floating islands in hot plum
  sauce, 396–7
Fluffy banana and pineapple
  mousse, 81
Fondue, chocolate fruit, 52–3
Fool, Boodles orange, 64–5
Fool, dried fruit, 363
Fool, rhubarb and orange,
  68–9
Fragrant mandarins with
  pistachio nuts, 449
Fragrant rice with dates, 354
French flan pastry, 11
Fresh citrus jelly, 348–9
Fresh figs with honey and
  wine, 447

Fresh fruit salad and almond
  curd, 451
Fresh fruit with caramel, 373
Fresh fruit with caramel
  rice, 356
Fresh fruit with mango
  sauce, 471
Fresh orange granita, 503
Fresh pineapple with
  coconut, 452
Fresh strawberry ice
  cream, 223
Fromage frais, 263
Frosted raspberry and coffee
  terrine, 253
Frozen apple and blackberry
  terrine, 488–9
Frozen strawberry mousse
  cake, 226
Frudités with honey dip, 206
Fruit and chocolate fondue,
  52–3
Fruit kebabs with mango
  and yogurt sauce, 88–9
Fruit, preparing, 14–17
Fruit purées, 267
Fruit salad with passion fruit
  dressing, 210
Fruit spice bread pudding,
  275
Fruit tartlets, 136–7
Fruited rice ring, 362
Fruits of the forest with
  chocolate creams, 208–9
Fruity bread pudding, 276

G
Gelatine, 18, 269

Génoise, 110–11
Gin and damson soufflés, 200
Ginger and honey syrup, 338
Ginger and kiwi sorbet, 490
Ginger and mango
  clouds, 423
Ginger and orange crème
  brûlée, 176–7
Ginger and peach paskha,
  426
Ginger baked papaya, 313
Ginger baked pears, 50–1
Ginger banana parkin, 103
Ginger baskets and ruby
  orange sherbet, 216–17
Ginger brandy mulled
  pears, 321
Ginger, watermelon and
  grapefruit salad, 207
Gingerbread upside-down
  pudding, 26
Glazed apricot sponge, 44–5
Glossy chocolate sauce, 21
Gooseberry cheese cooler, 440
Gooseberry and clotted
  cream ice cream, 219
Gooseberry crumble,
  crunchy, 46
Gooseberry and elderflower
  cream, 67
Grapefruit salad with
  Campari and orange, 459
Grapefruit sorbet, 491
Grapefruit, watermelon and
  ginger salad, 207
Grapes
  Grape cheese whips, 441
  Grape-yogurt jelly, 346–7
  Muscat grape frappé, 460
  Papaya and green grapes
    with mint syrup, 476
  Strawberries in spiced
    grape jelly, 344
Greek chocolate mousse
  tartlets, 162
Greek fig and honey
  pudding, 90–1
Greek honey and lemon
  cake, 104–5
Griddle cakes with mulled
  plums, 300–1
Ground rice pudding, 351

H
Hazelnut and nectarine
  meringues, 394
Hazelnut chocolate galettes, 76
Hazelnut ice cream, 227
Hazelnut pavlova,
  Australian, 127
Hazelnut-blueberry
  cheesecake, 108–9
Honey

Baked apples in honey and
lemon, 279
Fresh figs with honey and
wine, 447
Frudités with honey
dip, 206
Ginger and honey
syrup, 338
Honey and fig pudding,
90–1
Honey and lemon cake,
104–5
Hot blackberry and apple
soufflés, 435
Hot chocolate cake, 41
Hot chocolate zabaglione, 170
Hot mocha rum soufflés, 196
Hot plum batter pudding,
44–5
Hot quince soufflés, 192–3
Hot spiced bananas, 303

I
Ice cream
Banana and toffee, 220
Black Forest sundae, 242–3
Brandied fruit and rice, 239
Brown bread, 230
Buttermilk vanilla, 225
Chocolate, 224
Chocolate mint ice cream
pie, 245
Christmas cranberry
bombe, 485
Cinnamon and coffee
swirl, 235
Coconut, 234
Coffee ice cream with
caramelized pecans,
228–9
Fresh strawberry, 223
Gooseberry and clotted
cream, 219
Hazelnut, 227
Indian (Kulfi), 231
Italian fruit salad, 481
Mint, 236–7
Pineapple, 233
Praline ice cream in
baskets, 240–1
Rocky road, 238
Strawberry shortcake, 244
Summer fruit salad, 486–7
Turkish delight, 232
Iced coffee and nut
meringue, 249
Iced gin and damson
soufflés, 200
Iced mint chocolate
cooler, 255
Iced oranges, 502
Iced pear terrine with
chocolate sauce, 211

Iced pineapple crush, 454–5
Iced praline torte, 250–1
Indian ice cream (Kulfi), 231
Italian fruit salad and ice
cream, 481

J
Jam tart, 164
Jamaican fruit trifle, 184
Jelly, 269
Apricot and orange, 64–5
Clementine, 352
Fresh citrus, 348–9
Grapes in grape-yogurt,

346–7
Orange-blossom, 350
Raspberry and cranberry,
368–9
Raspberry and mint
bavarois, 366–7
Strawberries in spiced
grape jelly, 344

K
Key lime pie, 136–7
Kissel, 90
Kiwi ricotta cheese tart,
149
Kiwi sorbet, ginger and, 490
Kulfi, 231
Kumquat compote, 294

L
Lemons
Apple and lemon risotto
with poached plums, 58
Baked apples in honey, 279

Coconut layer cake, 116–7
Honey and lemon cake,
104–5
Lemon and lime sauce, 339
Lemon and orange tart, 150
Lemon chiffon cake, 412–3
Lemon granita, 504–5
Lemon hearts with
strawberry sauce, 428–9
Lemon meringue pie,
142–3
Lemon sorbet, 213
Mexican rice pudding, 353
Red berry tart with lemon

cream filling, 131
Soufflé with blackberries, 194
Soufflé with caramelized
almonds, 203
Tarte au citron, 152
Warm lemon and syrup
cake, 24
Limes
Banana, maple and lime
pancakes, 328
Key lime pie, 136–7
Lemon and lime sauce, 339
Lime sherbet, 215
Mango and lime sorbet in
lime shells, 497
Pineapple wedges with
allspice and lime, 456
Low-fat spreads, using, 265–7
Low-fat substitutes, 262–7
Lychee elderflower sorbet, 493

M
Magic chocolate mud

pudding, 37
Mango
Cold mango soufflés with
toasted coconut, 197
Fresh fruit with mango
sauce, 471
Fruit kebabs with mango
and yogurt sauce, 88–9
Mango and ginger
clouds, 423
Mango and lime sorbet in
lime shells, 497
Mango and passion fruit
gelato, 222
Mango sorbet, 214
Papaya and mango medley
with iced yogurt, 457
Sorbet with mango
sauce, 492
Spiced mango filo
fingers, 382
Maple coffee and pistachio
bombes, 248
Marbled cake, 119
Marbled Swiss roll, 125
Marzipan and yogurt with
nectarines, 308
Marzipan figs with dates, 472
Melon and strawberry
salad, 475
Melon cups, Persian, 448
Melon salad, mixed, 470
Meringue
Australian hazelnut
pavlova, 127
Blackberry brown
sugar, 395
Blackberry salad with rose
granita, 462–3
Blueberry and orange
salad, 464–5
Chocolate almond
meringue pie, 130
Floating islands, 92
Floating islands in hot
plum sauce, 396–7
Iced coffee and nut, 249
Lemon meringue pie,
142–3
Nectarine and hazelnut,
394
Pineapple and strawberry,
393
Queen of puddings, 36
Raspberry meringue
gâteau, 98–9
Raspberry vacherin, 398–9
Soft fruit pavlova, 378
Mexican fritters, spiced, 56–7
Mexican lemony rice
pudding, 353
Mince pies with orange
cinnamon pastry, 140

Mint and chocolate
cooler, 255
Mint ice cream, 236–7
Mint ice cream pie,
chocolate, 245
Mint raspberry bavarois,
366–7
Mint syrup with papaya and
green grapes, 476
Mississippi pecan pie, 158
Mixed fruit salad, 466
Mocha cream pots, 189
Mono-unsaturated fats, 260
Mousse
Bitter chocolate, 94
Chocolate mousse
strawberry layer cake, 120
Fluffy banana and
pineapple, 81
Frozen strawberry mousse
cake, 226
Greek chocolate tartlets, 162
White chocolate mousse
with dark sauce, 80
Muesli raspberry layer, 343
Mulled pears with ginger
and brandy, 321
Muscat grape frappé, 460

N
Nectarine and hazelnut
meringues, 394
Nectarines with Amaretto,
307
Nectarines, spiced, with
fromage frais, 309
Nectarines with marzipan
and yogurt, 308
Nougat and pistachio torte,
246
Nut and iced coffee
meringue, 249
Nut apricot filling and baked
apples, 278

O
Olive oil, 260, 262
Oranges
Apricot and orange jelly,
64–5
Apricot roulade, 410–11
Apricots with orange
cream, 68–9
Banana orange loaf, 102
Barbecued parcels, 310–11
Blueberry crêpe baskets,
336–7
Blueberry salad
meringues, 464–5
Boodles orange fool, 64–5
Chilled oranges in syrup, 345
Chocolate angel cake, 404–5
Chocolate mandarin

trifle, 178–9
Chocolate Scotch
pancakes, 25
Chocolate soufflé, 34–5
Creole ambrosia, 72
Devil's food cake with
orange frosting, 112
Fragrant mandarins with
pistachio nuts, 449
Fresh orange granita, 503
Ginger crème brûlée, 176–7
Grapefruit salad with
Campari, 459
Ice with strawberries, 501

Iced oranges, 502
Lemon and orange tart, 150
Mince pies with orange
cinnamon pastry, 140
Orange-blossom jelly, 350
Orange and date salad, 450
Orange rice pudding, 61
Orange yogurt brûlées, 420
Prune and orange pots,
438–9
Rhubarb fool, 68–9
Rhubarb water-ice, 500
Ruby orange sherbet in
ginger baskets, 216–17
Souffléed semolina, 436

P
Pancakes, 268
Apple and blackcurrant,
332
Banana, maple and lime,
328
Blueberry, 331
Cherry, 333

Chinese chestnut, 329
Chocolate and orange
Scotch pancakes, 25
Tropical fruit, 330
Papaya and green grapes
with mint syrup, 476
Papaya and mango medley
with iced yogurt, 457
Papaya baked with ginger, 313
Papaya skewers with passion
fruit coulis, 477
Passion fruit and apple
foam, 364–5
Passion fruit banana

whip, 186
Passion fruit brûlée, 422
Passion fruit coulis with
papaya skewers, 477
Passion fruit creams, 379
Passion fruit dressing with
fruit salad, 210
Passion fruit pineapple
salsa, 458
Passion fruit raspberry
swirls, 424
Pastry making, 10–13
Peaches
Baked with raspberry
sauce, 314
Blueberry pie, 132–3
Chocolate amaretti, 47
Coffee crêpes, 87
Cornflake-topped bake, 296
Ginger paskha, 426
Peach cobbler, 283
Peach Melba, 66
Peach pudding, 289
Stuffed with almond

liqueur, 315
Swiss roll, 408–9
Tart with almond cream,
146–7
Pears
Almond cream tart, 161
Apricot filo roulade, 384
Blushing pears, 324–5
Chocolate fudge
blankets, 33
Chocolate pear tart, 151
Fanned poached pears in
port syrup, 320
Ginger baked pears, 50–1
Iced pear terrine with
chocolate sauce, 211
Mulled with ginger and
brandy, 321
Poached in maple-yogurt
sauce, 322–3
Poached in red wine, 86
Spiced blueberry
parcels, 274
Warm pears in cider, 319
Pecan chocolate torte, 135
Pecan nuts with bread
pudding, 42
Pecan pie, 158
Pecans, caramelized, with
coffee ice cream, 228–9
Persian melon cups, 448
Petits pots de cappuccino, 175
Pina colada, blushing, 256–7
Pineapple
Barbecued with rum, 306
Fluffy banana mousse, 81
Fresh pineapple with
coconut, 452
Ice cream, 233
Iced pineapple crush, 454–5
Passion fruit salsa, 458
Perfumed pineapple
salad, 453
Pineapple flambé, 318
Pineapple wedges with
allspice and lime, 456
Pineapple with rum
custard, 185
Strawberry meringue, 393
Upside-down cake, 123
Pistachio and maple coffee
bombes, 248
Pistachio and nougat
torte, 246
Pistachio nuts and apricots
with yogurt, 371
Pistachio nuts with fragrant
mandarins, 449
Plums
Apple and banana scone
pie, 298–9
Apple and lemon risotto
with poached plums, 58

Chocolate crêpes with port, 32
Floating islands in hot plum sauce, 396–7
Griddle cakes with mulled plums, 300–1
Hot plum batter pudding, 44–5
Plum and custard creams, 190
Plum and port sorbet, 494
Plum filo pockets, 387
Poached pears in maple-yogurt sauce, 322–3
Poached pears in red wine, 86
Polyunsaturated fats, 261
Poppyseed custard with red fruit, 419
Portuguese rice pudding, 82
Praline and coffee soufflé, 201
Praline ice cream in baskets, 240–1
Praline torte, iced, 250–1
Prune and orange pots, 438–9
Prunes poached in red wine, 50–1
Pumpkin pie, American, 165

Q
Quark, 263
Queen of puddings, 36
Quick apricot blender whip, 437
Quince soufflés, hot, 192–3

R
Raisin and rum bananas, 304
Raspberries
Apples in rose syrup, 312
Baked peaches, 314
Coffee terrine, 253
Cranberry jelly, 368–9
Meringue gâteau, 98–9
Muesli layer, 343
Passion fruit swirls, 424
Raspberries and fruit purée, 372
Raspberry and mint bavarois, 366–7
Raspberry and redcurrant coulis, 18, 484
Sorbet with a soft fruit garland, 495
Tart, 148
Trifle, 181
Vacherin, 398–9
White chocolate cheesecake, 124
Red berry tart with lemon cream filling, 131
Redcurrant and raspberry coulis, 18, 484
Redcurrant filo baskets, 390

Rhubarb and orange fool, 68–9
Rhubarb chiffon pie, filo, 383
Rhubarb orange water-ice, 500
Rhubarb pie, 134
Rhubarb spiral cobbler, 297
Rhubarb-strawberry crisp, 27
Rice
Apple and lemon risotto with poached plums, 58
Brandied fruit and rice ice cream, 239
Caramel rice pudding, 60
Fragrant rice with

dates, 354
Fresh fruit with caramel rice, 356
Fruited rice ring, 362
Ground rice pudding, 351
Mexican lemony rice pudding, 353
Orange rice pudding, 61
Portuguese rice pudding, 82
Rice conde sundae, 83
Rice fruit sundae, 357
Rice pudding with mixed berry sauce, 355
Rich blackcurrant coulis, 342
Rich chocolate-berry tart, 154
Risotto, chocolate, 59
Rocky road ice cream, 238
Rose petal cream, 70–1
Rose petal strawberry paskha, 427
Ruby fruit salad, 468
Ruby grapefruit sorbet, 491

Ruby orange sherbet in ginger baskets, 216–17
Rum and raisin bananas, 304
Rum custard, pineapple with, 185
Rum glaze with barbecued pineapple boats, 306
Rum mocha soufflés, hot, 196
Russian blackcurrant pudding, 295
Russian fruit compote, 90–1

S
Sabayon, 19

Sachertorte, 126
Saturated fats, 260
Sauces
Baked apples with caramel sauce, 28–9
Baked peaches with raspberry sauce, 314
Brandy butter, 20
Butterscotch, 20
Chocolate fudge, 21
Coconut dumplings with apricot sauce, 316–17
Fresh fruit with mango sauce, 471
Fruit kebabs with mango and yogurt sauce, 88–9
Glossy chocolate, 21
Iced pear terrine with chocolate sauce, 211
Lemon and lime, 339
Lemon hearts with strawberry sauce, 428–9
Mango sorbet with mango sauce, 492

Rice pudding with mixed berry sauce, 355
Sabayon, 19
White chocolate mousse with dark sauce, 80
Sensational strawberries, 376
Sherbet, lime, 215
Sherbet, ruby orange in ginger baskets, 216–17
Shortcrust pastry, 10
Simple chocolate cake, 122
Skimmed milk, 263
Soft fruit pavlova, 378
Sorbets
Blackcurrant, 496
Chocolate with red fruits, 212
Ginger and kiwi sorbet, 490
Lemon, 213
Lychee and elderflower, 493
Mango, 214
Mango and lime in lime shells, 497
Mango with mango sauce, 492
Plum and port, 494
Raspberry with a soft fruit garland, 495
Ruby grapefruit, 491
Watermelon, 498–9
Soufflés
Amaretto, 191
Apple soufflé omelette, 195
Apple soufflé puddings, 434
Chilled coffee and praline, 201
Chocolate, 199
Chocolate and orange, 34–5
Chocolate soufflé crêpes, 198
Cinnamon and apricot, 432–3
Cold mango with toasted coconut, 197
Hot blackberry and apple, 435
Hot mocha rum, 196
Hot quince, 192–3
Iced gin and damson, 200
Lemon with blackberries, 194
Lemon with caramelized almonds, 203
Souffléed orange semolina, 436
Souffléed rice pudding, 430–1
Twice-baked mocha, 202
Spice and fruit bread pudding, 275

Spice and lime pineapple wedges, 456
Spiced bananas, hot, 303
Spiced date and walnut cake, 101
Spiced fruit platter, 467
Spiced fruits jubilee, 480
Spiced grape jelly, strawberries in, 344
Spiced mango filo fingers, 382
Spiced Mexican fritters, 56–7
Spiced nectarines with fromage frais, 309
Spiced pear and blueberry parcels, 274
Spiced pumpkin pie, 165
Spicy vanilla spread with barbecued bananas, 302
Sponge cake with fruit and cream, 110–11
Steamed chocolate and fruit puddings, 40
Sticky toffee pudding, 34–5
Strawberries
    Apple crumble, 287
    Chocolate mousse strawberry layer cake, 120
    Cointreau, 446
    Ice cream, 223
    Ice cream strawberry shortcake, 244
    Lemon hearts with strawberry sauce, 428–9
    Melon salad, 475
    Mousse cake, 226
    Orange ice, 501
    Pineapple meringue, 393
    Rhubarb crisp, 27
    Rose petal paskha, 427
    Roulade, 104–5
    Semi-freddo, 221
    Sensational, 376
    Spiced grape jelly, 344
Strudel, apple, 52–3
Stuffed peaches with almond liqueur, 315
Sultana and bread custard, 418
Sultana couscous puddings, 281
Summer berry crêpes, 334–5
Summer fruit salad ice cream, 486–7
Summer pudding, 358
Sunflower oil, 262
Syllabub, cherry, 70–1
Syrup
    Apples and raspberries in rose syrup, 312
    Banana, maple and lime pancakes, 328
    Carrot cake with maple butter frosting, 118

Chilled oranges in syrup, 345
Fanned poached pears in port syrup, 320
Ginger and honey syrup, 338
Maple coffee and pistachio bombes, 248
Papaya and green grapes with mint syrup, 476
Poached pears in maple-yogurt sauce, 322–3
Tropical fruits in cinnamon syrup, 88–9
Vermont baked maple custard, 188
Warm lemon and syrup cake, 24

T
Tangerine trifle, 180
Tarte au citron, 152
Tarte Tatin, 163
Thai fried bananas, 56–7
Three-fruit compote, 478
Tia Maria gâteau, 414–15
Tiramisù, 169
Toffee pudding, sticky, 34–5
Tofu berry brûlée, 421
Tofu berry cheesecake, 402
Treacle tart, 153
Trifle
    Chocolate mandarin, 178–9
    Coconut and coffee, 182–3
    Jamaican fruit, 184
    Raspberry, 181

Tangerine, 180
Tropical fruit filo clusters, 388–9
Tropical fruit pancakes, 330
Tropical fruit salad, 474
Tropical fruits in cinnamon syrup, 88–9
Turkish delight ice cream, 232
Twice-baked mocha soufflé, 202
Two-tone yogurt ring with tropical fruit, 360–1

U
Unsaturated fats, 260

V
Vanilla buttermilk ice cream, 225
Vanilla chocolate timbales, 425
Vanilla, coffee and chocolate stripe, 74–5
Vanilla spread, spicy, with barbecued bananas, 302
Vermont baked maple custard, 188

W
Walnut and apple crumble, 286
Walnut and date cake, spiced, 101
Walnut, date and chocolate pudding, 280
Warm lemon and syrup cake, 24

Warm pears in cider, 319
Watermelon, ginger and grapefruit salad, 207
Watermelon sorbet, 498–9
White chocolate mousse with dark sauce, 80
White chocolate parfait, 78–9
Wine
    Apricots in Marsala, 84–5
    Baked apples with red wine, 277
    Chocolate crêpes with plums and port, 32
    Fanned poached pears in port syrup, 320
    Fresh figs with honey and wine, 447
    Grapefruit salad with Campari and orange, 459
    Muscat grape frappé, 460
    Plum and port sorbet, 494
    Poached pears in red wine, 86
    Prunes poached in red wine, 50–1
Winter fruit salad, 469

Y
Yogurt, 263
    Apricots and pistachio nuts, 371
    Fruit kebabs with mango and yogurt sauce, 88–9
    Grapes in grape-yogurt jelly, 346–7
    Nectarines with marzipan, 308
    Orange yogurt brûlées, 420
    Papaya and mango medley, 457
    Poached pears in maple-yogurt sauce, 322–3
    Two-tone yogurt ring with tropical fruit, 360–1
    Yogurt toppings, 270–1

Z
Zabaglione, coffee cardamom, 174
Zabaglione, hot chocolate, 170
Zuccotto, 247